INSPIRE / PLAN / DISCOVER / EXPERIENCE

POLAND

POLAND

CONTENTS

DISCOVER 6

EXPERIENCE WARSAW 66

EXPERIENCE POLAND 118

NEED TO KNOW 312

Left: Magnets depicting Polish buildings
Previous page: Sunrise over the peaks of the Tatra Mountains

DISCOVER

The beautiful cityscape of Wrocław

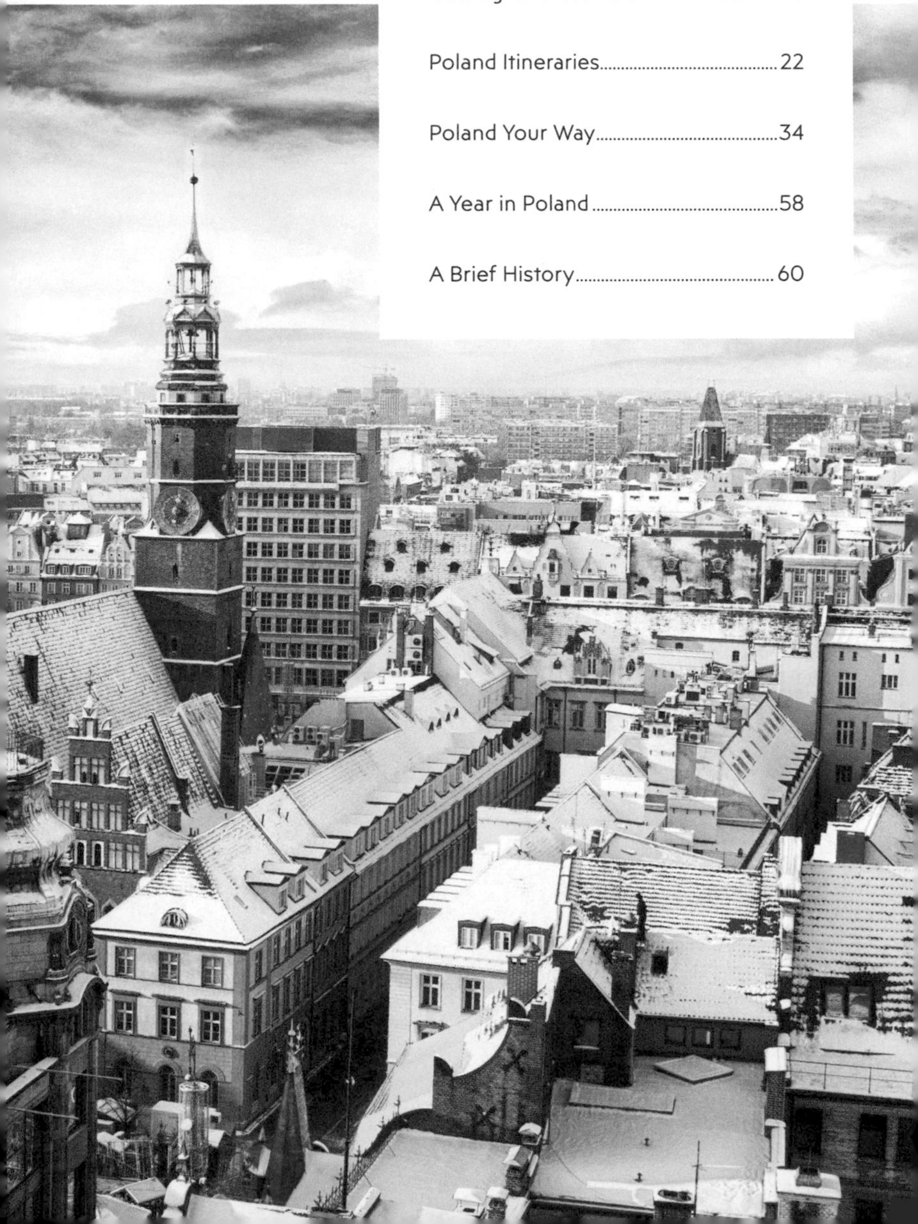

WELCOME TO
POLAND

Fairy-tale old towns and magical market squares. High-tech museums and quirky art galleries. Rugged mountains, beautiful beaches and dense forests. Mouthwatering comfort food and hipster bars filled with warming vodka. Whatever your dream trip to Poland entails, this DK Eyewitness Travel Guide is the perfect companion.

1 The magnificent market square in Poznań.

2 The striking exterior of the Museum of World War II.

3 A steaming bowl of ruby-red borscht.

4 A snowy village in the Tatra Mountains.

One of Europe's biggest countries, Poland is as famed for the cobbled streets and bohemian bars of enchanting Kraków as it is for the high-tech museums and trendy cafés of edgy Warsaw. But beyond this tale of two cities, there's so much more to discover. Compelling history can be found everywhere, from the once battle-scarred city of Gdańsk to the imposing fortified town of Zamość, built by knights. Medieval architecture and non-stop nightlife abound in artsy Wrocław and student-filled Toruń, while quirky street art and cool festivals are on the menu in post-industrial Łódź.

Beyond the cities, Poland's wild beauty is utterly undeniable. To the north stretch the golden beaches of the Baltic Coast, dotted with pretty fishing villages and spectacular sand dunes; to the south lie a sweeping chain of mountains, their ridges crisscrossed with hiking routes. In between you'll find rolling farmland, tranquil lakes, atmospheric wetlands and ancient forests, the latter home to magnificent bison. Imposing castles, opulent palaces and charming wooden churches are also scattered across the landscape, as are the scars of Poland's turbulent past.

The country's sheer size can threaten to overwhelm, but this guidebook breaks the country down into easily navigable chapters, with detailed itineraries, expert local knowledge and colourful, comprehensive maps to help you plan the perfect visit. Whether you're staying for a weekend, a week or longer, this Eyewitness guide will ensure that you see the very best Poland has to offer. Enjoy the book, and enjoy Poland.

REASONS TO LOVE
POLAND

Vibrant cities home to awe-inspiring architecture and non-stop nightlife. Ever-changing landscapes filled with fairy-tale castles and impenetrable forts. There are many reasons to love Poland; here are our favourites.

1 GOING UNDERGROUND

Some of the country's most fascinating history lies below ground. Delve under and discover Wieliczka's astonishing salt mines or the subterranean Nazi tunnels near Wałbrzych.

NOCTURNAL NEON 2

Under the Communists, Poland went wild for neon, with signs adorning everything from hotels to theatres. Most signs are now proudly displayed in museums and galleries.

3 ADVENTURES IN BIAŁOWIEŻA FOREST

This dense forest is one of the last remaining primeval woodlands in Europe. Try hiking or biking beneath its deep green canopy, keeping an eye out for a hairy bison or two.

BALTIC BEACHES 4

Poland's beautiful Baltic Coast is sprinkled with golden, endlessly sandy beaches, charming seaside towns, pretty fishing villages and towering sand dunes.

FAIRY-TALE KRAKÓW 5

Poland's former royal capital is utterly enchanting, from the magnificent Wawel and the elegant expanse of Rynek Główny to the cool cafés of Tytano and the late-night buzz of Kazimierz's bars.

PERFECT PIEROGI 6

These heaven-sent parcels of stuffed dough are incredibly moreish. Filled with everything from cottage cheese to fresh blueberries, this Polish staple is on every restaurant's menu.

ANCIENT CASTLES 7

Castles are scattered across the Polish landscape, from hill-hugging aristocratic residences to the red-brick bastions of the Teutonic Knights.

FAITH AND FERVOR 8

Synagogues large and small count among the country's most beautiful buildings, as do its magnificent big-city basilicas and remote wooden chapels.

9 POLISH NIGHTS

Poland loves to party. Places like Kraków and Wrocław are bursting with incredible nightlife, from underground clubs to hipster bars offering live music and craft beer.

10 VODKA SHOTS
Usually drunk neat, knocked back in one gulp and with a call of "Na Zdrowie!" ("Cheers!"), Poland's national tipple comes in many varieties and can be found at absolutely every social occasion.

SNACK TIME 11
Poles love their cafés and patisseries. Sample traditional *szarlotka* (spiced apple pie) or a slice of famously rich and tasty *sernik* (cheesecake), the national sweet of choice.

THE MAZURKA 12
Poland has many folk dances, but the mazurka – a fast-paced dance characterized by heel clicking and feet stamping – is undoubtedly the best known and most spectacular to watch.

EXPLORE
POLAND

This guide divides Poland into nine colour-coded
sightseeing areas, as shown on this map. Find
out more about each area on the following pages.

*Baltic
Sea*

○ Słupsk

○ Koszalin

POMERANIA
p270

Szczecinek ○

○ Człuchów

○ Świnoujście

○ Schwerin

○ Szczecin

Piła ○

○ Bydgoszcz

○ Gorzów Wielkopolski

GERMANY

○ Berlin

Gniezno ○

Potsdam ○

Poznań ○

○ Magdeburg

WIELKOPOLSKA
p196

○ Zielona Góra

○ Leszno

○ Żagan

○ Leipzig

Legnica ○

○ Wrocław

○ Dresden

SILESIA
p218

Opole ○

○ Kłodzko

**CZECH
REPUBLIC**

Ostrava ○

Brno ○

○ Bratislava

EUROPE

*North
Sea*

NORWAY

SWEDEN

FINLAND

ESTONIA

RUSSIA

LATVIA

DENMARK

*Baltic
Sea*

LITHUANIA

UNITED
KINGDOM

NETHER-
LANDS

BELARUS

GERMANY

POLAND

BELGIUM

CZECH
REP.

UKRAINE

SLOVAKIA

FRANCE

SWITZ.

AUSTRIA

HUNGARY

CROATIA

ROMANIA

SERBIA

ITALY

BULGARIA

SPAIN

GREECE

TURKEY

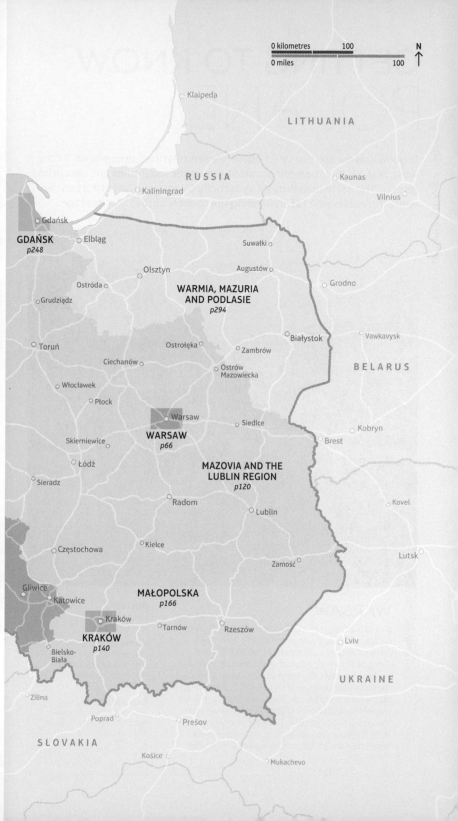

0 kilometres 100
0 miles 100
N

Klaipeda

LITHUANIA

RUSSIA

Kaliningrad

Kaunas

Vilnius

Gdańsk

GDAŃSK
p248

Elbląg

Suwałki

Augustów

Grodno

Vawkavysk

Olsztyn

Ostróda

**WARMIA, MAZURIA
AND PODLASIE**
p294

Grudziądz

Toruń

Ostrołęka

Zambrów

Białystok

BELARUS

Ciechanów

Ostrów
Mazowiecka

Włocławek

Płock

Warsaw

Siedlce

WARSAW
p66

Kobryn

Skierniewice

Brest

Łódź

Sieradz

**MAZOVIA AND THE
LUBLIN REGION**
p120

Radom

Lublin

Kovel

Częstochowa

Kielce

Zamość

Lutsk

Gliwice

MAŁOPOLSKA
p166

Katowice

Kraków

Tarnów

Rzeszów

Lviv

KRAKÓW
p140

Bielsko-
Biała

Žilina

UKRAINE

Poprad

Prešov

SLOVAKIA

Košice

Mukachevo

GETTING TO KNOW
POLAND

Beyond Kraków and Warsaw, Poland remains relatively unexplored. To the west, historic towns are surrounded by dramatic mountains and untouched forests. The north boasts bustling port-city Gdańsk and beautiful beaches, while the east is best for discovering the country's industrial heritage.

WARSAW

PAGE 66

One of the fastest-changing cities in Europe, Poland's capital is vibrant, dynamic and eclectic. Here, the restored historic architecture of the Old Town sits alongside ultra-modern skyscrapers and Communist-era concrete edifices – the most spectacular of which is the monumental Palace of Culture and Science. Elegant palaces and parks are plentiful, as are state-of-the-art museums, including the offbeat Neon Museum and thought-provoking POLIN. There are plenty of cool cafés to relax in, too, while the gritty-yet-bohemian neighbourhood of Praga offers incredible nightlife.

Best for
Amazing museums and non-stop nightlife

Home to
The Palace of Culture and Science, Royal Castle, POLIN Museum of the Polish Jews, Łazienki Park

Experience
Summer nights on the Vistula riverfront with its open-air bars and clubs

PAGE 120

MAZOVIA AND THE LUBLIN REGION

The rural antidote to Poland's bustling capital, this central swathe of the country is characterized by rolling farmland, sleepy villages and small towns. Lublin is a boisterous university city famous for its magical Old Town and summer street festivals. Other highlights include small-town synagogues, grand aristocratic palaces and the fortified town of Zamość. The unspoiled forest and lakes of Roztocze National Park provide a bucolic breather.

Best for
Historic towns, aristocratic palaces and traditional villages

Home to
Lublin, Zamość

Experience
Strolling the perfectly preserved streets of Kazimierz Dolny

PAGE 140

KRAKÓW

Poland's former royal capital features an array of memorable sights, from the set-piece Main Market Square to the extensive palace-complex of the Wawel. As well as hosting the country's highest concentration of churches and museums, the largely pedestrianized centre is a beautiful place to wander. Adding considerable character is Kazimierz, the former Jewish quarter that is now home to a famously unrestrained nightlife. Across the river, Podgórze, the former Jewish ghetto during World War II and home to Schindler's Factory, serves as a poignant reminder of the city's past.

Best for
Endless urban strolling in one of Europe's most splendid historical cities

Home to
The Wawel, Schindler's Factory and MOCAK, St Mary's Basilica

Experience
A night in Kazimierz, the bohemian quarter packed with restaurants and bars

→

PAGE 166

MAŁOPOLSKA

Running along Poland's southeastern border, Małopolska is packed with variety. It includes the country's biggest mountains, the snow-capped Tatras, as well as the bewitching green ridges of the Bieszczady hills. Nesting in the area's rolling green foothills are a rich variety of historical market towns and quiet villages. The region is particularly famous for its beautiful folk architecture: a rich collection of timber buildings are clustered around the mountain resort of Zakopane, while achingly pretty wooden churches are dotted throughout the southeast.

Best for
Poland's most varied and stunning landscapes

Home to
Łańcut Palace, Auschwitz-Birkenau Memorial Museum, Zakopane and Tatra National Park, Jasna Góra, Częstochowa

Experience
Hiking the beautiful bare ridges of the windswept Bieszczady hills

PAGE 196

WIELKOPOLSKA

Stately Poznań, the region's capital, is western Poland's main commercial and cultural hub, and contains one of the finest market squares anywhere in the country. The surrounding green plains of Wielkopolska make up one of the historical heartlands of the Polish nation – it was here in the Middle Ages that Poland was first founded. The cathedral city of Gniezno is where the Polish kings first accepted Christianity, and the surrounding area is celebrated for its Romanesque churches. Łódź, on the region's eastern boundaries, is a 19th-century textile town that is now a thriving centre of industrial heritage.

Best for
Romanesque architecture

Home to
Raczyński Palace, Poznań, Łódź, Gniezno Cathedral

Experience
A visit to the POW camp in Żagań that provided the real-life inspiration for Hollywood film The Great Escape

SILESIA

The Silesian capital Wrocław is one of Poland's major city-break destinations, and its elegant market square, extensive Old Town and nightlife scene can easily rival any in the country. The rest of the province embraces huge contrasts, from the forest-shrouded mountain resorts of the south to post-industrial conurbations like Katowice in the east. There is also history aplenty, with the Baroque interiors of Książ Castle, the Stara Kopalnia show-mine in Wałbrzych and the Nazi-built tunnels of the Riese Underground Complex all shedding light on a fascinating yet turbulent past.

Best for
Industrial heritage

Home to
Wrocław, Karkonosze Mountains, Kłodzko Valley

Experience
The grandeur of Książ Castle, arguably the most spectacular of Poland's aristocratic seats

→

PAGE 248

GDAŃSK

With its jumble of historic mansions, crumbling Gothic warehouses and blue-green canals, the Baltic port of Gdańsk is one of northern Europe's most evocative cities. The centuries-old Main Town, carefully restored following the destruction caused by World War II, is the city's historic heart, and is filled with charming cafés and pretty amber shops. The atmospheric waterfront is home to countless restaurants and the riveting Maritime Museum. Gdańsk is the main component of the "Tri-City", a unified conurbation that also includes Sopot, with its famous beach, and Gdynia, with its popular aquarium.

Best for
Canalside strolls

Home to
Church of St Mary, National Maritime Museum

Experience
A stroll along Gdańsk's charming main street, Ulica Długa

POMERANIA

PAGE 270

Stretching along Poland's Baltic coast, Pomerania is an area of beautiful white-sand beaches, rolling farmland and unspoiled lakes. There's a wide choice of seaside resorts on offer, with pretty fishing villages like Leba offering a folksy alternative to the ice cream parlours and ambling crowds of cities such as Kołobrzeg. Inland, the biggest draws are the medieval fortresses of the Teutonic Knights, the most spectacular of which is the imposing castle at Malbork. Medieval Toruń, once a former Teutonic stronghold, is today a vibrant university town with a hedonistic edge.

Best for
Red-brick castles and churches

Home to
Szczecin, Malbork Castle, Toruń, Kashubian Switzerland

Experience
Walking the dunes of the Słowiński National Park

PAGE 294

WARMIA, MAZURIA AND PODLASIE

Poland's southeastern corner is famous for undulating countryside. At its heart are the Great Mazurian Lakes, edged with resorts and criss-crossed by pleasure cruisers. The region's many canals and pristine rivers provide innumerable possibilities for kayakers and canoeists. The southeastern area is characterized by dense green woodland, most famously at Białowieża, site of the last remaining primeval forest in Europe and home to herds of majestic bison.

Best for
Tranquil lakes, meandering rivers and untouched forests

Home to
The Great Mazurian Lakes, Czarna Hańcza and Augustów Canal, Frombork Cathedral

Experience
Bison-watching in Białowieża's ancient forest

←

1 Interior of the Royal Castle.

2 POLIN Museum of the History of Polish Jews.

3 Monument to the Heroes of the Ghetto.

4 Palace on the Isle in Łazienki Park.

Poland offers endless options for exploration, from weekends spent discovering enchanting Old Towns to longer tours through dramatic landscapes. Wherever you choose to go, our handpicked itineraries will help you plan the perfect trip.

3 DAYS
in Warsaw

Day 1

Morning Get to grips with Polish history straight away on a tour of the Royal Castle (p74), then explore the nearby Cathedral of St John (p76), the final resting place of many famous Poles. From here, wander to the beautifully restored Old Town Square (p77) to enjoy classic Polish fare at U Fukiera (p79).

Afternoon Take a gentle stroll along Krakowskie Przedmiescie (p94), the city's set-piece boulevard that is lined with fine churches. Spend the rest of the afternoon admiring colourful folk exhibits at the Ethnographical Museum (p106).

Evening As the day draws to a close, make a beeline for Ulica Poznańska, a downtown street known for its bubbling bistro and bar scene. With a neon-lit exterior and cosy vintage interior, Prodiz Warszawski (www.prodizwarszawski.pl) is perfect for traditional, seasonal dishes.

Day 2

Morning Make your way to Plac Defilad, home to the gargantuan Palace of Culture and Science (p102) – it's viewing terrace offers awe-inspiring views over the city. Next up is the highly impressive National Museum (p90) where you can uncover Poland's leading collection of fine art and antiquities. For lunch, tuck in to grilled steak or fish at nearby Butchery & Wine (www.butcheryandwine.pl).

Afternoon Spend a relaxed afternoon roaming the paths of Łazienki Park (p110), Warsaw's largest green space. Take a boat ride on the peaceful lake to enjoy views of the elegant Palace on the Isle, then pay your respects to Poland's most famous composer at the Chopin Monument.

Evening As evening draws in, meander along the Vistula riverside path, lined with a profusion of food trucks and open-air bars. Nearby is Warszawa Powiśle (Zbigniewa Herberta 3B), a neon-lit bar much loved by locals.

Day 3

Morning Start your day at the POLIN Museum of the History of Polish Jews (p100), an absorbing introduction to Poland's Jewish history – a highlight is the exquisite painted ceiling of Gwoździec synagogue. The humbling Monument to the Heroes of the Ghetto is found next to the museum.

Afternoon Take the metro to Praga (p116), the 19th-century suburb found on the east bank of the Vistula. Fill your belly at Polish-Russian restaurant Skamiejka (Ząbkowska 37), then enjoy the fluorescent delights of the Neon Museum (p116), housed in the renovated Soho Factory.

Evening Eat in one of the Soho Factory's restaurants, then head back to the Praga to enjoy a tipple in one of the district's notoriously bohemian bars.

←

① Arcaded courtyard of the Royal Castle in the Wavel.

② Exhibition at Schindler's Factory and MOCAK.

③ Pizza being made by hand at Nolio.

④ St Mary's Basilica, floodlit in the evening.

3 DAYS
in Kraków

Day 1

Morning Start your first day in Kraków by exploring Rynek Główny, the city's photogenic market square. Dominating its centre is the magnificent Renaissance Cloth Hall (*p153*), beneath whose bulk lies the innovative Rynek Underground (*p153*), housing fascinating archaeological excavations. Emerging back into the light, visit Kraków's pride and joy, the sumptuously decorated St Mary's Basilica (*p152*).

Afternoon Stroll north along charming Ulica Floriańska (*p154*) towards the imposing Barbican (*p154*), detouring for a late lunch of fried pierogi at Milkbar Tomasza (*Ulica Świętego*). Spend the rest of the afternoon wandering through Planty park, a leafy ribbon of green that surrounds the Old Town – keep your eyes peeled for the fire-breathing dragon (*p148*).

Evening As the sun sinks, set your sights on the Tytano complex (*p160*); this former tobacco factory is now packed with some of Kraków's coolest restaurants, bars and clubs. Combat your carb-packed lunch with veggies at Veganic (*www.veganic. restaurant*), then enjoy local craft beers at Weźże Krafta (*www.wezze-krafta.ontap.pl*).

Day 2

Morning Begin the day by exploring the magnificent Wawel Hill (*p144*), the former home of Poland's kings – it'll take you the whole morning to explore this expansive complex. Afterwards, walk north through Planty park for lunch in the walled garden of Dynia Resto-Bar (*www.dynia.krakow.pl*).

Afternoon Wander back towards the Old Town's atmospheric University Quarter, home to the splendid Baroque Church of St Anne (*p155*). As sunset approaches, visit the Franciscan Church (*p156*): its beautiful stained-glass windows look even more spectacular when illuminated by the evening sun.

Evening After a busy day exploring the city, settle down at one of the restaurant terraces of the Main Market Square for an evening of people-watching.

Day 3

Morning Hop on a tram to Podgórze on the south bank of the Vistula, where Schindler's Factory and MOCAK (*p150*) provides a moving account of Kraków's sufferings under German occupation. Take time to reflect with a late-morning coffee at nearby BAL (*Ślusarska 9*), then cross back over the river to Kazimierz, formerly Kraków's Jewish quarter.

Afternoon Kazimierz's Nolio (*www.nolio. pl*), one of the city's best pizzerias, makes a good lunch stop. Afterwards explore the area's multicultural past, stopping in at the Old Synagogue (*p158*) before visiting the poignant Remuh Cemetary (*p159*).

Evening For dinner, munch on a delicious *zapiekanki* from one of the food stalls in Plac Nowy; both mouthwatering and unavoidably messy, these open baguettes are piled high with toppings like cheese and mushrooms. After, stick around in Kazimierz to enjoy the numerous vodka bars and clubs of this buzzing district.

1 The Monument to the Shipyard Workers.

2 The National Museum of Gdańsk.

3 Joseph Conrad statue in Gdynia.

4 Sopot's lovely pier.

3 DAYS
in Gdansk

Day 1

Morning Begin your exploration of this port-side city in the historic Main Town. Follow the Royal Way along Ulica Długa *(p261)*, a picturesque street lined with a number of fabulously restored merchants' houses. Towering over them is the magnificent Main Town Hall *(p263)*, home to the National Museum of Gdańsk. Spend an hour here, before having lunch in characterful café Mon Balzac *(Piwna 36/39)*.

Afternoon Ascend the tower of the monumental Church of St Mary *(p252)* for heartstopping views of the city. Back on earth, browse the amber shops of cobbled Ulica Mariacka *(p259)* as you wander towards the National Maritime Museum *(p254)*; there's enough here to fill a whole day, so look for the highlights.

Evening As night falls, cross the river to dine at Bazar *(www.restauracjabazar.pl)*, a canalside restaurant that offers traditional Polish cuisine with a modern twist.

Day 2

Morning Learn about Gdańsk's recent history at the Monument to the Shipyard Workers *(p256)*, which commemorates the brutally repressed strikes of 1970. Then explore the nearby European Solidarity Centre *(p256)*. Covering the history of non-violent protest, this centre pays special attention to the city's pioneering trade union, Solidarity *(p256)*.

Afternoon Enjoy a leisurely stroll back towards the city centre via the Raduna canal, stopping for fish and chips on the open-air terrace of A Nóz Widelec *(Plac Dominikański 1/2)*. Spend the rest of the afternoon browsing the Museum of World War II's compelling collection *(p257)*.

Evening Try craft beers at Café Lamus *(Ulica Lawendowa 8)*, the best of a knot of hipster bars on Ulica Lewandowa.

Day 3

Morning It's up early to explore Gdynia and Sopot, which alongside Gdańsk form the Tri-City. First stop is Gdynia *(p267)*, a relaxed town only 30 minutes away via the SKM train. When you arrive, make for the Museum of Emigration to explore the story of Poland's émigrés. After, amble down to the south pier to visit the statue of Polish-British writer Joseph Conrad.

Afternoon Jump on an SKM train bound for Sopot *(p266)*, a seaside town famous for its long sandy beach. Have a seafood snack at cult beachside café Bar Przystan *(www.barprzystan.pl)*, then meander along the beach to the pier; at 512-m- (1,700-ft) long, it offers beautiful ocean views.

Evening From Sopot, it's only 15 minutes on the SKM back to Gdańsk. You'll arrive in plenty of time to enjoy drinks on Ulica Piwna (literally "Beer Street") with its lively strip of bars – electic Joseph K *(p258)* is one of the best.

1

2

4

With a diverse landsacpe dotted with castles, country towns and wooden churches, southern Poland is the perfect place for a driving tour.

7 DAYS
in Southern Poland

Day 1

Morning Drive south from Kraków to Zakopane *(p178)*, a town surrounded by the majestic Tatra Mountains. On arrival, eat lunch at Polish-Swiss restaurant Mała Szwajcarja *(www.malaszwajcaria.pl)*.

Afternoon Stretch your legs with a hike in the nearby mountain valley of Dolina Białego *(p180)*, which offers an immediate taste of magnificent Alpine scenery.

Evening Back in town, indulge in a meal at Zakopiańska *(www.restauracjazakopianska. pl)*, housed in the historic Konstantynówka pension where Joseph Conrad once stayed.

Day 2

Morning Pack a picnic and spend the day touring the Tatra foothills. Head east past pretty highland villages to Lake Czorsztyn Enjoy a lakeside lunch and then admire the elegant wooden church at nearby Dębno.

Afternoon Experience the area's natural beauty with a raft ride down the picturesque Dunajec Gorge *(p194)*. Zip down the river in a kayak or drift along sedately in a traditional wooden boat.

Evening Head east to the sedate spa resort of Szczawnica, and enjoy dinner at chic Café Helenka *(www. cafe-helenka.pl)*.

Day 3

Morning Drive through the rolling Tatra foothills, stopping in at picturesque Nowy Sącz *(p187)* to explore one of Poland's largest open-air ethnographic museums. Pull in for lunch in the pretty town of Stary Sącz *(p188)*.

Afternoon Enjoy a leisurely drive along the scenic Poprad valley, where the river winds between steep green hills. End the day with a stroll around quaint 19th-century health resort Krynica *(p188)*.

Evening The French-inspired Koncertowa *(www.restauracjakoncertowa.pl)* restaurant in Krynica is one of the best in the region.

Day 4

Morning From Krynica, journey north through wooded hills to Gorlice *(p189)*, centre of fierce battles in World War I and home to a gripping local museum.

① Visitors on the Dunajec Gorge raft ride. ↑

② The resort town of Krynica.

③ The open-air ethnographic museum in Sanok.

④ Hikers strolling through the Tatra Mountains.

⑤ The charming town of Przemyśl.

Afternoon Admire the wooden churches at Sękowa and Kwiatoń, just south of Gorlice. Then nip up to Biecz (p188), one of Poland's best-preserved historic towns.

Evening Enjoy local food in Golice's charming Dark Pub (www.darkpub.pl).

Day 5

Morning Just east of Gorlice, the historic hilltop town of Sanok (p191) is your next stop, home to a spectacular open-air ethnographic museum.

Afternoon Continue northeast past rustic villages to reach Przemyśl (p190). Visit the regional museum with its fabulous collection of icons, followed by coffee and cake at renowned Café Fiore (p191).

Evening Amble along the town's cobbled streets and relax at Kawiarnia Libera (Rynek 26), a characterful bookshop-café.

Day 6

Morning Heading west this time, stop to explore Krasiczyn Castle (p190) and its beautiful park. Take the road southeast to Lesko and explore its evocative hilltop Jewish cemetery. Lunch at Pizzeria Roma (www.pizzaroma.pl) on the main square.

Afternoon After Lesko, enjoy a scenic ride past the Bieszczady mountains' (p192) wooded slopes to reach Wetlina, a village nestled beneath the stark bare hills of Połonona Wetlinska.

Evening Grab some grub at popular pub Baza Ludzi z Mgły (Wetlina 82).

Day 7

Morning Get your hiking boots on and strike uphill to the Połonina Wetlinska, a long mountain ridge that offers fabulous views of the Bieszczady range. Refuel at the Chata Puchatka mountain hut.

Afternoon Continue westward along the grassy ridge towards the summit of Smerek, from where you can descend south again to Wetlina.

Evening Wetlina's Chata Wędrowca restaurant (www.chatawedrowca.pl) is famous for serving gigantic pancakes with fruit; just the energy boost you need after a day in the hills.

←

1 Warsaw's Old Town at dusk.

2 Sołdek ship at the Gdańsk's Maritime Museum.

3 Poznan Cathedral at night.

4 The expansive Botanical Gardens in Wrocław.

2 WEEKS
in Poland

Day 1

Begin your two-week trip in Warsaw's Old Town Square, home to a statue of the city's iconic *Syrenka (p76)*. Then delve into Polish history at the Royal Castle *(p74)* and Cathedral of St John *(p76)*. Lunch on traditional Polish cuisine at Old-Town restaurant Stolica *(p79)* and then head southwest to spend the afternoon in the POLIN Museum of Jewish History *(p100)*, a tour-de-force of historical storytelling. Grab dinner at Signature on Ulica Poznanska, which is housed in a former Soviet embassy *(www.naturerestaurant.pl)*.

Day 2

Travel north across the green plains of northern Poland to the port-city of Gdańsk *(p248)*, grabbing a seafood lunch at Targ Rybny *(p257)* when you arrive. Discover Gdańsk's historic heart with a stroll down Ulica Długa *(p261)* and Długi Targ *(p262)*, lined with colourful merchants' houses. Cross the river to explore the National Maritime Museum's varied collection *(p254)*, before devouring pierogi at Nova Pierogova *(Ulica Szafarnia 6)*.

Day 3

Take a day trip from Gdańsk to the town of Malbork. Only a 30-minute drive away, it is the site of Poland's most complete medieval fortress complex *(p276)*, once home to the Teutonic Knights. Lunch at Bistro na Fali *(www.bistronafali.pl)*, a pleasant riverside restaurant with great views of the castle before motoring back to Gdańsk. Spend the afternoon at the Polish Post Office, site of a dramatic seige *(p258)*. End your busy day with a pint and plate of seafood at Gdański Bowke *(p257)*.

Day 4

Travel south along the Vistula river to the university town of Toruń *(p278)*. Stroll around the Old Town Square *(p278)* before lunching at the Kona Coast Café *(www.konacoastcafe.pl)*. Spend the afternoon exploring the house where astronomer Nicolaus Copernicus was born *(p280)*, then sample Toruń's famous *piernik* (gingerbread). As night falls, enjoy boutique beers and hearty food at the Jan Olbracht Browar Staromiejski *(www.browar-olbracht.pl)*, before strolling the banks of the Vistula.

Day 5

From Toruń make a beeline to cultural Poznań *(p202)*. Head straight for the Old Market Square *(p202)*, edged by brightly coloured merchants' houses, to lunch at the Ratuszova restaurant *(www.ratuszova.pl/en)*. After, wander through the riverside quarter of Ostrów Tumski *(p205)* to visit Poznań's magnificent cathedral *(p206)*. Then it's back to the main square for a slap-up meal at Brovaria *(www.brovaria.pl)*, followed by drinks and a gig at hipster favourite Meskalina *(www.meskalina.com)*.

Day 6

It's a two-hour drive south to Wrocław *(p222)*. On arrival, take a circuit of the beautiful market square *(p225)*, with its arresting Gothic Town Hall *(p225)*. Eat lunch on the garden terrace of the Bulka z maslem café *(p225)* and then admire the extraordinary Racławice Panorama *(p224)*, a huge circular painting celebrating an eighteenth-century battle. Spend the rest of the afternoon relaxing in the Botanical Gardens *(p228)*, before dining on refined Polish fare at JaDka *(p225)*.

→

Day 7

Make an early start for Oświęcim, site of the Auschwitz-Birkenau Memorial Museum (p174). Allow a whole day here to get the most from your visit: Auschwitz is found on the eastern outskirts of Oświęcim; the much larger Birkenau is a further 3 km (1.8 miles) to the east. In the late afternoon, make for the mountain resort of Zakopane (p178), passing through a landscape of increasingly imposing hills. Once you arrive, stretch your legs on Ulica Krupówka; Zakopane's main street is lined with plenty of great places for dinner.

Day 8

Gather picnic ingredients at the local market and set off for the Tatra National Park (p180), which starts on the southern fringes of town. Polana Palenica is the starting point for the 90-minute hike to Morskie Oko (p181), a high-altitude lake surrounded by an arc of grey peaks. Enjoy your lunch and then begin the hike back. Back in town, reward yourself with delicious Sicilian-inspired pizza at the Cristina Ristorante & Pizzeria (www.cristina.pl).

Day 9

It's up early to drive to Kraków (p140). On arrival, make a beeline for the Main Market Square to admire its magnificent Cloth Hall (p153) and Town Hall Tower (p153). Lunch in one of the square's pleasant pavement cafés, then cross the river to the Eagle Pharmacy (p161) to learn about the experiences of Kraków's Jews during World War II. Then make for buzzing Kazimierz, once the city's Jewish quarter, to sample Jewish food at Ariel (www.ariel-krakow.pl).

Day 10

Take the bus to Nowa Huta (p162) to spend a few hours exploring this fascinating town, built by the Communists as a model proletarian city. Back in Kraków, enjoy a plate of Poland's heartwarming dumplings at Love Pierogi (Jozefa Dietla 77), then jump on the tram to Kościuszko Mound (p162); this monument offers picture-perfect views of the city. Back in the Old Town, dine at Winoman (Bracka 15) where every dish served is designed to complement the wine on offer.

1 The gates at Auschwitz.
2 Morskie Oko lake in the Tatras.
3 Kraków's Main Market Sqaure.
4 Display at Zamość Museum.
5 Lublin's impressive castle.
6 Interior of Zamoyski Palace.

Day 11

Make the long drive from Kraków to the Renaissance town of Zamość (p128). Save yourself for lunch at Verona (www.verona cafe.pl) on the town's splendid main square. Dedicate your afternoon to Zamość's museum (p130), an excellent introduction to the town's history. Then take a gentle circuit of the park, which stretches around Zamość's magnificent star-shaped fortifications. Spend the evening at the town's legendary Jazz Klub Kosz (p131).

Day 12

It's not too far from Zamość to Lublin (p124), leaving you plenty of time to explore Lublin's gated Old Town. Huddled on a hill, it is home to a fascinating warren of alleys, churches and piazzas. Try Polish-Mediterranean fare at 16 Stolów (16stolow.pl) on the main square, then visit the castle (p125) to spy its fabulous fine-arts collection. After, stroll along the elegant 19th-century boulevard of Krakowskie Przedmeście, stopping at the huge oval-shaped bar ofthe Pijalnia Piwa pub (www.perla.pl) for dinner and drinks.

Day 13

Leave Lublin and head for Zamoyski Palace at Kozłówka (p138) and its unique museum of Socialist Realist art. Spend a couple of hours here before driving west to Kazimierz Dolny (p138), the beautifully preserved Renaissance town on the banks of the Vistula and enjoy a lunch in the garden of Zielona Tawerna (p139). Refuelled, make the climb up to the town's ruined castle, with expansive views over the river. Head back into town for a meal at arty Stara Łaźnia (www.restauracjalaznia.pl).

Day 14

Set off early for the drive back to Warsaw (p70), calling in at Puławy to take a look at the beautifully landscaped park of the Czartoryski family (p138). On arrival in the capital, seek out the Kafka café (p93) for a light lunch. From here it's only a short stroll to Warsaw's University Library (p92) whose leafy roof garden offers grand views across the Vistula. End your day (and your trip) with a couple of celebratory pints at Piw Paw (Foksal 16), which has 90 different types of beer on tap.

Hands-On Museums

Family-friendly, interactive museums are becoming something of a Polish trademark, and are a sure fire way to keep little ones entertained. One standout attraction is the Copernicus Science Centre *(p92)* in Warsaw, which provides activities for every age group, including mind-bending puzzles and educational play areas. Kids will also love the Hewelianum in Gdańsk *(p266)*, which teaches children about life and the universe, and offers the chance to roam around an 18th-century fort.

→

Children enjoy one of the exhibits at the Copernicus Science Centre

POLAND FOR
FAMILIES

With family at its heart, Poland is the perfect place for kids. Children will be enthralled by the country's castles and palaces, and there are plenty of awesome interactive museums to keep young minds occupied. Plus, Poland's stunning wildernesses are perfect for budding explorers.

The Great Outdoors

With emerald forests, expansive lakes and low-lying yet magnificent mountains, Poland is a veritable playground for kids. A gentle ride on one of the passenger steamers that crisscross the Great Mazurian Lakes *(p298)* is perfect for little ones, while older kids will enjoy Dunajec Gorge's popular raft ride *(p194)* which snakes between spectacular peaks. Kids of all ages can also enjoy mountain views by taking the scenic cable-car ride to Kasprowy Wierch's lofty peak *(p180)*; or by riding the funicular railway up to the Gubałówka Hill *(p178)*, site of a high-wire park.

→

Families beginning the Dunajec Gorge raft ride on traditional wooden boats

TOP 3 **PLAY PARKS IN POLAND**

Plac Wilsona, Warsaw
All the swings and climbing frames the kids could ever want, just a short hop away from the Plac Wilsona metro station.

Jordan Park, Kraków
This well-equipped playpark in one of Kraków's favourite green spaces also has a small boating lake.

Gdynia Beach
A cute playpark with climbing frames, slides and swings right on Gdynia's beautiful white-sand beach.

Travel Back in Time
Little time travellers can discover Poland's history thanks to the fun-filled historical reenactments that take place during summer. From medieval jousting at the Knights Tournament in Golub-Dobrzyń *(p290)*, to an action-packed reenactment of the siege of Malbork castle *(p276)*, there's enough here to keep everyone entertained.

→ The Knights' Tournament taking place at the 14th-century Teutonic castle in Golub-Dobrzyń, Pomerania

Awesome Entertainment
Keeping the kids amused is easy thanks to the country's incredible puppet theatres; one of the best is Teatr Groteska in Kraków, where puppetry is mixed with live action. The evening light shows at Warsaw's Multimedia Fountain *(p80)* will also leave kids wide-eyed, while the Magician's Festival in Lublin *(p59)* will astound the whole family with its tightrope walkers, buskers and circus entertainers.

← The spectacular light show at Warsaw's Multimedia Fountain

Remote Landscapes

The most hauntingly seductive highland area in the country, the Bieszczady mountains *(p192)* owe their allure to the long ridges covered by so-called *połoniny*. These meadows of tall grasses are a bewitching sight, as they change colour when blown by the wind. The villages here are sparsely populated, lending the area a remote, untouched feel.

←

The grass meadows changing colour at sunset in the Bieszczady mountains

POLAND FOR
NATURAL
WONDERS

From jagged mountains to ancient forests, the Polish landscape is both incredibly diverse and awe-inspiringly beautiful. With a total of 23 national parks, there's a wealth of natural beauty for visitors to get out and explore.

TOP 4 ANIMALS TO SPOT

Bison
Spot large herds in the Wolin and Białowieża national parks.

Lynx
The secretive wildcat is occasionally spotted in the Bieszczady hills.

Elk
These beasts thrive in the marshes and forests of eastern Poland.

Bears
Although they stay away from well-trodden paths, distant sightings are sometimes possible in the Tatra mountains.

Baltic Beaches

The most spectacular sight on the long expanse of Baltic coastline, with its endless stretches of white sand, are the huge shifting sand dunes in Slowinski National Park *(p286)*. These rise with Sahara-like majesty, and change shape yearly due to the action of the wind.

↑ Long stretches of sand beaches at windswept Slowinski National Park

Majestic Alpine Scenery

Marking Poland's border with Slovakia, the Tatra Mountains *(p178)* are the only truly alpine range in the country, characterized by granite peaks rising above the high-altitude and sloping meadows known as Haly. South-flowing streams have carved deep valleys edged by cliffs; it's here that many of the country's most epic hiking trails begin.

Rugged peaks and deep lakes at the spectacular alpine Tatra Mountains

Spellbinding Forests

The Białowieża forest *(p310)* is the last significant stretch of primeval forest in Europe, an enchanting emerald wonderland dense with oak, birch, alder and pine. The park is under strict protection, and large areas of the forest can only be visited with an official guide. Among Poland's many other magical woodlands is the Crooked Forest, an area of curved pine trees.

→

A snow-covered winter landscape at ancient Białowieża forest

Wonderful Wetlands

One of Poland's most enchanting wetland areas, Biebrza National Park *(p308)* is an important stopping-off point for hundreds of species of migrating birds in spring. Even if you're not a keen twitcher, an amble along the park's trails offers views of its waterways and covered peat bogs, as well as glimpses of elk and beaver. The park is at its best in spring.

Species like the godwit can be seen in the wetlands at Biebrza National Park

Fit for a King

Royal palaces have huge symbolic importance in a nation that was occupied by foreign empires for much of its modern history. Warsaw's opulent Royal Castle *(p74)* is a reconstructed marvel, while Wilanów Palace *(p112)* is a showcase of Polish Baroque. The Wawel *(p146)*, in Kraków, is a feast of Renaissance art.

←

The ornate Baroque façade of Wilanów Palace in Warsaw

POLAND FOR
CASTLES
AND PALACES

There is no better way to savour the grandeur of Polish history than by roaming the ramparts of its castles or admiring the interiors of its opulent palaces. Many have been superbly restored and now contain museums and galleries – they're the perfect places to transport you back to a fairytale past.

TOP 5 CASTLES ON THE EAGLES' NEST TRAIL

Ogrodzieniec
Said to be haunted by a huge black dog.

Olsztyn
An atmospheric ruin, with a dramatic brick tower *(p306)*.

Mirów
Once belonged to the Myszkowski family.

Bobolice
Built in the 14th century by Kazimierz the Great.

Pieskowa Skała
A well-preserved castle that dominates the Prądnik valley.

Teutonic Castles

If your idea of a castle is an impregnable-looking fortress, then the strongholds of the Teutonic Order will more than fit the bill. Poland's most famous example is Malbork *(p276)*, but imposing Golub-Dobrzyń *(p290)*, enchanting Nidzica *(p304)* and red-brick Frombork *(p302)* are equally impressive.

→

The Teutonic castle of Nidzica, strategically positioned at the edge of a lake

Hilltop Ruins

Małopolska was the heart of the Polish state in the 14th century, so it's not surprising that so many romantic hilltop ruins pepper its landscape. Many of the most evocative examples form the so-called Eagles' Nest Trail, a line of 25 striking castles straddling the limestone crags of the Kraków-Częstochowa uplands. Pick of the crop is Ogrodzieniec, a dramatic cluster of turrets at the uplands' highest point.

→

The arresting ruins of Ogrodzieniec Castle on the Eagles' Nest Trail

Aristocratic Seats

The lavish palaces and lush parks built by Poland's big landowning families are some of the country's most visited attractions. Top of the list is Łańcut *(p172)*, packed with paintings and sculpture.

←

The opulent interior of Książ Castle in Silesia

The lavish palace of the Raczynskis *(p200)* rivals anything else in Europe, as does Książ *(p240)*, the hilltop palace built by the Hochbergs.

Fortified Towns

By the 16th and 17th centuries, a new kind of fortified town, characterized by jutting bastions and multiple moats, had superseded the castle. Of these, the best preserved is Zamość *(p128)*; other examples include the Gora Gradowa in Gdańsk, now the Hewelianum museum *(p266)*, and the Boyen Fortress in Giżycko.

↑ The fortified town of Zamość, built in the 16th century

Polish Classics

Think of Polish food and you'll probably think of pierogi. These little parcels of dough are stuffed with a variety of fillings, from minced meat and onion, to cottage cheese and potato. Sample these in Kraków's cheap-and-cheerful milk bars, which used to be dining halls for Soviet-era workers. Don't forget to sample Poland's most famous street food, *zapiekanki*: these delectable toasted sandwiches consist of half a baguette smothered in tomato sauce, and topped with mushrooms and cheese.

→

Pierogi being served to happy punters at the Pierogi Festival

POLAND FOR
FOODIES

Forget all preconceptions about Polish cuisine being simple and stodgy. The country boasts an amazing variety of dishes, from tummy-warming appetisers and wonderfully creamy puddings to fabulously fresh seafood and celebratory platters of roast fowl.

Beautiful Beetroot

Poland is head over heels in love with beetroot. This mineral-rich vegetable is used in an array of Polish dishes, the most famous being borscht (*barszcz* in Polish), a truly heartwarming, dark ruby soup which is sure to feature on the menu of every restaurant. Classic borscht is usually light and clear, although other variations, such as Ukrainian borscht, can come with meat and chunky vegetables.

←

A warm bowl of borscht, Poland's best-loved soup, made from beetroot

VODKA

If you're meeting locals for the first time, be prepared to down a *wódka* shot - in fact, once a bottle is opened, it's de rigueur to finish the whole thing. You might be surprised to hear that vodka comes in many forms, not just the pure transparent version. Dabble with yellowish Żubrówka, flavoured with bison grass; sample the ruby-red Wiśniówka, made with cherries; or sip on the amber-coloured Żołądkowa Gorzka, flavoured with herbs.

Festive Fare

Here, it's not a celebration unless roast fowl and game are on the menu. Tender meats are frequently served with sweet fruit-based sauces: roast duck comes with apples, while wild boar is teamed up with forest berries. Honey and beer are used in the preparation of *golonka*, succulent pork knuckle stewed on the bone - this delicious dish is a national favourite.

← Duck, often paired with apples in Polish celebratory fare

Treats and Sweets

Patisseries are at the heart of Polish life, particularly served alongside coffee. Cake-making here is a high art; you won't know how to choose between mouth-watering *szarlotka* (apple pie with crumbly pastry) or delicious *sernik* (baked cheesecake), the nation's favourite desserts.

→ Sweet and savoury treats piled high at a Warsaw bakery

Remarkable Resistance

After World War II, Poland became a Communist satellite state of the Soviet Union. From 1980, resistance to this rule was led by trade union Solidarity (Solidarność), and eventually resulted in the country becoming democratic, a fight told at the stirring European Solidarity Centre *(p256)* in Gdańsk.

←

Community resistance celebrated at the European Solidarity Centre

POLAND FOR
HISTORY BUFFS

Delve into the story of Poland, with its repeating cycles of greatness, decline and rebirth, at the country's endlessly fascinating museums and historical sites. This history, particularly recent Nazi and Communist terror, has shaped the country and forged an incredible spirit of resistance.

TOP 4 FAMOUS WOMEN IN POLISH HISTORY

Marie Curie
The scientist won Nobel prizes in both physics and chemistry.

Emila Plater
Noblewoman Plater was a standard-bearer during the anti-Tsarist uprising of 1830.

Krystyna Skarbek
One of the top secret agents in the Allied forces in World War II.

Irena Sendlerowa
A resistance activist who smuggled thousands of Jewish children out of the Warsaw ghetto.

Deeper Underground

Journey into what feels like the centre of the earth at Wieliczka Salt Mine *(p186)* south of Kraków, where generations of miners have carved a magnificent underground city with halls, tunnels and chapels. Working-class history is also commemorated in the coal belt of Silesia, where the former mine of Stara Kopalnia *(p240)* is now a museum dedicated to telling the story of coal mining.

Bear Witness at Auschwitz-Birkenau

The Nazi extermination camp at Auschwitz-Birkenau (p174) is a unique and harrowing symbol of the horrors of the years surrounding World War II. The Auschwitz-Birkenau camp accounted for more victims than any other single site: an estimated 1.1 million people lost their lives here; of these, a staggering 90 per cent were Jewish. The bleak remains of the camp and the mountain of survivor testimony at the museum reveal the atrocities that were inflicted upon the prisoners interned here and stand as both a memorial and a record of the Holocaust.

$\rightarrow$

A guard tower at the extermination camp of Auschwitz-Birkenau

Warsaw and World War II

Few cities felt the impact of World War II as acutely as Warsaw, and a number of excellent museums tell this story. The Warsaw Uprising Museum (p114) is a tour-de-force, documenting the heroism of the city's 1944 uprising against the Germans, for which the city was almost totally razed to the ground.

$\leftarrow$

A gallery dedicated to Soviet occupation of the city at the Warsaw Uprising Museum

Memories and Memorabilia

Look beyond the big events of the past at social history museums in Poland, like the excellent Praga Museum (p116) in Warsaw, which conjures up the day-to-day life of a neighbourhood, and the Museum of Emigration (p266), which reveals how countless Polish families uprooted themselves in search of a better life.

$\uparrow$

The incredible grand hall at the underground Wieliczka Salt Mine

$\rightarrow$

The fascinating displays at the Museum of Emigration

Hit the Slopes

Zakopane (p178), Poland's prime skiing resort, is the perfect place for a snow-filled adrenaline rush. Boasting a big choice of black, red and blue runs, as well as plenty of nursery slopes with good tuition, it's great for expert skiers and beginners alike. It's also the best spot for cross-country skiing, with trails stretching out across the valley floor.

→

Skiers on the slopes of Kasprowy Wierch at Zakopane

POLAND FOR
ADVENTURERS

Poland is a big country for big adventures, with a range of outdoor activities offering everything from an adrenaline rush to the quiet contemplation of nature. Whether you're charging downhill on a mountain bike or indulging in an easy woodland walk, Poland offers you a breath of fresh air.

TOP 5 HIKING DESTINATIONS

Dolina Chochołowska
A narrow valley lined with pines, in the Tatra National Park (p178).

Słowiński National Park
A beautiful stretch of the Baltic Coast (p286).

Połonina Wetlińska
A mountain ridge with views of Bieszczady National Park (p192).

Vistula Riverbank
An easy route along Warsaw's right bank.

Royal Oaks Way
A gentle stroll through the primeval Białowieża Forest (p310).

Epic Hikes

Poland offers some of Europe's most spectacular hiking. The Tatra Mountains (p178) are ideal for multi-day, hut-to-hut hikes, with well-marked paths with stunning views of lush green valleys peppered with wooden houses. For one-day walks, nothing can beat the beautiful grey-brown hills of the Bieszczady range (p192).

Sleep Beneath the Stars

Poland features some truly stirring spots to camp. Łeba (p287), on the Baltic coast, offers a variety of sites wedged between sandy beach and deep green forest, while the Great Mazurian Lakes (p298) are ideal for peaceful waterside camping. The Tatra Mountains (p178) are home to an array of places to camp beneath the trees.

→

Camping in the verdant surroundings of the Tatra Mountains

Take to the Water

Northeastern Poland is ideal terrain for canoes and kayaks. The Great Mazurian Lakes (p298) provide opportunities for leisurely paddling, while the more ambitious can try a multi-day canoeing trip along the Krutynia River Trail or the Czarna Hańcza Trail (p300). On the Baltic coast, the resorts of Łeba (p287) and Hel (p288) offer the perfect conditions to try windsurfing, kitesurfing and wakeboarding.

←

Paddling along the beautiful Krutynia River Trail

On Two Wheels

Poland is a cyclist's dream, with marked routes crisscrossing the country. The Karkonosze National Park (p232), with its open moorland and emerald pine forests, is ideal for mountain bikers. The areas south and east of Kraków also offer spellbindingly scenic routes: few are more stunning than the Dunajec Gorge ride (p194). For a long-distance route, try the Green Velo Eastern Cycle Trail (www.greenvelo.pl), which winds through five magnificent national parks.

↑ Cycling through the dramatic Dunajec Gorge

↑ Hiking through the awe-inspiring scenery of the Tatra Mountains

A Song and a Dance
Poland sways to the sound of traditional music, and almost everywhere you go there will be a folk band playing in a main square, performing at weddings or touring the pavement cafés at tourist resorts. Keep an ear out for shows in big concert halls by professional troupes such as Mazowsze (from Warsaw) and Śląsk (from Silesia).

→

Noted folk group Śląsk performing an anniversary show

POLAND FOR
FOLKLORE

Traditional music, costume and design are still a vivid part of life in Poland, and church celebrations and saints' days in particular provide everyone with an excuse to dress up in their best traditional garb and dance the *oberek*. These numerous festivals are the perfect way to experience local customs.

TOP 4 POLISH DANCES

Mazurka
A quick-moving and zestful pairs' dance from central Poland.

Polonaise
A stately dance in which couples process through arches formed by the raised hands of others.

Krakowiak
This charming pairs' dance from Kraków involves a modicum of stamping and kicking.

Oberek
The fastest and most athletic of Polish dances, this features a lot of spinning, jumping and high kicks.

↑ A traditional house on display at the open-air museum in Sanok

Explore an Open-Air Museum
Sample life in a traditional Polish village by visiting an open-air ethnographic museum or *skansen*, where salvaged buildings have been painstakingly restored and re-erected. There is a spectacular example at Sanok where you can stroll around a reassembled 19th-century market square. Equally enchanting is the *skansen* in Nowy Sącz *(p187)*, where timber churches are spread across rolling meadows.

VAMPIRES IN KRAKOW?

Delve into the dark, night-time history of Kraków at the Rynek Underground museum *(p153)* on the Main Market Square, which displays a series of so-called vampire burials. The deceased were interred with their hands bound and their decapitated heads set between their feet. It is assumed that they were buried like this as a measure to stop them rising from the grave in search of blood.

Festivals and Fairs

From the traditional bold, stripy costumes worn by locals at the Corpus Christi processions in Łowicz, to the singing and dancing at one of Poland's annual fairs, like Hetman's Fair in Zamość, Poland's folk festivals are colourful affairs. If you have to choose just one, go to the summer International Highlanders' Folk Festival in Zakopane, which celebrates the music and dances of Poland's mountain communities.

↑ The annual process on the Corpus Christi saint's day in Łowicz

Folk Architecture and Design

Colourful folk traditions extend beyond singing and costumes into architecture and design. The ethnographic museums in Warsaw *(p106)* and Kraków *(p160)* are packed with examples of this creativity, from painted Easter eggs to detailed textiles.

Folk architecture is best experienced at Zalipie *(p186)*, where houses are decorated with paintings.

← Easter eggs painted in colourful traditional folk patterns

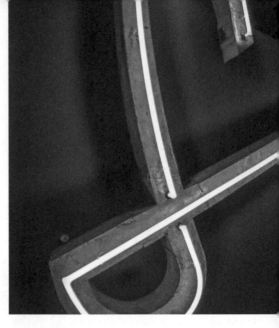

Neon Glow

If there is one thing that sums up Polish design then it's neon, the fizzing, flickering signage that used to adorn the façades of countless buildings across the country, from bars and hotels to restaurants and railway stations. Warsaw's thrilling Neon Museum *(p116)*, set up in 2005 by Polish photographer Ilona Karwinska and her husband, reveals what a great time Polish designers had with neon, creating flowing fonts that were perfectly suited to the medium's luminous tubes.

→

Examining the array of glowing signs at the Neon Museum in Warsaw

POLAND FOR
INSPIRATION

Poland has always been at the forefront of the arts, cultivating the avant-garde and creating breakthrough moments, as well as nurturing a talent for decoration and good design. Evidence of creativity is visible everywhere, and it's hard to come home from the country without feeling inspired.

Evocative Art Nouveau

Known as Młoda Polska, or "Young Poland", Polish Art Nouveau embraced theatre and poetry as well as art and design. Kraków is the best place to see it, with the Mehoffer House *(p156)* displaying a beautiful selection of paintings, furnishings, and the stained glass in which Mehoffer excelled. The leading artist and writer of the day was Stanisław Wyspiański, whose masterwork was the interior of Kraków's Franciscan Church *(p156)*.

←

A stained-glass window by Stanisław Wyspiański in the Franciscan Church

WITKACY

Paintings by Stanisław Ignacy Witkiewicz (1885–1939), popularly know as Witkacy, can be found at every major Polish gallery. After experimenting with various avant-garde movements, Witkacy set up a portrait studio in Zakopane *(p178)*. He produced penetrating psychological portraits of his sitters, as well as wild, surreal pictures full of distortion, aided by his intake of drugs. The amount of narcotics consumed by the artist was recorded in the corner of each canvas.

Revolutionary Films

From Andrzej Wajda's 1950s war trilogy to Krzystof Kieślowski's 1980s Decalogue series, nothing illustrates the creative tensions of Communist Poland better than the world of film. Learn more at the Museum of Cinematography *(p209)* in Łódź, home to a wealth of Polish cinematic treasures.

→

A still from Wajda's 1957 *Canal*, one of his war trilogy

Jazzing It Up

The Polish Jazz boom of the 1950s and 60s was a form of rebellion against the grey conformity of the Communist regime, led by icons including pianist Krzystof Komeda, saxophonist Zbigniew Namysłowski and trumpeter Tomasz Stańko. Today, the Polish jazz spirit still lives on in the cellar clubs of Kraków and in the famed Klub Kosz *(p131)* in Zamość.

→

A live jazz performance at a bar in Kraków

Peer into the Past at POLIN

To experience the grand panorama of Polish-Jewish history there is no place better than the POLIN Museum of the History of Polish Jews *(p100)*, built in the centre of the former Warsaw Ghetto. A spectacular slab of contemporary architecture, it offers an inspiring journey through ten centuries of history. A short stroll away is the Monument to the Heroes of the Ghetto *(p101)*, a compelling tribute to those brave individuals who fought in the Warsaw Uprising of 1943.

→

Exploring the exhibits at the POLIN Museum of the History of Polish Jews

POLAND FOR
JEWISH
HERITAGE

Established in the Middle Ages, Poland's Jewish community made a huge contribution to local industry and culture. While the treatment of Polish Jews during World War II is omnipresent, new museums and restored synagogues show a renewed appreciation of the country's Jewish heritage.

Stroll the Streets of Kazimierz

The lost world of Jewish Poland is at its most evocative in Kazimierz, the Kraków suburb that hosted a thriving Jewish community before World War II. The district featured heavily in the 1993 film *Schindler's List*, and the original Schindler Factory *(p150)*, now a compelling museum, is found just over the river in Podgórze.

←

Pavement cafés in Kazimierz, Kraków's old Jewish quarter

Did You Know?

At the outbreak of World War II, Poland was home to 3.3 million Jews.

THE STORY OF POLISH JEWS

Jewish traders and artisans began settling in Poland in the early Middle Ages; Polish rulers valued their skills and encouraged further immigration. Despite occasional pogroms, Poland was regarded as a relative safe haven for Jews, famous for its cosmopolitan culture and religious tolerance. Jews contributed to every level of Polish life, participating in the uprisings of the 19th century and serving in the Polish army in 1939. The vast majority of Polish Jews were murdered by Nazi Germany during World War II.

Jewish Industrialists

Visitors to Łódź will be struck by the vast red-brick factories built by 19th-century industrialists. Most successful of them all was Izrael Poznański, the Jewish magnate whose textile factory now serves as the Manufaktura shopping centre. You can visit Poznański's mansion, now the local history museum *(p209)*, or admire his extraordinary mausoleumd in the city's Jewish cemetery.

→

The Manufaktura shopping centre, housed in a former textile factory

Small Town Synagogues

Many of Poland's synagogues were destroyed in World War II although a significant number survive in the small towns of the east. Lovingly restored, they stand as colourful testimony to the richness of Jewish religious art. Admire the synagogue at Włodawa *(p132)*, with its brightly painted Torah Ark, or visit the one at Tykocin *(p308)*, with its lovely Baroque pulpit.

→

The decorative interior of the synagogue in Tykocin

Maestro, If You Please!

As you might expect from the country of Chopin and Szymanowski there is a lot of classical music on offer, including free piano concerts in Warsaw's Łazienki Park *(p110)*. But Poland is also a major centre of rock and pop, with Gdynia's massive Open'er Festival attracting international stars, while the edgy OFF Festival in Katowice *(p246)* is a major event in the indie music calendar.

→

Crowds watch a free piano performance taking place in Łazienki Park

POLAND FOR
FESTIVALS

Poland has a mind-bogglingly full calendar of festivals, with events covering just about every activity and art form you might think of. The big cities are powerhouses of arts and culture, while traditional folk celebrations take place in all corners of the countryside.

All the Fun of the Fair

Poland's traditional fairs go back to medieval times when artisans and traders would converge on city squares. The event with the longest history is St Dominic's Fair in Gdańsk, dating from 1260, which sees the Main Town filled with an abundance of craft stalls selling beautiful handmade goods. More modern in origin is Poznań's St Martin's Fair, when St Martin parades through town on a white horse, medieval jousts are reenacted, and the almond-filled St Martin's Day croissants (*rogale świętomarcińskie*) are devoured.

→

Visitors perusing the stalls at Dominic's Fair

Did You Know?

Every June Warsaw is home to an International Mime Art Festival.

Gorging on Gastronomy

Scrumptious food is one of Poland's strong points and gourmet events present a great way to see which of it will tickle your tastebuds. The all-day Breakfast Markets in Warsaw are held every summer weekend in an open-air location, with stalls loaded with local treats and deli products. The European Festival of Taste in Lublin *(p124)* allows visitors to sample the cuisine of the Lublin region, an eclectic mix of Polish, Belarusian, Ukrainian and Jewish traditions. Then there's the Good Taste Festival in Poznań, where street-food stalls are piled high with all manner of artisan cheeses, sausages and cakes, just perfect for nibbling on.

← A street food stall at Poznań's Good Taste Festival

TOP 3 FREE FESTIVALS

Ice Festival
Held in Poznań every December, this festival sees international artists make shining, glass-like ice sculptures in the main square.

Pol'and'Rock Festival
Previously known as Woodstock Station, this free event at Kostrzyn nad Odrą claims to be the biggest rock festival in Europe.

Dragon Parade
Huge, colourful dragons, made by locals, parade around Kraków's Main Market Square, before flying over the river illuminated by colourful fireworks and lasers.

Arting Around

Poland offers an array of awe-inspiring arts festivals, from the ever-popular New Horizons Film Festival in Wrocław *(p222)*, one of the year's biggest cultural events, to the Festival of Four Cultures in Łódź *(p208)*, an energetic celebration of the city's Polish, Jewish, Russian and German heritage.

↑ A parade taking place at Łódź's Festival of Four Cultures

Feeling Festive

Attracting the big names of international literature is the Conrad Festival *(www.conradfestival.pl)*, named after the Polish-born novelist Joseph Conrad. Held every October in Kraków, it boasts a packed programme of lectures and workshops. For a bit of literature by the beach, Sopot By The Book *(www.literacki sopot.pl)* holds a series of outdoor readings every August.

→

An event at Kraków's annual Conrad Festival

POLAND FOR
BOOKWORMS

Writers have played a key role in Poland's history, serving as the bearers of emancipatory ideas when political freedoms have been lacking. It's no surprise, then, that the country is a bookish kind of place, home to bookshop-cafés, literary festivals and plenty of nods to the nation's best-loved authors.

TOP 5 ESSENTIAL READS

Pawel Huelle, Mercedes Benz
A rollicking ride through Polish history.

Ryszard Kapuściński, Another Day of Life
Lyrical reportage from Angola.

Stanislaw Lem, Solaris
A Polish sci-fi classic.

Olga Tokarczuk, Flights
Award-winning book about travel.

Bruno Schulz, The Street of Crocodiles
Dreamy recollections of growing up.

Pause in Planty Park

Nowhere better sums up Poland's love affair with literature than Planty park in Kraków, where each bench has a plaque honouring one of the city's famous writers. Sit and share a sandwich with Nobel Laureate Wysława Szymborska, sip a takeaway coffee with prize-winning Olga Tokarczuk, or contemplate human nature with Anglo-Polish writer Joseph Conrad.

Enjoying the tranquil surroundings of Planty park ↑

Patriotic Poland

If you're a fan of historical epics, make sure you visit Poznan's fantastic Henryk Sienkiewicz Museum *(p203)*. Writing at a time when the country was partitioned, Sienkiewicz's historical novels drew on the heroic struggles of the nation's past as a way to inspire readers with hope for its future – his best-known title is *Quo Vadis* (1896), set in ancient Rome. The museum is packed with the books and personal effects of this Nobel-Prize-winning author, and is also a fascinating insight into the 19th-century literary world.

← A portrait of Henryk Sienkiewicz, the celebrated Polish novelist

NON-FICTION

Reportage and travel writing enjoy a special place in Polish literature, thanks in large part to 20th-century journalist Ryszard Kapuściński, the long-serving foreign correspondent whose books about Africa, South America and other trouble spots still enjoy a worldwide following. Heirs to Kapuściński's mantle include Jacek Hugo-Bader, a perceptive traveller through the landscapes of the former Soviet Union, and Mariusz Szczygieł, whose lifelong fascination with the Czech Republic has inspired a series of popular books.

Lounge in a Literary Café

The bookshop-café is something of a Polish tradition, especially in the university city of Kraków. One key address is Massolit *(www.massolit.com)*, a second-hand English-language bookstore where you can enjoy apple pie and espresso among the shelves. Alternatively, catch up with the non-fiction scene at Warsaw's Wrzenie Świata *(www.wrzenie.pl)*, which serves superb Sunday breakfasts.

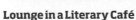

↑ Relaxing with a coffee in the bookshop-café Massolit in Kraków

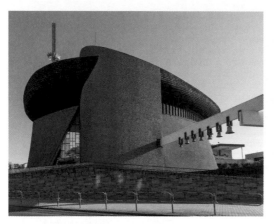

Sacral Symbols

The Polish Catholic Church was a keen supporter of Modernist trends. The most famous modern church is the Ark of the Lord in the Kraków suburb of Nowa Huta *(p162)*, combining rough concrete surfaces with an organic, curving profile. The nearby Maximilian Kolbe Church, built in 1983, is a startlingly angular contrast.

←

The rounded exterior of the Ark of the Lord church in Kraków

POLAND FOR
MODERNISTS

Poland isn't just about distant history; it's also about the shock of the new. The country's voracious appetite for Modernism left few cities untouched, with elegant Art Deco, gruff Communist-era Brutalism, and 21st-century neo-Modernism all clamouring for attention.

INDUSTRIAL HERITAGE

Poland has countless 19th-century industrial buildings and the repurposing of these imposing red-brick relics has had a transformational effect on many cities. One leading example is the former textile town of Łódź *(p208)*, where the Poznański factory now houses the MS2 Art Museum, Manufaktura shopping centre and Vienna House Andel's hotel. Even more spectacular is the Museum of Silesia in Katowice *(p246)*, where contemporary cubes of light rise up beside the pithead buildings of a former coal mine.

Brutal Buildings

For Brutalism at its best, look no further than Katowice *(p246)*. A showpiece of 1970s' urban planning, the city is famous for buildings like the Superjednostka, or "Super-Unit", a 187-m- (614-ft-) long block of flats inspired by the austere constructions of Le Corbusier. More breathtaking still is the city's Spodek, or "Flying Saucer", a futuristic domed sports hall that is nowadays a much-loved icon.

21st-Century Style

The early years of the 21st century witnessed a building boom in Poland, much of which was funded by grants from the European Union. New museums, stations and concert halls changed the face of the country. A prime example is the Museum of World War II (p257) in Gdańsk, an uncompromising building that leans sharply as if falling over. Most seductive of the concert spaces is Szczecin Philharmonic (p274), with towering white gables resembling the sails of tall ships.

→

The striking exterior of the Museum of World War II in Gdańsk

Keeping It Classical

Anyone with a passion for the geometric architecture of the 1920s and 30s will find a great deal to get excited about in Poland. The country is filled with Classic Modernist pieces, from the discreetly handsome Art-Deco Główna railway station in Gdynia (p267) to a whole suburb full of Bauhaus-inspired urban villas in Warsaw's Saska Kępa (p117).

←

Główna railway station in Gdynia

Communist Constructions

Come face to face with the ambiguities of Communist rule with a visit to the monumental Palace of Culture and Science (p102) in Warsaw, built in the early 1950s at a time when the country was in the grip of Stalinism. The nearby MDM residential district (p106), with Neo-Renaissance blocks adorned with Socialist Realist reliefs, is another piece of treasured socialist utopia.

↑ The eye-catching Spodek, a sports hall in Katowice

→

The Palace of Culture and Science in Warsaw, a city landmark

A YEAR IN POLAND

JANUARY

New Year's Day (*1 Jan*). Carol singers and well-wishers visit each other's houses.

△ **Epiphany** (*6 Jan*). The Three Kings of the nativity are celebrated with processions and masses. The initials "K + M + B" (Kaspar, Melchior and Balthazar) are chalked above doorways to ensure good fortune in the coming year.

FEBRUARY

Polish Maritime Festival, Kraków (*late Feb*). Europe's biggest festival of sea shanties.

△ **Fat Thursday** (*Feb or Mar*). The last Thursday before Lent is traditionally celebrated by eating doughnuts; there are big queues outside bakeries throughout the country.

MAY

△ **Corpus Christi** (*May or Jun*). Colourful religious processions take place throughout Poland, from carpets of flowers in Spycimierz to vibrant embroidered folk costumes in Łowicz.

Science Picnic, Warsaw (*May or Jun*). Europe's largest outdoor science festival, with live demonstrations and hands-on activities.

JUNE

△ **Midsummer's Eve** (*23 Jun*). Wreaths are thrown in rivers, and fireworks and lanterns are lit on the banks in a folk celebration that goes back to the pre-Christian epoch.

Open'er Rock Festival, Gdynia (*late Jun*). Huge international rock festivals, with big names performing on an airfield just outside the city.

SEPTEMBER

△ **Wratislavia Cantans, Wrocław** (*early Sep*). Festival of choral music from all epochs, with performances in the fabulous National Music Forum.

Sacrum Profanum, Kraków (*mid-Sep*). A contemporary music festival that embraces everything from string quartets to DJ culture, with performances in spaces all around the city.

OCTOBER

△ **Łódź Design Festival** (*early Oct*). A leading showcase for new design from Poland and further afield.

Warsaw Film Festival (*mid-Oct*). A major international event featuring independent movies from around the world.

MARCH

Misteria Paschalia, Kraków *(throughout)*. Held in the run-up to Easter, this is a festival of religious music throughout the ages.

△ **The Stage Songs' Review, Wrocław** *(late Mar)*. A celebration of quality songwriting, from the world of musicals and cabaret.

APRIL

Easter Monday *(Mar/Apr)*. Boys douse girls in water in an archaic spring fertility rite.

△ **Beethoven Easter Festival, Warsaw** *(Easter Week)*. Poland's largest classical music festival, this event celebrates the renowned composer with symphony and chamber concerts by international musicians.

Jazz on the Odra, Wrocław *(mid-Apr)*. One of Poland's oldest jazz festivals, featuring a galaxy of international guests.

JULY

Tauron New Music Festival, Katowice *(early Jul)*. Groundbreaking electronica and DJ sets in various venues around the city.

Magicians' Festival, Lublin *(late Jul)*. Conjurers, jugglers, acrobats and a host of other street entertainers converge on Lublin's Old Town for this fun-for-all-the-family outdoor festival.

△ **St Dominic's Fair, Gdansk** *(late Jul to mid-Aug)*. Crafts, local food and street music characterize an annual fair that dates back to medieval times.

AUGUST

△ **OFF Music Festival, Katowice** *(mid-Aug)*. Alternative rock festival in a park just outside the city.

Jewish Culture Festival *(late Aug)*. A celebration of Poland's traditional and contemporary Jewish culture, with concerts and film screenings.

NOVEMBER

△ **All Saints' Day** *(1 Nov)*. Cemeteries throughout Poland are lit up with candles as Polish families honour their dead.

Camerimage Film Festival, Bydgoszcz *(late Nov)*. An international film festival with a particular focus on cinematography and great cameramen.

St Andrew's Day (Andrzejki) *(29 Nov)*. According to folk tradition, St Andrew's day is a time of fortune-telling and prophecy.

DECEMBER

△ **Advent** *(throughout)*. From the first week in December, Christmas markets take over the squares and streets of Poland's cities. One of the most enjoyable is on the main market square in Kraków.

St Barbara's Day *(4 Dec)*. St Barbara is the patron saint of miners and her feast day is marked by processions and street parties in traditional mining areas.

A BRIEF
HISTORY

Polish history is one of Europe's most dramatic narratives, an important source of national pride and an enduring inspiration. Originating in the 10th century, the Polish state became one of Europe's great powers, before undergoing successive cycles of foreign occupation, resistance and rebirth.

Prehistoric Poland

In the prehistoric era Poland was almost totally covered by forest. The country's earliest inhabitants were hunters and gatherers living in loose tribal communities. Crop growers and animal herders began to appear in the 5th millennium BC. The Iron Age (750 BC) saw the emergence of fortified settlements; the most famous is Biskupin (p216) in Wielkopolska, a stock-aded settlement from around 650 BC. It is thought to have been a stop on the amber road, a trading route that took Baltic amber southwards and brought Mediterranean jewellery north.

1 A map showing Poland during the 16th century. ↑

2 The fortified settlement of Biskupin.

3 Statues of the Piasts, Poland's first rulers.

4 Polish king Władysław the Elbow-High.

Timeline of events

c1350 BC

Building of a Bronze-Age settlement at Trzcinica near Jasło, today famous as the "Carpathian Troy".

c650 BC

Building of Iron-Age fort at Biskupin in Wielkopolska.

c 500 AD

Slav tribes settle in Poland.

1025

Coronation of Bolesław the Brave, first king of Poland.

1079

Bishop (later Saint) Stanisław is killed in a fit of anger by King Bolesław the Bold.

The Emergence of a Polish State

Slav tribes began migrating from the east towards what is now Poland some time during the 6th century. The Vistulanians (Wiślane) settled around Kraków, while the Polonians (Polanie) established themselves in today's Wielkopolska. The ruling Piast family molded the Polonians into a strong political unit, which became the nucleus of the Polish state. Piast ruler Mieszko I (r 960-992) conquered the Vistulanians, and his son Bolesław the Brave (r 992-1025) was crowned king of Poland by Holy Roman Emperor Otto III, securing international legitimacy.

Rise of the Polish Medieval Kingdom

After a period of fragmentation in the 12th century, Władysław the Elbow-High (r 1261-33) used a combination of diplomacy and murder to reunite the country. He was the first Polish king to be crowned in Wawel Cathedral (p148). His son, Kazimierz the Great (r 1310-1370), reformed the state administration, launched an energetic programme of castle-building and extended his rule into modern-day Ukraine. He also assembled a glittering court at Kraków and guaranteed Jewish rights.

THE TEUTONIC ORDER

Formed in 1190 to aid the Crusaders, this military-religious order arrived in Poland in 1226 at the behest of Konrad of Mazovia. Establishing their capital at Malbork, their power grew and they began to challenge Poland's rulers. Defeated at the Battle of Grunwald in 1410, the Order recognized Polish sovereignty after the fall of Malbork in 1466.

1241

Tatar invaders defeat the Poles at the Battle of Legnica.

1320

Coronation of Władysław the Elbow-High.

1340-1366

Kazimierz the Great conquers Western Ruthenia (now western Ukraine).

1226

Konrad of Mazovia invites the Teutonic Order to Poland to defend his borders against the Prussians.

1309

The Teutonic Order makes Malbork their capital.

1

2

Poland Under the Jagiellonians

On the death of Kazimierz the Great, the Polish crown passed
first to Louis of Anjou, then to his daughter Jadwiga (1373–
1399). A pious woman, she reigned as the country's first female
monarch alongside her husband, the Grand Duke Jogaila of
Lithuania, Władysław II Jagiełło. Following her death, Jagiełło
extended the country's frontiers, turning Poland into one of
Europe's major players. His Jagiellonian descendants continued
his work, including his grand-nephew Kazimierz IV Jagiełło
(1444-1492), who secured Polish control over Prussia.

The Commonwealth of Two Nations

Until now a purely dynastic union, Poland's relationship with
Lithuania was cemented by the Union of Lublin in 1569 which
formed the so-called Commonwealth of Two Nations. The
Polish capital was moved from Kraków to Warsaw on account of
the latter's more central position. The union strengthened both
Poland's ability to withstand Moscow's growing power and the
position of the Polish and Lithuanian nobility. One of Europe's
most cosmopolitan states, it guaranteed religious equality.

THE GREAT EMIGRATION

Fleeing from Russian-
occupied Poland in the
19th century, many
Poles settled in Paris
and tried to build a
focus of Polish patri-
otism and culture
there. Among their
numbers were leading
rebel Prince Adam
Czartoryski and poet
Adam Mickiewicz.

Timeline of events

c 1400

Nawojka becomes
the first female
student to attend
Kraków University,
gaining entry by
dressing as a man.

1399

Death of Queen Jadwiga.

1473

Birth of Nicolaus
Copernicus.

1561

Livonia (western
Latvia) falls to the
Polish crown.

1596

The capital is moved
from Kraków to
Warsaw.

Decline and Partition

With the end of the Jagiellonian line, Polish kings were selected from the Swedish Vasa dynasty, starting with Sigismund III (his mother had been a Jagiellonian). However, tension between Catholic Poland and Protestant Sweden grew, and the Swedes finallly invaded in 1648. Poland fought back, but was left weak and surrounded by avaricious neighbours. The country was increasingly subject to the influence of Russia, who in 1774 engineered the First Partition of Poland. Following two further partitions in 1793 and 1795, Poland was completely swallowed up by its neighbours.

Poland Under the Partitions

Until World War I, Poland was divided between Russia, Austria and Prussia. Russian rule was severe, and there were major anti-Russian uprisings in 1830 and 1863. The Austrians offered a degree of political and cultural freedom, while Poles under Prussian rule were subjected to Germanization. Deprived of power, Poles turned to culture, in particular the epic poems of Adam Mickiewicz and historic novels of Henryk Sienkiewicz.

1 Queen Jadwiga, Poland's first female ruler ↑

2 The Union of Lublin by Jan Matejko.

3 The First Partition of Poland.

4 Renowned author Henryk Sienkiewicz.

Did You Know?
___
The invasion of Poland by Sweden became known as the "Swedish Deluge".

1655
Swedish armies repulsed by the Polish defenders of Jasna Góra monastery.

1793
The Second Partition provokes an armed uprising led by Polish patriot Tadeusz Kościuszko.

1849
Fryderyk Chopin dies in Paris aged 39.

1867
Birth of Poland's most renowned scientist, Maria Skłodowska-Curie.

1905
Henryk Sienkiewicz wins the Nobel Prize for literature.

World War I and the Independent Republic

Under Nationalist leader Józef Piłsudski, many Poles fought on the Austrian side during World War I, convinced an Austrian-German victory would rid them of foreign occupation. With the end of war in 1918, a Regency Council (comprising members of the Polish nobility and clergy) declared Poland independent, with Piłsudski its commander-in-chief. A succession of weak governments persuaded him to seize power in 1926, instituting the so-called Sanitation regime.

World War II

The secret Nazi-Soviet Pact paved the way for a joint invasion of Poland in 1939, and led to the start of World War II. Under Nazi rule, Poles were used as slave labour or simply shot, and Polish Jews were forced to live in appalling ghettos. The Soviets transported countless Poles to Siberia and murdered 20,000 army officers. When Hitler invaded the Soviet Union in 1941, more Jewish communities fell under Nazi control, presaging the introduction of the Final Solution. Six million Jews were murdered, mostly in death camps on Polish soil.

1 Nationalist leader Jozef Pilsudski. ↑

2 The concentration camp at Auschwitz.

3 Graffiti supporting trade union Solidarity.

4 Poland joins the NATO countries in 1999.

Did You Know?

Many Polish soldiers escaped in 1939 and fought bravely with the RAF and other Allied units.

Timeline of events

1917
Polish Nationalist leader Piłsudski is imprisoned by the Germans.

1939
Germany and the Soviet Union invade Poland.

1940
The most effective Hurricane squadron in the Battle of Britain is RAF 303, piloted by Poles.

1945
Soviet soldiers liberate Auschwitz.

1947
Communists and their allies win manipulated elections.

3

4

Communist Poland

With Poland overrun by the Red Army in 1945, Communism was imposed on an unwilling population. Student protests and ship-yard strikes during the 1960s and 70s created an atmosphere of unresolved social turmoil. The 1980 Gdańsk shipyard strike led to the formation of free trade union Solidarity, whose popular-ity paralyzed the regime. Although martial law was imposed in 1981-83, it caused constant unrest. At the Round Table Talks in 1989, the Communists met with Solidarity and finally agreed to elections, resulting in a landslide victory for the trade union.

Poland Today

The first post-Communist governments embarked on radical market reforms. These led to inflation and unemployment in the short term, but placed the economy on a sound footing for future decades. The last Russian forces left in 1993, leaving Poland free to join first NATO in 1999, then the European Union in 2004. Recent years have seen a sharpening of differences between a pro-EU, liberal centre-right, popular in the cities, and a Eurosceptic, populist right, favoured in the countryside.

WARSAW UPRISING

Poland's underground Home Army launched the Warsaw Uprising in August 1944. Initially liberating huge swathes of the city, the rebellion was then systematic-ally extinguished by the German army.

1970
Troops fire on striking shipyard workers in Gdańsk.

1978
Archbishop of Kraków Karol Wojtyła becomes Pope John Paul II.

1981
General Jaruzelski declares martial law.

1990
Solidarity leader Lech Wałęsa becomes President of Poland.

2015
Paweł Pawlikowski's film *Ida* wins an Oscar.

EXPERIENCE
WARSAW

Warsaw's historic City Walls at dusk

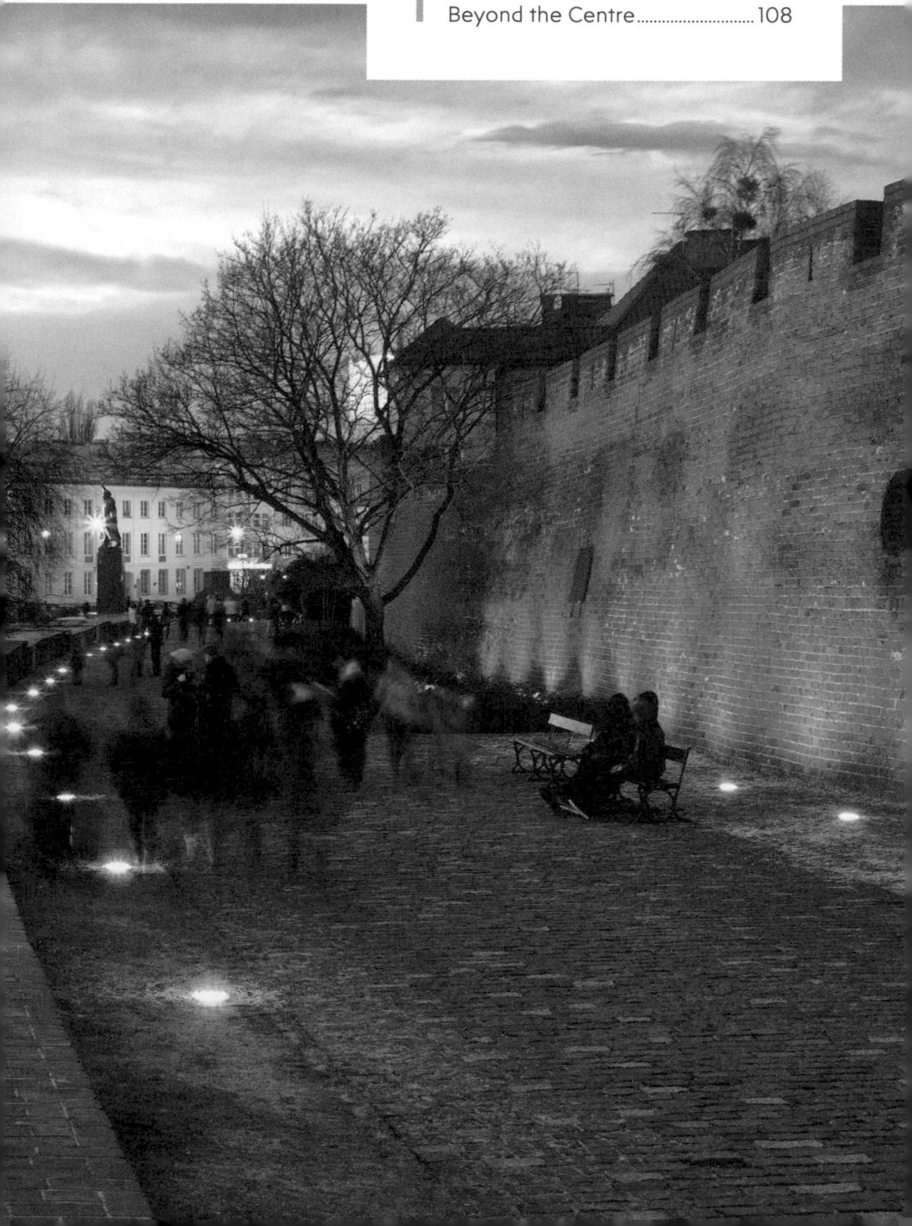

EXPLORE
WARSAW

This section divides Warsaw into three sightseeing areas, as shown on this map, plus an area beyond the city *(p108)*.

Park Traugutta

NOWE MIASTO

New Town Square

Church of St Kazimierz

THE OLD AND NEW TOWNS
p70

Old Town Square

POLIN Museum of the History of Polish Jews

Cathedral of St John

Ogród Krasińskich

Archaeological Museum

MURANÓW

Plac Teatralny

NOWOLIPKI

Plac Bankowy

Saxon Gardens

THE CITY CENTRE
p96

National Gallery of Contemporary Art

Park Mirowski

MIRÓW

ŚRÓDMIEŚCIE

Świętokrzyski Park

Plac Defilad

Palace of Culture and Science

Rondo Dmowskiego

| 0 metres | 500 |
| 0 yards | 500 |

N ↑

POLAND

WARSAW

PRAGA
PÓŁNOC

Warszawski
Ogród
Zoologiczny

Park
Praski

PRAGA

Vistula

STARE
MIASTO

Royal
Castle

MARIENSZTAT

Kazimierkowski
Park

Copernicus
Science Centre

Warsaw
University

**THE
ROYAL ROUTE**
p86

Vistula

Fryderyk Chopin
Museum

Park
Karola Beyera

Rondo
Charles de
Gaulle

National
Museum

SOLEC

Plac
Trzech
Krzyży

THE OLD AND NEW TOWNS

The Old Town (Stare Miasto), partially surrounded by medieval walls, is the oldest district in Warsaw. It was founded at the turn of the 13th and 14th centuries and its medieval urban layout survives to this day. The market square, with its colourful town houses and the Cathedral of St John, is the pride of the area. The New Town (Nowe Miasto), which is next to the Old Town, became a separate urban entity in 1408. Both the Old Town and the New Town were almost completely destroyed during the war and the reconstruction of these districts, including the Royal Castle, was an undertaking on a scale unprecedented in the whole of Europe. Today, after being rebuilt, these two areas are the most popular visitor attractions in Warsaw, particularly the Old Town, which pulsates with life until late evening.

THE OLD AND
NEW TOWNS

Kusociński
Park

Romuald
Traugutt
Park

SANGUSZKI

KONWIKTORSKA

WÓJTOWSKA

PRZYRYNEK

RAJCÓW

SAMBORSKA

BONIFRATERSKA

KONWIKTORSKA

FONDAMIŃSKIEGO

ZAKROCZYMSKA

Sapieha
Palace

Church of the
Visitation of the
Virgin Mary
10

MURA-
NOWSKA

SAPIEŻYŃSKA

Franciscan
Church

KOŚCIELNA

Church of
St Benon

Monument to
those Fallen and
Murdered in the East

2

BONIFRATERSKA

NOWE
MIASTO

PIESZA

Church of
St Kazimie.

14

FRANCISZKAŃSKA

CIASNA

KOŻLA

RYNEK
NOWEGO
MIASTA

3

12 New Town
Square

NOWINARSKA

11 Ulica Freta

STARA

Maria Skłodowska-
Curie Museum **13**

9 Church
of St Jacek

FRETA

MOSTOW

BONIFRATERSKA

GEN. WŁADYSŁAWA ANDERSA

THE CITY
CENTRE
p96

ŚWIĘTOJERSKA

Church of the
Holy Spirit

DŁUGA

6

WAŁOWA

ŚWIĘTOJERSKA

Barbican and
City Walls

KILIŃSKIEGO

Raczyński
Palace

3

Krasiński
Palace

PLAC KRASIŃSKICH

Monument
to the 1944
Warsaw Uprising
8

2

WĄSKI DUNAJ

ZAMENHOFA

Ogród
Krasińskich

Field
Cathedral

PODWALE

MIODOWA

DŁUGA

KAPITULNA

MIODOWA

GEN. WŁADYSŁAWA ANDERSA

BOHATERÓW GETTA

SCHILLERA

Pac
Palace
Capuchin
Church

MURANÓW

4

Archaeological
Museum

Independence
Museum

AL. SOLIDARNOŚCI

NOWY PRZEJAZD

DANIŁOWI

Ratusz Ⓜ

PLAC
TEATRALN

D   E   F

0 metres 250
0 yards 250
N ↑

THE OLD AND NEW TOWNS

Must Sees
❶ Royal Castle
❷ Cathedral of St John

Experience More
❸ Zygmunt's Column
❹ Old Town Market Square
❺ Museum of Warsaw
❻ Barbican and City Walls
❼ Adam Mickiewicz Museum of Literature
❽ Monument to the 1944 Warsaw Uprising
❾ Church of St Jacek
❿ Church of the Visitation of the Virgin Mary
⓫ Ulica Freta
⓬ New Town Square
⓭ Maria Skłodowska-Curie Museum
⓮ Church of St Kazimierz

Eat
① U Fukiera
② Stolica
③ Freta 33

BULWAR KARSKIEGO
WYBRZEŻE
GDAŃSKIE

V i s t u l a

BULWAR KARSKIEGO
WYBRZEŻE GDAŃSKIE

Old Gunpowder Magazine

BOLEŚĆ

BRZOZOWA
BUGAJ

Museum of Warsaw
❺
RYNEK STAREGO MIASTA
①

Adam Mickiewicz ❼ Museum of Literature

Old Town ❹ Market Square

STARE MIASTO

Jesuit Church

JEZUICKA

❷ Cathedral of St John

ŚWIĘTOJAŃSKA

ZAPIECEK

PIWNA

Church of St Martin

Zygmunt's Column
❸

Royal Castle
❶

GRODZKA

Blue Palace

Most Śląsko-Dąbrowski

PODWALE

SENATORSKA

PLAC ZAMKOWY

Branicki Palace

AL. SOLIDARNOŚCI

WYBRZEŻE
KOŚCIUSZKOWSKIE

THE ROYAL ROUTE
p86

KRAKOWSKIE PRZEDMIEŚCIE

Church of St Anne

SOWIA

MARIENSZTAT

Prymasowski Palace

KOZIA

BEDNARSKA

FURMAŃSKA

DOBRA

G

H

❶ 🛠 🏛 🍴 🏛

ROYAL CASTLE

📍 G3 🏠 Plac Zamkowy 4 🚌 116, 178, 180, 503 🚋 4, 13, 20, 23 🕐 10am–6pm
Tue–Thu & Sat, 10am–8pm Fri, 11am–6pm Sun 🚫 Mon, 2 & 6 Jan, Easter, 1 May,
Corpus Christi, 1 Nov, 24, 25 & 31 Dec 🌐 zamek-krolewski.pl

More of a palace than a fortified residence, the Royal Castle (Zamek Królewski) is one of Warsaw's most iconic sights and the Old Town's star attraction. It was constructed following Zygmunt III Vasa's decision to move the capital from Kraków to Warsaw in 1596.

The castle was originally built in the early Baroque style by the Italian architects Giovanni Trevano, Giacomo Rodondo and Matteo Castelli between 1598 and 1619, and incorporated the earlier castle of the Mazovian princes. The late Baroque façade overlooking the River Vistula dates from the time of August III, and the splendid interiors from that of Stanisław August. Completely destroyed by the Germans in World War II, the castle was reconstructed from 1971 to 1988, with donations of both money and works of art from Poles both at home and abroad. In 1980, the Royal Castle was registered as a protected UNESCO World Heritage Site.

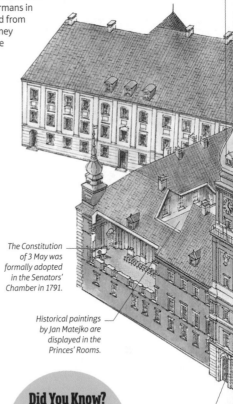

Clock Tower

The Constitution of 3 May was formally adopted in the Senators' Chamber in 1791.

Historical paintings by Jan Matejko are displayed in the Princes' Rooms.

Main entrance

↑ The Royal Castle, today a symbol of Polish independence

↑ The elaborately decorated interior of the Marble Room

Did You Know?

Before blowing up the castle, the Nazis looted it – taking even the central heating and parquet floors.

Timeline

1350
▽ Construction of the earliest castle on the site begins, including the Great Tower (now the Justice Court Tower).

1944
▽ The castle is completely destroyed by the German army during WW2; reconstruction only begins in 1971.

1598
△ Castle remodelled as a royal residence by King Zygmunt III Vasa, from the Swedish dynasty of Vasa, Poland's rulers at the time.

1980
△ The Royal Castle, together with the whole of the Old Town, becomes a UNESCO World Heritage Site.

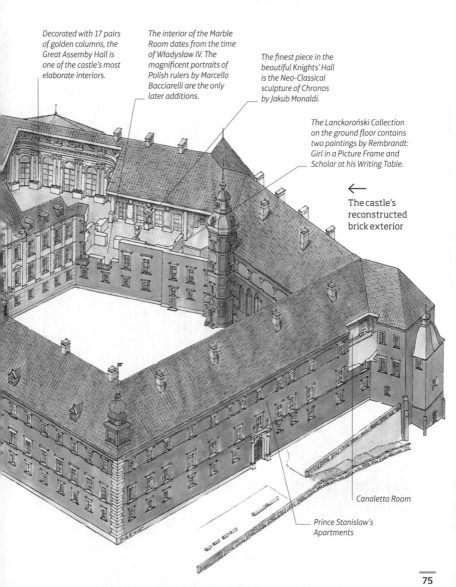

Decorated with 17 pairs of golden columns, the Great Assemby Hall is one of the castle's most elaborate interiors.

The interior of the Marble Room dates from the time of Władysław IV. The magnificent portraits of Polish rulers by Marcello Bacciarelli are the only later additions.

The finest piece in the beautiful Knights' Hall is the Neo-Classical sculpture of Chronos by Jakub Monaldi.

The Lanckoroński Collection on the ground floor contains two paintings by Rembrandt: Girl in a Picture Frame and Scholar at his Writing Table.

← The castle's reconstructed brick exterior

Canaletto Room

Prince Stanislaw's Apartments

2 🔄

CATHEDRAL OF ST JOHN

📍G3 🏛Ul Świętojańska 8 📞22 831 02 89 🚌116, 178, 222, 503 🚊4, 20, 23, 26 🕐10am–5pm Mon–Sat, 3–5pm Sun

This elegant cathedral is believed to be Warsaw's oldest church. Many famous Poles are buried in here, including the last king of Poland, Stanisław August Poniatowski, and Nobel prize-winning author Henryk Sienkiewicz.

The Cathedral of St John started life as a parish church at the beginning of the 15th century, only acquiring cathedral status in 1798. Over the years, successive rulers endowed it with new chapels and other elements. Important ceremonies have taken place here, including the coronation of Stanisław August Poniatowski in 1764 and the oath of allegiance to the Constitution of 3 May in 1791. The cathedral was seriously damaged in World War II when, during the Warsaw Uprising, the Nazis destroyed around 90 per cent of the building with explosives. The cathedral was later rebuilt, with its new façade designed by Jan Zachwatowicz in the spirit of Mazovian Gothic architecture.

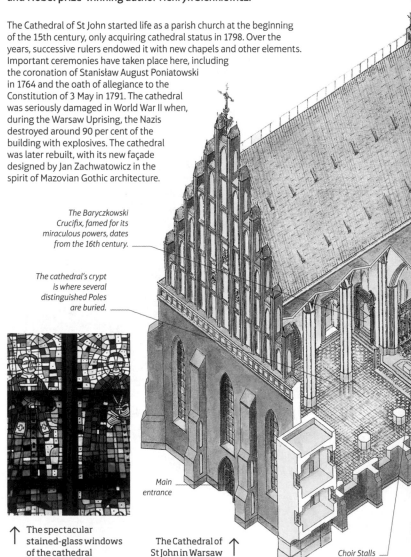

The Baryczkowski Crucifix, famed for its miraculous powers, dates from the 16th century.

The cathedral's crypt is where several distinguished Poles are buried.

Main entrance

↑ The spectacular stained-glass windows of the cathedral

The Cathedral of St John in Warsaw ↑

Choir Stalls

↑ The chancel, with the altar and carved wooden choir stalls

EXPERIENCE MORE

Zygmunt's Column

🔲 G3 🏛 Pl Zamkowy
🚌 116, 175, 180, 222, 503
🚋 20, 23, 26

Zygmunt's Column, found in the centre of Plac Zamkowy, is the oldest secular statue in Warsaw. It was erected in 1644 by Zygmunt III Vasa, who in 1596 had moved Poland's capital from Kraków to Warsaw. The monument, standing 22 m (72 ft) high, consists of a Corinthian granite column supported on a tall plinth, topped with a bronze statue of the ruler holding a cross in his left hand and a sword in his right. The figure is the work of Clemente Molli, and the whole monument was designed by Augustyn Locci the Elder and Constantino Tencalla, two Italian architects. Despite repeated damage, the statue was reconstructed and today retains its original appearance. The column itself has already been replaced twice; an older, fractured shaft can be seen on the terrace near the south façade of the Palace Under the Tin Roof.

④

Old Town Market Square

🔲 G3 🚌 116, 175, 190, 222, 503 🚋 4, 13, 20, 23, 26

Until the end of the 18th century, this square was the most important place in Warsaw. Most of the buildings date from the 1600s, giving the square its period character. In the centre there was once a town hall, a weigh house and stalls, all demolished in 1817. In their place now stands a statue of the Warsaw Mermaid (Syrenka); this mythical creature has been considered the city's protector ever since the Middle Ages.

Each row of houses bears the name of one of the people involved in the Four-Year Sejm, a reforming parliament which sat from 1788 to 1792. On the north side is the Dekerta row – named after Jan Dekert, a mayor of Warsaw in the 18th century. All the houses are interconnected and now host the Museum of Warsaw (p78), which reopened in 2017 after extensive restoration.

The Małachowski Family Tomb, carved in white marble, is based on a design by the Danish sculptor Bertel Thorvaldsen.

↑ The Warsaw Mermaid (Syrenka) statue at the centre of Old Town Market Square, illuminated at night

The Barbican and city walls that once protected the city's northern approach ↑

 5

Museum of Warsaw

📍 F3 🏛 Rynek Starego Miasta 28-42 🚌 116, 175, 222, 503 🚋 4, 13, 20, 23, 26 🕐 10am-7pm Tue-Sun 🌐 muzeumwarszawy.pl

Occupying historic houses on the northern side of Old Town Market Square, the Museum of Warsaw (Muzeum Warszawy) offers an engrossing record of the city and its citizens with a huge collection of artworks, costumes, domestic utensils and everyday objects. The core exhibition, entitled *The Things of Warsaw*, displays objects in themed rooms shedding light on the life and aspirations of the city's inhabitants. One room is devoted to the Warsaw Mermaid *(p77)*, showing

> **GREAT VIEW**
> **The Dung Mound**
>
> Until 1844 the grassy slope at the eastern end of Ulica Celna was used for the disposal of domestic and human waste. Nowadays the promenade at the top of the slope offers great views of the Vistula.

how depictions of the creature have evolved over the centuries. Elsewhere, a wealth of photographs and video material provide a pageant of street life in decades past.

 6

Barbican and City Walls

📍 F3 🏛 Ul Nowomiejska 🚌 116, 178, 185, 503

Warsaw is one of the few European capitals where a large portion of the old city wall survives. Construction of the wall began in the first half of the 14th century and continued in phases up to the mid-16th century. A double circumvalla-tion, reinforced with fortresses and towers, encircled the town. The earliest surviving part of the fortifications is the Barbican, erected around 1548 by Jan Baptist the Venetian, an Italian Renaissance architect who lived and worked in Poland. It was built on the site of an earlier outer gate and was intended to defend the Nowomiejska Gate (Brama Nowomiejska). The northern part of the building, in the form of a dungeon reinforced by four semicircular towers,

survived as the external wall of a town house. After World War II, parts of the wall were rebuilt and the Barbican was restored to its full scale.

 7

Adam Mickiewicz Museum of Literature

📍 G3 🏛 Ryek Starego Miasta 20 🚌 116, 190, 222, 503 🚋 4, 13, 20, 23, 26 🕐 10am-4pm Mon, Tue & Fri, 11am-6pm Wed & Thu, 11am-5pm Sun 🌐 muzeumliteratury.pl

A cluster of houses found on the eastern side of Old Town Market Square provide a home for this truly engaging museum (Muzeum Literatury im. Adama Mickiewicza) which celebrates the life and career of Adam Mickiewicz (1798-1855), Poland's most famous Romantic poet. Born in modern-day Belarus, educated in Vilnius and exiled first in Russia then Paris, Mickiewicz wrote a string of epic historic poems that filled Poles with hope and inspiration during a time of foreign occupation. The wide-ranging collection offers fascinating insights into 19th-century Poland.

⑧
Monument to the 1944 Warsaw Uprising

📍 F3 🏛 Pl Krasińskich
🚌 116, 178, 180, 222, 503

Built in 1989, this monument
commemorates the heroes of
the historic Warsaw Uprising.
It was sculpted by Wincenty
Kućma and the architect was
Jacek Budyn. The sculptures
represent soldiers – one group
defending the barricades, the
other going down into the
sewers that were used to
move around Warsaw during
the uprising. The entrance to
one sewer is still found near
the monument.

In front of this monument,
on the 50th anniversary of
the uprising, Richard Herzog,
President of the Federal
Republic of Germany, apolo-
gized to the Polish nation for
all the atrocities commited by
the Third Reich during World
War II, including the bloody
suppression of the uprising.

⑨
Church of St Jacek

📍 F2 🏛 Ul Freta 8/10
☎ 22 635 47 00 🚌 116,
178, 180, 222, 503

At the beginning of the 17th
century, while the Jesuits were
building a Baroque church in
the Old Town, the
Dominicans started
work on a Gothic

↑ Beautiful Gothic
features inside the
Church of St Jacek

chancel for the Church of
St Jacek (Kościół św. Jacka).
They returned to the Gothic
style partly because of the
conservatism of Mazovian
buildings and partly to give
the church the appearance of
age, so as to create an illusion
of the traditions of the order –
which had in fact only been
set up in Warsaw in 1603. When
work was interrupted by an
outbreak of plague in 1625,
the remaining monks listened
to confessions and gave com-
munion through holes drilled
in the doors. The work was
completed in 1639.

Interesting features inside
include the beautiful vaulting
above the aisles and the Gothic
chancel decorated with
stuccowork of the
Lublin type.

→
The Monument
to the 1944
Warsaw Uprising

Church of the Visitation of the Virgin Mary

📍F2 🏠Ul Przyrynek 2
📞22 831 24 73 🚌116, 178, 180, 222, 503

The brick tower of the Church of the Visitation of the Virgin Mary (Kościół Nawiedzenia NMP) rises over the roofs of the houses in New Town. This church is the oldest in this area. It was built at the start of the 15th century by the Mazovian princess Anna, wife of Janusz I the Old, and is reputed to stand on the site of a sacred pagan spot.

Damaged during World War II, it was subsequently rebuilt in the 15th-century Gothic style. The vaulting above the chancel was completed by medieval methods: that is, it was filled by hand, without the use of prefabricated moulds.

In the cemetery next to the church there stands a modern statue of Walerian Łukasiński (1786–1868), founder of the National Patriotic Society.

An inspiring statue of Nobel Prize-winning scientist Maria Skłodowska-Curie, holding a model of an atom, can be seen on the terrace next to the church. The statue was erected in 2014 on the 80th anniversary of the scientist's death. There are also magnificent views of the Vistula valley from this terrace.

Ulica Freta

📍F2 🚌116, 178, 180, 222, 503

The main road in the New Town, Ulica Freta developed along a section of the old route leading from Old Warsaw to Zakroczym. At the end of the 1300s, buildings began to appear along it, and in the 15th century it came within the precincts of New Warsaw (Nowa Warszawa).

Several good antique shops and cafés are on this street. The old boarding school at No 16, where Marie Curie was born, is now a museum *(p81)* dedicated to her.

INSIDER TIP
Multimedia Fountain Park

Set in a meadow below the Royal Castle *(p74)*, these fountains give a spectacular show Friday and Saturday evenings (Jun–Sep), with stirring soundtracks and images projected onto water.

New Town Square

📍F2 🚌116, 178, 222, 503

The heart of the New Town is the market square (Rynek Nowego Miasta). Once rectangular, it acquired its odd triangular shape after reconstruction. When the town hall, which stood in the centre of the square, was demolished in 1818, a splendid view of the Baroque dome which crowns the Church of St Kazimierz was opened up. Destroyed in 1944, the church was rebuilt in a manner reminiscent of the 18th century, though

 Fascinating photographs displayed at the Maria Skłodowska-Curie Museum

not exactly replicating the original. The façades of many buildings around the square are covered with interesting Socialist Realist murals. A charming 19th-century well can be found in the middle of the square.

Maria Skłodowska-Curie Museum

⊙ F2 ⌂ Ul Freta 16
🚌 116, 160, 222, 503
🚋 4, 13, 20, 23, 26 ⏰ Jun-Aug: 10am-7pm Tue-Sun; Sep-May: 9am-4:30pm Tue-Sun 🌐 muzeum-msc.pl

This small but inspiring tribute to the Nobel Prize-winning scientist is in an 18th-century building in which Maria's mother ran a girls' boarding school. The Skłodowski family lived in an annexe at the back and this was where Maria was born, although she only spent the first year of her life here before moving to Ulica Nowolipka, to the west. Period furniture, laboratory equipment, and Maria's own coat and hat all help to conjure up the pioneering

Cafés spilling out onto the cobbled Ulica Freta, with the church of St Jacek alongside

chemist's life and times. Films about Maria and the history of chemistry are presented to groups on request at an extra charge.

---

⑭
Church of St Kazimierz

⊙ F2 ⌂ Rynek Nowego Miasta 2 📞 22 841 21 31
🚌 116, 178, 180, 222, 503

The Church and Convent of the Order of the Holy Sacrament, designed by Tylman van Gameren, was built in 1688–92 by King Jan III Sobieski and Queen Maria Kazimiera. The remarkable domed building is distinguished by its clear Baroque architecture of classic

proportions. The interior, which was damaged in the war, has since been renovated. The most beautiful reconstructed feature is the tomb of Maria Karolina, Princesse de Bouillon. It was installed in 1746 by Bishop Andrzej Załuski and Prince Michał Kazimierz Radziwiłł, a well-known reveller who once, unsuccessfully, sought her hand in marriage. The tomb features a fractured shield and a crown falling into an abyss, references to the Sobieski coat of arms and the death of the last member of the royal line.

MARIA SKŁODOWSKA-CURIE (1867-1934)

Maria Skłodowska-Curie (Marie Curie) left Warsaw at 24 years old to study in Paris. Within a decade she had become famous as the co-discoverer of radioactivity. Together with her husband, Pierre Curie, she discovered the elements polonium and radium. She was awarded the Nobel Prize twice: first in 1903 for physics and then again in 1911 for chemistry.

MARIE CURIE STATUE

A SHORT WALK
THE OLD TOWN

Distance 1 km (half a mile) **Nearest metro** Ratusz Arsenał
Time 15 minutes

The Old Town Square (Rynek Starego Miasta) is surrounded on all sides by townhouses, rebuilt after World War II with great devotion. Remains of the former city walls give the ensemble an evocatively medieval feel. From spring to autumn the square is filled with café tables, and also becomes an open-air gallery of arts and crafts. There are several restaurants and bars squeezed into neighbouring streets, especially in Piwna and Jezuicka. As one of the most attractive places in Warsaw, the Old Town is not only popular with visitors but also a favourite place for local people, and makes for a lovely place to wander.

Did You Know?

The mermaid became Warsaw's protector after she was saved from imprisonment by a local fisherman.

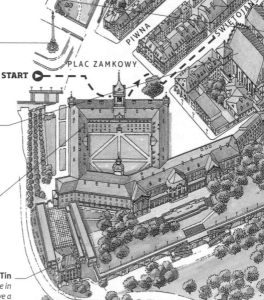

The striking modern crucifix of the **Church of St Martin** incorporates a fragment of a figure of Christ that was burned during the 1944 Warsaw Uprising.

The Baroque-Mannerist sanctuary of **Our Lady of Mercy**, patron saint of Warsaw, was rebuilt after World War II.

Zygmunt's Column (p77) is the oldest secular monument in Warsaw.

The **Cathedral of St John** (p76) was rebuilt in Gothic style after suffering damage during World War II.

The **Royal Castle**, formerly the home of Poland's rulers, was rebuilt in the 1970s and is today a symbol of Polish independence (p74).

The **Palace Under the Tin Roof** was the first house in the city of Warsaw to have a tin, rather than a tiled, roof.

↑ The red-brick barbican and city walls that surround Warsaw's Old Town

Locator Map
For more detail see p72

THE OLD AND
NEW TOWNS
The Old Town

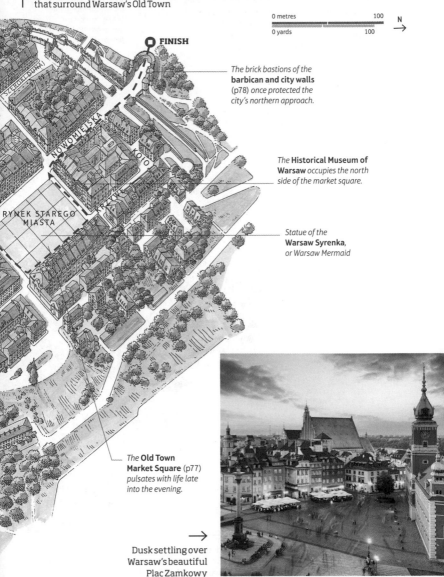

0 metres   100
0 yards   100

N →

● **FINISH**

The brick bastions of the **barbican and city walls** *(p78) once protected the city's northern approach.*

The **Historical Museum of Warsaw** *occupies the north side of the market square.*

Statue of the **Warsaw Syrenka,** *or Warsaw Mermaid*

The **Old Town Market Square** *(p77) pulsates with life late into the evening.*

→ Dusk settling over Warsaw's beautiful Plac Zamkowy

A SHORT WALK
NEW TOWN

Distance 500 m (530 yd) **Nearest metro** Dworzec Gdański
Time 10 minutes

The New Town took shape at the beginning of
the 15th century along the route leading from Old
Warsaw to Zakroczym. Of interest here are the Pauline,
Franciscan, Dominican and Redemptorist churches and
the Church of the Holy Sacrament, which were all rebuilt
after World War II, and the colourful reconstructed town
houses. Ulica Mostowa, the steepest street in Warsaw,
leads up to the fortress that defended one of
the longest bridges in 16th-century Europe.

Ulica Freta (p80) *is
the main thoroughfare
in New Town; freta
means an uncultivated
field or suburb.*

*The unusually elongated
interior of the* **Church of
St Jacek** (p79) *houses the
17th-century mausoleum
of the Kotowski family.*

*Every year, pilgrims gather
at the Baroque* **Church of
the Holy Spirit** *before
setting off to Jasna Góra
in Częstochowa.*

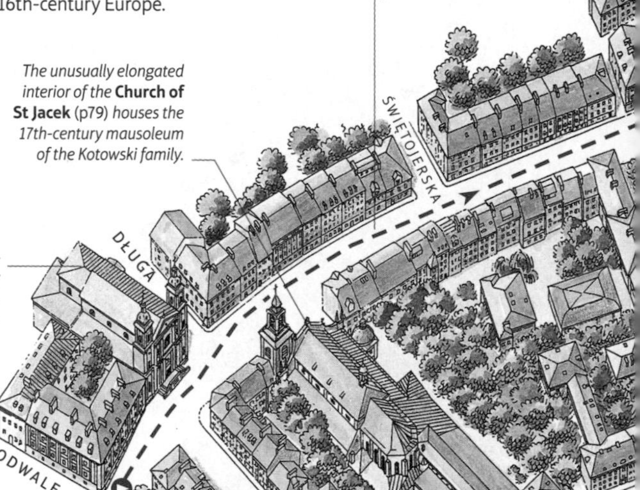

ŚWIĘTOJERSKA

DŁUGA

PODWALE

START

MOSTOWA

STARA

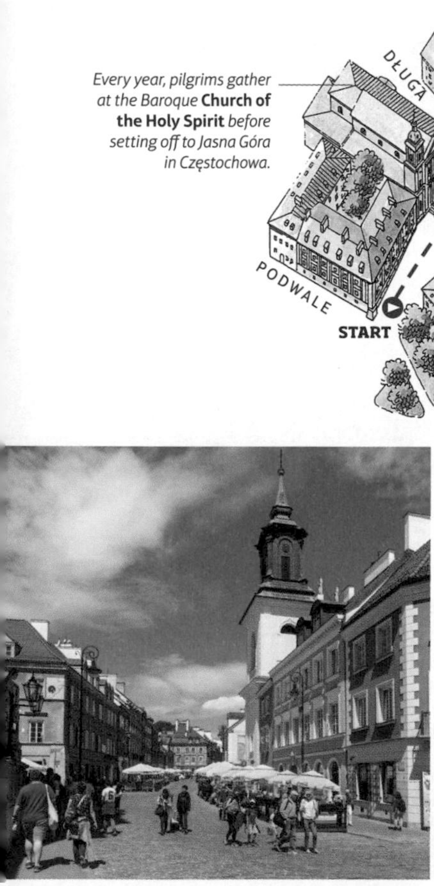

← Picturesque Ulica
Freta, the main street in
Warsaw's New Town

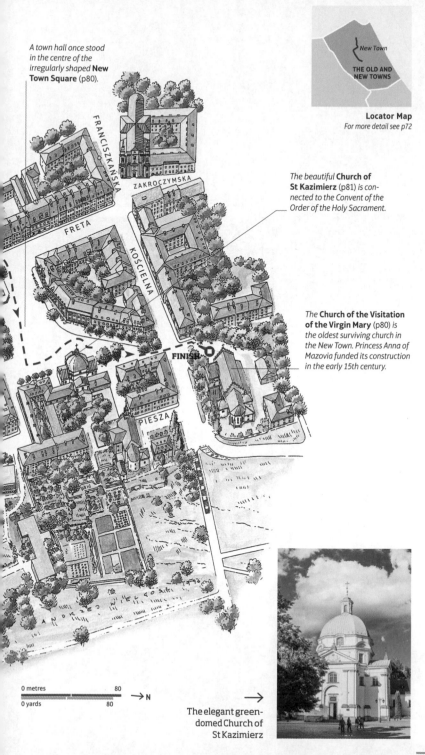

A town hall once stood in the centre of the irregularly shaped **New Town Square** (p80).

FRANCISZKAŃSKA

ZAKROCZYMSKA

FRETA

KOŚCIELNA

PIESZA

FINISH

ANDRZEJ WIELGOSKI

The beautiful **Church of St Kazimierz** (p81) *is connected to the Convent of the Order of the Holy Sacrament.*

The **Church of the Visitation of the Virgin Mary** (p80) *is the oldest surviving church in the New Town. Princess Anna of Mazovia funded its construction in the early 15th century.*

New Town

THE OLD AND NEW TOWNS

Locator Map
For more detail see p72

0 metres   80

0 yards   80

→ N

→ The elegant green-domed Church of St Kazimierz

THE ROYAL ROUTE

Stretching south from the Royal Castle, it was along this route (Trakt Królewski) that Poland's kings would move in procession whenever doing business in the capital. Aristocratic mansions, fine churches and government buildings grew up alongside this road, turning it into the city's most prestigious thoroughfare. The construction of royal palaces at Wilanów and Lazienki in the 18th and 19th centuries increased the amount of traffic along the Royal Route's length. The northernmost and oldest stretch of the route, called Krakowskie Przedmieście or "Krakow Suburb", has been a hub of politics and culture ever since the 1600s, and preserves its stately rows of Baroque churches and Neo-Renaissance palaces. Its Neo-Classical continuation Nowy Świat ("New World") has become the city's prime promenading ground due to its concentration of chic cafés and smart shops. The route continues with Aleje Ujazdowskie: once lined with the mansions of Polish nobility, the street was heavily damaged during World War II. Reconstructed following the end of the war, this broad leafy boulevard now sweeps past parks and embassies towards the southern suburbs.

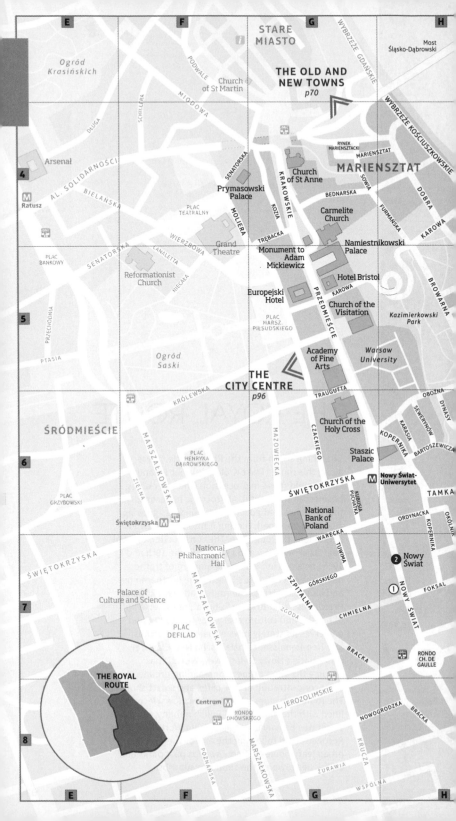

THE ROYAL ROUTE

Must See
❶ National Museum

Experience More
❷ Nowy Świat
❸ Copernicus Science Centre
❹ Warsaw University Library
❺ Fryderyk Chopin Museum
❻ Polish Military Museum

Eat
① Blikle Café
② Kafka
③ SAM

PRAGA

Vistula

Warsaw University Library ❹

Copernicus Science Centre ❸

Ⓜ Centrum Nauki Kopernik

Most Świętokrzyski

Most Średnicowy

Vistula

Most Poniatowskiego

Fryderyk Chopin Museum ❺

Sisters of Charity Monastery

Warszawa Powiśle

AL. 3 MAJA
AL. 3 MAJA

Polish Military Museum ❻

National Museum ❶

Stock Exchange

Church of St Alexandra

PLAC TRZECH KRZYŻY

Marshall Rydza Śmigłego Park

KSIĄŻĘCA

0 metres   300
0 yards   300

N

→

Visitors relaxing outside
the main entrance to the
National Museum

NATIONAL MUSEUM

J7 Al Jerozolimskie 3 10am-6pm Tue-Thu, Sat & Sun, 10am-9pm Fri
Mon, 1 Jan, Easter Sun, 1 and 3 May, Pentecost, Corpus Christi, 15 Aug, 1 Nov,
24-26 Dec 6, 8, 10, 13, 18 mnw.art.pl

The National Museum (Muzeum Narodowe) was previously known as the
Museum of Fine Arts, acquiring its present status in 1916. Despite wartime
losses, today it has a huge collection of works of art covering all periods
from antiquity to modern times.

First established in 1862, Warsaw's National Museum struggled at first to find a permanent home. However, following the end of World War I in 1918, the government decided the museum should play a prominent role in safeguarding the country's cultural heritage; as a result the Modernist building in which the museum currently resides was opened in 1938.

> **Today, the museum is home to an incredible collection, with over 830,000 works of art housed within its walls.**

Today, the museum is home to an incredible collection, with over 830,000 works of art housed within its walls, an abundance of paintings, sculptures, drawings, prints, photographs and coins. In fact, the museum has so many art works that, due to lack of space, not all the exhibits are on permanent display. The works held by the museum are by both Polish and international artists.

The National Museum also hosts a number of temporary exhibitions, which change throughout the year, as well as a variety of workshops, talks, film screenings, concerts and lectures.

Did You Know?

The National Museum is one of the oldest art museums in Poland.

GALLERY GUIDE

The collections are arranged on three floors. On the ground floor is the Professor Kazimierz Michałowski Faras Gallery, which contains examples of early Christian Nubian painting, while the Gallery of Medieval Art showcases medieval masterpieces. The first floor contains a gallery dedicated to 19th-century art, presenting the works of Polish artists in the context of their European counterparts. There are also galleries showcasing 20th and 21st century art, and Polish design. The third floor is dedicated to the Gallery of Old Masters, with artwork from the 15th to 18th centuries.

1 A visitor admires a painting in the Gallery of Old Masters.

2 This fresco of St Anne is one of the most stunning 10th-century wall paintings discovered by Polish archaeologists in Faras, Sudan.

3 A sculpture of Tytus Czyżewski by Polish artist Zbigniew Pronaszko.

EXPERIENCE MORE

2 Nowy Świat

⊘H7 ⊜E-2, 111, 128, 222 ⊞7, 8, 9, 22, 24 ⊗Nowy Świat-Uniwersytet

The street known as Nowy Świat (New World) forms part of the Royal Route, a medieval course leading from the castle to Wilanów Palace, and on to Krakow. Buildings started to appear along the road at the end of the 18th century and by the end of the 19th, Nowy Świat was an elegant street of cafés, restaurants, summer theatres, hotels and shops. After serious damage in World War II, it was only the Neo-Classical buildings that were reconstructed, although later buildings were also given pseudo-Neo-Classical features to preserve a uniform style.

Today, Nowy Świat is once again one of the most attractive streets in Warsaw, with expansive pedestrian areas and cafés with pavement gardens. To the north, it is linked to elegant Krakowskie Przedmieście *(p94)*, which is also part of the Royal Route.

3 Copernicus Science Centre

⊘J5 ⊘Wybrzeże Kościuszkowskie 20 ⊜118, 150, 506 ⊗Centrum Nauki Kopernik ⊘Hours vary, check website ⊘Mon & pub hols ⊚kopernik.org.pl

One of Poland's most visited attractions, the Copernicus Science Centre (Centrum Nauki Kopernik) opened in 2010. The centre allows visitors to discover the laws of science for themselves, and is constantly buzzing with school groups, families and individual visitors. More of a hands-on educational park than a traditional museum, it is filled with games, puzzles and interactive content that will appeal to children of all ages. There are special areas designated for toddlers and young children, as well as sections on biology and technology that keep teenagers and adults entertained. Visitors also can enjoy sweeping views of the River Vistula from its roof garden, which is open from May to

---

INSIDER TIP
Warsaw Palm

Rising above the Rondo Charles de Gaulle round-about, this artificial date palm is a symbol of Warsaw's multicultural past for artist Joanna Rajkowska, and an ironic nod to the city's main east to west street – Jerusalem Avenue.

October. Apart from the exhibitions, visitors can also go to the nearby Copernicus Planetarium, which shows films on astronomy with translations in English; a combined ticket is available.

---

4 Warsaw University Library

⊘H5 ⊘Dobra 56/66 ⊗Centrum Nauki Kopernik ⊘Apr-Oct: 8am-6pm daily (to 8pm May-Sep) ⊚buw. uw.edu.pl

Opened in 1999, Warsaw University Library is a popular visitor attraction thanks to its beautiful roof garden. Easily accessible by stepped walkways, the garden offers sweeping views across the

capital. It is planted with a variety of shrubs and grasses that are hardy enough to survive the city's cold and blustery conditions but also provide plenty of colour, from bright-green dwarf pines to silvery willows and yellow-flowering forsythia.The garden is closed between November and March.

Within the library's interior, the corridor-like atrium is open to non-readers and contains a lively collection of cafés and stalls selling postcards and posters.

↑ Contemporary gallery and high-tech exhibits at the Fryderyk Chopin Museum

EAT

Blikle Café
With its impressive array of cakes and tortes, Blikle has been an institution since it opened in the 1860s.

📍 H7 🏠 Ul Nowy Świat 35 📞 669 609 706

Kafka
A popular lunch spot for its menu of pastas, salads and soups, Kafka also impresses with colourful, chic design.

📍 H5 🏠 Ul Obożna 3 🌐 kawiarnia-kafka.pl

SAM
This bakery/café has an eclectic menu with Middle Eastern-inspired dips mingling with curry-spiced snacks.

📍 H5 🏠 Ul Lipowa 7a 🌐 sam.info.pl

 ←

The rooftop gardens of the Warsaw University Library, a green haven in the city

---

 ⑤

Fryderyk Chopin Museum

📍 H6 🏠 Ul Okólnik 1
🚌 111, 175, 178, 180, 503
🕐 11am–8pm Tue–Sun
📅 1 Jan, Easter, Corpus Christi, 1 Nov, 25 Dec
🌐 chopin.museum/en

Opened in 2010 to help mark the 200th anniversary of one of Poland's most famous sons, the Fryderyk Chopin Museum (Muzeum Fryderyka Chopina) is one of Warsaw's most visited museums. The collection takes up four floors of the splendid Gniński-Ostrogski Palace. Begun in 1681, it is one of Tylman van Gameren's grand masterpieces. The palace was constructed on top of a bastion, making it a fortress. According to legend, a golden duck lived under the palace, guarding its treasures.

Today the museum houses portraits, letters and auto-graph manuscripts, as well as the grand piano at which Chopin composed during the last two years of his life. Other exhibits include a gold watch presented to the ten-year-old Fryderyc by an admiring Italian singer and the passport that he used to enter England. It is also the home of the Chopin Society, and regular performances of Chopin's music take place here.

---

 ⑥

Polish Army Museum

📍 J7 🏠 Al Jerozolimskie 3
🚌 111, 117, 158, 507 🚃 7, 8, 9, 22, 24, 43 🕐 10am–5pm Wed, 10am–4pm Thu–Sun; outdoor exhibition until dusk 🌐 muzeumwp.pl

The Polish Army Museum (Muzeum Wojska Polskiego) contains a collection of Polish arms and armour spanning over 1,000 years. Most notable is the collection of armour from the early Middle Ages to the end of the 18th century. Exhibits include medieval jousting armour and an impressive collection of 17th-century armour of the Husaria, the Polish cavalry, with eagle wings, leopardskins and a mounted cavalryman in full regalia.

↑ Statue of a Polish pilot displayed at the Polish Army Museum

A SHORT WALK
KRAKOWSKIE PRZEDMIEŚCIE

Distance 1 km (half a mile) **Nearest metro** Ratusz Arsenał
Time 15 minutes

A walk along tree-lined Krakowskie Przedmieście, one of the most beautiful streets in Warsaw, takes you past magnificent palaces (now largely the home of government departments), pleasant restaurants, bars and cafés, green squares and little palaces with courtyards. On weekdays, Krakowskie Przedmieście is one of the liveliest streets in Warsaw, as students spill out of the University of Warsaw and the Academy of Fine Arts, both situated here.

Did You Know?

Krakowskie Przedmieście is often dubbed the "Champs Elysees" of Poland.

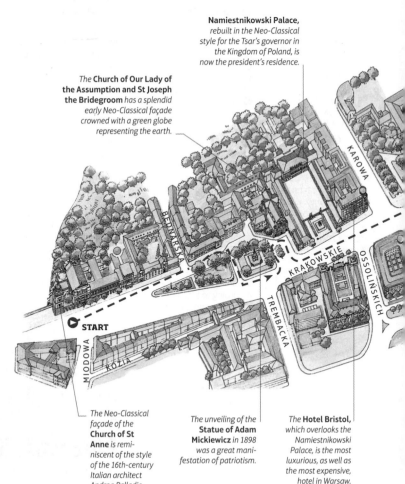

Namiestnikowski Palace, *rebuilt in the Neo-Classical style for the Tsar's governor in the Kingdom of Poland, is now the president's residence.*

The **Church of Our Lady of the Assumption and St Joseph the Bridegroom** *has a splendid early Neo-Classical façade crowned with a green globe representing the earth.*

START

The Neo-Classical façade of the **Church of St Anne** *is reminiscent of the style of the 16th-century Italian architect Andrea Palladio.*

The unveiling of the **Statue of Adam Mickiewicz** *in 1898 was a great manifestation of patriotism.*

The **Hotel Bristol,** *which overlooks the Namiestnikowski Palace, is the most luxurious, as well as the most expensive, hotel in Warsaw.*

↑ A beautifully ornate staircase found within the University of Warsaw

Locator Map
For more detail see p88

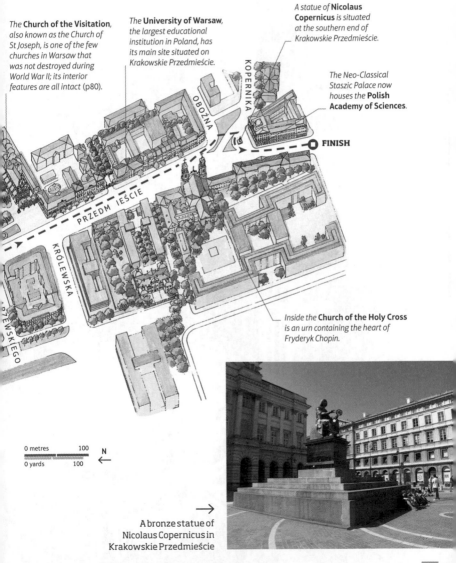

A statue of **Nicolaus Copernicus** *is situated at the southern end of Krakowskie Przedmieście.*

The Neo-Classical Staszic Palace now houses the **Polish Academy of Sciences**.

The **Church of the Visitation**, *also known as the Church of St Joseph, is one of the few churches in Warsaw that was not destroyed during World War II; its interior features are all intact (p80).*

The **University of Warsaw**, *the largest educational institution in Poland, has its main site situated on Krakowskie Przedmieście.*

○ **FINISH**

Inside the **Church of the Holy Cross** *is an urn containing the heart of Fryderyk Chopin.*

0 metres   100   N
0 yards   100

→ A bronze statue of Nicolaus Copernicus in Krakowskie Przedmieście

THE CITY CENTRE

From the late 18th to the mid-19th century, the area around Ulica Senatorska and Plac Teatralny was the commercial and cultural centre of Warsaw. Imposing Neo-Classical buildings with impressive colonnades can still be seen there and the Grand Theatre (Teatr Wielki) on Plac Teatralny is one of the largest buildings of its type in Europe. The Saxon Gardens (Ogród Saski), stretching through the centre of the district, are what remains of a former royal park that adjoined the Saxon king August II's residence. In the second half of the 19th century, the city's commercial centre moved to the area around Ulica Marszałkowska, prompted by the opening of Warsaw's first railway station in 1845. The city centre was completely trans-formed after the damage inflicted during World War II and today its principal landmark is the Palace of Culture and Science (Pałac Kultury i Nauki).

A · **B** · **C** · **D**

0 metres 400
0 yards 400
N

Umschlagplatz Monument
13

STAWKI

Monument to Those Fallen and Murdered in the East
15

STAWKI
NISKA
MIŁA
MIŁA
KARMELICKA
OKOPOWA
LEWARTOWSKIEGO
ZAMENHOFA
LEWARTOWSKIEGO
DUBOIS

Monument to the Heroes of the Ghetto

POLIN Museum of the History of Polish Jews **1**
NALEWKI

3

Cmentarz Żydowski

ESPERANTO
SMOCZA
ANIELEWICZA
PAWIA
ZAMENHOFA
KARMELICKA
DZIELNA
NOWOLIPKI

Pawiak Prison **14**
AL. JANA PAWŁA II

4

DZIELNA
NOWOLIPKI
NOWOLIPIE
KARMELICKA

MURANÓW

Town Hall

NOWOLIPIE
AL. SOLIDARNOŚCI
ORLA

5

AL. SOLIDARNOŚCI
OGRODOWA
ELEKTORALNA
ELEKTORALNA
ZIMNA
PTASIA

Mirowski Hall

THE CITY CENTRE

Must Sees
1 POLIN Museum of the History of Polish Jews
2 Palace of Culture and Science

Experience More
3 Archaeological Museum
4 Capuchin Church
5 Independence Museum
6 Plac Bankowy
7 Plac Teatralny
8 Saxon Gardens
9 National Gallery of Contemporary Art
10 Evangelical Church of the Augsburg Confession
11 Ethnographical Museum
12 Nożyk Synagogue
13 Umschlagplatz Monument
14 Pawiak Prison
15 Monument to Those Fallen and Murdered in the East

Stay
① Apple Inn
② Radisson Blu Centrum
③ Sofitel Victoria

ZELAZNA
KROCHMALNA
AL. JANA PAWŁA II
GRZYBOWSKA

2
Nożyk Synagogue **12**

TWARDA
MARIAŃSKA
ŁUCKA

Rondo ONZ Ⓜ
PANSKA
SLISK

PROSTA
ZELAZNA
CHAŁUBINSKIEGO

SIENNA

CHMIELNA
CHMIELNA

6

7

8

C · **D**

POLIN MUSEUM OF THE HISTORY OF POLISH JEWS

Q C3 **A** Ul Mordechaja Anielewicza 6 **🚌** 111, 180, 227 **⏰** 10am–6pm Mon, Thu & Fri (to 8pm Wed, Sat & Sun) **🚫** Mon, public hols **🌐** polin.pl/en

Housed in a breathtaking contemporary building, the country's largest Jewish heritage museum covers 1,000 years of the history of Polish Jews, from the first settlers in the Middle Ages to the present day.

The museum's fascinating displays illustrate how Poland became the centre of the Jewish diaspora. The centrepiece of the collection is the painted ceiling of a 17th-century synagogue that used to stand in Gwozdziec, east of Kraków. Overall this is a spectacular celebration of Jewish life and culture, although the tone becomes understandably more sombre as the exhibition turns to the Holocaust. The nearby Monument to the Heroes of the Ghetto (Pomnik Bohaterów Getta) symbolizes the heroic defiance of the Ghetto Uprising of 1943, which was planned not as a bid for liberty but as an honourable way to die.

JEWISH WARSAW

Before World War II, there were around 450,000 Jews living in Warsaw, out of a total city population of no more than 1,300,000. Warsaw had the second largest Jewish population after that of New York, and was a major centre of Jewish culture. The northern part of Warsaw, which was inhabited predominantly by Jews, was densely built up, with a large number of tenement blocks. Yiddish and Hebrew were the languages spoken here, as well as Russian, spoken by Jews who had fled Russia. The mass murder of Poland's Jews dramatically reduced Warsaw's Jewish population. Today, Warsaw is once again a hub of Jewish culture, with a yearly festival held to celebrate Jewish music, film and literature.

The striking exterior of ↑ POLIN Museum of the History of Polish Jews

← The curvy organic interior of the museum, designed by Rainer Mahlamäki

→ One of the fascinating exhibitions housed within the museum

Did You Know?
—
Muranów was chosen as POLIN's location because, prewar, the district was a hub of Jewish culture.

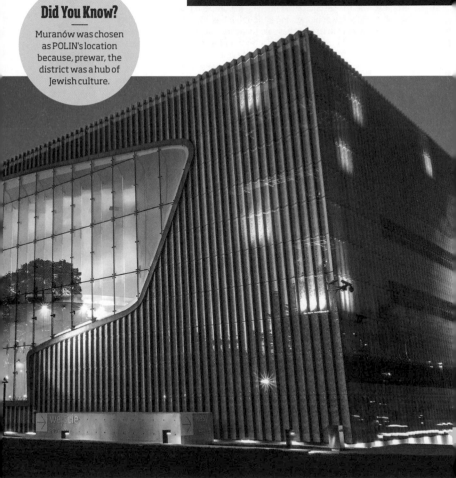

PALACE OF CULTURE AND SCIENCE

◉ F7 ⌂ Pl Defilad 1 🚌 109, 160, 227, 501 🚊 4, 17, 22, 35 Ⓜ Centre (Centrum) 🕓 Hours vary, check website 🌐 pkin.pl

Possibly the most recognized building in all of Warsaw, the monumental Palace of Culture and Science is an emblem of the city. This goliath is filled with an array of different venues, including a concert hall and two museums. One of its highlights is the viewing terrace, which offers spectacular views across the city; visit it at night, or even for a rooftop concert, for an unforgettable experience.

This enormous building – a gift for the people of Warsaw from the nations of the USSR – was built in 1952–5 to the design of a Russian architect, Lev Rudniev. At the time, this monument to "the spirit of invention and social progress" was the second tallest building in Europe. It resembles Moscow's Socialist Realist tower blocks, and although it has only 30 storeys, with its spire it is 230 m (750 ft) high. It is said to incorporate many architectural elements taken from stately homes after World War II. Despite the passage of time, this symbol of Soviet domination still provokes extreme reactions, from admiration to demands for its demolition.

The imposing exterior and *(inset)* interior of the Palace of Culture and Science ↑

TOP 5 VENUES TO VISIT

Viewing Terrace
Ride the lift to the top of the building for panoramic views.

Congress Hall
An elegant concert hall which hosts a variety of music concerts.

Dollhouse Museum
This charming museum is filled with over 100 historical dolls' houses.

Museum of Evolution
Dedicated to natural history, this museum contains dinosaur models the kids will love.

Kinoteka
A popular cinema showing both Polish and international films.

↑ The façade of the former arsenal, which now houses Warsaw's Archaeological Museum

EXPERIENCE MORE

Archaeological Museum

📍E4 🏛Ul Długa 52
🚆E-2, 107, 190, 503, 512
🚋4, 15, 20, 23, 26, 35, 70
Ⓜ Ratusz 🕐9am-4pm Mon-Fri, 10am-6pm Sun
🌐pma.pl

Housed in the former arsenal, the Archaeological Museum was built in the Baroque style between 1638 and 1647, during the reign of Władysław IV Vasa. It was here during World War II that boy scout soldiers of the Grey Ranks (Szare Szeregi) released 21 prisoners from the hands of the Gestapo; this brave action is commemorated by a plaque.

The museum displays exhibits from excavations carried out within both the country's prewar and present day borders. The exhibition on prehistoric Poland is highly recommended. One of the highlights of the medieval collections is a replica of the 12th-century door of Płock Cathedral (the original is in Velikiy Novgorod in Russia), decorated with striking Romanesque reliefs.

Capuchin Church

📍F4 🏛Ul Miodowa 13
🚌116, 174, 175, 180, 503

The Capuchin Church (Kościół Kapucynów), or Church of the Transfiguration, was built by Jan III Sobieski in gratitude for the Polish victory over the Turks at the Battle of Vienna in 1683. Building began in the same year under Izydor Affaita – probably to designs by Tylman van Gameren and Agostino Locci the Younger – and was completed by Carlo Ceroni in 1692. The façade recalls Rome's Capuchin church, while the interior houses urns containing the heart of Jan III and the ashes of the Saxon king, August II. Inside the crypt, there is an emotive nativity scene.

> **The Warsaw Capuchin church houses urns containing the heart of Jan III and the ashes of the Saxon king, August II.**

Independence Museum

⊙ E4 ⌂ Al Solidarności 62
☎ 22 826 90 91 ◰ 107, 111, 160, 503 ⊞ 13, 18, 20, 23, 26
Ⓜ Ratusz ⊙ 10am–5pm Wed–Sun

This elegant Baroque palace, surrounded by a major traffic artery, has the most beautiful mansard roofs in Warsaw and an oval bow-fronted façade. It was built in 1728 to a design by Jan Zygmunt Deybel. Since 1990 it has housed the Independence Museum (Muzeum Niepodległości), which covers the history of Polish battles and aspirations for independence from the Kościuszko Uprising to the modern day.

Plac Bankowy

⊙ E5 ◰ E-2, 107, 171, 190, 512 ⊞ 13, 18, 20, 23, 26, 35
Ⓜ Ratusz

Once a quiet little spot, Bank Square was radically altered after the construction of the East–West route and Ulica Marszałkowska. The most interesting buildings are on the west side of the square. The group of Neo-Classical buildings rebuilt after World War II were designed by Antonio Corazzi. The most impressive is the three-winged palace of the Commission for Revenues and Treasury, which today serves as a town hall.

Plac Teatralny

⊙ F4 ◰ 111

Before 1944, Plac Teatralny (Theatre Square) was the heart of Warsaw. The enormous Neo-Classical Grand Theatre (Teatr Wielki) on the south side was designed by Antonio Corazzi and Ludwik Kozubowski, and

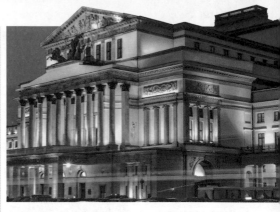

↑ The Neo-Classical Grand Theatre on Plac Teatralny, looking at its most stunning when illuminated at night

completed in 1833. Its façade is decorated with a frieze depicting Oedipus and his companions returning from the Olympian Games. The theatre was rebuilt and greatly enlarged after suffering war damage. Two statues stand in front of the building: one depicts Stanisław Moniuszko, the father of Polish opera, and the other is of Wojciech Bogusławski, who instigated the theatre's construction. Today it is the home of the country's National Opera and the National Theatre.

In 1848, the Russian composer Mikhail Glinka (1803–57) lived and worked in the house at No 2 Ulica Niecała, just off Plac Teatralny.

Saxon Gardens

⊙ F5 ◰ 102, 107, 160, 171, 174 ⊞ 4, 15, 18, 35

The Saxon Gardens (Ogród Saski), the oldest public park in the city, were laid out between 1713 and 1733 by August II, also known as August the Strong, to a design by Jan Krzysztof Naumann and

Mateus Daniel Pöppelmann. Originally the royal gardens adjoining Morsztyn Palace, they became the basis for a Baroque town-planning project in Warsaw known as the Saxon Axis (Oś Saska). In 1727 the Saxon Gardens became the first public park in Poland, and for two centuries they served as an alfresco "summer salon" for locals. At the time of August III, German architect Carl Friedrich Pöppelmann built a Baroque summer theatre here; this stood until 1772. Between 1816 and 1827, James Savage refashioned the gardens in the English style.

→

Fountains and colourful flowers on display in the Saxon Gardens

In 1870 they were graced by a huge wooden summer theatre, which was destroyed in September 1939, at the start of World War II. The gardens are now adorned with 21 Baroque sandstone statues, made by sculptors such as Jan Jerzy Plersch in the 1730s.

Saski Palace, which once stood in the gardens, was destroyed at the end of 1944. All that remains today is the Tomb of the Unknown Soldier, where the body of a soldier who fell in the defence of Lwów (1918–19) was interred on 2 November 1925.

National Gallery of Contemporary Art

☉F5 ⌂Pl Małachowskiego 3 ☷E-2, 102, 174 ☉Noon-8pm Tue-Sun ☒zacheta.art.pl

The Zachęta building, which houses the National Gallery of Contemporary Art, was built between 1899 and 1903 for the Society for the Promotion of Fine Arts. It was designed by Stefan Szyller, the leading architect of Warsaw's Revival period, a 19th- and early 20th-century architectural movement. It was conceived as a monumental building in the Neo-Renaissance style, with four wings (only completed in 1995) and an inner courtyard with a glass roof.

In order to promote the work of contemporary Polish artists, the society organized exhibitions and competitions, and purchased works of art. The Zachęta's permanent collections were transferred to the National Museum, and the building, as before, now serves as a venue for temporary exhibitions of modern art.

Evangelical Church of the Augsburg Confession

☉F6 ⌂Pl Małachowskiego 1 ☷102, 174 ☉By appt only, or during ceremonies ☒trojca.waw.pl

The Evangelical Church of the Augsburg Confession (Kościół św. Trójcy) was designed by Szymon Bogumił Zug and built in 1777–81. The Neo-Classical building is crowned by a dome 58 m (189 ft) high. The church is reminiscent of the Pantheon in Rome; however, this ancient model was merely a starting point from which Zug developed a unique design. The interior of the church features a vast barrel-vaulted nave with rectangular transepts. The west front features a massive Doric portico which is regarded as one of the outstanding examples of Neo-Classical architecture in Poland.

The west front features a massive Doric portico which is regarded as one of the outstanding examples of Neo-Classical architecture in Poland.

STAY

Apple Inn
A welcoming guesthouse with spacious rooms.

☉G7 ⌂Ul Chmielna 21 Lok 22B ☒appleinn.pl

㉋㉋㉋

Radisson Blu Centrum
Contemporary hotel that excels in attention to detail and comfort. Features a gym and indoor pool.

☉D6 ⌂Ul Grzybowska 24 ☒radissonblu.com

㉋㉋㉋

Sofitel Victoria
This striking white building has retained a retro-70s feel. Impressive indoor pool.

☉G5 ⌂Ul Królewska 11 ☒sofitel. accorhotels.com

㉋㉋㉋

Ethnographical Museum

📍 G6 🏛 Ul Kredytowa 1
🚌 102, 105, 107, 174
🕐 10am–5pm Tue, Thu
& Fri, 11am–7pm Wed,
noon–6pm Sat, noon–5pm
Sun 🚫 Mon & pub hols
🌐 ethnomuseum.pl

The Ethnographical Museum
(Państwowe Muzeum
Etnograficzne w Warszawie) is
housed in a Neo-Renaissance
building on the south side of
Plac Małachowskiego. It was
built in 1854–8 to a design by
Henryk Marconi, an Italian
architect who settled in
Warsaw. It recalls the Libreria

Sansoviniana in Venice, and
is one of the city's finest
buildings. The museum contains a fantastic display of
Polish folk costumes, folklore,
and arts and crafts. An entire
section of the museum is
dedicated to traditional Polish
musical instruments that
includes recordings of the
sounds the instruments originally produced. There is also
a small display on Judaica, as
well as collections of ethnic
and tribal art from around
the world, including Africa,
Australia and Latin America.

---

⑫ Nożyk Synagogue

📍 E6 🏛 Ul Twarda 6
🚌 109, 160, 178 🕐 9am–
40 mins before sunset Mon–
Thu & Sun, 9am–sunset
Fri 🌐 warszawa.
jewish.org.pl

Nożyk Synagogue was
founded by Zelman
and Ryfka Nożyk, who
in 1893 donated the
land on which it was to
be built. Later they left

HIDDEN GEM
The MDM Area

Stretching south of Aleja
Jerozolimskie, the MDM
estate (Marszałkowska
Dzielnica Mieszkanowa)
was built in the 1950s in
Stalinist Baroque style.
Many of the MDM area's
apartment blocks are
famous for their Social-
Realist frescoes.

half of their estate to the
Orthodox Jewish community.
The synagogue was built
between 1898 and 1902. The
interior has an impressive
portico, crowned by a metal
dome bearing the Star of
David, which contains the
Torah Ark. In the centre of the
nave is a raised pulpit known
as a bema. The nave is surrounded by galleries that
were originally intended for
female worshippers.

Today, this is the only active
synagogue in Warsaw. When it
was built, it was hidden away
in the heart of a housing estate,
amid high-rise buildings. After
the war, few of these were still

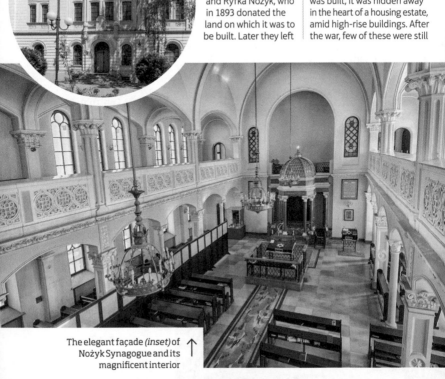

↑ The elegant façade *(inset)* of
Nożyk Synagogue and its
magnificent interior

Umschlagplatz Monument, at the spot where Jews were gathered for deportation

long-dead tree, covered with obituary notices for prisoners who died there.

 15

Monument to Those Fallen and Murdered in the East

📍D2 🏛Ul Muranowska
🚍116, 157, 178, 503
🚋6, 15, 18

This emotionally stirring monument, designed by Mirosław Biskupski, has the form of a railway wagon in which Poles were deported from the country into the Soviet Union during World War II. It is filled with crosses symbolizing the hundreds of thousands of Poles transported to the East and murdered in Soviet prison camps.

standing. During the Nazi occupation, the synagogue was closed for worship; the Germans used it as a warehouse. Reopened in 1945, it was eventually restored to its original condition (1977–83).

 13

Umschlagplatz Monument

📍C2 🏛Ul Stawki 🚍157
🚋15, 18, 33

The Umschlagplatz Monument, unveiled in 1988, marks the site of a former railway siding on Ulica Dzika. The German word *Umschlagplatz* translates as "collection point". It was from this location that some 300,000 Jews from the Warsaw Ghetto and elsewhere were summarily loaded onto cattle trucks and dispatched to almost certain death in the extermination camps. Among them was Janusz Korczak, an educator who despite multiple offers of sanctuary chose to remain with his group of Jewish orphans. Conditions in the ghetto were inhumane, and by 1942 more than 100,000 of the inhabitants had died. The simple yet moving monument, a collaboration between the architect Hanna Szmalenberg and the sculptor Władysław Klamerus, is made of blocks of black and white marble

resembling an open cattle truck and bearing the names of hundreds of Warsaw's Jews.

Between the Monument to the Heroes of the Ghetto, found at Plac Krasińskich, and the Umschlagplatz Monument runs the Trail of Jewish Martyrdom and Struggle. It is marked by 16 blocks of granite bearing inscriptions in Polish, Hebrew and Yiddish and the date 1940–43. Each block is dedicated to the memory of the 450,000 Jews from the Warsaw Ghetto murdered in the years 1940–3, to the heroes of the Ghetto Uprising in 1943 and to certain individuals from that time. The site of a bunker, in which the Uprising's commanders blew themselves up, has been specially marked.

 14

Pawiak Prison

📍C4 🏛Ul Dzielna 24/26
📞22 831 92 89 🚍107, 111, 180 🚋15, 18, 33, 35
🕐10am–5pm Wed–Sun

This prison was built in the 1830s by Henryk Marconi. It became notorious during the Nazi occupation, when it was used to imprison Poles and Jews arrested by the Germans. It now serves as a museum and houses photo displays, belongings of the prisoners and reconstructed cells. In front of the prison stands a

---

> **GHETTO UPRISING**
>
> The Nazis created the Jewish ghetto on 16 November 1940. The area was isolated with barbed wire fencing, which was later replaced with brick walls. Over 450,000 people were crowded into the ghetto: Jews from Warsaw and other parts of Poland, as well as gypsies. In March 1942, the Germans began to disband the ghetto, deporting over 300,000 people to the death camp in Treblinka. The Ghetto Uprising, which began on 19 April 1943, was organized by the secret Jewish Fighting Organization. Following the suppression of the Uprising, the Nazis razed the whole area to the ground.

BEYOND THE CENTRE

Move beyond the centre and visitors will discover what a varied city Warsaw is, a fascinating mosaic of different epochs and lifestyles. To the north of the Old and New Towns is the Warsaw Citadel, a vast red-brick complex built by 19th-century Russian occupiers and now home to some poignant museums. West of the Old Town is a vast region of post-World War II housing blocks, built on the ruins of districts destroyed by the Nazis in 1944. Although not exactly pretty, its well-planned residential neighbourhoods suggest that Socialist-era Warsaw was not as joyless as its critics might suggest. West of the city centre lies a brash stretch of 21st-century Warsaw, bristling with iconic sky-scrapers such as the baton-shaped Spire or the chisel-like Złota 44. Some of Warsaw's most evocative neighbourhoods lie east of the Vistula, where Praga is the only remaining part of the city that still looks much as it did in the 19th century.

Must Sees
1. Łazienki Park
2. Wilanów Palace

Experience More
3. Station Museum
4. Warsaw Uprising Museum
5. Katyń Museum
6. Centre for Contemporary Art
7. Gestapo Museum
8. Królikarnia Palace
9. Praga Museum
10. Orthodox Church of St Mary Magdalene
11. Neon Museum
12. National Stadium
13. Saska Kepa
14. Polish Vodka Museum

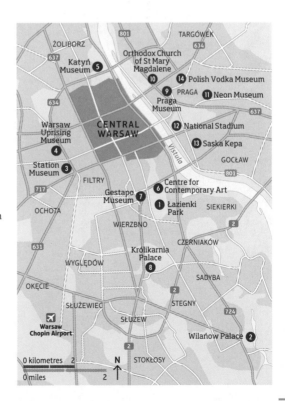

ŁAZIENKI PARK

🏛 Ul Agrykola 1 🚌 108, 116, 138, 166 🕐 Park: daily until dusk; Palace of the Isle, Myślewicki Palace & Old Orangery: mid-Apr-mid-Oct: 10am-6pm Tue-Sun; mid-Oct-mid-Apr: 9am-4pm Tue-Sun 🌐 lazienki-krolewskie.pl

This extensive park is an eternal oasis in the middle of the ever-changing capital. Its tree-lined paths and pretty lake make it a local favourite – in fact, half of Warsaw can be found strolling here at the weekend.

INSIDER TIP
Catch a Concert

Every summer by the Monument to Chopin, the park hosts outdoor concerts celebrating the music of this remarkable composer. First held in 1959, these performances are now a celebrated part of the city's cultural calendar.

Part of a great complex of heritage gardens, the park was home to a royal menagerie in the 17th century. In 1674, Grand Crown Marshal Stanisław Herakliusz Lubomirski acquired the park and altered part of the menagerie, building a hermitage and a bathing pavilion on an island. The pavilion gave the park its name (Łazienki meaning "baths"). In the 18th century, the park was owned by Stanisław August Poniatowski, who had it laid out as a formal garden. Lubomirski's baths were re-fashioned into a royal residence, Łazienki Palace, or Palace on the Isle, which is now a museum. There is an entrance charge for the Palace on the Isle, Myślewicki Palace and the Old Orangery.

1 The Art Nouveau Monument to Chopin, next to the lake, shows the composer sitting under a willow tree, seeking inspiration from nature.

2 The open-air Theatre on the Island took its inspiration from Greek amphitheatres.

3 The Old Orangery houses one of the few remaining 18th-century court theatres in the world.

EAT

Belvedere
This upmarket restaurant serves seasonal Polish cuisine in Łazienki Park's 19th-century New Orangery. This light and airy conservatory still houses an array of tropical plants – including a 100-year-old palm tree – so guests can dine surrounded by greenery.

⬛3 C5 ⬛Ul Agrykola 1 ⬛belvedere.com.pl

zł zł zł

←
The splendid Palace on the Isle on a crisp autumn day and *(inset)* one of its sumptuous rooms

2 ⊘ Ⓜ ▣ 🛍

WILANÓW PALACE

🏛 Ul SK Potockiego 10/16 🚍 E-2, 116, 164, 180, 317 🕐 Palace:
mid-Apr-mid-Oct: 9:30am-6pm daily, mid-Oct-mid-Apr:
9:30am-4pm Wed-Mon (first floor closed until 2020); Poster
Museum: 12pm-4pm Mon, 10am-4pm Tue-Sun 🖥 Palace:
wilanow-palac.pl; Poster Museum: postermuseum.pl

Just south of the city, set in lovely gardens and
parkland, stands Wilanów, one of Poland's most
important historic buildings. Built as a summer palace,
it looks at its best in that season, when the masonry
glows and the gardens are in full bloom.

Did You Know?
Wilanów is home to
some 800 pieces of
Chinese art collected
by its noble owners.

Wilanów was built at the end of the 17th century
as the summer residence of Jan III Sobieski.
This illustrious monarch, who valued family life
as much as material splendour (his wife bore
him 16 children), commissioned Augustyn
Locci to build him a modest country house.

> The finest artists, from both
> Poland and abroad, were
> commissioned to create the
> magnificent interiors.

Later the palace was extended and adorned by
renowned architects and sculptors, including
Michelangelo Palloni. The finest artists, from
both Poland and abroad, were commissioned
to create the magnificent interiors.

The gardens, recently revitalized, include a
beautiful parterre (a symmetrically laid-out garden connected by paths) and a 19th-century
rose garden, where concerts are held in summer. The grounds also contain a Chinese
Arbour, an orangery and a former riding
school that has been converted to house the
Poster Museum, the first of its kind in Europe.

The Paintings Gallery

▷ Originally a three-room apartment, the Paintings Gallery (usually referred to simply as the Museum) was reconstructed in the 19th century to house the palace's array of foreign paintings when the then-owner, the enlightened Stanisław Kostka Potocki, decided to allow the public to view the palace art. The Pompeii-pink walls and the ceiling murals with medallion portraits of great sculptors, architects and painters of the Renaissance, Baroque and Classicist periods are an allusion to typical 19th-century museum interiors. Two large cabinets contain fine Parisian silverware; smaller glazed cabinets between the windows contain 18th- and 19th-century bronzes, stoneware and porcelain.

King's Bedchamber

◁ Apart from serving its main purpose, the King's bedroom fulfilled an additional, stately role. In fact, it was the most important room in the residence, wherein the king received his visitors at audiences. The bed canopy is made of fabric brought back by Jan III Sobieski from his victory against the Turks at the Battle of Vienna in 1683. Look for the seasonal motifs and allusions celebrating summer, the time when the king would be in residence. Wall paintings depict idyllic rural scenes, and in the allegory of Summer on the ceiling, the goddess Aurora has been given the face of Jan III Sobieski's Queen Consort, Marie Casimire.

↑ The palace during summer, with the gardens in bloom

Queen's Bedchamber

In the enchanting Queen's bedroom, the seasonal theme is spring, possibly a flattering reference to her youthful beauty. As in the King's bedroom, there are paintings of tranquil rural scenes, but here they are taking place during spring instead of summer; an allegory of Spring adorns the ceiling, and the Regency mirror frames are decorated with symbolic vernal motifs. The walls are covered in patterned velvet dating to the early 18th century, in the then-fashionable Genoan style. On a chest of drawers are toilet articles that once belonged to Marie Casimire.

← One of many Classical statues in the gardens

The White Hall

▷ The White Hall in the southern wing, once the dining room, is the most sumptuous interior in the palace. Great wall mirrors facing the windows enhance the sense of light and spaciousness. At each end are magnificent fireplaces that still have their cast-iron plates carrying King August II's initials. Above the fireplaces there are two orchestra boxes, formerly used by court musicians and only discovered after World War II in the course of a conservation project. On the walls hang paintings of two of the kings from the Wettin dynasty, August II and August III, by Wilanów's court painter, Frenchman Louis de Silvestre.

EXPERIENCE MORE

3

Station Museum

🏠 Ul Towarowa 3
Ⓜ Rondo Daszyńskiego
🕐 10am–6pm daily
🌐 stacjamuzeum.pl

Celebrating the history of Polish railways, the Station Museum (Stacja Muzeum) occupies the site of Warsaw's main train station until 1975, when the current Warszawa Centralna opened.

Occupying four extensive rooms, the fascinating collection of models shows locomotives and rolling stock from throughout the ages. There are also some mobile dioramas. Outside in the courtyard is an extensive line of steam engines and vintage carriages parked on the railway tracks; children are invited to climb aboard some. Of particular interest is the armoured train, first used in the Russo-Polish War of 1920 and kept in service until World War II. The museum has a library that houses books on the subject of Polish railways.

4

Warsaw Uprising Museum

🏠 Ul Grzybowska 79 🚌 105, 109, 159 🚋 1, 8, 22, 24
Ⓜ Rondo Daszyńskiego
🕐 10am–6pm daily (to 8pm Thu) 🌐 1944.pl

This incredibly compelling museum, which opened in 2004 to commemorate the 60th anniversary of the Warsaw Uprising, is one of the most popular museums in the city.

A tribute to those who fought and died for Poland's independence, the museum recreates the atmosphere during those 63 days of military struggle, but it also shows what everyday life was like under Nazi occupation. The complicated international situation during the postwar years and at the time of the Uprising is portrayed in innovative displays that contain a wealth of photographs, films and audio recordings from eyewitnesses. Notable highlights include a full-size replica of a Liberator B-24J

Did You Know?

The Warsaw Uprising Museum is housed in a former tram power station.

bomber and a five-minute, 3D video that shows the wartime destruction of the city of Warsaw during an air raid.

5

Katyń Museum

🏠 Ul Jana Jeziorańskiego 4
📞 26 187 83 42 🚌 127, 176
🚋 1, 6, 16, 18 Ⓜ Dworzec Gdański 🕐 10am–5pm Wed, 10am–4pm Thu–Sun

Located in the red-brick battlements of the Citadela, a fortification built by the Russians in the 19th century, the Katyń Museum (Muzeum Katyńskie) commemorates the 20,000 Polish officers who

↑ Full-size model of a Liberator B-24J bomber displayed at the Warsaw Uprising Museum

The elegant Królikarnia Palace, surrounded by extensive gardens

were murdered by the Soviet security apparatus in 1940. When Polish army units surrendered to the invading Red Army in September 1939, the officers were separated from the other ranks and interned in camps in Western Russia. The majority of them were shot and then buried in mass graves the following spring. The moving, and at times harrowing, exhibition pays tribute to the victims and displays row upon row of personal effects retrieved from the graves.

Centre for Contemporary Art

🏠 Jazdów 2 🚌 E-2, 116, 138, 166, 411 🕐 Noon-7pm Tue-Sun (to 9pm Thu) 🌐 u-jazdowski.pl

The innovative Centre for Contemporary Art (Centrum Sztuki Współczesnej) organizes exhibitions of the work of artists from all over the world. The centre is housed in Ujazdowski Castle, an early Baroque fortification built at the beginning of the 17th century for Zygmunt III Vasa and his son Władysław IV. The castle's layout was spacious – it had an internal cloistered

---

> 💬 INSIDER TIP
> **Warsaw by Bike**
>
> Thanks to improved provision of cycle lanes, Warsaw is an increasingly easy city to explore by bike. A bike-hire network operated by Veturilo (veturilo.waw.pl) allows you to pick up and drop off bikes at points throughout the city.

---

courtyard and four towers – but its splendour was destined to be short-lived; the Swedish army sacked it in 1655 and it later changed hands repeatedly, being rebuilt many times. During World War II, Ujazdowski Castle was destroyed by fire and rebuilding of the castle only began in the 1970s.

Gestapo Museum

🏠 Al Szucha 25 📞 22 629 4919 🚌 E-2, 116, 180 Ⓜ Politechnika 🕐 10am-5pm Wed-Sun

When Warsaw was occupied by the Nazis during World War II, the Gestapo built an interrogation facility in the cellars beneath what is now the Ministry of Education. Today a museum, the site preserves many of the cells in their original state; these were once called "trams" because inmates were made to sit on rows of benches, waiting their turn to be taken away. The museum also provides chilling evidence of torture methods.

Królikarnia Palace (Pałacyk Królikarnia) owes its name – which means "rabbit hutch" – to the fact that it stands on the site of a rabbit farm that belonged to August II in the 1700s.

Królikarnia Palace

🏠 Ul Puławska 113a 🚌 218 🚊 4, 10, 14, 31, 35 🕐 11am-6pm Tue-Sun (to 8pm Thu) 🌐 krolikarnia. mnw.art.pl

Królikarnia Palace (Pałacyk Królikarnia) owes its name – which means "rabbit hutch" – to the fact that it stands on the site of a rabbit farm that belonged to August II in the 1700s. This exquisite little Neo-Classical palace is a square building topped by a dome, recalling Andrea Palladio's masterpiece, the Villa Rotonda, near Vicenza in Italy. Set in a garden on the slope of the escarpment in the district of Mokotów, it was designed by Dominik Merlini for Karol de Valery Thomatis, the director of Stanisław August Poniatowski's royal theatres. Since 1965 the Królikarnia Palace has been home to the fascinating Museum of Sculpture, which was previously named after the contemporary Polish sculptor Xawery Dunikowski and is dedicated to his works.

Praga Museum

Ul Targowa 50/52
Dworzec Wileński
10am–6pm Tue–Sun (to 8pm Thu)
muzeumpragi.pl

Opened in 2015, this museum (Muzeum Warszawskiej Pragi) is an engaging attempt to bring the social and cultural history of the district to life. The display includes an array of everyday objects, consumer goods and fashion items, as well as photographs of Praga in days gone by and a model of the suburb as it looked in the 19th century. The basement contains videos and audio recordings of local people reminiscing about their childhoods or recalling great events. Off the courtyard is a Jewish prayer house that once served traders at the nearby Różycki Market.

Orthodox Church of St Mary Magdalene

Al Solidarności 52
4, 13, 21, 23 Dworzec Wileński
11am–4pm Mon–Sat, 1–4pm Sun

During the Tsarist Russian occupation of Warsaw, the Praga district was where many Russian-speaking civil servants and military personnel lived. The Church (later elevated to cathedral status) of St Mary Magdalene was built in 1869 to serve their spiritual needs, and also to demonstrate to local Poles that Russian control was permanent.

Today the seat of the Bishop of Warsaw-Bielsk, it is the main Orthodox church in Poland. The five-domed structure was modelled on medieval Kiev churches. The interior is covered in murals portraying the principal saints, with particular prominence given to key figures in the Orthodox pantheon such as Emperor Constantine the Great and St Vladimir of Kiev.

Neon Museum

Ul Mińska 25
3, 6, 22 Noon–5pm Mon & Wed–Fri, 11am–6pm Sat, 11am–5pm Sun
neonmuzeum.org

Neon signs were one of the hallmarks of Polish cities during the Communist period. Commissioned by the regime to promote an appearance of affluence and glamour, they were created by some of Poland's finest architects and graphic designers.

Neon signs have been rediscovered as an important part in Poland's design heritage, thanks in part to Warsaw's Neon Museum. The team behind the museum first started collecting and renovating old neon signs in 2005, and opened a museum seven years later. The result is an incandescent collection of iconic signs advertising railway stations, restaurants, cinemas and shops – including many establishments that have long since disappeared.

The museum is part housed in the Soho Factory, a motorcycle and armaments works that is home to restaurants and design studios.

Did You Know?

Photographer Ilona Karwinska set up the Neon Museum after her "Polish Neon" exhibition.

↑ The eye-catching red-and-silver façade of the National Stadium, a major landmark

National Stadium

🏠 Al Poniatowskiego 1
🚋 7, 8, 9, 21, 24, 25
Ⓜ Stadion Narodowy
Ⓖ For guided tours only 2pm Mon-Fri, 2:30pm Sat & Sun 🌐 en.pgenarodowy.pl

Dominating the skyline on the eastern bank of the Vistula, the National Stadium (Stadion Narodowy) has become one of the defining buildings of modern Warsaw. It was built to serve as one of the key venues of the UEFA European Championships, co-hosted by Poland and Ukraine in 2012.

The stadium's distinctive appearance comes from the circle of outward-leaning spires, which support a mesh façade of eye-catching silver and red panels. Illuminated at night, it is an incredibly dramatic sight when viewed from the opposite bank of the river. As well as sporting events the stadium also hosts music concerts.

Guided tours of the stadium allow you to visit highly panoramic viewpoints in the upper tiers of the stands. You can also visit the changing rooms to see what goes on behind the scenes when the players are preparing for international matches.

←

The interior of St Mary Magdalene, Poland's main Orthodox church

13

Saska Kępa

🚋 7, 8, 9, 21, 24, 25

To the south of the National Stadium is a pleasant grid of residential streets known as Saska Kępa or "Saxon Meadow". The area was developed in the 1920s and 1930s, with the construction of row upon row of Bauhaus-inspired, Modernist urban villas. Much of its original architecture has survived, turning Saska Kępa into a unique monument to interwar lifestyles.

The district's main road, Ulica Francuska, is home to a growing number of cute cafés and restaurants. A statue outside No 11 honours Agnieszka Osiecka (1936-97), the songwriter who provided Polish pop music with a sophisticated, poetic edge.

↑ Photographing the various brands of vodka at the Vodka Museum

STAY

Autor Rooms
Pop art and modern design have transformed this renovated apartment into a chic B&B.

🏠 Ul Lwowska 17/7
🌐 autorrooms.pl

Hilton Warsaw
Classy skyscaper hotel in the heart of a high-rise district.

🏠 Al Grzybowska 63
🌐 hiltonhotels.com

Rialto
Every detail here is a faithful reproduction of Art Deco style.

🏠 Ul Wilcza 73
🌐 rialto.pl

14

Polish Vodka Museum

🏠 Ul Bialostocka
Ⓜ Dworzec Wileński
Ⓖ 10am-8pm Sun-Thu, 11am-9pm Fri & Sat
🌐 muzeumpolskiejwodki.pl

The Polish Vodka Museum (Muzeum Polskiej Wódki) is housed in the former Koneser vodka distillery, a collection of red brick buildings dating from 1897, and now the subject of post-industrial regeneration. A multimedia display takes visitors through the production process, revealing that true Polish vodka can only be made from potatoes or grains. It also explores the social and cultural importance of vodka in Polish society, and the way in which vodka has become a symbol of Polish identity abroad.

EXPERIENCE
POLAND

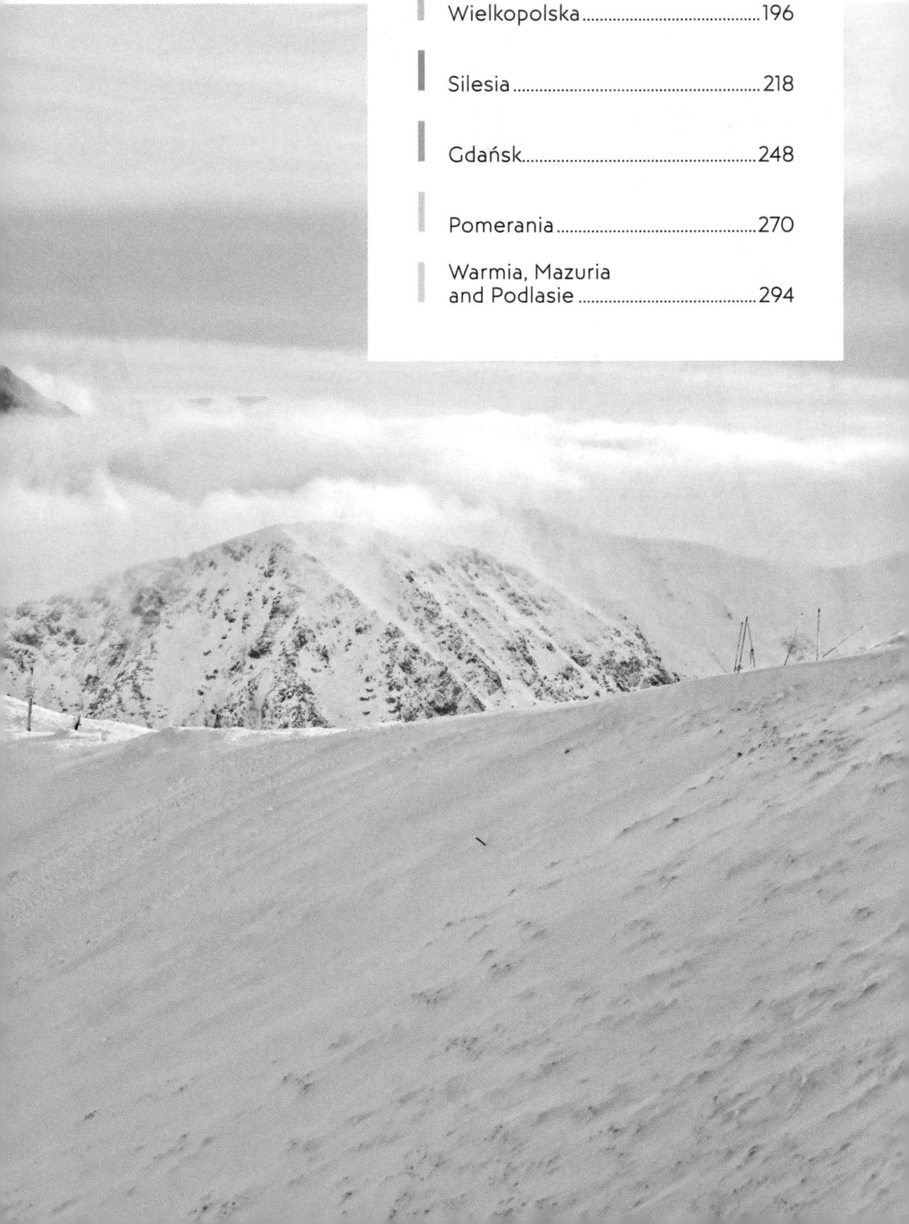

MAZOVIA AND THE LUBLIN REGION

For centuries, Mazovia was both culturally and economically one of the least-developed areas of the ethnically Polish lands of the Commonwealth of Two Nations *(p62)*. The Principality of Mazovia came into existence in 1138, during the division of Poland, and it preserved its independence for nearly 400 years. The area was then incorporated into the Kingdom of Poland in 1526 after the death of the last Mazovian princes and, in 1596, Sigismund III Vasa moved the capital of the Commonwealth of Two Nations from Kraków to Warsaw, in Mazovia. After the Congress of Vienna (1815), Mazovia and the Lublin region formed part of the Congress Kingdom, under Russian rule. In 1918, the whole area was returned to the reborn country of Poland. Today, in the east of Mazovia and in the Lublin region, farmsteads, with their humble cottages built to mimic the style of mansions, can be seen. The gently rolling Lublin region differs considerably from Mazovia, in terms of both landscape and culture, and has many excellent examples of Renaissance and Baroque architecture.

WARMIŃSKO-
MAZURSKIE

KUJAWSKO-
POMORSKIE

Brodnica
Działdowo
Mława
Przasnysz

Toruń
57
Orzyc
Inowrocław
A1
POMERANIA
p270
Sierpc
CIECHANÓW ⑩ ⑪ OPINOGÓRA
Wkra
10
Raciąż
Glinojeck
Maków
Mazowiecki
60
Włocławek
Drobin
50
PUŁTUSK ⑫
Strzelno
62
60
Płońsk
Wkra
MAZOWIECKIE
Serock
⑨ PŁOCK
62
61
Łąck
Warsaw Modlin Airport ✈
Konin
Vistula
Czerwińsk nad Wisłą
Legionowo
Koło
Wyszogród
Kampinoska Forest
A7
Wołomin
93
Brochów
⑬ ŻELAZOWA
WOLA
Warsaw
92
92
Sochaczew
2
91
A2
Warsaw Chopin
Airport ✈
A1
ŁOWICZ ⑮
⑭ NIEBORÓW
A2
79
Góra
ARKADIA ⑯
⑰ ŻYRARDÓW
Kalwaria
7
Skierniewice
50
WIELKOPOLSKA
p196
Grójec
Warka
Mogielnica
Pilica
58
Nowe Miasto
nad Pilicą
57
ŁÓDZKIE
Radom
12
Przysucha
12
Orońsk
Szydłowiec
Iłża
74
ŚWIETOKRZYSKIE
Kielce
Jędrzejów
Chielnik
57
73
Busko-Zdrój

MAZOVIA AND THE
LUBLIN REGION

Must Sees
① Lublin
② Zamość

Experience More
③ Chełm
④ Sobibór
⑤ Włodawa
⑥ Szczebrzeszyn
⑦ Roztocze National Park
and Zwierzyniec
⑧ Belzec Memorial Site and Museum
⑨ Płock
⑩ Ciechanów
⑪ Opinogóra
⑫ Pułtusk
⑬ Żelazowa Wola
⑭ Nieborów
⑮ Łowicz
⑯ Arkadia
⑰ Żyrardów
⑱ Treblinka
⑲ Kazimierz Dolny
⑳ Kozłówka
㉑ Radzyń Podlaski

↑ Lublin's beautiful Market Square, found within its romantic Old Town

①

LUBLIN

🅰 F5 ℹ Ul Jezuicka 1-3; www.lublintravel.pl

Lublin, the largest city in southeastern Poland, is buzzing with culture and peppered with historic buildings. It is also an important centre of academic life; its best-known seat of learning is the Catholic University of Lublin. Before World War II, the only Jewish college of higher education in Poland was located here. In 1944, after Lublin had been liberated from the Nazis, Poland's first Communist government, convened at Stalin's behest, arrived here on the tanks of the Red Army.

①

Old Town and Market Square

🅰 Rynek 12-13

The most attractive district of Lublin is the Old Town (Stare Miasto), situated on the edge of the escarpment. The area is reached through Kraków Gate (Brama Krakowska); one of the few remaining reminders of the fortifications which once surrounded Lublin, it has become a symbol of the city and is now home to an exhibition on local history. The Old Town is a maze of romantic lanes and alleys, lined with houses decorated with a mixture of Mannerist and Baroque ornamentation. Many of the buildings have Socialist Realist paintings dating from 1954, when the town was renovated to celebrate the tenth anniversary of the establishment of the Communist Lublin Committee.

At the centre of the Old Town is the Market Square, with Lublin's town hall. Here, the Crown Tribunal of the Kingdom of Poland once had its seat. In the 18th century, the town hall was rebuilt in the Neo-Classical style. Today its cellars house an exhibition on local history and are also part of Lublin's Underground Route, which runs along a series of 16th-century cellars; it is open by tour only (visit the Town Hall to book).

②

Cathedral of Saints John the Baptist and John the Evangelist

🅰 Pl Katedralny 📞 81 532 11 96 🕐 10am-4pm Tue-Sat

The interior of this former Jesuit church is a triumph of Baroque art. Trompe l'oeil frescoes painted by Joseph Mayer in 1756–7 depict scenes set against a background of illusory architecture. The most beautiful frescoes are those found within the cathedral treasury, including *Heliodorus Expelled from the Temple*.

💬 INSIDER TIP
Get Festive

Lublin hosts an array of fantastic family festivals, including the craft-filled Jagiellonian Fair in August *(www.jarmark jagiellonski.pl)* and the spellbinding Festival of the Magicians *(p59)* in July.

③ Dominican Church

📍 Ul Złota 9 🕐 Hours vary, check website 🌐 lublin.dominikanie.pl

The most magnificent place of worship in the Old Town is the Dominican church (Kościół Dominikanów), founded in 1342 and rebuilt in the 17th and 18th centuries. The finest of all its 11 chapels is the mid-17th-century Mannerist-Baroque Firlej Chapel. Its ribbed dome is an ambitious confection ascribed to the mason Jan Wolff. Since the 14th-century the church has housed a relic that is said to be part of the cross upon which Jesus Christ died.

④ Fortuna Cellar

📍 Rynek 8 🕐 Apr–Oct: 11am–7pm daily; Nov–Mar: 11am–5pm daily 📞 81 444 5555

Housed in the former wine cellars of a main-square tenement building, the Fortune Cellar (Piwnica pod Fortuną) is a museum honouring the multicultural heritage of Lublin, with audiovisual displays recalling the city's Catholic, Orthodox and Jewish communities. The walls and ceiling of the cellars are covered in beautiful murals from the 16th century, which depict mythological scenes. The museum's unusual name comes from a mural of the goddess Fortune, painted on the walls of a barrel-vaulted space where drinking parties were once held.

⑤ Lublin Castle

📍 Pl Zamkowy 1 🕐 Hours vary, check website 🌐 muzeumlubelskie.pl

Lublin Castle was built in the 14th century and remodelled in the Gothic style in 1823–6 for use as a prison. Within it is the city's most important historic building, the Chapel of the Holy Trinity (Kaplica Świętej Trójcy), a Catholic chapel whose interior is covered with Byzantine frescoes painted in 1418 by Orthodox artists. Among the saints and angels is a portrait of the chapel's founder, Władysław Jagiełło.

↑ Lublin Castle's beautiful Chapel of the Holy Trinity

The chapel is considered evidence of the cultural diversity of the Kingdom of Poland and the coexistence at this time of the Roman Catholic and Orthodox faiths. It is necessary to book in advance to visit the chapel. The castle also houses the Lublin Museum (Muzeum Lubelskie) which contains exhibitions of Polish paintings, folk art and weaponry.

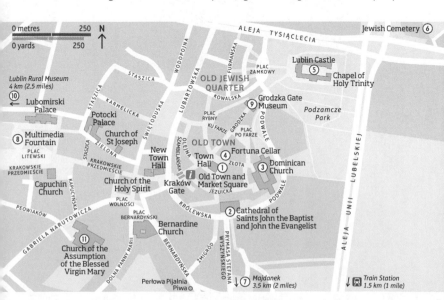

⑥ Jewish Cemetery

Ul Kalinowszczyna
⏰Daily

This atmospheric cemetery, built on the site of a former medieval fortress, is perched on a hill overlooking the Old Town. Established in 1555, the cemetery is evidence of the Jewish community that existed in Lublin for many centuries; this community was celebrated in the novels of Nobel Laureate Isaac Bashevis Singer (1904–91). Regarded as an important historical and religious site, this peaceful cemetery is filled with centuries-old gravestones.

⑦ State Museum at Majdanek

Droga Męczenników Majdanka 67 ⏰9am-6pm daily (to 4pm Nov-Mar)
🔒Public hols 🌐majdanek.pl

In 1941, the Nazis established a camp at Majdanek for Soviet prisoners of war, but it later

↑ A memorial exhibition at the moving State Museum at Majdanek

became a death camp, primarily for Jews. Of the 150,000 people who passed through Majdanek, 80,000 were murdered. The camp has been preserved as a museum and memorial to the victims.

⑧ Multimedia Fountain

Pl Litewski

The centrepiece of the newly rennovated and pedestrianized Plac Litewski, Lublin's multimedia fountain is a popular spot for locals to hang out at during the day. At night, the fountain is dramatically illuminated with a spectacular sound-and-light show; the displays are often based around different themes. Part of the fountain area is accessible to kids eager to splash around on warm summer days.

⑨ Grodzka Gate Museum

Ul Grodzka 21 ⏰Guided tours at 9:30am, 11am, 12:30pm & 2pm Mon-Fri
🌐teatrnn.pl

Located to the north of the Old Town, Lublin's Grodzka Gate (Brama Grodzka), also known as the Jewish Gate, once marked the boundary between the city centre, which was predominantly Catholic, and the Jewish quarter found immediately to the north.

Most of Lublin's Jews were murdered by the Nazis during World War II, and the Grodzka Gate – restored to its former glory following a period of dereliction – now holds an

↑ The wooden Greek Orthodox church at the Lublin Rural Museum

exhibition devoted to their memory. Filled with photographs and documentary evidence of this once-thriving community, the compelling display provides intimate insights into individual Jewish lives. The museum can be accessed by guided tour only.

⑩ 🏛 🏬

Lublin Rural Museum

🏠 Aleja Warszawska 96
🕐 Apr-Oct: 9am-5pm daily (to 6pm May-Sep); Nov-Mar: 9am-3pm Tue-Sun
🌐 skansen.lublin.pl

One of the biggest open-air museums in Poland, the Lublin Rural Museum celebrates the region's unique heritage and cultural diversity. Here you can see traditional rural buildings brought from nearby villages and small towns. There is a windmill from Zygmuntów and an elegant Greek-Catholic church from Tarnoszyn. The museum also includes a spectacular 18th-century manor from Żyrzyn, complete with its interior furnishings and surrounded by a picturesque garden. Another of its main attractions is a rebuilt market town from the early 20th century, which includes a main market square surrounded by an array of diffrent shops.

The museum also hosts educational events and celebrates regional festivals.

←

A colourful sound-and-light show takes place at Lublin's popular Multimedia Fountain

⑪

Church of the Assumption of the Blessed Virgin Mary

🏠 Ul Gabriela Narutowicza 6 🕐 Hours vary, check website
🌐 pobrygidkowski.pl

This church (Kościół Matki Boskiej Zwycięskiej) was founded by King Władysław Jagiełło (1386–1434) to commemorate his victory over the Teutonic Knights at the Battle of Grunwald in 1410. The church was home to nuns for hundreds of years; during Communist rule, it screened religious and historical films banned by the regime.

Visitors can also visit the church crypt and ascend the tower for views over the Old Town. Also worth a visit is the nearby Capuchin Church (kościół Kapucynów), found on Krakowskie Przedmieście.

Did You Know?

Lublin's Rusałka district is named after a water nymph who is said to haunt the area.

Cycling into Zamość's
historic centre through
the Szczebrzeska Gate ↑

2

ZAMOŚĆ

 G5 🚗🚌 ℹ **Rynek Wielki 13; www.turystyka.zamosc.pl**

Planned and built from scratch according to Italian concepts of the ideal town, Zamość is one of the best-preserved Renaissance towns in Europe. Conceived by powerful magnate Jan Zamoyski and designed by Bernardo Morando, it was constructed in the late 16th century. A programme of restoration was carried out in the 1970s, and today the Main Square remains as lively as ever with numerous cultural events.

①

Cathedral

🏛 **Ul Kolegiacka 1** 📞 **84 639 2614** ⏰ **Cathedral: 6am–7pm daily; Sacral Museum: May–Sep: 10am–6pm Mon–Fri, 1–6pm Sat & Sun (Oct–Apr by prior arrangement)**

With its graceful free-standing bell tower and elegantly pro-portioned façade, Zamość Cathedral is one of the best examples of Renaissance architecture in eastern Poland. Initiated in 1587 and com-pleted in the 1630s, it was one of the key buildings designed by Bernardo Morando, the chief architect of nobleman Jan Zamoyski. The airy interior features a distinctively deco-rated vaulted ceiling, and contains a late-Baroque main altar showing St Thomas kneeling before the resur-rected Jesus.

On the south side of the cathedral, the former deacon's house now holds the Sacral Museum (Muzeum Sakralne Katedry Zamojskiej). The museum displays an array of religious manuscripts, reli-quaries and coffin portraits (paintings of the deceased that were placed on the side of their caskets during the funeral procession).

②

Zamoyski Academy

🏛 **Ul Akademicka 8**

Founded in 1598, the Zamoyski Academy (Akademia Zamojska) was an important element in Zamoyski's plans for Zamość. It was intended to provide the sons of the landowning and mercantile elites with a broadly humanist, secular education. Completed in the 1630s, the academy building is an austere but handsome piece of Neo-Classical architecture, with an attractive garden courtyard in the middle. Turned into a barracks during the Tsarist occu-pation, it is now a secondary school.

1992

Zamość is declared a UNESCO World Heritage Site.

Rotonda

📍 Ul Męczenników Rotundy 🕐 May–Sep: 9am–8pm Tue–Sun

The barrel-shaped Rotonda is an artillery fort built by the Russians in the 19th century to extend the city's defences. In 1940 it was taken over by the German Gestapo, and for four years served as a site of imprisonment, torture and mass executions. Zamość's Nazi occupiers planned to settle German farmers on the fertile agricultural lands surrounding the city, and set about ethnically cleansing the local population. Polish peasants were deported, sent to work camps or simply shot. Polish community leaders (including priests and boy-scouts as well as teachers and lawyers) ended up at the Rotonda. An estimated 50,000 people passed through the prison here, of which 8,000 were murdered. The Rotonda is now a memorial to those who perished, with commemorative shrines and plaques placed in the individual rooms that line the central courtyard. White Graveyard crosses fill the surrounding park.

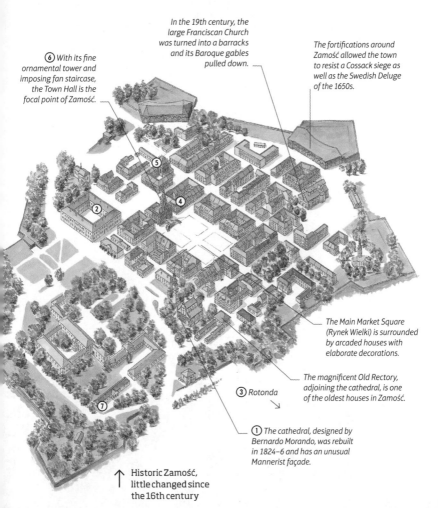

⑥ With its fine ornamental tower and imposing fan staircase, the Town Hall is the focal point of Zamość.

In the 19th century, the large Franciscan Church was turned into a barracks and its Baroque gables pulled down.

The fortifications around Zamość allowed the town to resist a Cossack siege as well as the Swedish Deluge of the 1650s.

The Main Market Square (Rynek Wielki) is surrounded by arcaded houses with elaborate decorations.

The magnificent Old Rectory, adjoining the cathedral, is one of the oldest houses in Zamość.

③ Rotonda

① The cathedral, designed by Bernardo Morando, was rebuilt in 1824–6 and has an unusual Mannerist façade.

↑ Historic Zamość, little changed since the 16th century

④

Zamość Museum

◨ Ul Ormianska 30
⊙ 9am–4pm Tue–Sun
ⓦ muzeum-zamojskie.pl

The Zamość Museum (Muzeum Zamojskie) occupies a handsome collection of former merchants' houses on the north side of the Main Square. The buildings have retained many of their wooden-beamed ceilings and delicately cut stone windowsills. Maps, models and engravings show the development of the town through the ages, while rich furnishings and oriental carpets serve as evidence of Zamość's role in East–West trade. There's also a display of Armenian costumes, revealing the historical importance of Zamość's Armenian merchant community, while a fascinating archaeological collection shows how local Gothic tribes used to periodically open the graves of the deceased in order to sacrifice tortoises, dogs, swans and rabbits in their honour. A selection of Naïve paintings by local villagers and vibrantly coloured traditional ceramics round off an absorbing and varied collection.

↑ Visitors relaxing outside Zamość's beautiful Renaissance synagogue

---

⑤

Synagogue

◨ Ul Pereca 14 ⊙ Mar–Oct: 10am–6pm Tue–Sun; Nov–Feb: 10am–2pm Tue–Sun
ⓦ fodz.pl

Jews constituted an important part of the Zamość community from the very beginning, when Jan Zamoyski invited Sephardic Jews from the Ottoman Empire to settle in his new town. Over time the community was increasingly dominated by Ashkenazi Jews from Eastern Europe, especially after 1648 when pogroms (organized persecutions) forced many to flee from nearby Ukraine.

Zamość's synagogue was built in 1610, and is a fine Renaissance structure with a beautifully restored interior that boasts a frieze of delicate floral carvings. The synagogue also houses a small multimedia museum with a display devoted to the history of Jews in Zamość.

⑥ Town Hall

🏛 Rynek Wielki 13
🕐 8am-6pm daily
🌐 turystyka.zamosc.pl

Designed in the 16th century by Bernardo Morando but much modified by his successors, Zamość's Town Hall (Ratusz) is a striking amalgam of Renaissance and early Baroque styles. The building's most arresting features are the sweeping, fan-shaped double stairway and the soaring double-domed spire, both of which were added in the late 18th century. The Town Hall is still home to the town council and also houses Zamość's Tourist Information Centre. In the basement there is an exhibition on the history of the building.

In a tradition that dates back to the town's founding, at noon every day in summer a trumpeter sounds a bugle call from the clock tower.

Did You Know?

Although the Town Hall looks symmetrical, its left-hand side is over 1 m (3 ft) wider than the right.

⑦ Arsenal Museum of Fortifications and Weaponry

🏛 Ul Zamkowa 2 🕐 May-Sep: 9am-5pm Tue-Sun; Oct-Apr: 9am-4pm Tue-Sun
🌐 muzeumarsenal.pl

For much of its history Zamość was an important military base, protected by the huge red-brick fortifications that still surround the town centre. This defensive role is explored in a three-part exhibition at the Arsenal Museum of Fortifications and Weaponry (Arsenał: Muzeum Fortyfikacji i Broni), a branch of the Zamość Museum housed in the former Arsenal in the southwest corner of town. Occupying the Arsenal building itself is a display covering pre-modern military history,

↑ A cannon at the Arsenal Museum of Fortifications and Weaponry

with a collection of sabres, pikes, muskets and cannons. Uniforms dating from the 19th century recall the days when Zamość was a border fortress, controlled first by the Austrians and then later by Tsarist Russia.

Warfare of the 20th century is examined in the Pavilion Beneath the Curtain (Pawilon pod kurtyną), a modern structure pressed against the town walls. Inside, a combination of original weaponry and multimedia exhibits is used to tell the story of Polish victories against the Bolsheviks in 1920, as well as the country's later defeat at the hands of Nazi and Soviet invaders in 1939. At the western end of the Arsenal complex is the Gunpowder Magazine (Prochownia), which shows films about the history of the imposing Zamość Fortress.

 INSIDER TIP
Zamość Jazz

Jazz Klub Kosz (Ul Szczebrzeska 3) has turned Zamość into a mecca for music fans. As well as gigs in its own premises, Kosz also organizes festivals on the Main Square in May and September.

 ←
The Town Hall, located at the heart of Zamość's beautiful Main Square

Looking over Chełm from the Basilica of the Virgin Mary on Castle Hill ↑

EXPERIENCE MORE

Chełm

⚑G5 🏛 𝑖 Ul Lubelska 63; www.itchelm.pl

Chełm is best known for its network of underground tunnels, which are the remains of the former **Chalk Mines** (Podziemia). The tunnels, which are on three levels, descend to a depth of 30 m (100 ft); visitors can walk along them, candle in hand. Note that visits are by guided tour only. During the 17th century, as many as 80 houses here had a direct entrance to the workings. Mining ended here in the 1800s.

Above ground, the town's most impressive building is the Piarist church. It was built by Paolo Fontana in 1753–63 and has an undulant façade, elliptical nave and imposing dome. The Baroque interior is decorated with paintings by Joseph Mayer.

The best view of Chełm is from the historic Castle Hill (Góra Zamkowa), where there are remains of a 13th-century princely castle. From here, the towers of Roman Catholic churches, the onion domes

of a Greek Catholic and an Orthodox ch urch, and a fine Baroque synagogue can be made out. A Jewish community, one of the earliest in Poland, settled here.

Chalk Mines
🎨🎨 **☐ Ul Lubelska 55a ☎ 82 565 25 30 ⏰ Tours at 11am, 1pm and 4pm daily ☒ Pub hols**

Sobibór

⚑G5 ☒ For restoration 🌐 sobibor-memorial.eu

In an area of forest some 10 km (6 miles) to the south of Włodawa, the Nazi death camp at Sobibór is where an estimated 200,000 Jews died. Most were from the eastern part of Poland, but there were also others from elsewhere in Nazi-occupied Europe. They were murdered when carbon monoxide fumes were fed into the closed chambers in which they were imprisoned. Before they left, the Germans destroyed these chambers, and their exact site was only confirmed by archeologists in

2014. Today, although little remains, there are information charts and signs marking the main sites of commemoration.

Włodawa

⚑G5 🚌 𝑖 Ul Partyzantów 25; um.wlodawa.eu

Quiet riverside Włodawa is a historical meeting point of Catholic, Orthodox and Jewish cultures. The 17th-century **Great Synagogue and Museum** is a masterpiece of provincial Baroque, with arcaded lower storeys and a multitiered copper roof. It's home to a colourful, richly carved Torah Ark as well as

> **HIDDEN GEM**
> **Park Life**
>
> The secluded Polesian National Park (Poleski Park Narodowy) is found 40 km (25 miles) northwest of Chełm. Explore its peat bogs, swamps and lakes, and try to spot animals like otters, beavers and bats.

a small prayer hall which houses an interesting ethnographic collection.

Nearby, on Ulica Klasztorna, is the twin-towered Church of St Louis (Kościół św. Ludwika), with Baroque ceiling paintings by Gabriel Sławiński. On Ulica Kościelna is the prim white 1890s Orthodox Church of the Nativity of the Virgin (Cerkiew pw. Narodzenia), an attractive onion-domed structure.

Great Synagogue and Museum

 Ul Czerwonego Krzyża 7 May-Jun: 10am-4pm Tue-Fri, 10am-2pm Sat & Sun; Jul-Sep: 10am-4pm Tue-Fri; Oct-Apr: 10am-3pm Tue-Fri muzeumwlodawa.pl

---

Szczebrzeszyn

G5 Ul Sądowa 3; 84 682 1060

Once an important medieval trading centre, Szczebrzeszyn went into decline after the foundation of Zamość, which is just 21 km (13 miles) away. The town huddles around the attractive Baroque Church of St Michael (Kościoł św. Mikołaja). Found nearby is an arcaded Renaissance synagogue with a two-tier roof typical of the Jewish prayer houses common in the east. The Jewish cemetery on the town's outskirts is among the oldest of its kind in Poland and contains some beautifully inscribed gravestones.

Roztocze National Park and Zwierzyniec

G6 Ul Słowackiego 2; zwierzyniec.info.pl

Covering more than 80 sq km (31 sq miles) of dense, rolling, forested terrain, Roztocze National Park is one of the prime recreation areas in eastern Poland, with numerous options for kayaking, hiking and boating.

The main entrance to the park is at the small town of Zwierzyniec, 30 km (19 miles) southwest of Zamość. The town originally developed around the summer palace of the 16th-century nobleman Jan Zamoyski. The **National Park Museum** (Ośrodek Edukacyjno-Muzealny RPN) found here has a range of multimedia displays introducing Roztocze's rich local animal and bird life.

Did You Know?

Some of the beech trees in Roztocze National Park have grown to a staggering 50 m (160 ft) tall.

The nearby national park gateway is the starting point for a number of different marked trails into the forest. Within the park, and only a short 20-minute stroll from Zwierzyniec, is Echo Lake; this tranquil body of water has a small sandy beach and is a very popular bathing spot in summer.

National Park Museum

Ul Plażowa 3, Zwierzyniec Apr-Oct: 9am-5pm Tue-Sun; Nov-Mar: 9am-3pm Tue-Sat roztoczanskipn.pl

---

Belzec Memorial Site and Museum

G6 Apr-Oct: 9am-5pm Tue-Sun; Nov-Mar: 9am-4pm Tue-Sun belzec.eu

About 40 km (25 miles) south of Zamość, the Nazi extermination camp at Bełżec was one of the main locations used in the mass murder of Poland's Jewish population, accounting for an estimated 430,000 victims. The site was bulldozed by the Nazis in 1943 and disguised as farmland. There is now a highly informative museum at the site, as well as an outdoor memorial where visitors have piled stones in memory of those who lost their lives here.

←

Inscribed gravestones in Szczebrzeszyn's Jewish cemetery

↑ Bust from a Bolesław
Biegas exhibition in the
Museum of Mazovia

Płock

D3 🚗🚌 *i* Ul Stary Rynek
8; www.turystykaplock.eu

This city, beautifully situated
on the high Vistula Bluff, is
best known today for its large
petrochemical plants. Its
history, however, goes back
many centuries. From 1075,
Płock was the seat of the
bishopric of Mazovia. Under
Władysław I (1079–1102) and
his heir Bolesław III Wrymouth
(1102– 1138), it was capital of
Poland and the favoured royal
seat. From 1138 to the end of
the 15th century, the Płock
and Mazovian princes resided
here, and, in the 12th century,
it was an important centre of
political and cultural life.

The buildings of old Płock
are relatively modest, but the
small Neo-Classical houses,
now restored, make a picturesque ensemble. Particularly
noteworthy, the Neo-Classical
town hall was built in 1824–7
to a design by Jakub Kubicki.
Here, on 23 September 1831,
during the uprising against
Russian rule, the final session
of the insurgent Sejm of the
Kingdom of Poland was held.
Another notable building is

the rather large Neo-Gothic
cathedral (1911–19) of the
Mariavite Church of Poland.
The Baroque church, the
Classical toll gates and the
remains of the Gothic city
walls are also worth seeing.

The most interesting part
of Płock is Tum Hill (Wzgórze
Tumskie), with its Renaissance
**Cathedral of Our Lady of
Mazovia** and castle remains.
Built in 1531–5, the town's
cathedral was the first large
Renaissance church in Poland.
It was established by Andrzej
Krzycki, Bishop of Płock, later
Primate of Poland and a noted
scholar and poet. Giovanni
Cini and Bernardino Zanobi de
Gianotis were the architects,
and later rebuilding was by
Gianbattista of Venice. The
interior has Renaissance and
Baroque tombstones, and in
a marble sarcophagus in the
Royal Chapel are remains
of Władysław I and his son
Bolesław III. The grand Neo-
Renaissance façade of the
cathedral, with its twin towers,
was built at the start of the
20th century to a controversial
design by Stefan Szyller, the
architect who was in charge
of the restoration work.

The **Diocesan Museum**
(Muzeum Diecezjalne) has a
rich collection of cathedral
treasures. Especially noteworthy are the gold vessels
and some liturgical textiles,
particularly the chasubles,

the oldest of which date from
the 1400s. The museum also
possesses woven sashes from
the old court dress of the
nobility. Sashes were often
made into vestments.

The **Museum of Mazovia**
(Muzeum Mazowieckie) is
located in a former monastery
and houses one of the largest
collections of Art Nouveau in
the world. Among the exhibits
can be found reconstructions
of domestic interiors, as well
as works of art, furniture, textiles and everyday objects
that were commonly used
during the period.

Sports facilities can be
found on Lake Włocławek,
a reservoir on the Vistula.
There is a stud farm at Łąck
9 km (5 miles) from Płock.

**Cathedral of Our Lady
of Mazovia**
🏠 Ul Mostowa 2 ⏰ 10am-
5:30pm Mon-Sat, 2-5:30pm
and between services Sun
🌐 katedraplock.pl

Diocesan Museum
♿🚻 🏠 Ul Tumska 3a
⏰ 10:30am-2pm Tue-Fri,
10am-6pm Sat 🌐 mdplock.pl

Museum of Mazovia
♿ 🏠 Ul Tumska 8 ⏰ May-
mid-Oct: 10am-5pm Tue-Sun;
mid-Oct-Apr: 10am-4pm
Tue-Sun 🌐 muzeumplock.eu

← The Krasiński mansion and its peaceful park in the town of Opinogóra

 12

Pułtusk

▲E3 🚌 **ℹ** Rynek 41, Town Hall Tower; pultusk.pl

Of all the small towns in Mazovia, Pułtusk has the most beautiful setting. Its historic centre, on an island formed by an arm of the River Narwa, has one of the longest market squares in Europe. The town hall, with a Gothic brick tower, houses the small Regional Museum. Of equal interest is the Gothic-Renaissance collegiate church, with barrel vaulting over the nave.

To the south of the market square is the castle of the bishops of Płock. Destroyed and rebuilt a number of times, it incorporates Renaissance, Baroque and Neo-Classical elements. After restoration work in the 1980s the House of the Polish Diaspora (Dom Polonii) was set up here. The castle is now the Hotel Zamek and visitors staying here can enjoy tennis, canoeing, rowing and horse riding; sledging parties also take place during the winter. The old-time Polish kitchen, which serves homemade fruit and berry liqueurs and home-baked sourdough bread, is recommended. Nearby, on the River Narwa, are water meadows and the White Forest (Puszcza Biała), with a rich variety of plants and wildlife, including more than 200 species of birds.

10

Ciechanów

▲E3 🚌 **ℹ** Ul Warszawska 34; www.umciechanow.pl

On the edge of Ciechanów stand the Gothic ruins of the Castle of the Mazovian Princes, built around 1420–30. The castle houses one of the exhibitions of the **Museum of the Mazovian Nobility** (Muzeum Szlachty Mazowieckiej).

In the town is the Gothic Church of the Annunciation, founded in the first half of the 16th century and rebuilt in the 17th; the 16th-century parish Church of the Nativity of the Blessed Virgin Mary; and a modest Neo-Gothic town hall. The low-rise apartment blocks near the railway station were built by the Nazis, who had intended to demolish the whole of Ciechanów and then build it anew.

Museum of the Mazovian Nobility

🎫 🏠 Ul Warszawska 61a
🕐 8am–4pm Tue–Sun (10am–6pm Jul–Aug)
🌐 muzeumciechanow.pl

→ The impressive Town Hall tower in historic Pułtusk

11

Opinogóra

▲E3 🚌

This tiny Neo-Gothic mansion, situated in a landscaped park, was built as a wedding gift for Count Zygmunt Krasiński (1812–59), a leading Romantic poet. Locals believe it was designed by French architect Eugène Emmanuel Viollet-le-Duc, although art historians attribute it to Henryk Marconi. It now houses the fascinating **Museum of Romanticism** (Muzeum Romantyzmu).

The parish church in the park is home to the mausoleum of the Krasiński family, where the poet is buried.

Museum of Romanticism

🎫 🎫 🏠 Ul Krasińskiego 9
🕐 May–Sep: 10am–6pm Tue–Sun; Oct–Apr: 8am–4pm Tue–Sun
🚫 Pub hols
🌐 muzeum romantyzmu.pl

→ Visitors exploring the fascinating Chopin Museum, Żelazowa Wola

 13

Żelazowa Wola

△E4 🚌

This Romantic manor, set in a verdant, well-tended park, is the birthplace of the famous composer Fryderyk Chopin (1810–49). At the time of his birth, however, it was no more than a thatched outbuilding in which Chopin's parents, Mikołaj and Justyna Tekla, rented a few rooms. In 1930–31, the building was converted into the **Chopin Museum** (Oddział Muzeum Fryderyka Chopina w Warszawie) and the park around it planted with trees and shrubs donated by horticulturalists from all over Poland. Inside, all kinds of objects associated with the great composer were assembled. During German occupation, many of these were looted by the Nazis, the music of Chopin was banned, and all pictures and busts of the composer were destroyed. After World War II, the manor was rebuilt, and in 1948 the museum was finally reopened to the public.

Near Żelazowa Wola lies the village of Brochów on the edge of the Kampinoska Forest (Puszcza Kampinoska). Chopin was christened in the Renaissance church here.

Chopin Museum

⊕ 🏠 Żelazowa Wola 15
🕐 Apr-Sep: 9am-7pm Tue-Sun; Oct-Mar: 9am-5pm
🔒 Pub hols 🌐 chopin.museum

 14

Nieborów

△E4 🚌 🕐 May & Jun: 10am-6pm daily; Jul-Apr: 10am-4pm Tue-Sun
🌐 nieborow.art.pl

Nieborów's Baroque palace was constructed by Tylman van Gameren between 1690 and 1696 for Primate Michał S Radziejowski, Archbishop of Gniezno. Radziejowski was a noted connoisseur of music, literature, art and architecture, and so was a client worthy of Tylman. A symmetric garden was also laid out. Around 1766, at the wish of a later owner, Prince Michal K Ogiński, the building's façade was adorned with a Rococo figure portraying a dancing Bacchus, with a bunch of grapes and a garland on his head. Ogiński is also famous for the construction of a canal in Belarus, which linked the Black Sea to the Baltic.

Between 1774 and 1945, the palace was the property of the aristocratic Radziwiłł family. It is famous for its fine furnishings, which include Antoine Pesne's portrait of the famous beauty Anna Orzelska, who was the natural daughter of August II (1697–1733), and the antique head of Niobe, celebrated in the poetry of Konstanty Ildefons Gałczyński (1905–53). This Roman head, carved in white marble after a Greek original, was given to Princess Helena Radziwiłłowa by Catherine the Great. In May and June, the palace is free to visit on Mondays; from July to April, free entry is on Tuesdays.

 15

Łowicz

△D4 🚗🚌 🚹 Stary Rynek 17; www.lowicz turystyczny.eu

The relatively small town of Łowicz, established in the 13th century, was the seat of

---

> 💬 **INSIDER TIP**
> **Chopin Concerts**
>
> From May to September, there are piano recitals held every weekend at the Chopin Museum in Żelazowa Wola. In warm, dry weather the windows are thrown open and the audience sits on benches outside.

one of the oldest castellanies in Poland. For centuries its castle (no longer standing) was the residence of the bishops of Gniezno, primates of Poland. The **Collegiate Church**, which was founded in the Middle Ages and rebuilt in the 17th century, contains many notable works of art. It also houses a number of tombs, the most illustrious occupant of one of them was the Primate Jakub Uchański (d 1581). Noteworthy features are a 16th-century alabaster carving by Jan Michałowicz of Urzędów and an early Neo-Classical frame by Ephraim Schroeger, from 1782–3.

The truly magnificent late Baroque high altar was made between 1761 and 1764 by Jan Jerzy Plersch to a design by Schroeger. It is considered by many to be one of the most original altars in Poland. The altar painting, crowned by an aureole and set between the pilasters of a narrow frame, makes a great impression on churchgoers and tourists alike.

Not far from the collegiate church is the old Piarist church (kościół Pijarów) – the Piarists were a Catholic order. Its late Baroque undulating façade, which dates from around 1729, is particularly eye-catching. The interior of the building has wonderful Baroque altars by Jan Jerzy Plersch.

On the other side of the Old Market Square, found within a former monastery and seminary for missionaries, is the **Łowicz Regional Museum** (Muzeum Ziemi Łowickiej) devoted to the folklore of the Łowicz area. Exhibits include Łowicz costumes of the 19th and early 20th centuries, paper cut-outs and folk embroidery. The museum is free to enter on Saturdays.

In the former chapel, built in 1689–1701 to designs by Tylman van Gameren and decorated with frescoes by Michelangelo Palloni, a collection of objects from the prehistoric Sarmatian culture are on display.

Łowicz comes alive during Corpus Christi, when local people dress in colourful traditional costumes to take part in a splendid procession that winds its way through the centre of town.

Collegiate Church
⌂ Stary Rynek 24 📞 46 837 32 66

Łowicz Regional Museum
♿ ⌂ Stary Rynek 5/7 🕐 9am–4pm Tue–Sun 🚫 Mon & pub hols 🌐 muzeumlowicz.pl

→

The temple of Diana in Arkadia's tranquil landscaped park

Arkadia

🅰 E4 🌐 nieborow.art.pl

Not far from Łowicz, found along the road to Nieborów, is Arkadia, a sentimentally romantic landscaped park. Laid out in 1778 by order of Princess Helena Radziwiłłowa, Arkadia's many attractions include a lake with two islands and a number of Romantic pavilions fancifully designed on historical or mythological themes by Szymon Bogumił Zug and Henryk Ittar.

Among ancient trees stand the High Priest's House, the Margrave's Cottage with Greek arch, the Gothic Cottage, the Grotto of the Sybil and the Aqueduct. The elegant Temple of Diana, perched in a pictur-esque position on the side of the lake, is one of the park's most beautiful buildings.

On some of the pavilion walls, fragments of decorative carving and stonework are mounted. These pieces were salvaged from the ruined Renaissance bishops' castle in Łowicz.

←

The colourful Corpus Christi procession through Łowicz

17 Żyrardów

🅰 E4 🅿 🅸 Ul 1 Maja 45; www.resursa.zyradow.pl

Some 60 km (37 miles) to the southwest of Warsaw, Żyrardów was a middle-of-nowhere village until the sudden emergence of a linen industry during the 1830s. The textile industry went into decline after 1989, but Żyrardów remains an outstanding example of a 19th-century factory town, with red-brick mills, houses and churches filling a grid-plan town centre. The **Museum of Western Mazovia** (Muzeum Mazowsza Zachodniego) has engaging exhibitions which cover the town's history, while the nearby **Linen Museum** (Muzeum Lniarstwa) contains displays of spinning machines inside what was once an old mill.

Museum of Western Mazovia

⊛ 🅲 Ul Karola Dittricha 1 🕒 8am–4pm Tue–Fri, 11am–4pm Sat & Sun 🆆 muzeum zyrardow.pl

Linen Museum

⊛ 🅲 Ul Karola Dittricha 18 🕒 10am–3pm Tue–Sun

SOCIALIST REALIST ART, KOZŁÓWKA

This doctrinal art style, developed in the Soviet Union under Stalin, was current in postwar Poland from about 1949 to 1955. Its theoretical principles were unclear and instructions given to the artists were what counted most. Party apparatchiks, buxom peasant women and muscular workers were the heroes. The largest collection in Poland of Socialist Realist art has been assembled at Zamoyski Palace.

↑ Memorial to the hundreds of thousands of Jews who were murdered in Treblinka

18

Treblinka

🅰 F3 🅿 🅸 Wólka Okrąglik 115, Kosów Lacki

Much of Warsaw's Jewish population was murdered at this SS-run death camp, 85 km (53 miles) northeast of the capital. A labour camp was established here in 1941 to exploit a nearby quarry. Of 20,000 Polish Jews, civilians and POWs sent here, about half died from torture, hunger or overwork. Treblinka II, with gas chambers, accounted for 700,000–900,000 deaths. The on-site **Treblinka Museum of Struggle and Martyrdom** includes an inspiring account of a 1943 breakout. Though the Nazis razed the buildings, marked paths point out key features. Take the train to Małkinia, then a short taxi ride to reach the camp.

Treblinka Museum of Struggle and Martyrdom

⊛ 🅿 🅲 Kosów Lacki 76 🕒 Apr–Oct: 9am–6:30pm daily; Nov–Mar: 9am–4pm daily 🆆 treblinka-muzeum.eu

---

19

Kazimierz Dolny

🅰 F5 🆕 🅸 Rynek 27; www. kazimierz-dolny.pl

This delightful little town, the favourite holiday resort of poets and painters, grew rich from the grain trade. A Gothic castle ruin with a high tower dominates the town. At its foot is the Renaissance Parish Church of Saints John the Baptist and Bartholomew.

The most attractive part of town is the market square, flanked by some richly ornamented Mannerist houses. Several 16th-century houses line Ulica Senatorska, which leads down to the Vistula. Also look out for the 18th-century former synagogue, the granaries on the riverbanks and the prewar villas.

About 10 km (6 miles) north at Puławy, located in a large landscaped park, is the former residence of the Czartoryski family. During the 18th century, Princess Izabella Czartoryska transformed the park into a shrine to Polish culture, filling it with symbolic buildings, such as the Temple of Sybil and the Gothic House.

20

Kozłówka

🅰 F5 🆕

The magnificent palace at Kozłówka is one of Poland's best-preserved aristocratic residences. Built between 1735 and 1742 in the Baroque style by Giuseppe Fontana, the palace later passed to the Zamoyski family, who rebuilt it and renamed it Zamoyski

Palace. In 1903, Konstanty Zamoyski legally ensured that it would remain in the family forever.

Konstanty Zamoyski was a likeable, well-educated connoisseur of the arts, and this is clearly visible in the rich decor and furnishings of the palace, which is today known as the **Zamoyski Palace and Museum**. Its entire contents have been preserved, making it Poland's finest collection not only of 19th-century art but also of everyday objects.

Most impressive of all is the collection of some 1,000 paintings, not originals but high-quality copies of great European masterpieces – the largest collection of its kind in Poland. The palace also has a unique gallery of Socialist Realist art.

The palace chapel, which was modelled on the Royal Chapel at Versailles, was built between 1904 and 1909 by Jan Heurich junior. The park surrounding the palace covers over 19 ha (47 acres).

Zamoyski Palace and Museum

⊗ ◻ Mar–Jun, Sep & Oct: 10am–4pm Tue–Sun; Jul & Aug: 10am–5pm Tue–Sun; Nov–Feb: 10am–3pm Tue–Sun ◻ muzeumzamoyskich.pl

---

21

Radzyń Podlaski

◻ F4 ◻◻ ◻ Jana Pawła II 2; 83 352 77 80

The splendid Potocki Palace in Radzyń Podlaski rivals Branicki Palace in Białystok,

the "Versailles of Podlasie" (*p294*). It was built for the ambitious Eustachy Potocki, who later became a general in the Lithuanian artillery. It was reconstructed in 1750–58, in the Rococo style by Giacopo Fontana. Dynamic carvings decorate the palace and adjacent orangery. It is currently under renovation.

The town itself is very pleasant and is home to the Church of the Holy Trinity (Kościół Świętej Trójcy), built in 1641 by Jan Wolff, the Zamoyski family's illustrious mason. The church contains the imposing red marble Renaissance tomb of Mikołaj Mniszech and his wife Zofia, and is possibly the work of Santi Gucci.

EAT

Zielona Tawerna
On a quiet street, this place is renowned for its imaginative take on Polish cuisine.

◻ Nadwiślańska 4, Kazimierz Dolny
◻ 81 881 0308

Various works of Socialist Realist Art at Zamoyski Palace and Museumm ↑

KRAKÓW

The earliest mention of Kraków in historical records dates from the middle of the 10th century. In 1000, it became a bishopric and around 1038 it assumed the importance of a capital. The city developed rapidly in the 14th and 15th centuries and acquired numerous Gothic churches and secular buildings that survive to this day. At the beginning of the 16th century, Kraków came under the influence of the Renaissance, and the Wawel Royal Castle, the Cloth Hall in the Main Market Square, and many mansions in the city were rebuilt in this style. The city gradually lost its significance, and in 1596 the capital was moved to Warsaw, though successive kings of Poland continued to be crowned and entombed in Wawel Cathedral. Under the Partitions of Poland, Kraków came under Austrian rule, which nevertheless permitted a relatively large degree of local autonomy. It thus began to assume the role of the spiritual capital for Poles. Kraków escaped significant damage during the two World Wars, and in 1978 UNESCO declared it a World Heritage Site.

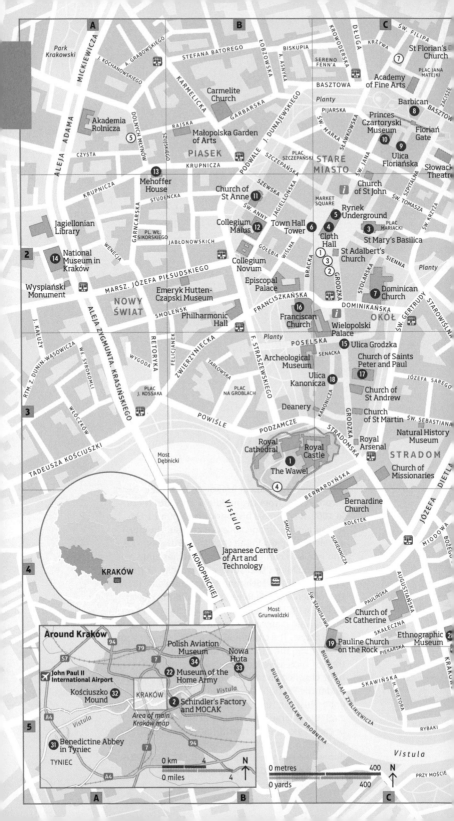

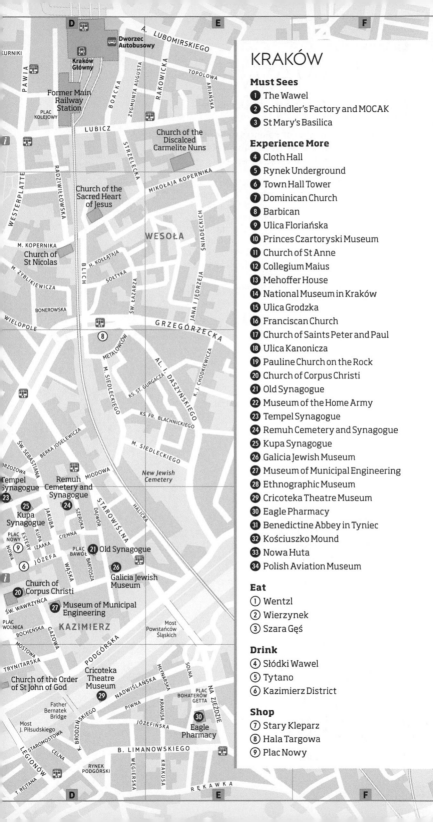

KRAKÓW

Must Sees
1. The Wawel
2. Schindler's Factory and MOCAK
3. St Mary's Basilica

Experience More
4. Cloth Hall
5. Rynek Underground
6. Town Hall Tower
7. Dominican Church
8. Barbican
9. Ulica Floriańska
10. Princes Czartoryski Museum
11. Church of St Anne
12. Collegium Maius
13. Mehoffer House
14. National Museum in Kraków
15. Ulica Grodzka
16. Franciscan Church
17. Church of Saints Peter and Paul
18. Ulica Kanonicza
19. Pauline Church on the Rock
20. Church of Corpus Christi
21. Old Synagogue
22. Museum of the Home Army
23. Tempel Synagogue
24. Remuh Cemetery and Synagogue
25. Kupa Synagogue
26. Galicia Jewish Museum
27. Museum of Municipal Engineering
28. Ethnographic Museum
29. Cricoteka Theatre Museum
30. Eagle Pharmacy
31. Benedictine Abbey in Tyniec
32. Kościuszko Mound
33. Nowa Huta
34. Polish Aviation Museum

Eat
1. Wentzl
2. Wierzynek
3. Szara Gęś

Drink
4. Słódki Wawel
5. Tytano
6. Kazimierz District

Shop
7. Stary Kleparz
8. Hala Targowa
9. Plac Nowy

THE WAWEL

◉ B3 ⌂ Wawel Hill ◷ Hours vary, check website
Ⓦ wawel.krakow.pl

For centuries the symbol of Poland's national, cultural
and spiritual identity, the royal complex of buildings
occupying Wawel Hill is revered by Poles.

The Vistulanians were the first to build a citadel on this
limestone outcrop, with successive dynasties developing
and extending the site. The impressive fortifications
encircle a number of buildings, among them the magnificent Renaissance Royal Castle *(p146)* and the Gothic
Royal Cathedral *(p148)*. Once the site of coronations and
royal burials, the Royal Cathedral is regarded by Poles as
a spiritual shrine. The Royal Castle, found beside it, was
previously the seat of Poland's royals and remains to this
day an enduring symbol of national identity.

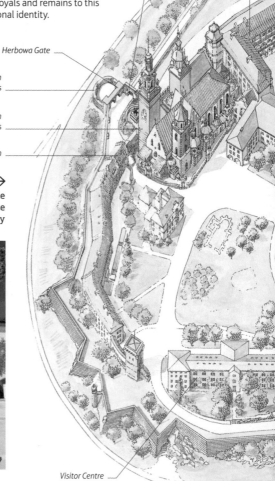

*The Royal Castle,
incorporating the walls of
older Gothic buildings*

Vasa Gate

Herbowa Gate

*Defensive position
on the fortifications*

*The Royal Cathedral, lined with
royal burial chapels*

Cathedral Museum

→

**The Wawel, seat of the
government since
the 11th century**

Visitor Centre

↑ The turrets and cupolas
of the Royal Cathedral

Other Highlights

Fortifications on the Wawel

▶ The Wawel's systems of fortification have been demolished and renewed several times since the Middle Ages - right up to the 20th century. Only fragments of the oldest Gothic fortifications remain, but three towers raised in the second half of the 1400s survive; they are known as the Sandomierska Tower, the Senators' Tower and the Thieves' Tower (below which dungeons served as a prison). Of the fortifications dating from the 16th to the 17th centuries the most interesting is the Vasa Gate. Since 1921 it has been crowned with a monument to the 18th-century national hero Tadeusz Kościuszko, leader of an uprising in 1794; his defeat resulted in Poland's Third Partition. The Wawel continued to play a defensive role into the 19th century, and a relatively well-preserved system of fortifications dating from the late 18th to mid-19th centuries can still be seen today.

Cathedral Museum

This museum is located in buildings near the cathedral and contains a valuable collection of pieces from the cathedral treasury. Here visitors can admire liturgical vessels and vestments, including the magnificent robe of Stanisław August Poniatowski (1764-95), the last king of Poland; another superb example is the chasuble of Bishop Piotr Kmita, which dates from 1504 and is ornamented with quilted embroidery depicting scenes from the life of St Stanisław. The museum also contains replicas of funeral regalia, royal swords and trophies from battles won. Look out for the sword of Zygmunt II, the last of the Jagiellonian kings, which was ceremoniously broken in two places at his funeral.

"Lost Wawel" Exhibition

◀ For anyone interested in medieval archaeology, this exhibition is a real delight. Various finds from archaeological excavations on the Wawel Hill are exhibited here in a display that charts the development of the Wawel over a considerable period of time. It also includes a virtual image of the Wawel buildings as they existed in the early Middle Ages, and a partially reconstructed pre-Romanesque chapel of Saints Felix and Adauctus, dedicated to the Blessed Virgin (Saints Felix and Adauctus); built at the turn of the 11th century, the chapel was discovered during research work carried out in 1917. There is also a collection of beautiful glazed ceramic tiles dating from the 16th and 17th centuries. They were taken from the stoves that were once used to heat the palace.

"Lost Wawel" Exhibition

Bernardyńska Gate

Sandomierska Tower

Royal Castle

One of the most magnificent Renaissance residences in Central Europe, the Wawel Royal Castle was commissioned for Zygmunt I, the penultimate ruler of the Jagiellonian dynasty. Built in 1502–36, the four-winged palace was designed and constructed by the Italian architects Francisco Fiorentino and Bartolomeo Berrecci, and incorporates the 14th-century walls of a Gothic building that once stood on the site. After the royal court was transferred from Kraków to Warsaw in 1609, the palace fell into neglect, deteriorating further under the Swedish occupation of the early 18th century and throughout the era of the Partitions. At the beginning of the 20th century, the castle was returned to the city of Kraków by the occupying Austrian army, and an extensive programme of restoration began. Following World War II, the castle was decreed a national museum; today the palace's Italian-inspired interiors are returned to their former glory, housing vast collections of priceless royal treasures.

$\longrightarrow$

The castle's Italianate arcaded inner courtyard

> **CASTLE GUIDE**
>
> Part of the ground floor, as well as the halls on the first and second floors of the castle's east and north wing, are open to visitors. Items from the Royal Treasury and Royal Armoury are displayed on the ground floor, and the vast Oriental collection fills the first floor of the west wing.

→ Fine tapestries and carpets adorn the lavish Royal Apartments

← An ornate silver eagle, among the collections of the Royal Treasury

DRINK

Słódki Wawel
Set amid the castle grounds, with a pleasant terrace overlooking the river, this café and chocolaterie makes the perfect spot to enjoy a hot chocolate after wandering Wawel.

📍B3 🏛Zamek Wawel 9
🌐wawel.com.pl

Did You Know?

In 1796 the castle was converted into barracks for the Austrian army.

↑ Kraków's imposing Royal Castle on a sunny day

Royal Cathedral

Wawel Hill's spectacular cathedral, known as the Cathedral of Saints Stanisław and Wacław, is one of the most important churches in Poland. Before the present cathedral was erected (1320–64), two earlier churches stood on the site. The traditional coronation and burial site of Polish monarchs, the cathedral has many fine features. Its series of chapels founded by rulers and bishops, the most beautiful being the Renaissance Zygmunt Chapel, were constructed between 1517 and 1533 by Florentine architect Bartolommeo Berrecci. The royal tombs in both the cathedral and the Crypt of St Leonard are a remnant of the 11th -century Romanesque Cathedral of St Wacław, and the final resting place of Polish kings – among them Jadwiga, Poland's first female monarch – as well as national heroes and revered poets.

Zygmunt Bell (1520) is the largest bell in Poland; its diameter is over 2 m (6 ft).

The top of the 14th-century clock tower is decorated with statues of saints and a fine Baroque dome, added in 1715.

THE LEGEND OF THE KRAKÓW DRAGON

According to legend, ancient Kraków was threatened by a cattle-eating dragon that lived in a cave beneath Wawel Hill. It is said that the dragon was slain by King Krakus (or in some accounts by a humble cobbler, Skuba) who tricked the beast into eating a sulphur-filled sheepskin. Today, a brass dragon statue guards the cave at the foot of Wawel Hill.

Main entrance

→
The cathedral exterior, a mix of Gothic and Romanesque styles

→
Baroque oak stalls lining the chancel leading to the grand high altar

In front of the grand high alter are Baroque oak stalls, made around 1620.

A silver coffin holding relics of St Stanisław, the bishop of Kraków, was cast in 1669–71 by Pieter van der Rennen, a goldsmith from Gdańsk.

Zygmunt Chapel, which contains the tombs of the two last Jagiellonian kings, is the jewel of Italian Renaissance art in Poland.

Baroque sarcophagi in the Royal Tombs were made for members of the royal Vasa dynasty.

↑ The Roman Catholic Cathedral of Saints Stanisław and Wacław

Did You Know?

In 1079, King Bolesław accused St Stanisław of treason, and condemned the bishop to dismemberment.

② ◈ ◈ ▢ ▣

SCHINDLER'S FACTORY AND MOCAK

⬤ B5 **⬤** Ul Lipowa 4 **⬤** 3, 19, 24 **⬤** Schindler's Factory: Apr-Oct: 9am–8pm daily (to 4pm Mon, to 2pm first Mon of month), Nov–Mar: 10am–6pm daily (to 2pm Mon); MOCAK: 11am–7pm Tue-Sun **⬤** Schindler's Factory: mhk.pl; MOCAK: mocak.pl

Located in the former industrial district of Zabłocie, next to Podgorze, Schindler's Factory is a symbol of humanitarian courage. In 1943, the factory's German owner, Oskar Schindler, saved over 1,000 Jews from deportation to the death camps by employing them in his factory and claiming that they were essential to the running of his business.

The factory, now part of the Historical Museum of the City of Krakow *(p153)*, features an exhibition entitled "Krakow Under Nazi Occupation 1939–45". Everyday life for Krakow's inhabitants – from the last prewar summer of 1939 through the Nazi occupation until the arrival of the Red Army in January 1945 – is illustrated using original documents, radio and film recordings, photographs and multimedia installations. The fate of the Jewish population is a major theme, though lives of other citizens are also covered in detail, notably the arrest and murder of prominent members of the city's intellectual and political elite. Poignant exhibits include Schindler's desk and a wall of photographs of those that Schindler saved.

A section of the building now houses MOCAK (Museum of Contemporary Art in Krakow), whose main exhibition halls display the cream of Polish contemporary art.

SPIELBERG'S SCHINDLER'S LIST

Based on Thomas Keneally's novel *Schindler's Ark*, Steven Spielberg's 1993 film *Schindler's List* brought the story of factory-owner Schindler to a global audience. Most of the filming took place in Kraków, using real-life locations in Kazimerz and Podgórze as much as possible. Scenes set in Plaszów concentration camp were shot in a nearby quarry, because the Plaszów skyline had changed too much. Much of the film's extraordinary power is due to Oscar-winning Polish cinematographer Janusz Kamiński.

Did You Know?

After his death in 1974, Schindler was burried in the cemetery on Mount Zion in Jerusalem.

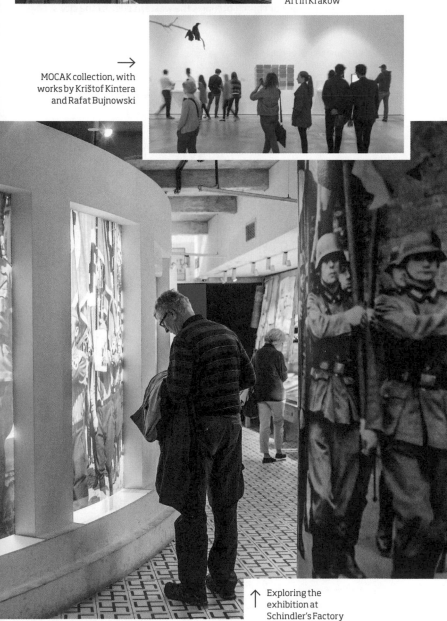

← MOCAK Museum of Contemporary Art in Kraków

→ MOCAK collection, with works by Krištof Kintera and Rafał Bujnowski

↑ Exploring the exhibition at Schindler's Factory

ST MARY'S BASILICA

⦿ C2 🏠 **Pl Mariacki 5** 🚌 **124, 152, 304, 424, 502** 🚋 **1, 3, 18, 24, 52**
🕐 **11:30am–6pm daily (from 2pm Sun)** 🌐 **mariacki.com**

The imposing St Mary's Basilica (Kościół Mariacki) was built by the citizens of Kraków to rival the Royal Cathedral on Wawel Hill. One of Kraków's most iconic sights, this spectacular church occupies the western edge of the city's expansive Main Market Square (Rynek Główny).

Construction of the church began in 1355, but work on the vaulting and the chapels continued until the mid-15th century, and the lower tower was not completed until the early 16th century. This great basilica contains an exceptional number of important works of art, including the magnificent Gothic altarpiece carved by German sculptor Veit Stoss in 1477–89 (currently undergoing renovation).

Hejnał Tower

The sandstone crucifix by Veit Stoss is a fine example of 15th-century sculpture.

↑ The decorative blue and gold interior of St Mary's Basilica

Did You Know?

The Altarpiece of Veit Stoss is the world's largest Gothic altarpiece.

Main entrance

This pentagonal Baroque porch was built in the mid-18th century to a design by Francesco Placidi.

This large ciborium, in the form of a Renaissance church, was made by Giovanni Maria Padovano around 1552.

The famous trumpet call - the Hejnał - is sounded hourly from the church's magnificent tower. The call is left unfinished, in tribute to a medieval trumpeter shot while sounding the alarm of an attack on the city. The Hejnał is broadcast live by Polish radio daily at noon.

↑ The Cloth Hall standing at the centre of Market Square, illuminated in the evening

Gothic stained-glass window made around 1370

The altarpiece of Veit Stoss measures 11 m (36 ft) wide and 13 m (42 ft) high.

Visitors' entrance

 The spectacular St Mary's Basilica in Kraków's Main Market Square

EXPERIENCE MORE

4 Cloth Hall

📍C2 🏛Rynek Główny 1/3
🚌124, 152 🚋3, 4, 7, 13

Set in the Main Market Square, the Cloth Hall (Sukiennice) replaces an earlier Gothic trade hall dating from the 1300s. Destroyed in a fire, then rebuilt by Giovanni Maria Padovano, it owes something of its present appearance to Tomasz Pryliński's Romantic-style restoration (1875–9). The **Sukiennice Gallery**, a branch of the National Museum in Kraków (Muzeum Narodowe w Krakowie or MNK) *(p156)*, is housed on the upper floor.

Sukiennice Gallery
⏲🕙10am–6pm Tue (to 4pm Sun) 🌐mnk.pl

5 Rynek Underground

📍C2 🏛Rynek Główny 1
🕙Apr–Oct: 10am–10pm daily (to 8pm Mon, to 4pm Tue); Nov–Mar: 10am–8pm daily (to 4pm Tue) 🔒2nd Mon of month 🌐mnk.pl

This high-tech museum, tracing the story of the city, is found under the Main Market Square. The underground vaults contain displays on transportation and trade, as well as archaeological finds. The museum cleverly blends modern technology with interactive exhibits and more traditional displays.

6 Town Hall Tower

📍B2 🏛Rynek Główny 1
🚌124, 152, 304 🚋4, 13, 19

The Gothic tower, crowned by a Baroque cupola, that dominates the Main Market Square is the only remaining vestige of the City Hall, built in the 14th century and pulled down in the first half of the 19th. The tower is now a branch of the **Historical Museum of the City of Krakow** (Muzeum Historyczne Miasta Krakowa or MHK) dedicated to the history of the city from the Middle Ages to present day; it is also a venue for the Ludowy Theatre. The city's history is further documented in the Museum of the History of the Market, in the crypt of the neighbouring Church of St Wojciech.

Historical Museum of the City of Krakow
🕙Apr–Oct: 10:30am–6pm daily; Nov–Dec: 11am–5pm daily 🌐mhk.pl

⑦ Dominican Church

📍 C2 ⬚ Ul Stolarska 12
📞 12 423 16 13 🚊 1, 3, 6, 8, 13, 18 🕐 6:30am–8pm daily

The origins of the Dominican Church (Kościół Dominikanów) go back to the second half of the 13th century. Rebuilt a number of times, by the middle of the 1400s it had become the magnificent Gothic building that still stands today. A number of mortuary chapels were also added; many of them are major works of Renaissance and Baroque art in their own right, with rich decorations and furnishings. Of particular note are the Baroque chapel of the Zbaraski family, at the west end of the north aisle, and the Mannerist chapel of the Myszkowski family, in the first bay of the south aisle. The church was badly damaged by a great fire that swept through the city in 1850, although it was promptly restored.

⑧ Barbican

📍 C1 ⬚ Ul Basztowa 🚊 124, 152, 304, 502 🚊 2, 4, 7, 14 🕐 Apr–Oct: 10:30am–6pm daily 🌐 mhk.pl

Now a branch of the MHK, the Barbican (Barbakan) is one of the remaining elements of

Did You Know?

The Barbican used to be encircled by a 24-m- (78-ft-) wide moat.

Kraków's medieval defences. The double ring of walls that once surrounded the city was built in stages from 1285 to the beginning of the 15th century. Most of the circum-vallation was pulled down in the 19th century. The Barbican was built in 1498–9, when the city's defences were strengthened in response to advances in military tactics and equipment. It protected the Florian Gate, to which it was connected by an under-ground passage. The latter's route is marked by a change in the colour of the paving stones.

⑨   Ulica Floriańska

📍 C1 🚊 124, 152, 304, 502 🚊 2, 14, 18, 19, 20, 24

This charming street in the Old Town is full of restaurants, cafés and shops. It leads from the Main Market Square to the Florian Gate and was once part of the Royal Route, along which rulers would ride on their way from Warsaw to their coronation in Kraków. At No 41 is **Matejko House**

(Dom Matejki), the birthplace of the painter Jan Matejko (1838–93). He spent most of his life here and a collection of his paintings, as well as his studio, is on display. The museum is part of the MNK.

At the end of the street, the Florian Gate is one of the few surviving remnants of the city's medieval fortifications, along with a section of the city wall and three towers.

Matejko House

  🕐 9am–4pm Tue–Fri, 10am–6pm Sun, 10am–4pm Sun 🌐 mnk.pl

⑩  Princes Czartoryski Museum

📍 C1 ⬚ Ul św Jana 19 🚊 124, 152, 304, 502 🚊 2, 4, 18, 24, 30 🚫 Closed for renovation until 2020 🌐 mnk.pl

This relatively small museum has one of the most interesting art collections in Poland. Once the private collection of the Czartoryski family, the collection was later taken to Paris, and then to Kraków, where it was put on public view.

The museum is closed for long-term renovations. Some of its most famous artworks, however, are on display at buildings belonging to the National Museum (*p156*). Leonardo da Vinci's painting *Lady with an Ermine* (c 1485) is in the National Museum, while Rembrandt's atmos-pheric *Landscape with the Good Samaritan* (1638) is in the **Europeum**.

Europeum

📍 Plac Sikorskiego 6 🕐 9am–4pm Tue–Fri, 10am–6pm Sat, 10am–4pm Sun) 🌐 mnk.pl

←
The 15th-century Barbican, based on Arabic designs

↑ The beautiful interior of the Roman Catholic Church of St Anne

⑪
Church of St Anne

📍 B2 🏛 Ul św Anny 11 ☎ 12 422 53 18 🚌 124, 152, 504 🚊 2, 8, 13, 18, 20 🕐 1:30-7pm Tue-Thu, 9am-7pm Sat, 2-7pm Sun

In the narrow Ulica św. Anny, it is impossible to miss the imposing Baroque façade of the twin-towered Church of St Anne (Kościół św. Anny). The architect was Tylman van Gameren. In designing the façade, he acknowledged that any view of it would be acutely foreshortened by virtue of the narrowness of the street. The church was erected between 1689 and 1703, although work on the decoration was not completed until much later.

The interior has murals by Karol and Innocenti Monti and a fine high altar by Baldassare Fontana. The painting of St Anne that adorns it is by Jerzy Eleuter Siemigonowski.

In the south transept is the shrine and reliquary of St John of Cantinus, a 15th-century theologian and the patron of St Anne's.

---

⑫ 🚴 Ⓜ 🖥
Collegium Maius

📍 B2 🏛 Ul Jagiellońska 15 🚌 124, 152, 504 🚊 2, 13, 18, 20 🕐 Apr-Oct: 10am-5:20pm Tue & Thu, 10am-4:20pm Mon, Wed, Fri, 10am-1:30pm Sat; Nov-Mar: 10am-2:20pm Mon-Fri (to 1:30pm Sat) 🌐 maius.uj.edu.pl

The Collegium Maius is the oldest surviving college of the Jagiellonian University, which grew from the Kraków Academy established by Kazimierz the Great in 1364. Queen Jadwiga, wife of Władysław Jagiełło, donated her personal fortune to the academy in 1399.

In the second half of the 15th century the Collegium Maius acquired new premises, which incorporated the walls of several older buildings. Its present appearance is largely due to a 19th-century restoration in a Romantic style, although the building's Gothic structure survives. Copernicus *(p280)* would have undoubtedly walked in the cloistered courtyard when he was a student here. In the Jagiellonian University Museum are numerous exhibits documenting the rich history of the university.

While taking a guided tour is compulsory for the Collegium Maius, there is no need to book in advance. Note, though, that payment is in cash only.

The Collegium Maius, ↓ a college of the Jagiellonian University

13

Mehoffer House

🔲 A1 🏠 Ul Krupnicza 26 🚌 4, 8, 13, 14, 24 🕐 10am–6pm Tue-Sat (until 4pm Sun) 🌐 mnk.pl

This small museum, part of the MNK (Muzeum Narodowe w Krakowie), is located in the house where Józef Mehoffer, the leading Art Nouveau stained-glass artist, lived from 1932 until his death. It has furnishings made by Mehoffer, as well as some of his artistic works, including the captivating *Portrait of the Artist's Wife*. The house was the birthplace of the artist and writer Stanisław Wyspiański (1869–1907).

EAT

Wentzl
Traditional Polish fare with a French twist is served in 19th-century elegance.

🔲 C2 🏠 Rynek Główny 19 🌐 restauracjawentzl.pl

złzłzł

Wierzynek
Said to be the oldest restaurant in Kraków, Wierzynek remains true to its culinary traditions.

🔲 C2 🏠 Rynek Główny 15 🌐 wierzynek.pl

złzłzł

Szara Gęś
Feast on roast goose and venison in this outstanding, opulent restaurant.

🔲 C2 🏠 Rynek Główny 17 🌐 szarages.com

złzłzł

14

National Museum in Kraków

🔲 A2 🏠 Al 3 Maja 1 🚌 124, 144, 152, 173 🚊 20 🕐 10am–6pm Tue-Sat, 10am–4pm Sun 🌐 mnk.pl

The enormous edifice that dominates this part of the city is the main building of Kraków's National Museum (MNK). Construction began in the 1930s but was not finished until 1989.

The exhibits are divided into three main sections. The first is devoted to the applied arts. The second comprises an interesting collection of militaria, while the third has an important collection of 20th-century painting and sculpture. The work of the artists of the Young Poland movement is particularly well represented.

15

Ulica Grodzka

🔲 C3 🚊 1, 6, 8, 10, 13, 18, 20

A variety of interesting buildings give picturesque Ulica Grodzka, winding from the Main Market Square to the Wawel, a truly historical atmosphere. At No 53 is the cloistered courtyard of the Collegium Luridicum, a law college founded in the 15th century and rebuilt in 1718. A little further along rises the façade of the Church of Saints Peter and Paul, with the white stone tower of the 13th-century Romanesque Church

of St Andrew (Kościół św. Andrzeja) gleaming behind it. The latter's walls conceal an earlier, late 11th-century building whose interior was altered around 1702. The adjacent Baroque building is the former Catholic Church of St Martin (Kościół św. Marcina). Built between 1637 and 1640 for the Discalced Carmelites, it is now owned by the Evangelical Church of the Augsburg Confession.

16

Franciscan Church

🔲 B2 🏠 Pl Wszystkich Świętych 5 🚌 124, 152, 304, 502 🚊 1, 6, 8, 10, 13 🕐 10am–4pm Mon-Sat, 1:15pm–4pm Sun & hols 🔔 During services 🌐 franciszkanska.pl

The origins of this Gothic Franciscan church go back to the 13th and 15th centuries,

→

The Franciscan Church, adorned with stunning stained glass and murals although rebuilding in the 17th and 19th centuries has considerably altered its appearance. The church, however, is renowned more for its interior decoration than for its architecture and attracts many visitors from all over the world.

A number of interesting features from different ages have been preserved, although the most notable are the Art Nouveau murals and stained-glass windows by Stanisław Wyspiański, dating from around 1900. The chancel and transept are decorated with a vertiginous scheme featuring entwined flowers, heraldic motifs and religious scenes. The stained-glass windows are monumental compositions of great expressive power and represent one of the highest achievements of the Art Nouveau stained-glass movement. Particularly impressive is *God the Father – Let There Be!*, which shows the figure of God creating the world.

The cloisters are lined with murals that include the Gallery of Krakóvian Bishops, in which the finest portrait is that of Bishop Piotr Tomicki, painted by Stanisław Samostrzelnik some time before 1535.

↑ Visitors admiring the Baroque façade of the Church of Saints Peter and Paul

 17

Church of Saints Peter and Paul

📍 C3 🏛 Ul Grodzka 52a
📞 12 422 65 73 🚋 6, 8, 10, 13, 18 🕐 9am-7pm Mon-Fri, 9am-5:30pm Sat, 1:30-5:30pm Sun

The Church of Saints Peter and Paul (Kościół sw. Piotra i Pawła) is one of the most beautiful early Baroque churches in Poland. It was built for the Jesuits soon after their arrival in Krakow. Work began in 1596, but after a structural disaster in 1605, the church was almost completely rebuilt to the design of an architect who remains unknown to this day.

The church is enclosed by railings, topped with figures of the 12 apostles, dating from 1715–22. The interior of the building contains fine stuccowork and rich Baroque furnishings. The high altar and the organ screen, by Kacper Bażanka, are noteworthy.

Among the many funerary monuments, the most striking is the black-and-white marble tomb of Bishop Andrzej Tomicki, dating from 1695–6.

 18

Ulica Kanonicza

📍 C3 🚋 1, 8, 10, 13, 20

This street formed the last stretch of the Royal Route leading towards Wawel. From the 14th century onwards it was lined with the houses of Kraków's canons, who were given the use of these houses for life when they took up office in the Chapter of Kraków. Each successive inhabitant modernized their house. As a result, Gothic houses acquired arcaded Renaissance courtyards, Baroque doorways or Neo-Classical façades. The canons could afford to spend lavishly owing to their elite status within the church. The great diversity of architectural styles found within the gently curving Kanonicza Street gives it a picturesque character.

19
Pauline Church on the Rock

📍C4 🏛Ul Skałeczna 15
📞12 619 09 00 🚌504 🚊6, 8, 10, 13 🕐Church: 9am–5pm Mon–Sat; Crypt of Honour: Apr–Oct: 9am–5pm daily, Nov–Mar: by appt

The impressive Baroque Pauline Church on the Rock (Kościół Paulinów na Skałce), with its adjoining monastery complex, was built in 1733–42 by Gerhard Müntzer in collaboration with Antoni Solari. The present church was preceded by two earlier buildings. St Stanisław, the Bishop of Kraków, was murdered at the foot of the altar of the Romanesque church, the first to be built on the site.

The interior includes Baroque stuccowork by Jan Lehnert. The crypt was converted by Teofil Żebrawski into a pantheon to Polish writers and artists, including the painters Jacek Malczewski (1854–1929) and Henryk Siemiradzki (1843–1902), the writers and poets Józef Ignacy Kraszewski (1812–77), Adam Asnyk (1839–97) and Wincenty Pol (1807–72), and the artist, writer and designer Stanisław Wyspiański (1869–1907).

Nearby on Ulica Skałeczna is the beautiful Gothic Convent and Church of St Catherine (Kościół św. Katarzyny), begun in the mid-14th century. Once belonging to the Augustinian order, it was deconsecrated

Did You Know?

During World War II, the Nazis used the Old Synagogue as a warehouse.

and used as a warehouse. Of the original features only the high altar remains.

20
Church of Corpus Christi

📍D4 🏛Ul Bożego Ciała 26 🚌504 🚊6, 8, 10, 13 🕐7am–7pm daily
🌐bozecialo.net

The mighty Gothic Church of Corpus Christi was built as the parish church of the town of Kazimierz, which was founded by Kazimierz the Great in the 14th century. Work on the church began around 1340, continuing into the early 15th century. The basilica-like interior contains some fine works of art in the Baroque style, including the magnificent high altar of 1634–7, with its painting of *The Birth of Christ* by Tomasso Dolabella, a fine mid-18th-century pulpit, and stalls dating from 1632,

→

Tombstones in the Remuh Cemetery, some dating from the 16th century

originally built for the monks (although the church has been in the care of canons since the 15th century). The monastery is on the north side of the church.

21
Old Synagogue

📍D4 🏛Ul Szeroka 24
🚌184, 504 🚊3, 19, 24, 69

Constructed by Matteo Gucci in the mid-16th century in the Renaissance style, the Old Synagogue replaced an earlier Gothic synagogue that burned down in 1557. In the Hall of Prayer you will find a reconstructed bema (raised orator's platform) and Torah Ark.

The synagogue houses the **Museum of Jewish History**, a branch of the MHK. The displays consist of artifacts used in Jewish rituals, and documents relating to the history of Kraków's Jews and their extermination during the Nazi occupation in World War II.

Museum of Jewish History
♿ 📞12 431 05 45 🏛Apr–Oct: 10am–2pm Mon, 9am–5pm Tue–Sun; Nov–Mar: 10am–2pm Mon, 9am–4pm Tue–Thu, Sat & Sun, 10am–5pm Fri 🌐mhk.pl

Torah Ark and the bema, rebuilt as a replica of the original, have survived.

Behind the synagogue is one of the most important Jewish cemeteries in Europe. Despite the damage that the cemetery suffered during World War II, many of the tombstones have survived. Fragments of the shattered tombstones have been built into the cemetery wall abutting Ulica Szeroka.

This part of town was immortalized in Spielberg's film *Schindler's List*. The district now has shops and kosher restaurants; also here is the home of Helena Rubinstein, founder of the eponymous cosmetics business.

㉒ Museum of the Home Army

 B5 🏛 Ul Wita Stwosza 12 🚌 105, 129, 179, 405, 501 🚊 3, 5, 17, 47 🕐 11am–6pm Tue–Sun 🖥 muzeum-ak.pl

Housed within an imposing 19th-century command post, the compelling Museum of the Home Army (Muzeum Armii Krajowej) is devoted to all aspects of Polish resistance during World War II. It is a complex and detailed story, movingly told with the aid of photos, weaponry and personal recollections.

Poland's underground Home Army liberated huge swathes of territory from the Germans in the summer of 1944, only to be treated with suspicion by the Red Army advancing from the East. Having fought against the Nazis, many Polish resistance fighters were imprisoned by the Soviets: a betrayal that left a profound mark on Poland.

←

The sacred sanctuary of Pauline Church on the Rock

㉓ Tempel Synagogue

📍 D4 🏛 Ul Miodowa 24 📞 12 430 54 11 🚌 184 🚊 3, 9, 12, 22, 52 🕐 10am–4pm Sun–Thu, 10am–dusk Fri

The newest of the synagogues in Kazimierz, the Tempel was built in the Neo-Renaissance style between 1860 and 1862. It is used by non-Orthodox Jews. Inside note the stained-glass and period decoration. Concerts are occasionally held at the synagogue.

㉔ Remuh Cemetery and Synagogue

📍 D4 🏛 Ul Szeroka 40 📞 12 429 57 35 🚌 184, 504 🚊 3, 19, 24 🕐 9am–6pm Sun–Fri (to 4pm Oct–Apr)

The humble prayer house known as the Remuh is one of two synagogues in Kraków that are still in use. It was built around 1557 by Izrael ben Józef for his son Mojżesz Isserles, a famous scholar, rabbi and reputed miracle worker, known as Remuh. Inside, the Renaissance

㉕ Kupa Synagogue

📍 D4 🏛 Ul Miodowa 27 📞 12 429 5735 🚊 3, 19, 24 🕐 Sun–Fri

Dating from the 16th-century, the outwardly plain Kupa synagogue has a vibrant interior, thanks to wall paintings executed in the 1920s and only recently restored. Depicting zodiac symbols and views of holy cities, they are best viewed in the women's section of the synagogue, reached by ascending an outdoor staircase.

26
Galicia Jewish Museum

📍D4 🏛Ul Dajwór 18
🚋3, 19, 24 🕐10am-6pm
daily 🌐galiciajewish
museum.org

Housed in a restored prewar factory, the Galicia Jewish Museum was founded in 2004 by photographer Chris Schwartz to commemorate the once-thriving Jewish culture of southeastern Poland. Schwartz's evocative photographs of synagogues and graveyards are crammed into the exhibition halls. The museum also hosts a variety of changing exhibitions dedicated to Jewish historical themes.

↑ The elegant façade of Kraków's Renaissance Town Hall

DRINK

Tytano

This handsome redbrick complex, a former cigarette factory, has been given a new lease of life as a hip new eating and drinking venue. Its courtyard is packed with bars, many of them sporting cool minimalist décor and serving the best of local craft beers.

📍A1 🏛Ul Dolnych Młynów 10
🌐tytano.org

Kazimierz District

Found just south of the Old Town, the Kazimierz district offers a dizzying choice of cafés and bars which cater for pretty much every taste - from candlelit bohemia to cocktails and DJs.

📍D4 🏛Kazimierz

27
Museum of Municipal Engineering

📍D4 🏛Ul Św Wawrzyńca 15 🚋3, 19, 24 🕐Jun-Sep: 10am-6pm Tue, Thu & Sun, 10am-4pm Wed, Fri & Sat; Oct-May: 10am-4pm Tue-Sun 🌐mimk.com.pl

This charming museum is located in a late-19th-century former tram depot. The fascinating collection consists of motor cars through the ages, including many Polish-made vehicles that are no longer around. For kids, there are hands-on displays of maths, science and future technology like virtual reality, and a large collection of trams parked in the tram shed.

28
Ethnographic Museum

📍C4 🏛Plac Wolnica 1
📞12 379 60 23 🚌504
🚋6, 8, 10, 13 🕐10am-7pm
Tue-Sun 🚫Pub hols

Kazimierz's Renaissance Town Hall is now home to the engaging Ethnographic Museum. Reconstructions of rooms from the 19th and 20th century display a rich collection of exhibits, including costumes from all over Poland, traditional Kraków Christmas cribs, folk art and musical instruments. There is also a section covering the seasonal folk festivals once celebrated by both Christians and Jews, and a fantastic display of re-created house interiors on the ground floor.

29
Cricoteka Theatre Museum

📍D5 🏛Ul Nadwiślańska 2-4 🚋3, 19, 24 🕐11am-7pm Tue-Sun 🌐cricoteka.pl

Opened in 2014, this diverse museum and research centre is dedicated to the work of Tadeusz Kantor (1915–1990), the avant-garde artist, set

The Cricoteka Theatre Museum exhibits stage props (including creepy mannequins), costumes and a video footage archive of classic Cricot 2 performances.

designer and theatre director who founded the Cricot 2 theatre company in 1955 (*p160*). A major figure in the 20th-century theatre reform, Kantor created drama that was socially profound, absurd, subversive and exceptionally funny, and he went on to enjoy much critical success both at home and abroad.

The Cricoteka Theatre Museum exhibits stage props (including creepy mannequins), costumes and a video footage archive of classic Cricot 2 performances. There are also temporary exhibitions. As if paying homage to Kantor's experimental approach, the waterside building housing the theatre is an attraction in itself – a V-shaped, shimmering structure of rusted metal which hovers on stilts above a 19th-century former electricity plant.

Eagle Pharmacy

30 🕎 🕎

📍 E5 🏛 Pl Bohaterów Getta 18 🚋 3, 19, 24 🕐 10am–2pm Mon, 9am–5pm Tue–Sun 🌐 mhk.pl

Located on the southern side of the River Vistula, the suburb of Podgórze was chosen to be a ghetto by the Nazis in 1941, and the city's Jewish population was relocated here as a result.

Declining to be moved from the area, Dr Tadeusz Pankiewicz, a Polish pharmacist, continued to run his pharmacy; it was the only one left operating in the ghetto. As well as providing medication, often for free, the Eagle Pharmacy (Apteka pod Orlem) became a social hub for the Jewish population.

Dr Pankiewicz documented his experiences in a moving book entitled *The Krakow*

↑ Poignant mementos of the ghetto found in the Eagle Pharmacy

Ghetto Pharmacy. In this memoir, Pankiewicz describes how he and his staff risked their lives to undertake numerous clandestine operations: smuggling food and information, and offering shelter on the premises for those Jews facing deportation to the camps.

Now a small but fascinating museum, the pharmacy (a branch of the MHK) has been re-created to look as it did during the war. Multimedia displays, as well as photographs and personal effects hidden in drawers and cupboards, recount the devastating stories of those forced to live in the ghetto during the Nazi occupation.

Did You Know?
—
Dr Pankiewicz is recognized as one of the Righteous Among the Nations for his brave deeds.

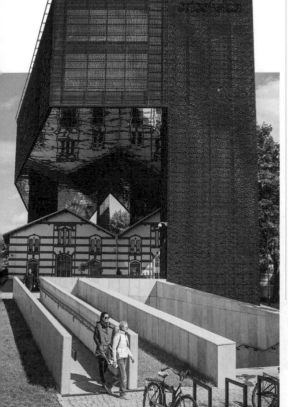

←
The extraordinary building that plays host to the Cricoteka Theatre Museum

Benedictine Abbey in Tyniec

A5 **Ul Benedyktyńska 37** **112** **9am–5pm Mon–Fri, 10am–6pm Sat & Sun (to 4pm daily Nov–Apr)** **tyniec.benedyktyni.pl**

This impressive abbey is set on a high chalky outcrop overlooking the River Vistula. The history of the abbey goes back to the mid-11th century. Originally, a Romanesque basilica stood on the site, but it was replaced in the 15th century by a Gothic church. The present Baroque abbey was built in 1618–22. Although in the course of its stormy history the church has lost

many fine and valuable features, it still retains its monumental Baroque altars.

Kościuszko Mound

A5

The tree-lined Aleja Jerzego Waszyngtona leads to the Kościuszko Mound on Sikornik Hill. At its foot, the Chapel of St Bronisława marks the site of the hermitage of the eponymous nun. The chapel was erected between 1856 and 1861 in the Neo-Gothic style.

The Kościuszko Mound was built between 1820 and 1823 to commemorate the leader of the insurrection of 1794. The monument was inspired by the mounds of mythical Polish rulers, Krak and Wanda, located in the Kraków environs. The construction of the mound

became a patriotic endeavour and the monument itself a destination for national pilgrimages. It offers incredible views of the city. Fortifications at the foot of the mound were constructed after 1850 as part of a project to transform Kraków into a massive fortress. These fortifications now house temporary exhibitions.

Nowa Huta

B5 **502** **4, 10, 22**

Kraków was considered an anti-Communist town in the aftermath of World War II due to its patriotic, intellectual and clerical traditions. To challenge this, the Communist regime began to industrialize the region in an effort to increase the working-class population. At the end of the 1940s, the regime ordered a giant steelworks and new adjoining city – named Nowa Huta (New Steelworks) – to be constructed. Designed by Tadeusz Ptaszycki, this "model

The Benedictine Abbey in Tyniec above the Vistula, and *(inset)* the abbey's wooden well

↓

Communist town" was built in the Socialist Realist style, complete with wide, tree-lined avenues spreading out from a monumental central square. The regime intended that this new town would be the antithesis of the historic city of Kraków and a powerful symbol of Communist capability and strength, as well as a working class enclave. Rather ironically, during the period of Martial Law (1981–3), Nowa Huta became notorious for anti-regime protest.

The building of churches was completely banned within the town. It was only after years of campaigning by the people of Nowa Huta that the construction of these religious buildings finally began in the 1970s. Among these, the Ark of God is an outstanding piece of modern sacral Polish architecture.

The **Nowa Huta Museum**, a branch of the MHK, hosts fascinating exhibitions on the new town's history. Exhibitions about life during the Communist period are also held at the **PRL Museum** (Polish People's Republic or Polska Rzeczpospolita Ludowa in Polish), which documents the history of the Marxist state that existed from 1952 to 1990.

Nowa Huta Museum

📷 🅰 Os Słonecznie 16
🕐 Apr-Oct: 9:30am-5pm Tue-Sun; Nov-Mar: 9am-4pm Tue, Thu & Sat, 10am-5pm Wed 🌐 mhk.pl

PRL Museum

📷 🅰 Os Centrum E1
🕐 10am-5pm Tue-Sun
🌐 mprl.pl

↑ A 1918 German plane on display at the Polish Aviation Museum

Polish Aviation Museum

📍 B5 🅰 Al Jana Pawła II 39
🚋 4, 5, 9, 10, 52 🕐 9am-5pm Tue-Sun 🌐 muzeum lotnictwa.pl

This absorbing museum is located on the historic Rakowice-Czyżyny airfield, one of the oldest military airfields in Europe (it was established in 1912) and the second largest in Poland prior to World War II. The museum has a modern pavilion which features one of the best collections of early 20th-century aircraft. The collection consists of more than 200 aircraft including prewar Polish fighter planes, Spitfires, German Albatrosses and Soviet Kakaruzniks. There is also a fascinating exhibit in the museum of 22 rare aeroplanes that were once part of Hermann Göring's personal collection. In addition, there are several displays in neighbouring hangars and a large open-air section.

A great way to explore the collection is with one of the museum's knowledgeable guides; these tours need to be booked in advance.

A SHORT WALK
MAIN MARKET SQUARE

Distance 600 m (655 yd) **Nearest bus stop** Kraków
Główny **Time** 10 minutes

This huge market square (Rynek Główny) was laid out when
Kraków received its new municipal charter in 1257. One
of the largest in Europe, it bustles with life all year round.
In summer, pedestrians find themselves negotiating the
maze of café tables that surround the square, along with a
host of shops, antique dealers, restaurants, bars and clubs.
There are also many interesting museums, galleries and
historic sights, including some splendid Renaissance and
Baroque houses and mansions.

Rynek Underground
*museum (p153) offers
tours of the maze of
medieval tunnels and
chambers beneath
the square.*

SŁAWKOWSKA

ŚW. JANA

The Renaissance **Cloth
Hall** *(p153) replaced an
earlier Gothic market hall;
today its upper floor
houses a gallery exhibiting
19th-century art.*

SZCZEPAŃSKA

RYNEK
GŁÓWNY

The Gothic **Town Hall
Tower** *(p153) is the only
remaining part of the former
City Hall; there is now a café
in the basement.*

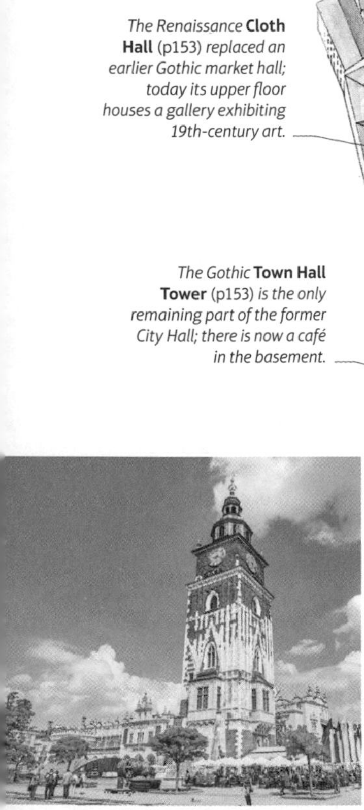

SZEWSKA

ŚW. ANNY

WIŚLNA

↑ Kraków's striking City
Hall Tower in the Main
Market Square

↑ The awe-inspiring interior of St Mary's Basilica

Locator Map
For more detail see p142

0 metres   80   N
0 yards   80

The spectacular **St Mary's Basilica** *(p152), the main parish church in Kraków, is renowned for its asymmetrical twin towers.*

START

The **Church of St Barbara,** *dating from the late 14th century, contains many treasures, including a 15th-century Gothic pietà.*

No 8 is known as the **House under the Lizards** *for the engraved stone sign above its entrance.*

Did You Know?

Each winter, Rynek Główny is host to Christmas markets and Yuletide celebrations.

St Wojciech is a small but splendid Romanesque church. One of the oldest stone churches in Poland, it pre-dates the planning of this vast square and is all but lost in it.

FINISH

Cafés and shops line the street of Grodzka, which leads to Wawel Castle.

MAŁOPOLSKA

During the 9th century, the Vistulanian tribe established a state in Małopolska. For centuries, this area was the heart of Poland. However, its importance waned at the end of the 16th century, when the capital of the Republic was moved from Kraków to Warsaw. After the Partitions of Poland, Małopolska went into a gradual decline. While Galicia, its southern part, came under Austrian rule, its northern part was incorporated into the Russian Empire. When Galicia gained autonomy within the Austro- Hungarian Empire, Galician towns, and especially Kraków, became important centres of Polish culture, retaining their identity despite a succession of annexations. Not until 1918, when Poland at last regained its independence, did Małopolska again become part of the Polish state. The region, home to some of Poland's most awe-inspiring scenery, is dotted with pretty towns, ruined castles, great monasteries and picturesque wooden churches. In the idyllic surrounds, folk customs survive and flourish, nowhere more than in the Podhale region.

MAŁOPOLSKA

Must Sees

1. Jasna Góra, Częstochowa
2. Łańcut Castle
3. Auschwitz-Birkenau Memorial and Museum
4. Zakopane and Tatra National Park

Experience More

5. Henryk Sienkiewicz Museum, Oblęgorek
6. Kielce
7. Holy Cross Mountains
8. Ujazd
9. Wadowice
10. Sandomierz
11. Kalwaria Zebrzydowska
12. Leszczyński Castle, Baranów Sandomierski
13. Wieliczka Salt Mine
14. Żywiec
15. Tarnów
16. Dębno Podhalańskie
17. Zalipie
18. Nowy Sącz
19. Stary Sącz
20. Krynica
21. Biecz
22. Gorlice
23. Krosno
24. Krasiczyn Castle
25. Przemyśl
26. Sanok
27. Jarosław
28. Rzeszów

Ostrowiec Świętokrzyski

MAZOVIA AND THE LUBLIN REGION
p120

Zamość

LUBELSKIE

Opatów

8 UJAZD

10 SANDOMIERZ

Klimontów

Kurozwęki

Tarnobrzeg

Stalowa Wola

Nisko

Bilgoraj

12 BARANÓW SANDOMIERSKI

Mielec

Kolbuszowa

Sokołów Małopolski

Leżajsk

Sieniawa

Lubaczów

Pava Ruska

Rzeszów–Jasionka International Airport

ŁAŃCUT CASTLE

Przeworsk

Dębica

RZESZÓW 28

2

JAROSŁAW 27

Korczowa

Yavoriv

Pilzno

Radymno

PODKARPACKIE

Strzyżów

Krzywcza

Kołaczyce

21 BIECZ

KROSNO 23

19

Brzozów

KRASICZYN CASTLE 24

25 PRZEMYŚL

Dukla

Rymanów

26 SANOK

Zagórz

Lesko

Sambir

UKRAINE

Carpathian Mountains

Komańcza

Ustrzyki Dolne

Svidnik

Bieszczady National Park

Ustrzyki Górne

Tarnica 1,346 m (4,416 ft)

1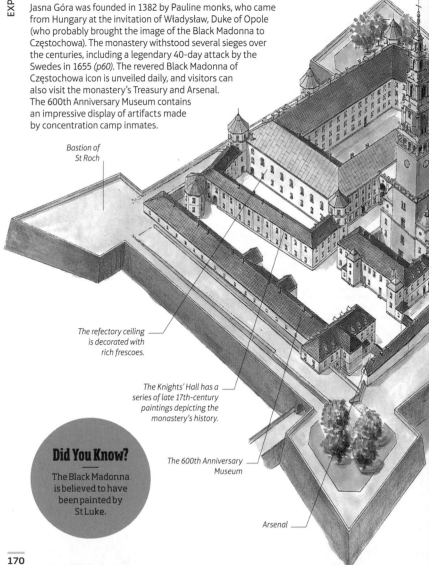

JASNA GÓRA, CZĘSTOCHOWA

🅐 D5 🚄🚌 🏛 Ul Kordeckiego 2, Częstochowa 🕐 5am–9:30pm daily 🌐 jasnagora.pl

The monastery of Jasna Góra in Częstochowa is the most famous shrine of the Virgin in Poland and the country's greatest place of pilgrimage – for many, its spiritual capital. The image of the Black Madonna of Częstochowa, to which miraculous powers are attributed, is Jasna Góra's most precious treasure.

Jasna Góra was founded in 1382 by Pauline monks, who came from Hungary at the invitation of Władysław, Duke of Opole (who probably brought the image of the Black Madonna to Częstochowa). The monastery withstood several sieges over the centuries, including a legendary 40-day attack by the Swedes in 1655 *(p60)*. The revered Black Madonna of Częstochowa icon is unveiled daily, and visitors can also visit the monastery's Treasury and Arsenal. The 600th Anniversary Museum contains an impressive display of artifacts made by concentration camp inmates.

Bastion of St Roch

The refectory ceiling is decorated with rich frescoes.

The Knights' Hall has a series of late 17th-century paintings depicting the monastery's history.

Did You Know?

The Black Madonna is believed to have been painted by St Luke.

The 600th Anniversary Museum

Arsenal

1 The Lubomirski Gate is one of four gateways that allow entry into Jasna Góra monastery.

2 The Black Madonna of Częstochowa is the most important icon of the Catholic faith in Poland.

3 Jasna Góra monastery has a large collection of votive art; the basilica also features vibrant stained-glass windows.

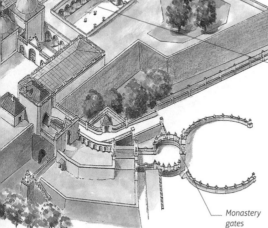

The Black Madonna

The outdoor altar, where services are held for the pilgrims.

Basilica of the Holy Cross and the Nativity of the Virgin Mary

The Treasury, where gold and silver vessels, vestments, tapestries and votive offerings are on display.

The Chapel of the Last Supper, designed by Adolf Szyszko-Bohusz in the 20th century.

Confessional

Monastery gates

↑ The impressive monastery complex of Jasna Gora, in the town of Częstochowa

STATIONS OF THE CROSS

Located within what was once the monastery's moat - now a lush green, leafy park - are the 14 Stations of the Cross. These bronze sculptures of religious figures stand atop plinths of granite, and were designed by the architect Stefan Szyller and created by the sculptor Pius Weloński in 1900–13. Every day, groups of pilgrims gather here to attend a religious service.

② 🏛 🥾 🍴 ☕ 🛍 🛒

ŁAŃCUT CASTLE

🅰F6 🏠 Ul Zamkowa 1, Łańcut 🚌🚆 🕐 Feb-May, Oct & Nov: noon-3pm Mon, 9am-3pm Tue-Sat, 9am-4pm Sun; Jun-Sep: noon-3pm Mon, 9am-3pm Tue-Fri, 10am-5pm Sat & Sun 🚫 Jan, Easter, 3 May, Corpus Christi, 1 & 11 Nov, Dec 🌐 zameklancut.pl

This magnificent fortified residence, surrounded by beautiful gardens, dominates the town of Łańcut. Now a museum, the building's opulent interiors are a delight to explore.

After purchasing the town of Łańcut in 1629, powerful magnate and Polish nobleman Stanisław Lubomirski went about building this spectacular castle-palace – work was completed in 1641. After 1775 the castle was extended and the interiors remodelled. The Neo-Classical Ballroom and the Great Dining Room were created during this period, and the magnificent gardens with their many pavilions laid out. Modernized from 1889 to 1914, the palace is one of the most beautiful aristocratic houses in Poland and attracts numerous visitors.

The statue in the Column Room is of young Henryk Lubomirski, Stanisław's grandson.

 HIDDEN GEM
Baroque Synagogue

Just outside the castle park is the 18th-century Old Synagogue, famous for its vividly decorated interior. It is filled with rich stuccowork, frescoes and a spectacular bema (pulpit) with a brightly painted canopy.

The Mirror Room's walls are lined with Rococo panelling brought back to Łańcut by Izabella Lubomirska – probably from one of her visits to France.

Library

The impressive fortified residence of Łańcut Castle ↑

↑ The castle's beautiful Baroque façade during early autumn

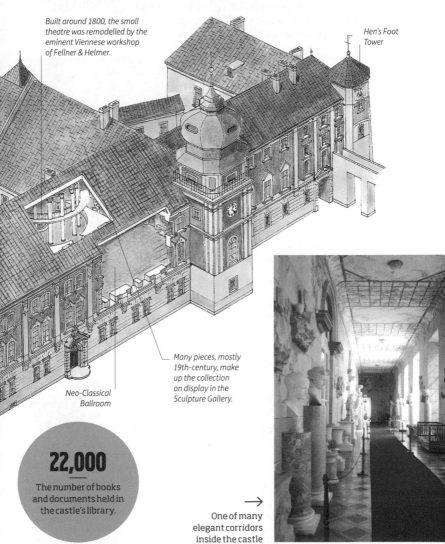

Built around 1800, the small theatre was remodelled by the eminent Viennese workshop of Fellner & Helmer.

Hen's Foot Tower

Neo-Classical Ballroom

Many pieces, mostly 19th-century, make up the collection on display in the Sculpture Gallery.

22,000

The number of books and documents held in the castle's library.

→ One of many elegant corridors inside the castle

3

AUSCHWITZ-BIRKENAU MEMORIAL AND MUSEUM

♀D6 🏠Oświęcim 🚌From Kraków Bus Station 🕐Jan & Nov: 7:30am–3pm; Feb: 7:30am–4pm; Mar & Oct: 7:30am–5pm; Apr, May & Sep: 7:30am–6pm; Jun, Jul & Aug: 7:30am–7pm; Dec: 7:30am–2pm 🚫1 Jan, Easter Day, 25 Dec 🌐auschwitz.org

More than a million people visit Auschwitz every year, to pay their respects to the estimated 1.1 million people murdered here in the Nazis' quest for their Final Solution – the extermination of the Jews. Now a UNESCO World Heritage Site, it has been preserved as a museum and memorial to its victims.

Auschwitz opened in 1940 on the site of a former Polish army barracks. Originally built to incarcerate Polish political prisoners, it became a camp for Soviet prisoners of war, many of whom died of malnourishment, overwork or torture. Further buildings were added in the spring of 1941 as the number of prisoners dramatically increased. From 1942 onwards, Auschwitz II – Birkenau – was built to deal with the vast numbers of Jews brought to be murdered as part of the Nazis' Final Solution. While Birkenau (p176) was the main concentration and extermination camp, Auschwitz was the administrative centre; it was here that the Nazis conducted sickening experiments on their prisoners and built the first gas chamber, using the pesticide Zyklon B as an instrument of mass murder. Six more gas chambers were to be built at Birkenau.

When Germany's defeat seemed inevitable, the Nazis made hasty attempts to destroy the camps and thus the evidence of their activities, but much remains at both sites to bear witness to this most atrocious of crimes.

↑ A reconstruction of the wall near Block 11 used for summary executions

↑ A display showing the discarded shoes of people murdered at the camp

1940

▲ Oświęcim chosen as the site of the Nazis' new concentration camp; first deportation of German Jews into Nazi-occupied Poland.

1942

▲ The implementation of the Final Solution is agreed at the Wannsee Conference, and mass deportation to Auschwitz begins.

1944

▲ As the Soviet Army closes in, the SS begin destroying evidence of the camp and its machinery of death.

1945

▲ Most prisoners evacuated on a "Death March" on 18 January; Soviet soldiers liberate Auschwitz's remaining prisoners on 27 January.

VISITING THE CAMPS

Auschwitz and Birkenau are 3 km (2 miles) apart, on the western suburbs of the town of Oświęcim (Auschwitz in German). Buses and trains taking visitors to the camps will have Oświęcim listed as their destination. A shuttle bus runs frequently between the two sites, leaving from the Auschwitz Information Centre. Advance booking online of tickets and tours is advised.

"Work Sets You Free", the
tragic message seen by ↑
prisoners entering the camp

Auschwitz II – Birkenau

Birkenau was opened in March 1942 in the village of Brzezinka, where the residents were evicted to make way for it. The camp grew steadily to become the largest of all the camps in Nazi-occupied Europe, housing 90,000 prisoners by mid-1944.

While many other camps were built for slave labour, Birkenau was primarily a place of extermination. It housed most of Auschwitz's machinery of mass murder, and the whole process was carried out systematically and on an enormous scale. In the six gas chambers in use at different stages of the camp's construction, over one million people were killed, 98 per cent of whom were Jewish. Victims included people from over 20 nations. The purpose of the remaining buildings on the site are now for remembrance.

The camp grew steadily to become the largest of all the camps in Nazi-occupied Europe, housing 90,000 prisoners by mid-1944.

→
"Hell's Gate", the infamous entrance through which prisoners arrived by train

Memorial wall of photographs in the "sauna", where new arrivals were deloused and disinfected ↑

1 A pile of suitcases stolen from the prisoners comprises one of the museum's harrowing and moving exhibits.

2 The camp's primitive wooden barracks had lines of bunks inside, and were crammed with up to 600 prisoners at a time.

3 One of the ponds in the camp's surrounds, where tons of ash, the remains of multiple victims, were dumped.

THE LIBERATION OF THE CAMPS

With the war all but lost, in mid-January 1945 the Nazi leaders gave the order for the camps to be destroyed. So rapid was the collapse of the German army, however, that much of Birkenau remained intact. More than 56,000 inmates were evacuated by the Nazis and forced to march west; many died en route. When the Soviet army entered the camps on 27 January 1945, they found just 7,000 survivors.

4

ZAKOPANE AND TATRA NATIONAL PARK

🅐 D7 🚉🚌 🈺 Ul Kościuszki 17; www.zakopane.pl

Lying on the boundary of Tatra National Park, Zakopane is one of Poland's most popular holiday destinations. This attractive town has long been regarded as the country's winter capital, on a par with alpine resorts as an upmarket winter sports and leisure centre. Its surrounding mountains are equally popular with summer visitors, lured by the network of hiking trails and the breathtaking scenery surrounding Mount Kasprowy Wierch and Morskie Oko lake.

Gubalówka Funicular to Gubalówka Hill

Rising above Zakopane to the north, the green ridge of Gubalówka Hill is famous for its superb views of the Tatra peaks. A funicular railway runs up the hill from just behind Zakopane's central market, a ride that takes around three minutes. At the top of the hill there are plenty of marked trails offering easy walking, and a dry toboggan run that's popular with children.

Willa Oksza Gallery of 20th-Century Art

🏠 Ul Zamoyskiego 25
🕐 10am-6pm Wed-Sat, 11am-4pm Sun 🌐 muzeum tatrzanskie.pl

One of the most beautiful houses designed by artist and architect Stanisław Witkiewicz, creator of the "Zakopane Style" of architecture, is the Willa Oksza. Built in 1895, it now serves as a gallery devoted to 20th-century art.

Zakopane was a popular resort among Polish artists, especially before World War I when the town was a ferment of creativity.

The Szymanowski Museum

🏠 Ul Kaprusie 8 🕐 10am-5pm Tue-Sun 🌐 mnk.pl

From the 1930s until his death, Polish composer Karol Szymanowski (1882-1937)

← Visitors strolling through the picturesque town centre of Zakopane

spent most of the year in the idyllic wooden house known as the Willa Atma. The house is now a museum devoted to Szymanowski's life and works, with period furnishings and personal effects mingling with touchscreen computers and multimedia displays. The exhibition devotes particular attention to *Harnasie* (1935), a ballet inspired by folk tales of Tatra mountain brigands.

④

Tatra Museum

⌂ Ul Krupówki 10
🕒 10am–6pm Tue–Sat, 9am–3pm Sun 🌐 muzeum tatrzanskie.pl

The Tatra Museum (Muzeum Tatranskie) eloquently tells the story of how Zakopane came to occupy a central place in Polish culture. Photographs and mementos recall how the town was "discovered" by 19th-century Polish doctors, who concluded that the fresh mountain air would make it the perfect health resort. This, combined with Zakopane's rustic character – traditional music and dress could still be heard and seen on the streets – drew city folk in droves, and a host of pensions and sanatoria were opened to cater for them. The town became a major meeting-point for Polish society, with cultural figures spending weeks or months here every year. The museum's exhibits, including re-creations of traditional interiors, paint a vivid picture of what this time was like.

↑ Learning about the fascinating history of Zakopane in the Tatra Museum

⑤

Museum of the Zakopane Style: Willa Koliba

⌂ Ul Kościeliska 18
🕒 9am–5pm Wed–Sat, 9am–3pm Sun
🌐 muzeumtatrzanskie.pl

In the years before World War I, a group of Polish architects led by Stanisław Witkiewicz developed a house-building style based on the traditional timber dwellings found in the Zakopane region. The Willa Koliba, designed by Witkiewicz in 1892, is a key example of this "Zakopane Style". Inside the house are models and sketches of other structures built in the style, and a display of portraits by Witkiewicz' son Stanisław Ignacy Witkiewicz.

The related **Museum of the Zakopane Style: Inspirations** displays folk crafts from the region and reveals how they influenced modern furniture and interior design.

Museum of the Zakopane Style: Inspirations
⊛ ⌂ Droga do Rojów 6 🕒 9am–5pm Wed–Sat, 9am–3pm Sun
🌐 muzeumtatrzanskie.pl

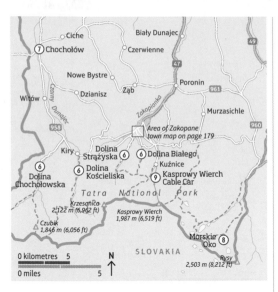

AROUND ZAKOPANE

⑥ The Mountain Valleys

The border of Tatra National Park lies on the southern outskirts of Zakopane. The massif is riven with scenic valleys (known as *doliny*), and it is here that some of the most popular hiking trails are to be found. Some of them are within walking distance of Zakopane; others are served by a regular minibus.

The closest valley to town is woody Dolina Białego; follow the trail along a stream. Running parallel to the west is the picturesque Dolina Strążyska, with a broad path passing gurgling cataracts and the Siklawica Waterfall (Wodospad Siklawica). The path climbs up to the meadow of Hala Strążyska, which has superb views of the higher Tatra peaks. Combining this trail with the one through Dolina Białego makes for a good day-long circular walk.

Around 6 km (4 miles) west of Zakopane, Dolina Kościeliska is characterized by steep rocky sides pitted with caves. After about 4 km (3 miles) of gradual ascent, the path along the valley becomes steeper as it climbs towards the Hala Ornak mountain hut. Sitting at 1,100 m (3,500 ft), it serves hot food and refreshments.

A further 2 km (1 mile) west of Dolina Kościeliska, Dolina

Chochołowska is arguably the most spectacular of the valleys, with steep sides darkened by dense pines. Nonetheless, the ascent is sufficiently gentle to ensure that it is a good family walking destination. The main target for hikers is the Polana Chochołowska mountain hut, which sits at 1,146 m (3,800 ft) and is just over 7 km (4 miles) from the valley entrance.

---

⑦ Chochołów

Along the main street of this 16th-century village stand traditional wooden cottages, the best examples of the region's highland architecture. The cottage at No 75 dates from 1889 and is open to the public. It has "white" and "black" rooms, and houses the **Museum of the Chochołów Insurrection**, which took place in 1846 against Austrian rule. Chochołów has a local custom that involves cleaning the walls of the building once a year until they are white.

Museum of the Chochołów Insurrection
🕙 🏠 Chochołów 75
🕙 10am–2pm Wed–Sun
🌐 muzeumtatrzanskie.pl

→
Hiking through the spectacular scenery of Tatra National Park

Surrounded by stark grey peaks, the high-altitude lake of Morskie Oko (Eye of the Sea) is the most visited attraction in the Tatra National Park.

⑧ Morskie Oko

Surrounded by stark grey peaks, the high-altitude Morskie Oko ("Eye of the Sea") is the largest lake in Tatra National Park, and its most visited attraction for its spectacular beauty. It lies at the end of a 9 km (6 mile) paved trail from Polana Palenica, around 15 km (9 miles) east of Zakopane. Horse-drawn carts are available to take visitors up the scenic, forest-shrouded trail, although most people choose to walk. There is a hut serving refreshments beside the lake, and a choice of trails leading round the shore and up into the mountains.

Did You Know?

According to legend, an underground passage once connected Morskie Oko to the sea.

⑨ Kasprowy Wierch Cable Car

🕐 **Hours vary, check website** 🌐 **pkl.pl**

The settlement of Kuźnice, 3 km (2 miles) south of Zakopane, is the start of the cable-car ride to Kasprowy Wierch, the highest of the mountains in Zakopane's immediate vicinity at 1,987 m (6,500 ft). The ascent takes about 15 minutes and offers superb views – however, it's a very popular ride so it is advisable to buy tickets in advance from one of the automatic machines in central Zakopane. The summit boasts a stunning panorama of the ridges that make up the central part of the Tatra chain. From here you can walk back to Zakopane via the Hala Gąsienicowa meadow. Experienced walkers can use Kasprowy Wierch as the starting point for a number of high-altitude hikes, either westwards to Mount Giewont or east towards the challenging terrain of Orła Perć.

STAY

Art & Spa

Roomy doubles and apartments in an elegant mansion.

🏠 Ul Kościuszki 18, Zakopane
🌐 artandspa.pl

Sabała

Comfortable accommodation in the heart of Zakopane.

🏠 Ul Krupówki 11, Zakopane
🌐 sabala.zakopane.pl

Konstantynówka

A lovely Zakopane-style building, with hillside forest views.

🏠 Ul Jagiellońska 18, Zakopane 📞 18 533 0363

Willa Hueta Hotel

A great base for touring northern Małopolska.

🏠 Ul Juliusza Słowackiego 25, Kielce
🌐 willahueta.pl

EXPERIENCE MORE

5

Henryk Sienkiewicz Museum, Oblęgorek

⚐E5 **⌂** Aleja Lipowa 24 🚌 **⊙** Apr-Oct: 9am-5pm Tue-Sun; Nov-Mar: 8am-3pm Tue-Sun 🔳mnki.pl

The leafy village of Oblęgorek is home to a small manor house which belonged to the famous Polish writer Henryk Sienkiewicz; it was given to him as a gift from the nation in 1900. An eclectic building with a tall circular tower, its interior remains as it was when the author lived and worked here. Today it houses the fascinating **Henryk Sienkiewicz Museum**, and there is an exhibition on his life and work on the first floor. In 1905 Sienkiewicz was awarded the Nobel Prize for Literature for his historical novel *Quo Vadis*.

6

Kielce

⚐E5 🚊🚌 **𝒊** Ul Sienkiewicza 29; www.um.kielce.pl

In a city whose beauty has been defaced by postwar buildings, the **Former Palace of Kraków Bishops** stands out like a jewel, an exceptional example of a well-preserved 17th-century aristocratic town house. The early Baroque façades and corner towers are almost intact, the decoration of the first-floor rooms is well-preserved, and the marble doorways and beamed ceilings are original.

The palace was constructed in 1637–41, probably by royal architect Giovanni Trevano, for the then Bishop of Kraków, Jakub Zadzik. During the reign of Zygmunt III, it was this exceptional clergyman who was in charge of the Republic's foreign policy, successfully making peace with Russia and establishing a long-standing ceasefire with Sweden.

The period interiors form part of the National Museum; there is also an excellent gallery of Polish painting here.

Next to the palace is the cathedral, built on the site of an earlier church of 1632–5, in the time of Bishop Zadzik.

The **Kielce Historical Museum**, a few streets over, has an attractive display of photographs, old postcards, domestic furnishings and a scary-looking 19th-century dentist's chair. If you have children in tow, the **Museum of Toys and Play** is a highly enjoyable museum packed with dolls and fluffy toys from the past alongside model trains, cars and rockets.

At the **Ethnographic Park** in Tokarnia, part of the Kielce Rural Museum, several dozen wooden village buildings from around Kielce are laid out over 4.2 sq km (1.6 sq miles).

The ruins of a 13th-century castle dominate the town of

↑ Kielce Cathedral and the Former Palace of Kraków Bishops

Chęciny, which is found 15 km (9 miles) west of Kielce. Just north of Chęciny is Paradise Cave (Jaskinia Raj), which contains some spectacular stalactites and stalagmites.

Former Palace of Kraków Bishops

◎◎ 🅐 Pl Zamkowy 1 🅞 May–Aug: 10am–6pm Tue–Sun; Sep–Apr: 9am–5pm Tue–Sun 🅒 6 Jan, Easter, Corpus Christi, 1 Nov, 24–26 & 31 Dec 🅦 mnki.pl

Kielce Historical Museum

◎ 🅐 Ul Swietego Leonarda 4 🅒 41 340 5520 🅞 9am–4pm Tue–Sun

Museum of Toys and Play

◎ 🅐 Pl Wolnosci 2 🅞 9am–5pm Tue–Sun 🅦 muzeum zabawel.eu

Ethnographic Park

◎ 🅐 Tokarnia 303 🅞 Hours vary, check website 🅦 mwk.com.pl

→

Boulders of a stone run, a geological feature of the Holy Cross Mountains

---

7

Holy Cross Mountains

 E5 🅡🖂 ℹ 41 367 64 36 or 41 367 60 11

Part of the Małopolska Uplands, these are among the oldest mountains in Europe. Eroded over thousands of years, the stunning range is neither high nor steep, but it is exceptionally rich in minerals, which have been exploited since ancient times, witnessed by the remains of prehistoric mines and furnaces. The Łysogóry range, with Mount Łysica its highest peak

Did You Know?

By passing sentences of impalement, Prince Wiśniowiecki earned himself the nickname *Palej* (The Impaler).

at just 612 m (2,000 ft), lies within the Świętokrzyski National Park. Only vestiges remain of the primeval forest of firs that once covered the range, badly damaged by acid rain in the 1970s and 1980s. In ancient times Łysa Góra, the second-highest peak, was a place of pagan worship. Its slopes are covered with broken rock.

The Benedictine abbey in Święty Krzyż atop Łysa Góra, built in the 12th century and later extended, has predominantly Baroque and Neo-Classical features and contains paintings by the 18th-century artist Franciszek Smuglewicz. The cloisters and vestry, with late Baroque frescoes, date from the 15th century. The 17th-century domed chapel of the Oleśnicki family is its most outstanding feature. The relic of the Holy Cross, kept in the chapel, attracts crowds of pilgrims. In the crypt beneath the chapel is a glass coffin containing the supposedly mummified body of Prince Jeremi Wiśniowiecki. In his 1884 novel *With Fire and Sword* Henryk Sienkiewicz portrayed this magnate as a saviour and hero of battles against Ukrainian insurgents in 1648. History judges him less kindly as an unimaginative politician and a brute.

Bodzentyn, to the north, is worth a visit for its 18th-

century Gothic parish church, with an altar from Kraków's Cathedral of Saints Stanisław and Wacław, and the stately ruins of the Bishops' Palace.

8

Ujazd

 E5 🖂

The main attraction in Ujazd are the ruins of **Krzyżtopór Castle**. Built for the Palatine Krzysztof Ossoliński, it is one of the most eccentric residences of its time in Europe. Attacked during the Swedish Deluge *(p63)*, the castle fell into neglect and for 300 years it was plundered by surrounding villages for building material. However, the ruins are still extremely impressive.

The Mannerist and Baroque collegiate church in Klimontów, 13 km (8 miles) east of Ujazd, is something of an architectural curiosity. Begun in 1643, the church's elliptical nave with galleries is an unusual combination, and the columns, sunk into niches hollowed out in the pillars, are equally uncommon.

Krzyżtopór Castle

🅞 8am–4pm daily (to 6pm daily Sep–Nov, to 8pm daily Apr–Aug) 🅒 1 Jan, Easter, 1 Nov, 25–26 Dec 🅦 krzyztopor.org.pl

Wadowice's Church of the Presentation of the Virgin Mary ↑

9 Wadowice

 D6 🚌 🚆 *i* Ul Koscielna 4; www.it.wadowice.pl

Karol Wojtyła, who became Pope John Paul II in 1978, was born in Wadowice in 1920. His childhood home is now the **Museum of the Holy Father John Paul II** containing items relating to his early life in the town, as well as access to the small apartment on the first floor where his family resided.

He was christened in the late Baroque Church of the Presentation of the Virgin Mary (Kościół Ofiarowania NMP), near the Market Square. The church, built in 1791–8, s now classed as a minor basilica. The tower, with Baroque cupola, was built by Tomasz Pryliński in the late 19th century. Inside there is a Chapel dedicated to Saint John Paul II and in the presbytery are eight portraits of saints canonised by him.

Museum of the Holy Father John Paul II

🏛 Ul Kościelna 7 🕐 Apr & Oct: 8:30am–4:30pm; May–Sep: 8:30am–5:30pm; Nov–Mar: 8:30am–2:30pm
🌐 domjp2.pl

10 Sandomierz

 F6 🚌 🚆 *i* Rynek 12; www.sandomierz.pl

This small, ancient town has a charming Market Square surrounded by elegant buildings. In the centre stands the splendid 14th-century town hall, which now houses a branch of the **Regional Museum**. There are further exhibits in the castle and the museum also runs an underground tour.

The town's most important building is the magnificent cathedral. The 15th-century Ruthenian-Byzantine frescoes in its chancel depict scenes from the lives of Christ and the Virgin.

The 13th-century Church of St James (Kościół św. Jakuba) is an exceptionally fine late-Romanesque aisled basilica. Its ceramic decoration and the beautiful portal are evidence that it was built by master craftsmen from Lombardy. The remains of 49 Dominican friars murdered by Tatars in 1260 lie in the Martyrs' Chapel.

The **Diocesan Museum** is within the Gothic house of Jan Długosz (1415–80), the celebrated chronicler of

Poland. It features religious paintings and sculptures from the Middle Ages to the 19th-century, including a *Madonna with the Christ Child* by Lucas Cranach the Elder.

Regional Museum

🚻 🏛 Market Square
🕐 Hours vary, check website
🌐 zamek-sandomierz.pl

Diocesan Museum

🚻 🏛 Ul Długosza 9
📞 15 833 26 70 🕐 May–Sep: 9am–4:30pm Tue–Sat, 1:30–4:30pm Sun; Oct–Apr: 9am–3:30pm Tue–Sat, 1:30–3:30pm Sun

EAT

Bistro Podwale

Occupying a former apple cellar, this relaxing bistro offers a selection of seasonal soups, salads and mains.

🏛 F6 🏛 Ul Podwale Dolne 8a, Sandomierz 🌐 bistropodwale.pl

Si Senor

This chic Spanish-themed place prides itself on an excellent choice of Mediterranean fish and seafood.

🏛 E5 🏛 Ul Kozia 3, Kielce 🌐 si-senor.pl

Tatrzańka

Much-loved by locals, this old-school café-restaurant is the place to go for delicious pastries and meat-and-veg lunches.

🏛 E6 🏛 Ul Krakowska 1, Tarnów 🌐 kudelski.pl

> **Due to its architectural ornamentation, featuring spheres, rosettes and strange creatures, the castle is thought to have been designed by Santi Gucci.**

Kalwaria Zebrzydowska

🅐 D6 🏛️🚌
ℹ️ Ul Bernardyńska 46; www.kalwaria.eu

Kalwaria Zebrzydowska is the oldest and most unusual calvary in Poland. It was commissioned in 1600 by Mikołaj Zebrzydowski, the ruler of Krakow.

The calvary, built between 1605 and 1632, consists of 40 chapels, scattered across the forest-covered hills of the 527-m- (1,729-ft-) high Mount Żar. The most distinctive of these chapels are the work of the Flemish architect and goldsmith Paul Baudarth. Some have unusual shapes: the House of the Virgin Mary takes the form of the Mystic Rose, and the House of Caiaphas that of an ellipsis.

The large Baroque monastery church dates from 1702, while the monastic buildings were constructed by Baudarth and Giovanni Maria Bernadoni in 1603–67.

During Holy Week there are passion plays performed at the calvary. The Feast of Assumption is celebrated here in August.

Leszcyński Castle, Baranów Sandomierski

🅐 F6 🏛️🚌 🕐 Ul Zamkowa 20 🕐 Apr-Sep: 9am-6pm daily; Oct: 9am-5pm daily; Nov-Mar: 9am-4pm Tue-Sun 🌐 baranow.com.pl

Situated close to the Vistula, the small town of Baranów Sandomierski is best known for the beautiful Leszczyński Castle. It was built on the east bank of the river for the Leszczyński family in 1591–1606. The castle is without a doubt one of the finest examples of Mannerist architecture in all of Poland. The castle consists of four wings arranged around a rectangular arcaded court-yard. The grand exterior staircase and the façades, with their elaborate attics giving the impression of a massive (but in fact rather delicate) curtained wall, are striking. The square tower in the central façade serves a purely decorative purpose. Due to its architectural ornamentation, featuring spheres, rosettes and strange creatures, the castle is thought to have been designed by Santi Gucci, a noted architect. The castle is also home to a golf course and the Magnate's Restaurant. The latter, housed in the castle's cellars, serves up traditional Polish cuisine.

A museum, located on the ground floor, contains furni-ture and suits of armour, as well as other objects from the castle's heyday. There are also exhibits relating to the history of sulphur exploitation in the huge quarries nearby.

← Leszczyński Castle's elegant courtyard in Baranów Sandomierski

Wieliczka Salt Mine

🅰 E6 🚌🚆 🅰 Ul Daniłowicza 10 🕐 Apr–Oct: 7:30am–7:30pm; Nov–Mar: 8am–5pm 🚫 1 Jan, Easter, 1 Nov, 24–26 Dec 🌐 wieliczka-saltmine.com

Wieliczka is famous for its ancient Salt Mine, which opened 700 years ago and is still in operation. The mine is unique in the world for its corridors and chambers, which are carved out of rock salt, and is now listed as a UNESCO World Heritage Site.

The 2-km- (1.5-mile-) long route through the network of underground galleries reaches a depth of 135 m (442 ft), with a stable temperature of 13–14° C (55–57° F). Highlights

include the Chapel of St Kinga, with altarpieces, chandeliers and sculptures made of salt. The Staszic Chamber has the highest ceiling and a sub-terranean sanatorium.

The Salt Mine Castle at Ulica Zamkowa 8 is also worth a visit, too. From the 13th century right up until 1945 it was a base for the manage-ment of the salt mine. Today it houses a museum with, among other things, a collec-tion of antique salt mills.

Did You Know?

The mine at Wieliczka is one of the world's oldest salt mines still in operation.

⑭
Żywiec

🅰 D7 🚌🚆 𝒊 Ul Zamkowa 2 🌐 zywiec.pl

This town is associated with one of the best locally brewed Polish brands of beer and is a perfect starting point for trips out into the Beskid Żywiecki Mountains. The Żywiecki lake, with watersports facilities, is another local attraction. Folk traditions thrive here; a high point is Corpus Christi, with a

procession featuring women in traditional dress. Sights of interest include the Market Square, the Town Museum and the Church of the Nativity of the Virgin Mary (Kościół Narodzenia Najświętszej Marii Panny). Not far from the Market Square is the Gothic Church of the Holy Cross (Kościół św. Krzyża). Other buildings of note are the Renaissance castle and the 19th-century palace. The latter was built by the Habsburgs when they gained ownership of the town in the 19th century.

⑮
Tarnów

🅰 E6 🚌🚆 𝒊 Rynek 7; www.it.tarnow.pl

The medieval layout of the old town in Tarnów is perfectly preserved. The town hall, in the centre, dates from the 15th century and was remodelled in the second half of the 16th. Tarnów's grandest building,

 EXPERIENCE Małopolska

the late Gothic Cathedral of the Nativity of the Virgin Mary (Katedra Narodzenia NMP), was built in 1400. Its Diocesan Museum is worth a visit.

↑ An old wooden house in Zalipie, prettily decorated with traditional floral paintings

Dębno Podhalańskie

E7 🚌

This pretty village is home to the larch timber Parish Church of St Michael the Archangel (Kościół parafialny św. Michała Archanioła). Built in the mid-15th century, it is one of the most highly regarded examples of wooden Gothic architecture in Europe, and is also notable for its ceiling, walls and furnishings, which are covered with wonderfully colourful geometric, figural and floral motifs.

Around 30 km (17 miles) north, Chabówka is the site of Poland's largest open-air railway museum. It has an array of steam and diesel locomotives, alongside several vintage passenger carriages.

← One of the huge chambers created by salt extraction at the Wieliczka Salt Mine

Zalipie

E6 🚌🚐 ℹ️ www.dommalarek.pl

The picturesque village of Zalipie has a truly unique folk art tradition: cottages, barns, wells and fences are painted with colourful floral, animal, geometric and other motifs. The painters are usually the women of the village. Every year in June, a competition called the Painted Cottage is organized and exhibitions of paintings are held.

Nowy Sącz

🅰️ E7 🚌🚐
ℹ️ Ul Szwedska 2; www.ziemiasadecka.info

Set amid low hills, about 100 km (62 miles) southeast of Kraków, this town is the main administrative centre of the Beskid Region. Next to the lively main square, the **Regional Museum** (Muzeum Okręgowe) is rich in religious paintings from local village churches. The well-preserved 17th-century **Synagogue** is now used as a contemporary art gallery. Around 4 km (2.5 miles) from the centre, the **Sącz Ethnographic Park**

(Sądecki Park Etnograficzny) is an open-air museum featuring traditional buildings from all across the region. Next to it is the **Galician Market Town** (Miasteczko Galicyjskie), in which the main square of a 19th-century market town (based loosely on Stary Sącz) has been carefully recreated and is complete with workshops giving fascinating demonstrations of local crafts.

Regional Museum
♿ 🏠 Ul Lwówska 3
🕐 9:30am–3pm Tue–Thu, 9am–5pm Fri, 9am–4pm Sat & Sun (free Sat) 🌐 muzeum.diecezja.tarnow.pl

Synagogue
♿ 🏠 Ul Joselewicza 12
🕐 10am–3pm Wed & Thu, 10am–5:30pm Fri, 9am–2:30pm Sat & Sun
🌐 muzeum.sacz.pl

Sącz Ethnographic Park
♿ 🏠 Ul Wienawy-Długoszewskiego 🕐 May–mid-Oct: 10am–6pm Tue–Sun; mid-Oct–Apr: 9am–3pm Tue–Sun
🌐 muzeum.sacz.pl

Galician Market Town
♿ 🏠 Ul Lwówska 226
🕐 May–mid-Oct: 10am–6pm daily; mid-Oct–Apr: 9am–4pm daily
🌐 muzeum.sacz.pl

The church of the Convent of the Order of St Clare in Stary Sącz ↑

 Biecz

 E7

In the 16th century this small town was one of the most important centres of cloth manufacture in Poland. It is dominated by the town hall tower, built in 1569–81, and the Parish Church of Corpus Christi (Kościół farny Bożego Ciała). The church, built at the turn of the 15th century, is one of the most magnificent in the region, reconciling the Gothic tradition with the new canons of the Renaissance. The Renaissance house at Ulica Węgierska 2 is home to Brecz's Regional Museum.

STAY

Śnieżka
This friendly hotel, set in an interwar mansion, has small but well-equipped rooms.

E7 Ul Lewakowskiego 22, Krosno hotelsniezka.pl

zł zł zł

Małopolanka
A genteel old-school hotel in the town centre, with a small spa and a café.

E7 Bulwary Dietla 13, Krynica malopolanka.eu

zł zł zł

Grand Hotel Boutique
Contemporary quarters a short walk from the main square.

F6 Ul Dymnickiego 1, Rzeszów grand-hotel.pl

zł zł zł

 Stary Sącz

E7 Rynek 5; wstarymsaczu.pl/en

This charming Galician town has a cobbled Market Square and some very fine buildings including the Convent of the Order of St Clare (Klasztor Sióstr Klarysek), founded in 1208. The Gothic church was consecrated in 1280 and the vaulting dates from the 16th century. Its altars, with stucco-work by Baldassare Fontana, and a pulpit from 1671 showing a depiction of the Tree of Jesse, complement the church's modern decoration.

Krynica

E7 Ul Zdrojowa 4/2; krynica.pl

Well-equipped with sanatoria and pump rooms, Krynica is one of the largest and most modern health and ski resorts in Poland. Fashionable and luxurious prewar boarding houses stand next to old wooden villas, the best known of which is the Art Nouveau "Patria". The New Sanatorium near the pedestrian promenade (Deptak) and the Great Pump Room are also worth a visit.

The work of the amateur painter Nikifor is displayed in the **Nikifor Museum** housed in the "Romanówka" villa.

Encircling the town are tree-covered mountains; Mount Jaworzyna is the higest at 1,114 m (3,654 ft). It can be reached by cable car, from Czarny Potok. In winter, this is a skier's paradise. Remote areas are inhabited by lynxes, wolves and bears, so exercise caution if away from the established trails.

Nikifor Museum
Bulwary Dietla 19
18 471 53 03 10am–1pm & 2–5pm Tue–Sat, 10am–3pm Sun Pub hols

Gorlice

A E7 🚌🚃 **i** Rynek 2;
www.gorlice.pl

Gorlice grew in importance
when industrial pioneer
Ignacy Łukasziewicz opened
an oil refinery here in 1853.
In World War I the city saw
fierce battles between Tsarist
Russia and Austria-Hungary;
as a result, military graveyards
encircle the outskirts. Located
just off the main square, the
Regional Museum (Muzeum
Regionalne) exhibits World
War I memorabilia.

Sękowa, 7 km (4 miles)
south, is home to the wooden
**Church of Saints Philip and
James** (Kościół św. Filipa i św.
Jakuba), with a steep shingle
roof and a squat bell tower.

In Kwiatoń, about another
20 km (12 miles) south of
Gorlice, is the beautiful
St Parascheva Church
(Cerkiew św. Paraskewy), a
veritable masterpiece of 17th-
century architecture.

Regional Museum

⊛ **A** Ul Wąska ⏰ 9am-
4pm Tue-Fri, 10am-2pm
Sat & Sun

Church of Saints Philip
and James

A Sękowa 13 **w** sekowa.
rzeszow.opoka.org.pl

St Parascheva Church

A Kwiatoń **C** 660 105 342
⏰ 9am-1pm & 1:30-5pm Wed,
9am-1pm & 1:30-6pm Thu-
Sat, noon-5pm Sun

Krosno

A F7 🚌🚃 **i** Rynek 5;
13 432 77 07

Once the centre of the Polish
oil industry, Krosno has more
to offer than industrial history.
The finest monument is the
Oświęcim Chapel in the Gothic
Franciscan church. Completed
in 1647, it is decorated with
exquisite stuccowork by
Giovanni Battista Falconi.
The Market Square is lined by
old arcaded houses. Just off
the main square, the **Glass
Heritage Centre** (Centrum
Dziedzictwa Skla) celebrates
local industry with demonstrations of glass blowing and
a display of items that were
made at the town's renowned
glass works. Note that the
last admission is two hours
before closing.

In Odrzykoń, just 10 km
(6 miles) north, the ruined
Kamieniec Castle was the
setting for *Revenge* (1834),
a comedy by 19th-century
writer Count Aleksander
Fredro, its plot involving a
dispute over the hole in the

> ## WOODEN
> ## CHURCHES
>
> Southeastern Poland is
> extraordinarily rich in
> wooden churches, and
> many are in villages of
> the Carpathian foot-
> hills. Built by Catholic,
> Orthodox and Uniate
> communities, they are
> just as intricate and
> expressive as any brick
> or stone edifice. Many
> follow East European
> models, with onion
> domes and icon-filled
> interiors. The variety is
> due to the nature of the
> cosmopolitan congre-
> gations living in such
> close proximity.

wall dividing the courtyard
of the castle. In the geological
park near the castle is a group
of sandstone and shale
structures known as Prządki
(the Spinners), which have
unusual shapes.

Located around 15 km
(9 miles) east of Krosno,
Iwonicz Zdrój and Rymanów
are popular health resorts.

At Dukla, around 18 km
(11 miles) south of Krosno,
there is the Baroque Mniszcha
Palace, which today houses
a historical museum, and an
18th-century Bernardine
church, featuring the charming
Rococo tomb of Maria Amalia
Brühla Mniszkowa.

In Bóbrka, 12 km (7 miles)
south of Krosno, an industrial
skansen has been created in
what is certainly one of the
oldest oil wells in the world,
established in 1854.

Glass Heritage Centre

⊛⊛⊛ **A** Ul Blich 2 ⏰ Jul-
Aug: 10am-6pm Mon-Sat,
11am-6pm Sun; Sep-Jun:
9am-5pm Mon-Sat, 11am-
5pm Sun **w** miastoszkla.pl

The colourful fountain
found in Krosno's charming
Market Square

24

Krasiczyn Castle

F7 **Mid-Apr–mid-Oct: 9am–4pm daily; mid-Oct–mid-Apr: by appt only** **krasiczyn.com.pl**

Krasiczyn is one of the most magnificent late-Renaissance castles in the old Ruthenian territories of the Polish crown. Building began in 1592 on the site of an earlier castle and was completed in 1608. The architect was Galeazzo Appiani. It has an arcaded courtyard, with a clock tower over the gate and four stout cylindrical corner towers. The Divine Tower contains a chapel, while the Papal Tower is crowned by a dome and parapet symbolizing the papal tiara. The Royal Tower has a crown-shaped dome and the Tower of the Gentry is topped by sword pommels.

The Baroque sgraffito on the walls is very striking, with mythological scenes on the upper tier; there are portraits of both nobles and the kings of Poland on the central tier;

and medallions with the busts of Roman patricians on the lowest tier. Little of the interior's original decoration survives, as it was destroyed by fire in 1852, on the eve of the marriage of a later owner, Duke Leon Sapieha.

In Krzywcza, 10 km (6 miles) west of Krasiczyn, stand the ruins of the castle of the Kącki family. About 12 km (7 miles) south of Krasiczyn, in Posada Rybotycka, is Poland's only stone-fortified Uniate church. In Kalwaria Pacławicka, the 18th-century Franciscan monastery has about a dozen chapels marking the Stations of the Cross. Passion plays are performed here on Good Friday and many processions and plays are organized during the year for different church festivities.

25

Przemyśl

F7 **Ul Grodzka 1; www.przemysl.pl**

The history of this picturesque city, located on a hill by the banks of the River San, goes back to prehistoric times. In the Middle Ages it was a regional capital and lay on a busy trade route. The object of dispute between Poland and Ruthenia, it became part of Poland in 1340.

During World War I, the strongly fortified city held out against the besieging Russian army, and the fortifications from that time survive. From 1939 to 1941 the River San, which flows through the city, constituted a border between territory held by the Soviet Union and Germany.

The cathedral, remodelled in 1718–24, is predominantly in Baroque style; of its earlier Gothic form only the chancel remains. Notable features of the interior include the Renaissance tomb of Bishop Jan Dziaduski, by Giovanni Maria Padovano, and the late Gothic alabaster figure of the Virgin from Jacków. Near the cathedral are the Baroque Church of the Discalced Carmelites and the former Jesuit church, now Uniate, dating from 1627–48. The castle, founded by Kazimierz the Great in the 1340s, stands on a hill above the city; its tower offers a panorama of the city and the San Valley.

EXPERIENCE Małopolska

Sumptuous interior of
an old Orthodox church
at Sanok Skansen

Sanok Skansen
 Ul Rybickiego 3
Apr: 9am-4pm daily;
May-Sep: 8am-6pm daily;
Oct: 8am-4pm daily; Nov-
Mar: 9am-2pm daily
skansen.sanok.pl

㉗
Jarosław
F6 www.
jaroslaw.pl

This city owes its wealth to its
location on the River San and
the trade route from the East
to Western Europe. In the 16th
and 17th centuries, the largest
religious fairs in Poland were
held here – one was even
attended by Władysław IV,
who mingled with merchants.

The **Jarosław Museum** is in
the Orsetti House, built in the
16th century in the style of an
Italian Renaissance palazzo,
reflecting the wealth of the
city's merchants. It was
extended in 1646, and is
crowned with a Mannerist
parapet. The town hall, with
coats of arms on the corner
towers, stands in the centre
of the broad Market Square.

Jarosław Museum
Orsetti House, Rynek 4
9am-5pm Tue-Sat (to 4pm
Oct-May), 10am-6pm Sun
muzeum-jaroslaw.pl

㉘
Rzeszów
F6 Rynek 26;
www.rzeszow.pl

The dominant building here
is the Gothic Church of Saints
Stanisław and Adalberg, from
the 15th century but with a
later Baroque interior. The
former Piarist Church of the
Holy Cross (Kościół św.

㉖
Sanok
F7 Rynek 14; www.
sanok.pl

A key staging post on trade
routes from Kraków to L'viv,
Sanok was fortified by medieval kings. Before World War II
it had a mixed population of
Poles, Jews, Lemkos and
Ukrainians, and was a cultural
centre for the latter.

The surviving keep of the
castle holds the wide-ranging
Sanok Castle Museum, with
local folklore, Orthodox and
Uniate icons, and fantastical
artworks by surrealist painter
Zdzisław Beksiński. Along the
north bank of the River San is
Sanok Skansen, displaying
buildings associated with all
the area's ethnic and religious
groups. It also features a
19th-century market square
with original shops and
houses of the region.

Sanok Castle Museum
 Ul Zamkowa 2 Apr-
Oct: 8am-noon Mon, 9am-
5pm Tue-Sun; Nov-Mar:
8am-noon Mon, 9am-5pm
Tue & Wed, 9am-3pm Thu-
Sun muzeum.sanok.pl

Visitors exploring the
magnificent courtyard
of Krasiczyn Castle

EAT

Café Fiore
A legendary patisserie
serving some of
Poland's best cakes.

F7 Ul Kazimierza
Wielkiego 17 B, Przemyśl
cukierniafiore.pl

Stary Browar
Rzeszowski
A brewery with grilled
meats and local beers.

F6 Rynek
20-23, Rzeszów
browar-rzeszow.pl

Karczma Jadło
Karpackie
A folk restaurant with
hearty regional dishes.

F7 Rynek 12, Sanok
13 464 67 00

Krzyża), and the Baroque
monastery and Bernardine
church of 1624–9 are also
worth a visit. The latter has
the unfinished mausoleum of
the Ligęz family, who were
members of Poland's nobility.
The family once owned the
town's castle; it later passed
into the ownership of the
Lubomirskis, who surrounded
it with bastions in the 17th
century. The Market Square,
with an eclectic town hall, is
also interesting.

Highlights of the **Muzeum
Miasta Rzeszowa** include
the gallery of 18th- to 20th-
century Polish painting and
a collection of glass, china
and faïence.

Muzeum Miasta Rzeszowa
Ul 3 Maja 19
Hours vary, check website
mhmr.muzeum.rzeszow.pl

A DRIVING TOUR
BIESZCZADY MOUNTAINS

Length 195 km (120 miles) **Stopping-off points** Ustrzyki Górne; Lesko **Terrain** Mountainous, with good roads

The Bieszczady Mountains, together with the neighbouring Beskid Niski, are the wildest in Poland. Tourists return with blood-curdling tales of coming face-to-face with bears and wolves, or discovering a skeleton in the forest undergrowth. Needless to say, these stories are often exaggerated. Before World War II, the region was densely populated by Ukrainians and ethnic groups known as the Boyks and the Lemks. After the war, because of fighting and resettlements, the area was slowly deserted, and farming had largely disappeared from the region by the 1970s. Pastures and burned-out villages became overgrown as the forest encroached and wild animals returned to the mountains. It is a spectacular destination to explore, and collect some tales of your own.

Zagórz, the starting point for hiking trails into the Bieszczady Mountains, is dominated by the ruins of the hilltop Baroque Church of Discalced Carmelites.

*The charming town of **Lesko** has many fantastic buildings, including a castle and a Baroque synagogue housing a museum.*

*Cardinal Stefan Wyszyński, Primate of Poland, was sent into exile to **Komańcza** by Communist authorities in 1955. The village had been deserted after World War II.*

Sanok

Niebieszczany

Zagórz
START

Lesko

Mokre

Karlików

Czaszyn

Hoczew

Szczawne

FINISH
Komańcza

Baligród

Chryszczata 998 m (3,274 ft)

Nowy Łupków

Wołosań 1,071 m (3,514 ft)

Cisna

Kołonice

Balnica 712 m (2,336 ft)

↑ The unique shapes of wooden Orthodox churches found in the region

Did You Know?

There are thought to be 150 brown bears living in Bieszczady National Park and its surrounding areas.

← Wild mountain ranges at
Bieszczady National Park,
a UNESCO biosphere area

MAŁOPOLSKA
*Bieszczady
Mountains*

Locator Map
For more detail see p168

*The highest dam in Poland, at
82 m (269 ft) high and 664 m
(2,178 ft) long, was built at* **Solina***.
The reservoir is ideal for sailing, and
is surrounded by forests.*

The village of **Rownia** *has a
distinctive wooden Orthodox
church, as do many of the old
Boyk and Lemk villages in the
Bieszczady Mountains.*

Wańkowa

Olszanica

Lake
Myczkowskie

Ustrzyki Dolne

Solina

Równia

Zadwórze

Polańczyk

Lake
Solina

Łabiska
618 m (2,028 ft)

Jawarniki
909 m (2,982 ft)

Wołkowyja

Czarna Górna

Terka

Hulskie
846 m (2,775 ft)

San

Lutowiska

Wetlina

Trohaniec
939 m (3,080 ft)

Zatwarnica

Procisne

Kalnica

Smerek
1,222 m (4,009 ft)

Pszczeliny

Połonina
Wetlińska

Połonina
Caryńska

Bereżki

Tarnawa
Niżna

Bieszczady

National

Park

Ustrzyki Górne

Tarnica
1346 m (4,416 ft)

Wołosate

Kiczera Beniowska
861 m (2,825 ft)

The elongated **Połonina Wetlińska**
*ranges, with their picturesque alpine
meadows, are a characteristic feature
of the Bieszczady Mountains. The most
interesting, 1,250 m (4,100 ft) up, are
Caryńska and Wetlińska.*

Bieszczady National Park
*protects wild native forests, and
is part of the UNESCO East
Carpathian International
Biosphere Reserve. The main
tourist base is the small
village of Ustrzyki Górne.*

0 kilometres   10

0 miles   10

N
↑

A RIVER TOUR
THE DUNAJEC

Length 2.5 hours **Stopping-off points** Kąty is the starting point for river tours; tours end at Szczawnica, a health resort with shops and restaurants

The famously beautiful Pieniny Mountains has mountain gorges cut through by the Dunajec river. Rafting along the river here is one of the most popular attractions in the area. Start your journey by driving around dramatic castle ruins before heading to the river at Kąty for a guided tour. At first the rafts move calmly, but as the waterway starts to twist and turn, the water becomes rougher, a wild journey which lasts for about 8 km (5 miles). The trip ends in Szczawnica, a famed health resort.

MAŁOPOLSKA

● *The Dunajec*

Locator Map
For more detail see p168

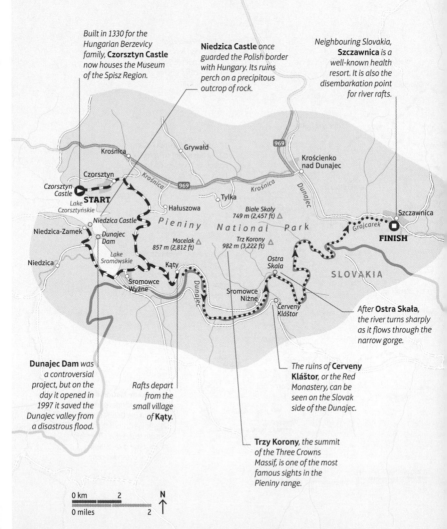

Built in 1330 for the Hungarian Berzevicy family, **Czorsztyn Castle** now houses the Museum of the Spisz Region.

Niedzica Castle once guarded the Polish border with Hungary. Its ruins perch on a precipitous outcrop of rock.

Neighbouring Slovakia, **Szczawnica** is a well-known health resort. It is also the disembarkation point for river rafts.

Dunajec Dam was a controversial project, but on the day it opened in 1997 it saved the Dunajec valley from a disastrous flood.

Rafts depart from the small village of Kąty.

The ruins of **Cerveny Kláštor**, or the Red Monastery, can be seen on the Slovak side of the Dunajec.

After **Ostra Skała**, the river turns sharply as it flows through the narrow gorge.

Trzy Korony, the summit of the Three Crowns Massif, is one of the most famous sights in the Pieniny range.

↑ Rafting along the Dunajec river as Trzy Korony looms above

WIELKOPOLSKA

Wielkopolska (Greater Poland) is the cradle of Polish statehood. It was here in the mid-10th century that the Polonians, the strongest of the Polish tribes, set up an enduring state. It was also here that the Piast dynasty, the first Polish dynasty, emerged to rule the country in the 10th century. At the time of the Thirty Years' War of 1618–48, the region was settled by large numbers of dissenting Germans, particularly from neighbouring Silesia. Their Protestant faith set them apart from the existing inhabitants, who were Catholics. During the Partitions of Poland, Wielkopolska was divided: the larger western part fell under Prussian rule, and the smaller eastern part came under Russian control. In the second half of the 19th century the Prussian part of Wielkopolska was subjected to repeated, but unsuccessful, campaigns of Germanization. At the end of 1918, an insurrection broke out here, resulting in almost the entire region being reincorporated into Poland. The years of Soviet domination that followed World War II saw economic hardship, although the local state-owned farms worked more efficiently than those in other parts of the country. Many of the region's palaces and country mansions also survived Communist rule in better condition than was the case elsewhere. Despite a turbulent history, Wielkopolska's unique identity and customs continue to live on in its towns and villages, and its capital, Poznań, is an ebullient cultural centre, abounding in historic buildings.

WIELKOPOLSKA

Must Sees
1 Raczyński Palace
2 Poznań
3 Łódź
4 Gniezno Cathedral
5 Wielkopolska's Romanesque Architecture

Experience More
6 Łagów
7 Leszno
8 Rydzyna
9 Kórnik
10 Ostrów Lednicki
11 Biskupin
12 Gołuchów
13 Kalisz
14 Antonin
15 Łęczyca
16 Zielona Góra

POMORSKIE

Grudziądz

Świecie

A1

5

16

22

A1

15

Bydgoszcz Ignacy Jan
Paderewski Airport
Bydgoszcz

Toruń

5

KUJAWSKO-
POMORSKIE

Żnin

Gniewkowo

Vistula

15

11 BISKUPIN

Inowrocław

WIELKOPOLSKA'S
ROMANESQUE ARCHITECTURE

5 Strzelno

Brzeşc
Kujawski

4 GNIEZNO
CATHEDRAL

Lubień
Kujawski

MAZOWIECKIE

Września

25

91

A1

60

92

Słupca

Kłodawa

A2

Konin

92

Kutno

92

MAZOVIA AND THE
LUBLIN REGION
p120

Koło

Rychwał

A2

ŁĘCZYCA 15 Tum

Ozorków

25

Turek

14

Pleszew

12

Warta

Zgierz

Skierniewice

12 GOŁUCHÓW

Aleksandrów
Łódzki

3 ŁÓDŹ

72

Rawa
Mazowiecka

13 KALISZ

Warta

Pabianice

A1

Ostrów
Wielkopolski

12

Sieradz

S8

Łask

Tuszyn

ŁÓDZKIE

14 ANTONIN

Złoczew

91

S8

Ostrzeszów

Piotrków Trybunalski

Opoczno

11 S8

Bełchatów

74

Kępno

45

74

Sulejów

74

Wieluń

91

Przedbórz

OPOLSKIE

Kluczbork

91

Radomsko

74

Częstochowa

MAŁOPOLSKA
p166

94

46

46

Lubliniec

ŚLĄSKIE

Visitors wandering through
the delightful French Gardens
facing the rear of the palace ↑

RACZYŃSKI PALACE

B4 Świątniki nad Wartą, Ul Arciszewskiego 2, Rogalin May & Jun: 9:30am–4pm Tue–Fri, 10am–5pm Sat & Sun; Jul & Aug: 10am–5pm Tue–Sun; Sep–Nov & mid-Jan–Apr: 9:30am–4pm Tue–Sun mnp.art.pl

Raczyński Palace, in the village of Rogalin, is one of the most magnificent buildings in Wielkopolska. This elegant palace is surrounded by elegant gardens and magical woodland.

A lovely tree-lined drive flanked by stables and carriages leads to the main palace building. It was begun in around 1770 for Kazimierz Raczyński, Palatine of Wielkopolska and Grand Marshal of the Crown. It was designed in the Baroque style, but during construction the architectural ornamentation was abandoned. The imposing main building, however, retains its late Baroque solidity. In 1782–3 curving colonnades were added on each side to give the building a more fashionable Neo-Classical character, complemented by annexes in the Palladian style. A drawing room and grand staircase designed by Jan Chrystian Kamsetzer were added in 1788–9. A nearby pavilion built in 1909–12 contains a collection of European and Polish paintings dating from about 1850 to the early 20th century, including works by Jacek Malczewski and Jan Matejko's *Joan of Arc*.

THE OAKS OF ROGALIN

Surrounding the palace, Rogalin park has one of the largest protected oakwoods in Europe, with some of its oak trees almost 600 years old. The three largest trees, named after the legendary Slavic brothers Lech, Czech and Rus, stand in a meadow off the park's main avenue. Rus's girth is an impressive 9.15 m (30 ft) around.

←
One of the elegant rooms found within the palace, restored following the damage caused by looting during World War II

→
The Classical St Marcellinus Church holds the Raczyński family mausoleum

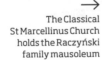

②

POZNAŃ

A B3 **X** Ul Bukowska 283/285 **R** Dworzec Główny
i Stary Rynek 59; cim.poznan.pl

Poznań, the capital of Wielkopolska and its largest city, has long been historically significant. In the 10th century it was the capital of the emerging Polish state and the seat of the first bishopric in Poland. Today a thriving commercial centre with major trade fairs, Poznań still has many historic buildings, particularly in the Old Town with its spectacular town hall. A visit to the late 19th-century quarter is also rewarding.

①

Old Market Square

The Old Market Square (Stary Rynek) is the bustling heart of the Old Town, dominated by the Renaissance town hall. It is surrounded by town houses with colourful façades, whose ground floors are mainly filled by restaurants and cafés, permanently busy from spring to autumn. The square is also a venue for cultural events.

Some of the houses in the Old Market Square were destroyed during the battles for Poznań near the end of World War II in 1945, and were rebuilt, but others escaped serious damage. They include Mielżyński Palace, which dates from 1796–8, and Działyński Palace, both in the Neo-Classical style.

The centrepiece of the Old Market Square is the Baroque Proserpine Fountain (1766), which depicts the abduction of the ancient Roman fertility goddess Proserpine by Pluto, ruler of the underworld.

②

Działyński Palace

A Stary Rynek 78 **W** bkpan.poznan.pl

This elegant Neo-Classical palace was built in the late 18th century for Władysław Gurowski, Grand Marshal of Lithuania, the façade topped with a sculpture of a large eagle and figures of Roman soldiers. Inside, the columned Red Room is particularly worth a look. The building is now used as a library, theatre, and concert hall.

③

Town Hall

A Stary Rynek 1
© Museum of the History of Poznań: 9am–3pm Tue–Thu, noon–9pm Fri, 11am–6pm Sat & Sun (free on Sat)
W mnp.art.pl

Poznań's town hall is one of the finest municipal buildings in Europe, built by the Italian architect Giovanni Battista di

> **INSIDER TIP**
> ### Old Town Art
> The notable street artist Noriaki is from Poznań, and his signature character can be spotted all over the Old Town. The best place to see his work is the corner of Szkolna and Paderewskiego streets.

←
The personality-filled multicoloured town houses in the Old Market Square

Quadro in 1550–60. It has three tiers of arcades, topped by a large clock tower. The façade is decorated with portraits of the kings of Poland. At noon each day two clockwork goats emerge from tower doors 12 times to butt heads. Inside, the ceiling of the lavish Great Hall is covered with intricate paintings.

④

Henryk Sienkiewicz Literary Museum

🏛 Stary Rynek 84 ☎ 61 852 2496 ⏰ 9am–5pm Tue-Fri, 9am–4pm Sat ✖ Sun

Occupying the 18th-century Quadro House on the north side of the Rynek, the Henryk Sienkiewicz Literary Museum (Muzeum Literackie im Henryka Sienkiewicza) is a

tribute to the Polish author who won the Noble Prize for Literature in 1905. Books and personal effects add up to an engaging portrait of the author. One display is devoted to the films inspired by his works, including the much-loved 1951 classic *Quo Vadis*.

⑤

Przemysław Castle

🏛 Góra Przemysła 1 ⏰ 9am–3pm Tue-Thu, noon–9pm Fri, 11am–6pm Sat & Sun (free on Sat) 🌐 mnp.art.pl

Little remains of the original castle built by Przemysław II in the 1200s. The reconstructed castle that now stands on the site houses the Museum of Applied Art, and its collection spans from the Middle Ages to the present, containing items from religious artifacts to television sets by Polish designers. A lift takes visitors to the tower, which provides a sweeping panorama of the city centre.

STAY

IBB Andersia
This centrally located hotel, in one of Poznań's tallest buildings, offers modern rooms with sweeping urban views. Facilities include a pool, spa facilities and gym.

🏛 Pl Andersa 3
🌐 andersiahotel.pl

ⓩⓩⓩ

Blow Up Hall 5050
The design of this cult hotel was partly inspired by pop art from the 1960s. Guests are given a smartphone which acts as both a room key and concierge.

🏛 Ul Kościuszki 42
🌐 blowuphall5050.com

ⓩⓩⓩ

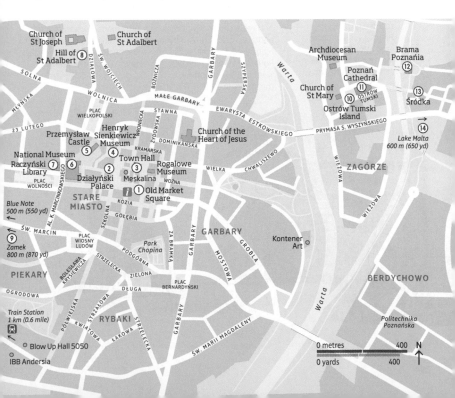

⑥

National Museum

🏛 Al Marcinkowskiego 9 🕐 9am-3pm Tue-Thu, noon-9pm Fri, 11am-6pm Sat & Sun (free on Sat) 🌐 mnp.art.pl

The National Museum is housed in what was originally the Neo-Renaissance Prussian Friedrich Museum. Its fine collection of Polish painting includes medieval art of the 12th to 16th centuries as well as work by artists in the Young Poland movement, such as Jacek Malczewski (1854–1929). In the European collection, the most outstanding pieces are by Dutch and Flemish painters, with Joos van Cleve and Quentin Massys among their number.

THE POZNAŃ TRADE FAIR

The trade fair area, in the city centre, has been the venue for the Poznań International Trade Fair since 1921. It takes place in June, when the city throngs with corporate visitors. The symbol of the Trade Fair is the steel needle atop the Upper Silesian Tower, built in 1955. When the tower itself was built in 1911, to a design by Hans Poelzig, it was considered by critics to be a masterpiece of modern concrete architecture.

⑦

Raczyński Library

🏛 Pl Wolności 19 🕐 9am-8pm Mon-Sat 🌐 bracz.edu.pl

The Raczyński Library's grand façade of columns sets it apart from any other building in Poznań. Although the library's architect is unknown, it is thought to have been built by the French architects and designers Charles Percier and Pierre Fontaine. The idea for a library was initiated by the visionary aristocrat Count Edward Raczyński in 1829, who wanted to turn Poznań into a "New Athens"; the library was to be a centre of culture and "a shrine of knowledge". A seated figure of Hygeia, the ancient Greek goddess of health, with the features of Konstancja z Potockich, Raczyński's wife, was installed in front of the library in 1906.

⑧

Hill of St Adalbert

The hill is said to be the spot where, 1,000 years ago, St Adalbert gave a sermon before setting off to evangelize the Prussians. There are now two churches on the summit: the Discalced Carmelites' Church of St Joseph, built by Cristoforo Bonadura the Elder and Jan Catenaci in 1658–67, and the small Gothic Church of St Adalbert. At the latter, the crypt contains the remains of great figures in the history of Wielkopolska, including Józef Wybicki (1747– 1822), who wrote the national anthem, and scientist Paweł Edmund Strzelecki (1797–1873). The ultramodern glass, concrete and stainless steel entrance to the crypt is a striking contrast to the rest of the building.

↑ The soaring steel Monument to the Victims of June 1956 in Zamek

⑨ Zamek

The city once had a ring of 19th-century fortifications, but when this was demolished the space was used for government buildings. Designed by the German town planner Josef Stübben, these were built in 1903–14 and today stand amid gardens, squares and avenues. Dominating the scene is the Kaiserhaus, built for Kaiser Wilhelm II in the 1900s. The castle was renovated by the Germans during World War II; little survives of its original splendour apart from. Today, the structure houses a cultural centre.

In Plac Mickiewicza, next to the castle, stands the moving Monument to the Victims of June 1956. Unveiled in 1981, it commemorates the violent suppression of the workers' uprising in Poznań in 1956.

←

People enjoying the courtyard outside the National Museum

⑩ Ostrów Tumski

Ostrów Tumski (the Island of Tumski), with its many notable buildings, is the oldest part of Poznań. The area is dominated by the Gothic towers of the cathedral, which contains many fine works of art. Nearby, the small Gothic Church of St Mary (Kościół halowy NMP) was built in the years 1431–48 for Bishop Andrzej Bniński by Hanusz Prusz, a pupil of the notable late medieval architect Heinrich Brunsberg.

In the gardens on the other side of Ulica ks. l. Posadzego stand a number of canons' and vicars' houses which are charming in appearance – if a little neglected. One of these houses contains the superb collections of the **Archdiocesan Museum**. Among exquisite hoards of religious art on display at this small museum, there are medieval paintings and sculptures, along with pieces of Gothic embroidery and some fine kontusz sashes.

DRINK

Kontener Art
Set in a row of former freight containers by the banks of the Warta river, this summer-season bar hosts live gigs, DJs and art events. An inner courtyard is strewn with deckchairs and filled with sand.

🅐 Ul Ewangelicka
🆆 kontenerart.pl

Blue Note
Located inside the Zamek cultural centre, Blue Note is one of Poland's foremost jazz venues, hosting top-notch concerts by local and international guests. It also serves as an intimate and mellow bar on non-gig nights.

🅐 Ul Kościuszki 76/78
🆆 bluenote.poznan.pl

Meskalina
Situated in a main square alleyway, this popular and bohemian venue serves boutique beers and inexpensive snacks. It's also one of the best alternative rock venues in town.

🅐 Stary Rynek 6
🆆 meskalina.com

The most outstanding pieces include *Madonna of Ołobok*, a Romanesque-Gothic statue dating from 1310–29.

Nearby, the late Gothic Psalter (or Psalm singer's house), which was built in around 1520, has fine stepped and recessed gables.

Archdiocesan Museum
🅐 Ul Lubrańskiego 1
🕐 10am–5pm Tue–Fri, 9am–3pm Sat 🔒 Public hols
🆆 muzeum.poznan.pl

⑪
POZNAŃ CATHEDRAL

🏠 Ul Ostrów Tumski 17 🕐 Mid-Mar–mid-Nov: 9am–5pm Mon–Fri;
mid-Nov–mid-Mar: 9am–4pm Mon–Fri 🚫 Closed during mass, services
and concerts 🌐 katedra.archpoznan.pl

The double towers of this spectacular Gothic edifice rise high over Ostrów
Tumski (Cathedral Island). Rebuilt and remodelled over hundreds of years,
the cathedral is Poznan's oldest historical monument.

The first church on this site, a pre-Romanesque
basilica, was built in 966, shortly after Poland
adopted Christianity; the country's first rulers
were buried there. In 1034–8 the basilica was
destroyed during pagan uprisings and the
campaign of the Czech prince Brzetysław.
Completely rebuilt in the Romanesque
style, it was later remodelled in Gothic
and Baroque fashion during the 14th
and 15th centuries. After suffering
war damage, it was restored to its
earlier Gothic form. It is home to
some beautifully sculpted tombs.

Main entrance

↑ The impressive double
towers of Poznań's
Gothic Cathedral

↑ The gilded interior of the
Golden Chapel, home to the
tombs of Poland's first kings

↑ The magnificent Poznań
Cathedral, found on
Ostrów Tumski island

↑ One of the fascinating interactive multimedia displays in Brama Poznania

The late Gothic polyptych on the high altar was brought to the cathedral in 1952.

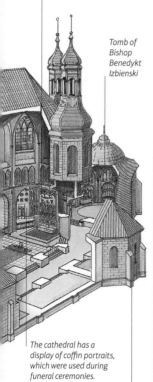

Tomb of Bishop Benedykt Izbieński

The cathedral has a display of coffin portraits, which were used during funeral ceremonies.

The Golden Chapel, built in 1834–41, contains the tombs of two of Poland's first rulers, Mieszko I and Bolesław the Brave.

⑫ ⑬

Brama Poznania

🏛 Gdanska 2 🕐 9am-6pm Tue-Fri, 10am-7pm Sat & Sun 🌐 bramapoznania.pl

Housed in a cube-like concrete building, just across the water from Ostrów Tumski, this stunning contemporary museum opened in 2013. It narrates the history of Ostrów Tumski through an engaging series of themed multimedia displays that are more like art installations than traditional museum exhibits.

⑬

Śródka

🚊 3, 4, 8, 17

Situated on the east bank of the Warta River, just beyond Ostrów Tumski, the compact suburb of Śródka was a separate town until it became part of Poznań in 1800. Of all the city's neighbourhoods it has most retained a small-town feel, with a knot of narrow streets arranged around a small market square. Dominating one side of the square is the celebrated

"Śródka Story" (Opowieść śródecka). Designed by local artist Radosław Barek in 2015, this colourful mural provides some idea of what the Śródka district looked like in the past. Today the area is famed for its pretty cafés and bistros.

⑭

Lake Malta

🚊 3, 4, 8, 17

Southeast of Śródka is Lake Malta (Jezioro Maltańskie), a 2-km- (1.2-mile-) long reservoir that is the city's main area for outdoor recreation. It gets its name from the Knights of Malta, the religious-military order once based at the Church of St John of Jerusalem Outside the Walls (Kościół pw. św. Jana Jerozolimskiego za Murami), a handsome red-brick structure which still stands near the lake's north-western shoulder. Surrounded by a foot- and cycle-path, and with a narrow-gauge railway along its northern shore, the lake is popular year-round. The beach on its southern shore, backed by open-air cafes and restaurants, is particularly busy in summer.

3

ŁÓDŹ

D4 **Pl Sałacińskiego** **Al Włókniarzy 227**
Ul Piotrkowska 28; cit.lodz.pl

The centre of Polish textile production, Łódź developed at an astonishing rate during the Industrial Revolution. As documented in *The Promised Land* (1899) by Nobel Prize-winning author Władysław Reymont, it became a place of great contrasts, with vast wealth existing alongside abject poverty. This contrast is still evident today in Łódź's architecture; factories and mansions sit beside ramshackle houses of factory workers.

1

Ulica Piotrkowska

The city's main thoroughfare is Ulica Piotrkowska, Poland's longest pedestrianized street, lined with restaurants, shops, cafés and banks. The section most worth exploring extends from Plac Wolności to Aleje Piłudskiego. Outside the Hotel Grand at Piotrkowska 72, a line of stars is embedded in the pavement in honour of Andrzej Wajda and other film directors associated with the Łódź Film School. Arranged at irregular intervals along the street are statues commemorating other famous people from the city, including poet Julian Tuwim, pianist Artur Rubinstein and author Władysław Reymont.

Behind the town houses are brick factory buildings, many of them now converted into stores. A particularly great example is the factory at Piotrkowska 137/139, which was built in 1907 for the cotton manufacturer Juliusz Kindermann by the architect Gustav Landau-Gutenteger. It features a gold mosaic frieze depicting an allegory of trade. In Plac Wolności there is a monument to hero Tadeusz Kościuszko from 1930, rebuilt after its destruction in 1939 and now a favourite meeting place for the city's youth.

2

EC1 Science and Technology Centre

Ul Targowa 1/3 **9am-7pm Tue-Fri, 10am-8pm Sat & Sun** **ec1lodz.pl**

Occupying the cavernous halls of a pre-World War I power station, the EC1 Science and Technology Centre (Centrum Nauki i Techniki) has multi-media and hands-on displays relating to life, the universe and everything inbetween. As well as science-related temporary exhibitions there is also a planetarium and a centre devoted to comic strips and animated films.

3

Central Museum of Textiles

Ul Piotrkowska 282 **9am-5pm Tue-Wed & Sun, 12-7pm Thu-Sat** **Mon** **cmwl.pl**

Located in the so-called White Factory (Biała Fabryka), which was opened by industrialist Ludwik Geyer in 1838, the Central Museum of Textiles (Centralne Muzeum Włókiennictwa) has a well-presented history of the Łódź

The EC1 Science and Technology Centre, in an old power station

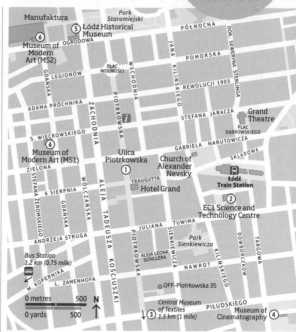

weaving industry. Working machines and displays on the manufacturing process are shown alongside material on fashion and design.

---

④

Museum of Cinematography

◻ Pl Zwycięstwa 1
🕙 10am-5pm Tue, 9am-4pm Wed & Fri, 11am-6pm Thu, Sat & Sun (free on Tue)
🌐 kinomuzeum.pl

Situated in the eclectic palace of textile manufacturer Karol Scheibler, this museum is dedicated to Polish cinema, with a rich collection of films and film posters from the earliest days of cinematography to modern times. It also documents the works of Łódź's renowned film school, whose graduates include the directors Roman Polański and the much-praised cameraman

---

DRINK

OFF Piotrkowska 35
One of the most exciting examples of post-industrial regeneration in Łódź is found at Piotrkowska 138/140, where the Ramisch cotton factory has been transformed into a nightlife quarter of bars and restaurants. It's particularly lively on summer evenings when the courtyard fills with merrymakers.

◻ Piotrkowska 138/140
🌐 offpiotrkowska.com

Witold Sobociński. The palace is fascinating to explore, with numerous decadent rooms.

---

⑤

Łódź Historical Museum

◻ Ul Ogrodowa 15 🕙 10am-4pm Tue-Thu, noon-6pm Fri-Sun 🌐 muzeum-lodz.pl

This museum is located in Poznański Palace beside a group of factory buildings. This eccentric palace, with twin cupolas, was built in stages from 1888 onwards, and has a grand staircase, a series of private apartments, beautifully restored reception rooms, and belle époque furniture. The museum is dedicated to life in the city from the end of the 19th century to the start of World War II, and has a number of re-created rooms. There are also exhibits associated with the pianists Władysław Kędra and Artur Rubinstein, who were both born in Łódź.

Alongside the palace stands a former spinning mill, a vast Neo-Renaissance edifice designed by Hilary Majewski in 1876.

---

⑥

Museum of Modern Art

◻ MS1: Ul Więckowskiego 36; MS2: Ul Ogrodowa 19
🕙 10am-6pm Tue, 11am-7pm Wed-Sun (free Thu)
🌐 msl.org.pl

The Museum of Modern Art has two branches, MS1 and MS2. The first is housed in another of Izrael Poznański's palaces, this one built in imitation of a Florentine Renaissance palazzo. This is usually used for high-profile temporary exhibitions.

MS2 is in part of the restored factory complex, now known as Manufaktura, and contains one of Poland's best collection of modern art, featuring the likes of Hans Arp and Piet Mondrian.

④ ⟨⟩ Ⓜ 🏛

GNIEZNO CATHEDRAL

🅐 C3 🏛 Ul Wzgórze Lecha Gniezno 🚆🚌 🕐 May-Oct: 9am-5pm Mon-Sat;
Nov-Apr: 9am-4pm Mon-Sat 🚫 Closed during services, noon-1pm 🌐 gniezno.eu

This imposing Gothic cathedral occupies a special place in the country's history – from 1025 to the 14th century Poland's first royal rulers were crowned here. The cathedral contains several elaborate tombs, a chapel decorated with beautiful Baroque paintings and a pair of exquisite 12th-century bronze doors.

This 14th-century cathedral (Archikatedra Wniebowzięcia NMP) stands on the site of two earlier churches, a 10th-century pre-Romanesque church and a mid-11th-century Romanesque church. Gniezno was the capital of Poland when the first church was built, and Princess Dąbrówka was buried here in 977. The site's importance increased further in 997 when the relics of St Adalbert were laid here; the cathedral's bronze doors depict scenes from his life.

The Baroque cupolas are 20th-century reconstructions of the 1779 originals.

↑ The red-brick exterior of the cathedral

↑ The cathedral's elegant nave, with the Shrine of St Adalbert

ST ADALBERT

St Adalbert (St Wojciech in Polish) was a bishop from Prague. In 977, on Bolesław the Brave's orders, he left Poland for the heathen lands of Prussia, where he was martyred for trying to convert the locals to Christianity. Bolesław bought the saint's body from the Prussians, giving them in return its weight in gold, and laid the remains in Gniezno. Pope Sylvester II acknowledged the bishop's martyrdom and canonized him.

Gniezno's impressive ↑ cathedral, with its double towers

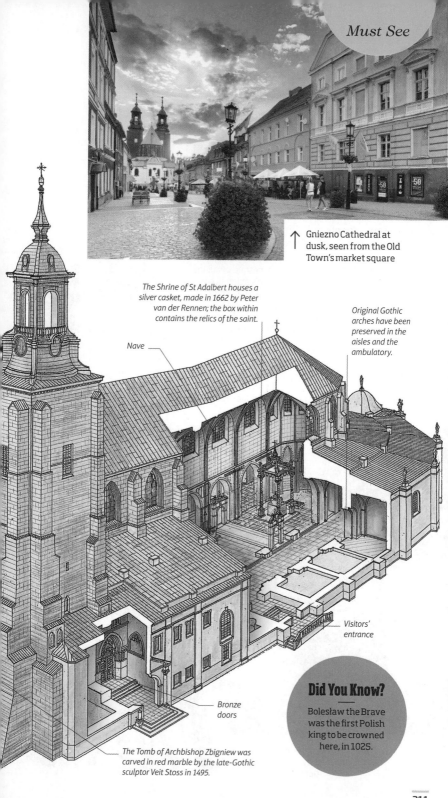

↑ Gniezno Cathedral at dusk, seen from the Old Town's market square

The Shrine of St Adalbert houses a silver casket, made in 1662 by Peter van der Rennen; the box within contains the relics of the saint.

Original Gothic arches have been preserved in the aisles and the ambulatory.

Nave

Visitors' entrance

Did You Know?

Bolesław the Brave was the first Polish king to be crowned here, in 1025.

Bronze doors

The Tomb of Archbishop Zbigniew was carved in red marble by the late-Gothic sculptor Veit Stoss in 1495.

211

5

WIELKOPOLSKA'S ROMANESQUE ARCHITECTURE

🅐C3 🔒 Gniezno: Rynek 14, 61 428 4100; Inowrocław: Ul Królowej Jadwigi 3, www.inowroclaw.home.pl

The birthplace of the Polish nation, Wielkopolska's verdant landscape is peppered with a wonderful array of Romanesque buildings, from pretty churches to legendary towers.

A tour of pre-Romanesque and Romanesque buildings in Wielkopolska might start at Gniezno's magnificent cathedral *(p210)*, and then take in the elegant churches in both Trzemeszno and Mogilno. The finest Romanesque architecture in Poland is to be found in Strzelno, including the Rotunda of St Procopius and the Church of the Holy Trinity, a pair of remarkable Romanesque pillars found within its interior. Another town of interest is Kruszwica, home to the legendary "Mouse Tower" where King Popiel got his come-uppance. There's also the beautiful 13th-century Church of Our Lady in the resort town of Inowrocław.

The Romanesque "Mouse Tower", overlooking Lake Gopło in Kruszwica ↑

① The picturesque Church of the Holy Trinity in Strzelno is home to 12th-century carvings depicting personifications of the virtues and vices of Christian tradition.

② The historic Church of Our Lady in Inowrocław was constructed on the orders of the town's dukes.

③ The dramatic Rotunda of St Procopius, dating from the turn of the 13th century, is found in the pretty town of Strzelno.

Did You Know?

The "Mouse Tower" was in fact built nearly 500 years after King Popiel's death.

THE LEGEND OF KING POPIEL

Ruling over the Polonians during the 9th century, King Popiel was feared by his people due to the atrocities he committed, so they decided to depose him. Popiel fled to his tower but his rebellious subjects follwed him, turned into mice and then devoured him.

EXPERIENCE MORE

⑥ Łagów

 ▲A3 🚌🚇 **ℹ** www.lagow.pl

Pretty Łagów is situated in woodland between lakes Łagów and Ciecz. The tower of its 14th-century castle, built by the Knights Hospitallers, affords a magnificent view, as does the 19th-century tower of the Neo-Classical Church of St John the Baptist (Kościoł św. Jan Chrzciciela), dating from 1726. Around the town are also remains of the 15th-century town walls.

Nearby Łagów Nature Park contains protected areas of woodland and wild flowers. About 16 km (10 miles) east of the town are the remains of fortifications erected by the Germans just before World War II. The surviving corridors and bunkers are now inhabited by thousands of bats.

⑦ Leszno

 ▲B4 🚌🚇 **ℹ** Ul Słowiańska 24; www.leszno.pl

In the 17th century Leszno gave asylum to the religious dissidents fleeing the ravages of the Thirty Years' War (1618–48) in Silesia. Apart from Lutheran Protestants, they included the Bohemian Brethren, who founded the Arian Academy that gained renown across Europe. One of its members was Jan Amos Komeński (Commenius), a prominent philosopher of the Reformation.

The town burned in 1707, so none of its buildings predate the 18th century. The Baroque town hall was built just after the fire to Pompeo Ferrari's designs. Found beside the market square is the distinctive Baroque parish church built by Jan Catenaci at the turn of the 18th century. It has a delightful façade, with Baroque altars and tombs inside. Ferrari also designed the former Lutheran Church of the Holy Cross (Kościoł luterański św. Krzyża), which was built after 1707.

The **Regional Museum**'s finest collection is in the Polish Portrait Gallery, and features 18th-century coffin portraits of the Bohemian Brethren. Also part of the museum is an art gallery housed in a former synagogue on Ulica Narutowicza 31, which celebrates the heritage of Leszno's Jewish population.

 HIDDEN GEM
Lush Landscape

Wielkopolska National Park (Wielkopolski Park Narodowy) offers a compact but varied landscape of low hills, lakes and forest, with well-marked trails.

Regional Museum

 📍 Pl Metziga 17 🕐 9am–4:30pm Tue, 9am–2:30pm Wed–Fri, 10am–2pm Sat, 2pm–6pm Sun (free on Tue) 🌐 muzeum.leszno.pl

⑧ Rydzyna

▲B4 🚇🚉 **ℹ** www.rydzyna.pl

This small town is dominated by a palace, built in the 15th century. Its present late Baroque appearance dates from after 1737; further building work was carried out by Karl Martin Frantz in 1742, when paintings by Polish painter Wilhelm Neunhertz were added to the ballroom ceiling. These were added in honour of the palace's owner, Prince Józef A Sułkowski. A member of a noble family of relatively low rank, he was catapulted to success at the court of August III, but fell from the king's favour in 1738 and was replaced by Henryk Brühl. The ballroom was destroyed by fire in 1945.

The palace remained in the possession of the Sułkowskis into the early 20th century, when it was sold to Prussian rulers. It is now a hotel. Rydzna's Market Square is

←

Pedalo boats on peaceful Lake Łagów, surrounded by verdant woodland

Neo-Gothic Kórnik Castle in beautifully landscaped grounds ↑

lined with Baroque houses, the town hall and two Baroque churches: the Parish Church of St Stanisław (Kościoł św. Stanisława) designed by Karl Martin Frantz and Ignacy Graff in 1746–51, and the Protestant church, dating from 1779–83, also by Graff.

Kórnik

⚠C4 🏛🚌 **ℹwww. kornik.pl**

This pretty town is home to the truly picturesque **Kórnik Castle**, set on an island and surrounded by a landscaped park. Its present appearance dates from the 19th century, when it was rebuilt in the English Neo-Gothic style by Karl Friedrich Schinkel.

The castle's original interior survives: the Moorish Hall is decorated in the style of Spain's Alhambra Palace and the dining room ceiling is covered with the coats of arms of all the Polish knights who fought at the Battle of Grunwald (1410). A Turkish inscription on the ceiling of one hall honours Turkey's refusal to recognize the Partitions of Poland. The castle also has a collection of

18th- and 19th-century porcelain, and became the repository of art treasures once kept at Czartoryski Palace in Puławy (p138). To acquire the library at Puławy, Tytus Działyński persuaded his son Jan to marry Izabella, the heiress to the Czartoryski fortune. The castle has a library and a museum which includes a display of 16th- to 19th-century Polish and foreign paintings, as well as sculpture, drawings and an intriguing array of militaria, including a complete suit of armour. The Kórnik Library contains manuscripts by Polish poets and a substantial collection of prints and maps. In the park, an arboretum has many rare species of trees.

Several holiday villages are scattered along the shores of lakes Kórnik and Bnin, to the south of Kórnik. The best known is Zaniemyśl which has a bathing beach and a holiday camp. Edward Island has a 19th-century pavilion in the style of a Swiss chalet.

Kórnik Castle

🏰 Ul Zamkowa 5 ☎ 61 817 00 81 🕐 Mar, Apr & Oct–mid-Dec: 10am–4pm Tue–Sun; May–Sep: 10am–5pm Tue–Sun 🚫 Pub hols, Easter, 1 Sep, mid-Dec–Feb

Ostrów Lednicki

⚠C3 🏛🚌 **🕐1 Nov–14 Apr**

This small island in Lake Lednickie has a special religious significance as the place where Poland is believed to have officially adopted Christianity.

During the 10th century a fortified town stood on the island, surrounded by earth ramparts which enclosed the earliest known Christian buildings in Poland. In the 19th century, archaeologists uncovered the foundations of a rotunda, a rectangular hall identified as a baptistery and palace, and a church. The town is assumed to have been the seat of the Piasts. The baptism of Poland, by which the country adopted Christianity, is believed to have taken place in this baptistery in 966. The island, as a result, has now become the **Museum of the First Piasts**, where you can view the archaeological findings.

Museum of the First Piasts

♿ 🏰 Lednogóra 🕐 Hours vary, check website 🚫 Mon & Oct–mid-Apr 🌐 lednicamuzeum.pl

←
The elegant French Renaissance-style Gołuchów castle

11 Biskupin

C3 9am-4pm daily (to 5pm Apr & Oct, to 6pm May-Sep) 1 Jan, Easter, Sun, 1 Nov, 25 Dec biskupin.pl

Found on an island in Lake Biskupinskie, this archaeological site showcases the remains of a 2,500-year-old Iron Age fortified settlement. Built entirely of wood, this settlement was inhabited for about 150 years by people of the Lusatian culture. It was surrounded by a stockade and a wall of earth and wood 6 m (18 ft) high. Access was over a bridge and through a gateway. More than 100 houses were built in 13 terraces, and the streets were paved with wood.

When the water level rose, the lake flooded the houses and covered the settlement in silt, so the site was abandoned. Rediscovered in 1934 by a local teacher, Walenty Szwajcer, it is the earliest known settlement in Poland and one of Europe's most interesting prehistoric sites. Some of the buildings have been reconstructed and there are pens with small ponies, goats and sheep similar to those that the original inhabitants would have kept.

The annual Archaeology Gala features exhibitions and workshops in which artifacts are made according to prehistoric methods.

12 Gołuchów

C4 en.goluchow.pl

The castle here looks as if it belongs in the Loire Valley. Although built in the mid-16th to 17th centuries, its present exterior, ordered by Izabella Czartoryska and her husband, Jan Działyński, dates from 1872–85. Izabella, educated in France, wished to turn the residence into a "paradise on earth" and plans were made in 1871 by French architect Eugène Viollet-le-Duc. The **Castle Museum** contains European and Oriental works of art from the Działyński family's collection.

Found in Dobryczy, 23 km (14 miles) west of Gołuchów, is the Neo-Classical residence of Augustyn Gorzeński, a freemason, built in 1798–9.

Castle Museum

Ul Działyńskich 2 May-Sep: 10am-4pm Tue-Sat, 10am-6pm Sun; Oct-Apr: 9am-4pm Tue-Fri, 10am-4pm Sat & Sun (tours free on Tue) mnp.art.pl

13 Kalisz

C4 Ul Zamkowa www.cit.kalisz.pl

Kalisz, a settlement on the amber route between the Baltic Sea and Rome, has ancient origins. Although mentioned as Calisia by Ptolemy in his *Geography* of AD 142–7, a town was not established here until the 13th century, and did not really develop until the 15th century, when it became a provincial capital. During the Partitions of Poland, this was the furthest outpost of the Russian Empire. In 1914, after the start of World War I, the town was bombarded by the Prussian artillery. Rebuilding began in 1917, and today's city centre, the town hall and the Bogusławski Theatre around the Market Square date from that time. Earlier buildings that survive include the Gothic Cathedral of St Nicholas (Katedra św. Mikołaja), and the late Baroque Church of the Assumption (Kościół Wniebowzięcia NMP). The Bernadine monasteries and the late Renaissance Church of the Annunciation (Kościół Nawiedzenia NMP) are also worth a visit.

14 Antonin

C4

When Duke Antoni Radziwiłł asked Karl Friedrich Schinkel to build him a hunting lodge, it was an unusual commission for an architect used to city planning. The small larchwood building, dating from 1822–4, has a cruciform plan and a central octagonal hall which is surrounded by galleries supported by a large central pillar. It was here that, in 1827, Chopin taught Wanda,

→
The ornate interior of the Church of the Assumption, Kalisz

Duke Radziwiłł's daughter, and fell in love with her. The piano on which the great composer played was used for firewood by Red Army soldiers billeted in the lodge. Now a hotel, the lodge is also a venue for concerts and festivals in honour of Chopin.

The village of Bralin, 36 km (22 miles) to the north, has a wooden church, Na Pólku, dating from 1711.

Łęczyca

 D4 🚌🚆

This royal castle was built in 1357 by Kazimierz the Great; it was the third to be raised in the town. Little is known of the first; the second was the seat of rulers of another duchy.

The castle, with its brick tower, served as a jail for imprisoned aristocrats. The **Regional Museum** within it contains artifacts from prehistoric times to the present day. The main attraction is the unusual exhibition dedicated to the devil Boruta, legendary guardian of the treasure hidden in the castle's cellar.

In Tum, 3 km (2 miles) from Łęczyca, there is a splendidly preserved Romanesque church with a remarkable 12th-century fresco of *Christ in Glory*.

Regional Museum
⊛⊛⊛ 🚪 Ul Zamkowa 1
🕐 Hours vary, check website
🚫 Pub hols 🖥 muzeum leczyca.pl

---

16 Zielona Góra

🅰 A4 🚌 ℹ Stary Rynek 1; www.cit.zielona-gora.pl

Southwestern Wielkopolska's main city, Zielona Góra was little damaged in World War II and retains a well-preserved 19th-century centre. The city lies at the heart of a major wine-producing region, celebrated by displays in the **Lubuskie Regional Museum** (Muzeum Ziemi Lubuskiej). Occupying a low hill just southeast of the centre, the **Wine Park** (Park Winny) is cloaked in vineyards. At the summit of the hill is a **Palm House** (Palmiarnia) containing exotic plants, an aquarium

 INSIDER TIP
Ride the Rails

Notheast of Zielona Góra, lakeside Wolsztyn is the last place in Europe with working steam locomotives. Regular services still run, with extra routes available on summer weekends.

and good views of the city from its gallery. Also worth visiting is the half-timbered Church of Our Lady of Częstochowa (Kościół Matki Boskiej Częstochowskiej), with a galleried interior rich in wood-carved features.

Lubuskie Regional Museum
⊛ 🚪 Al Niepodleglosci 15
🕐 11am-5pm Wed-Fri, 10am-3pm Sat, 10am-4pm Sun
🖥 zl.zgora.pl

Wine Park
⊛⊛⊛ 🚪 Ul Zamkowa 1
🕐 May-Sep: 10am-5pm Tue-Sun (from 11am Sat & Sun)

Palm House
⊛ 🚪 Ul Wroclawska 12
🕐 10am-11pm daily

SILESIA

The stormy history of Silesia (Śląsk) and the great variety of cultural influences that have flourished here have given this region a rich heritage. Initially held by the Bohemian crown, it passed into Polish control around 990. When Poland was split into principalities, Silesia began to gain independence, yet it returned to Bohemian rule in the 14th century. During the Reformation, many of its inhabitants were converted to Lutheranism. The Thirty Years' War (1618– 48) inflicted devastation on Silesia, bringing in its wake the repression of Protestantism. Seized by Prussia in 1742, it wasn't until after 1945 that nearly all of historical Silesia joined Poland, and its German population was deported. Poles who had been resettled from the country's eastern provinces (which had been annexed by the Soviet Union) took their place. Silesia remains today an utterly enchanting region, not only for the breathtaking beauty of its soaring mountain landscapes but also for its outstanding architecture, including medieval castles and grand Renaissance manor houses.

SILESIA

Must Sees
1. Wrocław
2. Karkonosze Mountains
3. Kłodzko Valley

Experience More
4. Lubiąż Abbey
5. Bolesławiec
6. Legnica
7. Legnickie Pole
8. Żagań
9. Lwówek Śląski
10. Krzeszów
11. Jelenia Góra
12. Jawor
13. Wałbrzych
14. Bolków
15. Riese Underground Complex
16. Świdnica
17. Trzebnica
18. Otmuchów
19. Oleśnica
20. Henryków
21. Paczków
22. Góra Świętej Anny
23. Nysa
24. Opole
25. Cieszyn
26. Pszczyna
27. Katowice
28. Gliwice
29. Chorzów
30. Brzeg

The cheery and colourful rooftops of Wrocław's reconstructed Old Town ↑

①

WROCŁAW

⊙ B5 **i** Przejście Żelaźnicze 1; www.visitwroclaw.eu

This cosmopolitan city bears the stamp of several cultures. Founded by a Czech duke in the 10th century, a Polish bishopric was established here in the 19th century. It then became the capital of the duchy of the Silesian Piasts, before coming under Czech rule in 1335. In 1526, it was incorporated into the Habsburg Empire, and in 1741 was transferred to Prussian rule. Although the destruction of World War II left most of the city in ruins, reconstruction has been successful.

①

Wrocław University

🏛 Pl Uniwersytecki 1
🕐 Aula Leopoldina: 10am-4pm Mon, Tue & Thu, 10am-5pm Fri-Sun 🖥 uni.wroc.pl

Established as an academy by Emperor Leopold I in 1702, the university was granted its current status in 1811. Many of its alumni have gained renown. They include nine Nobel laureates, among them the nuclear physicist Max Born (1882–1970), who won for physics in 1954.

Designed by Tausch, an Italian architect and painter, the centrepiece of this imposing Baroque building is the Aula Leopoldina, the assembly hall, of 1728–32. It is adorned with frescoes by Christopha Handk and figural sculptures by Franz Joseph Mangoldt. The hall is currently closed for renovation.

②

Church of the Holy Name of Jesus

🏛 Pl Uniwersytecki 1 📞 71 344 94 23 🕐 Mar-Jun, Sep & Oct: 11am-3:30pm; Jul & Aug: 10:30am-5:30pm 🚫 Closed during services

This beautiful church (Kościół Najświętszego Imienia Jezus),

erected for the Jesuits in 1689–98, is an example of Silesian Baroque church architecture. The fine interior was built in 1722–34 by Tausch and the vaulting decorated by Viennese artist Rottmayer in 1704–6.

③ Cathedral of St Mary Magdalene

Ul Szewska 10 · 71 344 19 04 · 9am–noon & 4–6pm daily

The great Gothic Cathedral of St Mary Magdalene (Katedra św Marii Magdaleny) was gradually erected between about 1330 and the mid-15th century, incorporating the walls of a 13th-century church that had previously stood on the site. Inside the basilica is a Renaissance pulpit dating from 1579–81 by Friedrich Gross, as well as a Gothic stone tabernacle and tombstones of various periods. The portal on the north side is a very fine example of late-12th-century Romanesque sculpture. It was taken from a demolished Benedictine monastery in Olbina and added in 1546. The spectacular tympanum, depicting the Dormition of the Virgin, is now found on display in the National Museum.

④ National Forum of Music

Pl Wolności · nfm.wroclaw.pl

The National Forum of Music (Narodowe Forum Muzyki or NFM) was built in 2015 to serve as a state-of-the-art concert hall for the city's prestigious Philharmonic Orchestra. Without a doubt a scene-stealing building, its asymmetrical brown-grey façade is designed to look like the body of an enormous stringed instrument. It rises above the very elegant Plac Wolności, a large plaza where patches of glass paving reveal medieval ruins below. Concerts regularly take place within the hall.

WROCŁAW'S DWARVES

Scattered throughout the city, dwarf statuettes, represent one of Wrocław's more unusual civic symbols. The city's adoption of the dwarf is largely in tribute to the 1980s anti-Communist group Orange Alternative (Pomorańczowa Alternatywa), who used a stencilled graffiti image of a dwarf as their symbol. As these statuettes grow in number, their original subversive focus has been replaced by a simple desire to bring cheer to the streets; Images of these folk legends are also now found on souvenirs.

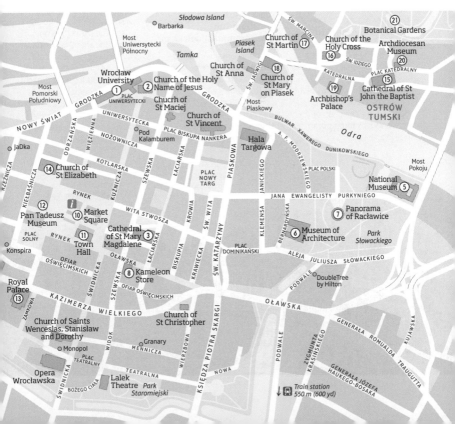

INSIDER TIP
Wrocław Craft

Producing craft beer ever since the Middle Ages, Wrocław remains one of the best cities in Poland for beer. Spiż (*www.spiz.pl*), beneath the town hall, was one of the first boutique breweries set up in post-Communist Poland.

National Museum

🏛 Pl Powstańców Warszawy 5 🕐 Apr-Sep: 10am-5pm Tue-Fri, 10am-6pm Sat & Sun; Oct-Mar: 10am-4pm Tue-Fri, 10am-5pm Sat & Sun 🌐 mnwr.art.pl

The ground floor of this fascinating museum contains a variety of examples of Silesian and Gothic art, including the tombstone of Henry IV, the Good, dating from 1300. The first floor has a collection of delightful 16th- and 17th-century paintings, including works by the Silesian artist Michael Willmann (1630–1706) and wooden sculptures by Thomas Weissfeldt (1630–1712). The second floor is devoted to a selection of artworks by contemporary Polish artists.

Museum of Architecture

🏛 Ul Bernardyńska 5 🕐 11am-5pm Tue, Fri-Sun, 10am-4pm Wed, noon-7pm Thu 🌐 ma.wroc.pl

This impressive group of monastic buildings, previously a Benedictine Church and Monastery (Kościół i Klasztor pobernardyński) that was constructed in 1463–1502, now houses Poland's only Museum of Architecture. The monastery is of interest for its late Gothic cloisters and the Church of St Bernard of Siena, a towering Gothic basilica with a typically Baroque gable.

Panorama of Racławice

🏛 Ul Purkyniego 11 🕐 Apr-Oct: 8am-7pm daily; Nov-Mar: 9am-4:30pm Tue-Fri (to 6:30pm Sat, to 5:30pm Sun) 🌐 panoramaraclawicka.pl

The panorama depicts the Battle of Racławice of 4 April 1794, when the Poles defeated the Russians. At 114 m (374 ft) long and 15 m (46 ft) high, it took artists Jan Styka and Wojciech Kossak nine months to paint. Unveiled in 1894 in Lviv, in Ukraine, it was brought to Poland in 1946 and put on display in Wrocław in 1985.

⑧

Kameleon Store

🏛 Ul Szewska 6

This store (Dom Handlowy Kameleon) is an unusual building on the corner of Ulica Szewska and Ulica Oławska. Its semicircular bay, formed of rows of windows, juts out dramatically. It was built as a retail store for Rudolf Petersdorf in 1927–8.

⑨

White Stork Synagogue

🏛 Ul Włodkowica 9 🕐 10am-5pm Mon-Thu, 10am-4pm Fri, 11am-4pm Sun 🌐 wroclaw.jewish.org.pl

Located in a courtyard that was once the heart of the city's Jewish quarter, the White Stork Synagogue (Synagoga pod Białym Bocianem) is Wrocław's only surviving Jewish house of prayer. Its interior decoration, destroyed during Kristallnacht in 1938, has been beautifully restored. The synagogue now contains a display on Jewish history and is once again used for religious services.

Wrocław's picturesque market square, lined with colourful houses ↑

 ⑩
Market Square

Rynek

Wrocław's Market Square is the second largest in Poland, after that of Kraków. In the centre stands the magnificent town hall; the houses around the square date from the Renaissance to the 20th century. The most attractive side of the square is the west, featuring the late Baroque House of the Golden Sun at No 6, built in 1727 by Johann Lucas von Hildebrandt, and the House of the Seven Electors, its paintwork dating from 1672.

⑪
Town Hall

Ul Sukiennice 14/15 Museum of Bourgeois Art: 10am–5pm Wed–Sat, 10am–6pm Sun mmw.pl

The building is one of the most important examples of Gothic architecture in Central and

←

Visitors admiring the monumental Panorama of Racławice

Eastern Europe. The town hall's southern façade was embellished with Neo-Gothic stone carvings in around 1871. Inside are impressive vaulted halls, the largest being the triple-aisled Grand Hall on the ground floor, and several impressive late Gothic and Renaissance doorways.

The building is home to the Museum of Bourgeois Art, containing the works of local artists, as well as pieces by renowned painters Andy Warhol and Salvador Dalí.

⑫
Pan Tadeusz Museum

Rynek 6 10am–6pm Tues–Sun muzeumpan atadeusza.ossolineum.pl

One of Wrocław University's proudest possessions is an original manuscript of *Pan Tadeusz*, the epic poem published by national poet Adam Mickiewicz (1798-1855) in 1834. Built to house the manuscript and explain its context, the Pan Tadeusz Museum (Muzeum Pana Tadeusza) evokes the patriotic struggles of 19th-century Poland through a mixture of mementoes, paintings, costumes and touchscreen digital content.

EAT

Bulka z maslem
A homely café that excels in soups, salads and burgers.

Ul Włodkowica 8a

zł zł zł

JaDka
Offering classic Polish fare, this restaurant's barrel-vaulted brick ceilings and subdued lighting make for a truly atmospheric dining experience.

Ul Rzeźnicza 24/25 jadka.pl

zł zł zł

Konspira
Filling Polish staples are served in this themed restaurant based around the anti-Communist movements of the 1980s.

Pl Solny 11 konspira.org

zł zł zł

↑ The awe-inspiring interior of the Cathedral of St John the Baptist on Ostrów Tumski

Royal Palace

🏛 Ul Kazimierza Wielkiego 34/35 🕐 10am–5pm Tue–Fri, 10am–6pm Sat–Sun
🌐 mmw.pl

This Baroque palace, enclosed by a court of annexes, was built in 1719. After 1750, when Wrocław came under Prussian rule, it became a residence for the Prussian kings. On the side facing Plac Wolności, only a side gallery remains of the Neo-Renaissance palace that was built in 1843–6.

The Royal Palace is now home to the main branch of the City Museum of Wrocław, with three separate exhibitions on offer. The first covers a selection of the building's royal apartments, which were painstakingly re-created following the destruction the palace suffered during World War II. There's also a fascinating exhibition on the city's

> **INSIDER TIP**
> **Views from the Water**
>
> Take a trip on one of the passenger steamers that cruise Wrocław's Odra River to spy great views over both the historic Old Town and the towering spires of Ostrów Tumski.

history from the Middle Ages to modern day. Possibly the star of the collection is the Beyersdorf Room, which is beautifully decorated in 17th-century Dutch tiles.

Church of St Elizabeth

🏛 Ul św Elżbiety 📞 71 343 16 38

The large tower dominating the market square is that of the Church of St Elizabeth (Kościół św. Elżbiety), one of the largest churches in all of Wrocław. The Gothic basilica was built in the 14th century on the site of an earlier church, although the tower was not completed until 1482. It became a Protestant church in 1525. Since 1946 it has been a garrison church.

The church has suffered damage from a succession of wars, fires and accidents. A fire in 1976 destroyed the roof and the splendid Baroque organ. Fortunately, more than 350 epitaphs and tombstones have survived, forming a remarkable exhibition of Silesian stone-carving from Gothic to Neo-Classical times.

→

Cathedral of St John the Baptist and Church of the Holy Cross on the river

Cathedral of St John the Baptist

🏛 Pl Katedralny
🕐 Cathedral: daily; tower: hours vary, check website
🚫 Cathedral: closed during services 🌐 katedra.archidiecezja.wroc.pl

One of the most beautiful buildings on all of Ostrów Tumski (Cathedral Island), the Cathedral of St John the Baptist (Archikatedra św. Jana Chrzciciela) showcases a

combination of styles from different periods. The presbytery was built some time between 1244 and 1272; the basilica was built in the first half of the 14th century; and the west tower was completed even later. Around three-quarters of the cathedral was destroyed in World War II, and most of the present building is the result of postwar reconstruction. The east end, with its interesting chapels accessible from the presbytery, survives in its original form. The beautiful Chapel of St Elizabeth in the south aisle was built in the Roman Baroque style by Giacomo Scianzi in 1680. The interior of the chapel is also the work of Italian artists: the tomb of Cardinal Frederyk, a Hessian landowner whose burial chapel this became, is by Domenico Guidi. The altar is by Ercole Ferrata.

The presbytery contains a spectacular late-Gothic polyptych of 1522, which was brought from Lubin, and some beautiful Baroque choir stalls that were previously housed in a church of the Premonstratensian order.

Did You Know?
———
Ostrów Tumski used to be an island, but the river surrounding it was filled in during 1810.

The cathedral also has an observation point in one of its towers, which offers incredible views over Ostrów Tumski, including the nearby Church of the Holy Cross, and over the water to Wrocław's charming Old Town.

———

Church of the Holy Cross

🏛 Pl Kościelny 📞 71 322 25 74

The two-tiered Church of the Holy Cross (Kościół św. Krzyża), one of the few split-level churches in the whole of Europe, was established in 1288 by Henry IV, also known as Henry the Pious. Building continued in the 14th century, and the south tower was finally completed in 1484. The lower church has had a turbulent history: it has been robbed several times, was used as a stable by invading Swedes, and was heavily damaged during World War II. The church has been used by Uniates since 1956.

The upper church, a narrow nave with a transept, was badly damaged during the course of World War II, when most of its interior fittings were lost; it was reconstructed following the conflict. The tombstone dedicated to the church's founder has been moved to the National Museum, but the original tympanum, depicting the ducal couple admiring the heavenly Throne of Grace, can still be seen in the north aisle. The 15th-century triptych over the high altar comes from a church in Świny.

Found just outside the church is an 18th-century statue of John of Nepomuk.

Church of St Martin

🏛 Ul św. Marcina 67–68

The first ecclesiastical building raised on the site now occupied by the tiny Church of St Martin (Kościół św. Marcina) was a stronghold chapel that was erected at the turn of the 11th century. The present church dates from the late 13th century but was rebuilt after World War II because it had suffered major damage. The present building consists of an octagonal nave and an unfinished presbytery.

Church of St Mary on Piasek

🏛 Ul Najświętszej Marii Panny 1

The rather forbidding bulk of the Church of St Mary on Piasek (Kościół NMP na Piasku) dominates Piasek Island. The church was constructed for canons regular in the second half of the 14th century on the site of a 12th-century Romanesque building whose tympanum is built into the wall over the sacristy in the south aisle.

The Church of St Mary suffered extensive damage in World War II, but some impressive features survive. The asymmetrical tripartite rib vaulting over the aisles is unusual. The church also houses a fine collection of Gothic altars brought here from other churches in Silesia.

Archbishop's Palace

🏛 Ul Katedralna 11
🚫 Closed to visitors

The present archbishop's residence, once the home of the canons of the cathedral, is a relatively plain building that was reconstructed from a more splendid Baroque edifice in 1792. The old bishop's palace, which stands at Ulica Katedralna 15 nearby, is a fine Neo-Classical building dating from the second half of the 18th century, although three 13th-century wings from the earlier palace remain.

One of the tranquil areas found in the Botanical Gardens →

Archdiocesan Museum

🏛 Ul Kanonia 12 📞 71 322 17 55 🚫 Closed for restoration until further notice

The Archdiocesan Museum (Muzeum Archidiecezjalne) stands among a group of buildings dating from three historical periods. The earliest of these is the elegant Gothic-Renaissance chapterhouse built in 1519–27, which has fine portals and arcades. The later Baroque chapterhouse was completed in 1756. The purpose-built Neo-Gothic museum, libraries and archives of the archdiocese were built in 1896. The museum contains an important and growing collection of Silesian religious art that dates back to the Gothic period. In addition to the altars and sculptures on display, it also showcases one of the earliest cabinets in the world, dating from 1455. Due to ongoing resoration works, the museum is currently closed to visitors.

THE BRIDGES OF WROCŁAW

Situated on the River Odra, the city of Wrocław boasts more than 100 bridges crossing numerous streams, canals and inlets. The oldest is the Piasek Island bridge, dating from 1845; each side of the bridge is guarded by a statue, one of St Jadwiga and the other of St John the Baptist. The best known bridge is Grunwaldzki Suspension Bridge, dating from 1908-10, which under German rule was named the Kaiserbrücke.

(21)
Botanical Gardens

🏛 Ul H Sienkiewicza 23
🕐 Apr & Sep: 9am-6pm daily; May-Aug: 9am-7pm daily; Oct: 9am-5pm daily
🚫 Nov-Mar 🌐 ogrod botaniczny.wroclaw.pl

Wrocław boasts the most attractive botanical gardens in all of Poland. They were established in 1811 by two professors from the University of Silesia in Katowice, and after being totally destroyed in World War II, were then-reverently re-created.

The gardens' central area contains picturesque ponds fashioned from what was an arm of the River Odra when Ostrów Tumski was still an island. There are also palms, as well as an alpine garden, cactuses, fountains and bridges peppered throughout the gardens. In addition, there is a 19th-century model of the geology of the Silesian town of Wałbrzych.

The gardens contain around 7,000 different plant species; a bust of the Swedish botanist Carolus Linnaeus (1708–78), dating from 1871, stands among the greenery.

The gardens also host a number of different events throughout the year, including hands-on workshops and a classical music concert, plus talks and discussions from experts on different gardening topics.

The botanical gardens are a favourite with locals, who can be found relaxing within its leafy expanse at the weekends. A branch of the gardens, which has an extensive arboretum, has been established in Wojsławice, near Niemcza.

> The gardens' central area contains picturesque ponds fashioned from what was an arm of the River Odra when Ostrów Tumski was still an island.

DRINK

Barbarka
Situated on a boat, this bar offers views of the historic university buildings across the water.

🏛 Wyspa Słodowa 6
📞 607 898 089

Mleczarnia
Full of antique furnishings, Mleczarnia is perfect for a mellow evening of candle-lit drinking.

🏛 Ul Włodkowica 5
🌐 mle.pl

Pod Kalamburem
This legendary bar boasts an Art Nouveau-inspired interior.

🏛 Ul Kuźnicza 29a
🌐 kalambur.org

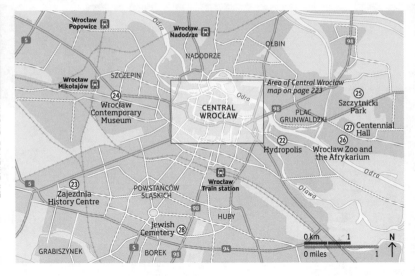

Wrocław Popowice

Wrocław Nadodrze

OŁBIN

NADODRZE

SZCZEPIN

Wrocław Mikołajów

 Wrocław Contemporary Museum

Area of Central Wrocław map on page 223

CENTRAL WROCŁAW

Odra

PLAC GRUNWALDZKI

Szczytnicki Park

25

Centennial Hall 26

22 Hydropolis

Wrocław Zoo and the Afrykarium

Olawa

5

23 Zajezdnia History Centre

POWSTAŃCÓW ŚLĄSKICH

98

Wrocław Train station

HUBY

Oława

98

Jewish Cemetery 28

GRABISZYNEK

5

BOREK 98

94

0 km   1

0 miles   1

N ↑

AROUND WROCŁAW

22

Hydropolis

🏠 Ul Na Grobli 19-21
🕐 9am-6pm Mon-Fri,
10am-8pm Sat & Sun
🌐 hydropolis.pl

Located halfway between the Old Town and the Centennial Hall, this Neo-Gothic water tank from 1893 has been turned into an ultramodern museum dedicated to water. The museum has 64 inter-active installations that take visitors on a journey from the Big Bang to nucleosynthesis and the formation of planets to the origin of Earth's water.

23

Zajezdnia History Centre

🏠 Ul Grabiszyńska 184
🕐 Hours vary, check
website 🌐 zajezdnia.org

Located in a former tram depot west of the centre, this engrossing museum deals with social life and popular culture, as well as the city's main political events. Its starting point is 1945, when

Wrocław (until then German Breslau) was emptied of its German population after World War II and then repop-ulated with Polish immigrants. The story of how they built a new life and culture in the war-devastated city is told through an engaging mixture of personal effects and visuals. Particular attention is given to the 1980s, a decade when Wrocław was a hotbed of anti-Communist subversion.

24

Wrocław Contemporary Museum

🏠 Pl Strzegomski 2A
🕐 10am-6pm Mon,
noon-8pm Wed-Sun
🌐 muzeumwspolczesne.pl

A short tram ride west of the centre, this museum (Muzeum Współczesne Wrocław or MWW) hosts cutting-edge contemporary art exhibitions in the stark concrete shell of a World War II anti-aircraft tower. It is worth visiting for the top floor café, which has stunning views back towards the city centre.

🔍 HIDDEN GEM
The Werkbund Estate

Built during the 1930s, this experimental area just east of Szczytnicki Park was filled with geometric modern villas. Some can still be seen on streets such as Ullica Kopernika.

25

Szczytnicki Park

This extensive park dates back to the 18th century. Its southern end is marked by a horseshoe-shaped lake with a group of fountains in the middle. During spring and summer evenings (April-September) the spraying fountains are accompanied by a truly spectacular sound-and-light show. One of Szczytnicki Park's distinctive features is its delightful Japanese garden, made for the World's Fair in 1913, which has been painstakingly restored with the help of Japanese gardening experts. The footbridges and pathways that run among the pavilions and plants make a charming setting for a leisurely walk.

26

Wrocław Zoo and the Afrykarium

🏛 Ul Wróblewskiego 1–5
🕐 Hours vary, check website 🌐 zoo.wroclaw.pl

South of Szczytnicki Park, this zoo is the oldest, largest and most-visited zoo in Poland. Much of its current popularity is due to the Afrykarium, a specially designed habit for African lake- and ocean-dwelling creatures which opened in 2014.

 27

Centennial Hall

🏛 Wystawowa 1 📞 71 347 51 00 🕐 9am–4pm, except during trade fairs and sports events

This hall (Hala Stulecia) was intended to be the centrepiece of an exhibition commemorating the centenary of the coalition's victory over Napoleon at Lipsk. It was designed by Max Berg and built in 1911–13. At the time of its construction, it was considered as one Europe's finest modern buildings. The centre of the hall is covered by a reinforced concrete dome with a diameter of 65 m (200 ft). It is lit by a sophisticated method, as the openwork design inside the stepped tambour consists of rows of windows that can be shaded or uncovered as required. The hall has functioned as a concert hall and theatre, and today is used for sports events and trade fairs. It has been named a UNESCO World Heritage Site.

 28

Jewish Cemetery

🏛 Ul Ślężna 37/39 📞 71 791 59 03 🕐 10am–dusk daily (to 6pm summer) 🔒 Jewish holidays

This is one of the few Jewish cemeteries in Poland that escaped destruction during World War II. First opened in 1856, it was the burial place of many celebrated citizens of Wrocław, including the socialist politician Ferdinand Lassalle, the painter Clara Sachs and the parents of Sister Theresa Benedicta of the Cross, born in Wrocław as Edith Stein.

STAY

DoubleTree by Hilton
Occupying a curvy contemporary building, this hotel's social spaces have an organic feel.

🏛 Ul Podwale 84
🌐 doubletree3.hilton.com

Monopol
This 19th-century hotel has preserved its fin-de-siecle elegance, with plush and well-appointed rooms.

🏛 Ul Heleny Modrzejewski 2
🌐 monopolwroclaw.hotel.com.pl

Granary
This lovingly restored, high-gabled granary building houses luxurious suites with kitchenettes.

🏛 Ul Mennicza 24 b
🌐 granaryhotel.com

↑ People relaxing in front of the Centennial Hall's distinctive form

KARKONOSZE MOUNTAINS

🅰A5/B5 📍Around 20 km (12 miles) S of Jelenia Góra
🌐kpnmab.pl

This spectacular range – whose name translates as the Giant Mountains – is a haven for outdoor adventurers. Hikers traverse its many footpaths year-round; in winter skiers come to enjoy the pistes.

The Karkonosze Mountains are the highest in the Sudeten chain, and their upper parts are a national park, recognized by UNESCO as a World Biosphere Reserve. Mount Sniezka, a relatively accessible hike, is the goal for many walkers. In the lower parts of the mountains are attractive small spa towns, such as Karpacz and Szklarska Poręba (the latter famous for its glassmaking), as well as Cieplice and Sobieszów in Jelenia Góra district (p238). The Karkonosze National Park Ecological Education Centre, found in the nearby town of Jelenia Góra (Ulica Okrzei 28), has an array of interactive exhibts on the diverse ecology and fascinating geology of the area.

① Hikers admire the view from Mount Sniezka, which is the highest point of the Silesian Ridge, a series of mighty peaks that dominate the entire Karkonosze range.

② A carved wooden statue of a Liczyrzepa, the guardian spirit of the Karkonosze Mountains, watches over the range from the town of Karpacz.

③ A Norwegian stave church can be seen in Karpacz; it was sold by the people of Vang, Norway to the King of Prussia in the 1840s.

Did You Know?
—
Mouflons, small feral sheep imported from Corsica and Sardinia in the 19th century, still thrive here.

↑ Visitors enjoying a winter hike on the snowy paths of Mount Sniezka

The weathered sandstone peaks of the Table Mountains ↑

3

KŁODZKO VALLEY

🅰 B6 🏠 Around 90 km (56 miles) S of Wrocław ℹ Pl Bolesława Chrobrego 1, Kłodzko 🌐 klodzko.pl

This spectacular valley is home to brilliantly green forested landscapes, dotted with rocky outcrops and spectacular castles. Its charming towns are renowned for their architecture, intriguing museums and grand 19th-century spas. The area also offers countless opportunities for skiing, mountain climbing and caving.

The largest valley within the Sudety mountain range, the Kłodzko Valley is one of the most beautiful landscapes found in Silesia. The tranquil Nysa Kłodzka river winds through its rolling, verdant hills, while impressive mountain ranges encircle its edges, among them the unsual, stony slabs of the Table Mountains (Góry Stołowe). As well as an abundance of natural beauty, the valley is also famous for its array of pretty spa towns,

perenially popular with the locals of Wrocław – found just to the north – as a weekend break spot. The charming town of Kłodzko itself, with its impressive fortress, is another of the valley's highlights. While there's plenty to keep you entertained above ground, try delving below, too. The area is home to the remains of a fascinating gold mine, as well as a huge network of subterranean caves, known as the Bear's Cave, just perfect for exploration.

Did You Know?

The Table Mountains are home to a giant rock crevice referred to locally as "hell".

Kłodsko Valley highlights

Kłodzko ▷

Located at the heart of the Kłodzko valley, this was for centuries a border town disputed by neighbouring Polish, Czech and German states. It is dominated by the hilltop Kłodzko Fortress (Twierdza Kłodzko), built during Austrian and Prussian rule in the 17th and 18th centuries. Tours are given by staff wearing period costume. Visitors can admire the view from the ramparts, which are 11 m (36 ft) thick at some points, and see a historical display, which takes in the role of the fortress as a Gestapo prison during World War II. There is also a network of underground tunnels to explore. In the town below is a Gothic stone bridge dating from 1390 and decorated with statues of saints. The Kłodzko Regional Museum (Muzeum Ziemi Kłodzkiej) is famous for a huge collection of timepieces that were made in local factories.

Table Mountains

The Table Mountains (Góry Stołowe) are an unusual geological phenomenon – the strange shapes of the sandstone and marl hills were created by erosion. At Szczeliniec Wielki and Błędne Skały, fissures form natural mazes.

Gold Mine

Enticing over 250,000 tourists every year, this gold mine (Kopalnia Złota) is one of the biggest attractions of the region. Designed for children, it offers an underground waterfall, a "Titanic" boat tour, and the opportunity to pan for gold and cast gold bars.

Wambierzyce

◁ This village is an ancient town of pilgrimage. The Pilgrimage Church dates from 1695-1710. In the village and nearby hills are more than 130 Stations of the Cross.

Bear's Cave

Formed 50 million years ago, Bear's Cave (Kletno), the largest in the Sudeten range, has 3 km (2 miles) of subterranean passages on four different levels with stalactites and stalagmites in a variety of shapes.

Spa Towns ▷

The valley is home to a number of elegant spa towns. World-renowed Polanica Zdrój was founded in the 19th century and is considered to be one of the area's most attractive spa towns. The health spa of Duszniki Zdrój contains a number of interesting sights, including the Baroque pulpit in the Church of Saints Peter and Paul (Kościół św. Piotra i Pawła), by Michael Kössler, and a historical paper mill. Near the quaint spa town of Kudowa Zdrój is the 18th-century Chapel of Skulls (Kaplica czaszek); this rather morbid chapel contains 3,000 skulls and other bones of victims of the Thirty Years' War (1618-48).

INSIDER TIP
Take the Train

Make the short train trip (30 km/18 miles) from Kłodzko to the pretty spa town of Kudowa, on the Czech border. The route winds its way over rolling hills, offering spectacular views of the area's lovely and unspoiled highland landscape along the way.

EXPERIENCE MORE

4

Lubiąż Abbey

🅐B5 🅞Pl Klasztorny 1
🚌🚍 🅞Apr-Sep: 9am-6pm
daily; Oct-Mar: 10am-3pm
daily 🅦fundacjalubiaz.
org.pl

The tiny village of Lubiąż is
the home of Lubiąż Abbey, a
gigantic Cistercian monastic
complex situated on the high
bank of the River Odra. A
group of Cistercian monks
settled in Lubiąż in 1175,
building a Romanesque
church followed by a Gothic
basilica, of which the twin-
tower façade and ducal chapel
remain. The present abbey
dates from 1681–1715. After
World War II, it was used as a
warehouse for unsold books,
mostly works by Lenin. Its
restoration began in the mid-
1990s with an exhibition of
Silesian sculpture. You can
also visit the refectory, with
its beautifully painted ceiling,
and the Ducal Hall, which is a
magnificent example of the
late Baroque style, its purpose
being to glorify the faith and
the feats of the ruling
Habsburg dynasty.

5

Bolesławiec

🅐A5 🅡 🅘Pl Piłsudskiego
1C; www.boleslawiec.pl

Founded in 1190 by Bolesław
the Tall to mine recently discovered gold, this town is
today more famous for its
ceramic production. Immediately recognizable due to its
brightly coloured dots and
stripes, this folk-inspired ware
is both highly practical and an
ideal souvenir. The Museum of
Ceramics (Muzeum Ceramiki)
reveals the secrets of the
potters' art and the history of
ceramics. The main square,
with its elegantly restored
town hall and surrounding
mansions, is one of the
prettiest in Poland.

SHOP

Manufaktura

Several places in
Bolesławiec make
and sell traditional
ceramics, but the best is
the flagship store of the
Manufaktura company.

🅐B4 🅞Ul Gdańska 30,
Bolesławiec 🅦polish-
pottery.com.pl

6

Legnica

🅐B5 🅡 🅘Brama
Głogowska; www.
portal.legnica.eu

After Wrocław and Opole, this
is Silesia's third largest city.
It is a large administrative
centre and copper-mining
town, as evidenced by the
fascinating displays in the
Copper Museum. The **Parish
Church of John the Baptist**
(Fara św. Jana Chrzciciela)

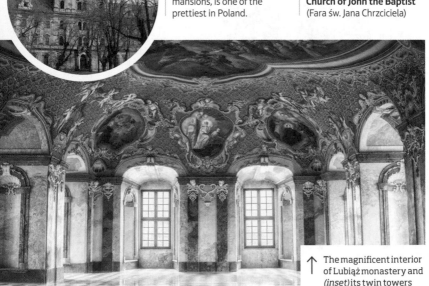

↑ The magnificent interior
of Lubiąż monastery and
(inset) its twin towers

→
The grand Baroque palace housing Żagań's Cultural Institute

is one of the most beautiful Baroque shrines in Silesia, built for the Jesuits in 1714–27. The presbytery of the original church was converted into a chapel, the Mausoleum of the Silesian Piasts (1677–8).

In the northern part of the Old Town, the Dukes' Castle has medieval origins and was remodelled many times. The fine Renaissance gate was added by George von Amberg in 1532–3.

In the Market Square stand the Baroque town hall, from 1737–46, which has a theatre, and the Gothic **Cathedral of Saints Peter and Paul** (Katedra św Piotra i Pawła), built in the 14th century and preserving a 13th-century baptismal font. In the centre of the square are eight narrow arcaded houses known as the Herring Stalls and, at No 40, the 16th-century Under the Quail's Nest House, with sgraffito decoration.

Copper Museum
 Ul Partyzantów 3 10am–5pm Tue–Fri, 11am–5pm Sat museum-miedzi.art.pl

Parish Church of John the Baptist
Ul Zbigniewa i Michała 1 76 724 41 88

Cathedral of Saints Peter and Paul
Ul św. Piotra 2a 500 245 557

⑦
Legnickie Pole
B5

It was here in this small village that a great battle between the Poles, led by Henry II the Pious, and the Tatars took place on 9 April 1241. Despite

the Turks' defeat of the Poles and the death of the Polish commander, westward Tatar expansion was prevented. The **Museum of the Battle of Legnica** details this event.

The Baroque Benedictine abbey, dating from 1727–31, is the main attraction. The abbey church, dedicated to St Jadwiga, has an elliptical nave, fine furnishings and undulating vaulting covered with trompe l'oeil paintings by Cosmas Damian Asam.

Museum of the Battle of Legnica
 Pl Henryka Pobożnego 3 76 858 23 98 11am–5pm Wed–Sun

⑧
Żagań
A4 Ul Szprotawska 4 um.zagan.pl

Żagań is home to a beautiful Baroque palace with a Neo-Classical interior that now houses the Cultural Institute, the 14th-century Franciscan Church of Saints Peter and Paul (Kościół św. Piotra i Pawła), built in the Gothic style, and the Church of the Assumption (Kościół Wniebowzięcia NMP), with its finely furnished interior.

Just south of Żagań was the location of several German Prisoner of War (POW) camps used during World War II, one

of which (Stalag Luft III) was the site of the real-life escape attempt that inspired the Hollywood film *The Great Escape*. The **POW Camps Museum** (Muzeum Obozów Jenieckich) at the site contains a fascinating exhibition on life inside the camp system. A well-signposted network of paths leads to the site of the escape tunnels.

POW Camps Museum
Ul Lotników Alianckich 6 Mar–Oct: 10am–4pm Tue–Fri, 10am–5pm Sat–Sun; Nov–Feb: 10am–3pm Tue–Sat

---

THE GREAT ESCAPE
The legendary breakout of POWs from Stalag Luft III took place in 1944. Led by Squadron Leader Roger Bushell, air officers dug three tunnels (Tom, Dick and Harry) under the camp wire. Guards discovered two of them, but 76 prisoners were able to escape through "Harry" on 24 March 1944. Three succeeded in reaching neutral countries; the others were recaptured and 50 of them were shot. The story was immortalized by the 1963 Hollywood film *The Great Escape*, starring Steve McQueen.

The picture-perfect town hall, found in the Market Square of Lwówek Śląski

⑪ Jelenia Góra

🅰B5 🔲🚌 ℹ Pl Ratuszowy 6/7; 9am-7pm daily (to 8pm Jun-Sep); www.jeleniagora.pl

At the foot of the Karkonosze Mountains, Jelenia Góra is a favourite tourist destination and a major starting point for hikers. Granted city status around the end of the 13th century, the town was once renowned for its textiles, with delicate batiste and voile exported as far as Africa and America. It was also one of the main centres of engraved glassware, and in the **Regional Museum** you can view the largest collection of decorative glassware in the whole of Poland. A traditional Karkonosze hut nearby houses an ethnographical exhibition.

The historic centre is the Market Square, its Baroque town hall surrounded by arcaded town houses. In Ulica Maria Konopnicka, east of the Market Square, is the **Church of Saints Erasmus and Pancras** (Kościół św. Erazma i Pankracego), a Gothic basilica of the late 14th to early 15th centuries featuring late-Gothic vaulting and a Baroque altar depicting the Transfiguration. The line of the old defensive walls here is marked by a chapel.

On Ulica 1 Maja, on the same axis, is the Church of Our Lady, with two penitentiary crosses on the outer walls. The street then leads to the Baroque former Protestant **Church of the Holy Cross**

⑨ Lwówek Śląski

🅰A5 🔲🚌 ℹ Pl Wolności 1; www.lwowekslaski.pl

This small town in the foothills of the Izerski Mountains is set on a precipice overlooking the River Bóbr. Remnants of the stone walls that once surrounded it can still be seen.

The town's centrepiece is its Gothic-Renaissance town hall. Built in the 15th century, it was restored in 1902–5, when the arcades around the building were added. Several historic town houses stand in the pretty Market Square.

The twin-towered Church of the Assumption (Kościół Wniebowzięcia) has an imposing Romanesque façade from the 13th century, although the main body of the church was not added until the early 16th century. The Gothic chapel on the south side, dating from 1496, has vaulting with beautiful 16th-century frescoes.

The 16th-century castle at Płakowice, 2 km (1 mile) south of Lwówek Śląski, is one of the finest Renaissance castles in Silesia.

⑩ Krzeszów

🅰B5 🔲🚌

This tiny village in the Góry Kamienne Mountains has one of the most picturesque groups of historic buildings in Poland. The most impressive collection is found within the **Sanctuary of Our Lady of Grace**, a magnificent abbey complex. Located here is the Church of St Joseph (Kościół św. Józefa); built by Cistercian monks in 1690–96 it contains frescoes by Michael Willmann. The monks also built the Church of the Blessed Virgin Mary (Kościół NMP Łaskawej), in 1727–35. The interior is decorated with vertiginous trompe l'oeil paintings by Georg Wilhelm Neunhertz; sculptures by Anton Dorazil and Ferdinand Maximilian Brokoff make the pilasters, cornices and vaulting appear to float in mid-air.

Behind the presbytery the Mausoleum of the Silesian Piasts (Mauzoleum Piastów Śląskich) contains the Gothic tombs of Bolko I (d 1301) and Bolko II (d 1368), dukes of Świdnica-Jawor. Figures of their wives, Agnieszka and Beatrycze, stand opposite the tombs. On the wall is an epitaph by the son of Bolko II, the last of the Piast dynasty.

Sanctuary of Our Lady of Grace

📞 75 742 32 79 🕒 May-Oct: 9am-6pm daily; Nov-Apr: 9am-3pm daily

> **At the foot of the Karkonosze Mountains, Jelenia Góra is a favourite tourist destination and a major starting point for hikers.**

(Kościół św. Krzyża), known also as the Church of Peace. Built by Martin Franze in 1709–18, it has a triple tier of galleries and ceiling frescoes by Felix Anton Scheffler and Jozef Franz Hoffman. The integrated altar and organ loft is striking.

The town's boundaries were expanded in 1976 so that it includes the pretty town of Sobieszów, which is home to the Karkonosze National Park Ecological Education Centre *(p232)*. Cieplice, famous for its hot springs since the 13th century, also falls within Jelenia Góra. It is home to the intriguing **Natural History Museum**, which contains giant models of insects, exhibits on the area's geology and a reconstructed courtyard of a Cistercian abbey.

Regional Museum
⊘ ☐ Ul Matejki 28
☉ 9am–5pm Tue–Sun
Ⓦ muzeumkarkonoskie.pl

Church of Saints Erasmus and Pancras
☐ Pl Kościelny 1-2 ☎ 75 752 21 60

Church of the Holy Cross
☐ Ul 1 Maja 45 ☎ 75 642 32 82

Natural History Museum
⊘ ☐ Ul Cieplicka 11a, Cieplice
☉ Jan–Oct: 9am–4pm Tue–Sun; Dec: 9am–3pm Tue–Sun
☒ Nov Ⓦ muzeum-cieplice.pl

---

⑫

Jawor
 B5 ☐ 🚍 🛈 Rynek 3; 76 870 33 71

Many of this town's buildings were painstakingly restored following World War II, something which has enhanced its historic atmosphere.

The most picturesque building is the **Evangelical Church of Peace** (Kościół Pokoju), one of three "peace churches" erected in Silesia after the Peace of Westphalia. Built in 1654–6 by Andreas Kempner, to a design by Albrecht von Säbisch, it is now a UNESCO World Heritage Site. With the church in Świdnica *(p241)*, it is among the world's largest timber-framed structures. Other

notable buildings are the 14th-century Church of St Martin (Kościół św. Marcina) and the late 15th-century Church of St Mary (Kościół Mariacki). The best place to finish a walk around the town is the Market Square, lined by arcaded Baroque houses.

Evangelical Church of Peace
☐ Park Pokoju 2 ☉ Apr–Oct: 10am–5pm Mon–Fri; Nov–Mar: by advance booking only Ⓦ kosciolpokojujawor.p

---

STAY

Czoch Castle Hotel
A turreted medieval castle turned stately home is one of Silesia's most romantic hotels.

 A5 ☐ Sucha 59-820 Leśna Ⓦ hotelewam.pl

ⓩⓩⓩ

→ Jelenia Góra's pretty town square, surrounded by 18th-century buildings

Wałbrzych

A B5 **f** Rynek 9
w cit.walbrzych.pl

A coal-mining centre until the 1990s, this town has more recently found fame from the legend of the missing Nazi Gold Train. The centre has some fine 19th-century buildings on its two main squares, but the main sight is the former mine of **Stara Kopalnia** (Old Mine), with underground workings to be explored and a tower with panoramic views. The town is also a centre for ceramics and its **Porcelain Museum** has displays on Delft and Dresden alongside local wares.

Around 8 km (5 miles) north of Wałbrzych is **Książ Castle**, the largest residential building in Silesia. This huge edifice was built on a rocky hilltop overlooking the surrounding wooded countryside. The late 13th-century Gothic castle of Prince Bolko I was rebuilt in the mid-16th century for the Hochberg family, who continued to own it until World War II. Tours explore its sumptuous interiors, while an alternative trail visits parts of the castle and garden associated with English society beauty Daisy von Pless (1873–1943), who married Count Hans Heinrich XV of Hochberg in 1891. Tunnels below the castle, built during World War II can also be visited. The castle's extensive grounds feature rose gardens, topiary and fountains, with a palm house around 1 km (0.5 miles) to the southeast.

Stara Kopalnia
 Q Ul Piotr Wysockiego 29
Q 10am–6pm daily
w starakopalnia.pl

Porcelain Museum
Q Ul 1 Maja 9 **Q** 10am–4pm daily (to 6pm Wed)
w muzeum.walbrzych.pl

Książ Castle
Q Ul Piastów Śl **Q** Apr–Oct: 9am–5pm Mon–Fri, 9am–6pm Sat & Sun; Nov–Mar: 10am–3pm Mon–Fri, 10am–4pm Sat & Sun **w** ksiaz.walbrzych.pl

---

Bolków

A B5 **Q** **w**

The great towering Castle of the Dukes of Świdnica-Jawor is the main feature of this small town. Built from the mid-13th to the mid-14th century, it was sacked and destroyed several times, before being rebuilt in the Renaissance style. Today it houses the **Castle Museum**. The beautiful Gothic Church of St Jadwiga (Kościół św. Jadwigi) is also worth a visit.

In Świny, 2 km (1 mile) north of Bolków, there are the haunting and atmospheric ruins of a 14th-century castle.

Visitors strolling around the lawn fronting the impressive Książ Castle

---

Castle Museum
Q Ul Zamkowa 1 **C** 75 741 32 97 **Q** May–Sep: 9am–4:30pm Tue–Fri, 9am–5:30pm Sat & Sun; Oct–Apr: 9am–3:30pm Tue–Fri, 9am–4:30pm Sat & Sun (Nov–Mar: to 3:30pm Sat & Sun) **Q** Pub hols

---

Riese Underground Complex

A B5 **w**

Beneath the Góry Sowie (Owl Mountains) southeast of Wałbrzych lies a huge complex of tunnels built by the Nazis during World War II. Excavated by slave labour and given the code-name Riese – meaning "Giant" – they served as an underground factory in

The beautifully ornate interior and *(inset)* elegantly simple exterior of the wooden Church of Peace in Świdnica

which V2 rockets and other secret weapons were made. The **Osówka Underground City** (Podziemne Miasto Osówka) at Sierpnica offers guided tours of one section and to the east, the **Walim Drifts: Rzeczka Complex** (Sztolnie Walimskie: Kompleks Rzeczka) provides tours of an underground factory, thought to have been a rocket plant.

Osówka Underground City

⊕ ⊕ ⊖ 🚗 Ul Świerkowa 29d, Sierpnica 🕐 10am-4pm daily (to 5pm Mar-Oct) 🌐 osowka.pl

Walim Drifts: Rzeczka Complex

⊕ ⊕ 🚗 Ul 3-ego Maja 26, Walim 🕐 9am-5pm Mon-Fri, 9am-6pm Sat & Sun (to 7pm May-Sep) 🌐 muzeum.walbrzych.pl

16 Świdnica

🅰 B5 🚉 🚌 *i* www.swidnica.pl

For almost 100 years, Świdnica was the capital of an independent duchy. The town minted its own coins and was renowned for its beer – its history is well illustrated in the **Museum of Old Trade**.

From the pretty market square, with its fine Baroque plague column, Ulica Długa, the main street, leads to the 14th-century Cathedral of Saints Stanisław and Wenceslas (Katedra św. Stanisława i Wacława), a richly furnished Gothic building. The town's most impressive building is the wooden **Church of Peace** (Kościół Pokoju), one of two surviving Protestant "peace churches" built after the Peace of Westphalia that ended the Thirty Years' War (1618–48).

Museum of Old Trade

⊗ 🚗 Rynek 37 📞 74 852 12 91 🕐 May-Sep: 10am-5pm Tue-Fri, 11am-5pm Sat & Sun; Oct-Apr: 10am-4pm Tue-Fri, 11am-5pm Sat & Sun

Church of Peace

🚗 Pl Pokoju 6 📞 74 852 28 14 🕐 Apr-Oct: 9am-6pm Mon-Sat, noon-6pm Sun; Nov-Mar: 10am-3pm Mon-Sat, noon-3pm Sun

---

THE GOLD TRAIN

Local legend tells of a train laden with gold looted by the Nazis that was hidden in a secret tunnel in the Wałbrzych region in 1945. International attention was sparked in 2015 when a group of treasure hunters claimed to have established its location. Excavations revealed nothing, but this has done nothing to dim the legend's appeal. In an area full of Nazi-era tunnels, the Gold Train remains an irresistable local symbol.

INSIDER TIP
Trzebnica Aquapark

With fountains, wave pools and water slides, this aquapark *(www. trzebnicazdroj.eu)* can keep the kids going for hours. There are also indoor activities. Saunas and spa facilities are for adults in need of a pamper.

⑰ Trzebnica

Ⓐ B5 🚌🚃 ❗www. trzebnica.pl

In 1203 Jadwiga, Henry I's wife, brought an order of Cistercian monks from Bamberg, located in Germany, to Trzebnica, and helped them build a monastery. She was buried there and, after her canonization in 1267, the monastery became an important place of pilgrimage. It underwent a period of major rebuilding during the 17th century, obliterating its Romanesque architecture, although the tympanum of the main portal retains a fine relief of around 1230 representing the Old Testament figures David and Bathsheba. The impressive Gothic chapel of St Jadwiga contains her Baroque-style tomb, dating from 1677–8.

⑱ Otmuchów

 Ⓐ B6 🚌🚃

Otmuchów has a picturesque setting between two lakes, Lake Głębinowskie and Lake Otmuchówskie. In spring and summer the town is filled with flowers, partly as athe result of the spring flower festival that is held here.

From the 14th century until 1810, Otmuchów belonged to the bishops of Wrocław. Its historic buildings are all in close proximity around the sloping Market Square. On the lower side is the Renaissance town hall, built in 1538, with a later tower. On the upper side is the Baroque parish church of 1690–96, and the Palace of the Bishops of Wrocław. The adjacent palace, known as the Lower Castle, was the bishops' secondary residence.

⑲ Oleśnica

 Ⓐ C5 🚌🚃 ❗www. olesnica.pl

The most impressive building in Oleśnica is the **Castle of the Dukes of Oleśnica**. While the Gothic interior is original, the exterior, with its circular corner tower, is the result of rebuilding from 1542 to 1610 by Italian architects. The castle retains ornamental gables in the attic rooms, in the wings and on the galleries supported on brackets overlooking the courtyard. Attached to the castle is the delightful palace of Jan Podiebrad, built in 1559–63.

The exterior of the Castle of the Dukes of Oleśnica ↓

A pleasant way of rounding off a visit to Oleśnica is to walk through the old quarter to the Gothic Church of St John the Evangelist (Kościół św. Jana Ewangelisty). Beside the presbytery is a chapel built in memory of the dukes of Wurtemberg, and containing the tombs of Jan and Jerzy Podiebrad. Other elements include the Mannerist pulpit and the Gothic stalls from the late 15th and early 16th centuries. Remnants of castle walls, with the tower of the Wrocławski Gate, and the town's Neo-Classical town hall, rebuilt after World War II, are other features of interest.

Castle of the Dukes of Oleśnica

🏛 Ul Zamkowa 4 📞 71 314 20 12 🕐 8am–5pm daily

20
Henryków

🏛 B5 🚉🚌

This small town is best known for its **Cistercian church**, founded in

1227 by Henryk the Bearded. Abbey allotments separate the church and monastery from the street, so that access to the church is by way of a series of gates. The church, originally Gothic, was rebuilt in the early 14th century and remodelled in the Baroque style by Matthias Kirchberger in 1687–1702. Prominent features of the elegant Baroque interior are the high altar, with *The Birth of Christ in the Vision of St Bernard of Clairvaux* by Michael Willmann, and the large, highly ornamented choir stalls. A plague column outside the church depicts the four archangels. Other points of interest include the extensive monastery and the scenic park laid out at the rear of the monastery in the early 18th century. A pretty summerhouse stands in the park.

Cistercian Church

🏛 Pl Cystersów 1 📞 74 810 51 35 🕐 10am–3pm daily (to 4pm Jul & Aug)

↑ One of the towers that punctuate the walls surrounding Paczków

21
Paczków

🏛 B6 🚉🚌 ℹ Wojska Polskiego 23 🌐 paczkow.pl

Completely surrounded by a medieval wall set with towers and gates, Paczków has been dubbed the "Carcassone of Silesia" after the medieval walled city found in southwest France. Founded in 1254, Paczków's old town retains its original street layout. It contains many distinctive town houses, alongside an impressive Neo-Classical town hall and the Church of St John (Kościół św. Jana), an originally Gothic church that was rebuilt in the Renaissance style in 1529–36 and fortified for defensive purposes.

> ## Did You Know?
> Paczków's fortified walls are almost 4,000 ft (1,200 meters) long and include 19 towers.

Monument to the Silesian uprisings of 1919–21, in Góra Świętej Anny

㉒
Góra Świętej Anny

 C6 🏛 ℹ www.swanna.com.pl

Góra Świętej Anny is a place of pilgrimage for Catholics and a centre of commemoration of the Silesian uprisings that took place in 1919–21.

The impressive Pilgrimage Church of St Anne was built here by members of the Gaschin-Gaszyński family in the second half of the 1600s. The Stations of the Cross that make up the 18th-century Calvary are placed around the church and monastery. The Calvary draws large numbers of pilgrims.

During the Third Silesian Uprising in May and June 1921, two major battles were fought in the mountains near Góra Świętej Anny. These are commemorated by a commanding monument carved by Xawery Dunikowski and others in 1955 on the side of the mountain. It sits above a huge amphitheatre that was constructed in 1930–34. Found on the site is the fascinating **Museum of the Uprising**, which contains records relating to the events.

Museum of the Uprising
⊛ 🏛 Ul Leśnicka 28
📞 77 461 54 66 🕐 9am–3pm Tue–Fri, 10am–4pm Sat & Sun (free Sat) 🚫 Dec–Feb: Sun

㉓
Nysa

 C6 🏛🚆 ℹ Ul Piastowska 19; www.nysa.eu

Founded in 1223, this town was once the capital of the dukes of Wrocław and the see of the duchy of Nysa (Niesse). In the 16th and 17th centuries it became the residence of the Catholic bishops of Wrocław, who were driven there from Ostrów Tumski during the Reformation. After 1742 the Prussians enclosed the town with ramparts.

Despite suffering massive destruction during World War II, Nysa retains a number of interesting and historic buildings. Dominating the pretty town centre is the Gothic **Basilica of Saints James and Agnieszka** (Basilica św. Jakuba i Agnieszki), with a separate belfry dating from the early 16th century. The well beside it, referred to locally as the Beautiful Well, is covered with unusual wrought ironwork and dates from 1686.

Also of interest to visitors are the impressive bishop's palace, which dates from 1660–80, and the old manor, which stand beside a group of Jesuit buildings. The palace is now home to the spectacular **Town Museum**. It contains a fine collection of European painting, including pictures from the studios of Lucas Cranach the Elder (1472–1553) and Hugo van der Goes (around 1440–82)

The late Baroque **Church of Saints Peter and Paul** (Kościół św. Piotra i Pawła) was built by Michael Klein and Felix Anton Hammerschmidt in 1719–27 for the Canons Regular of the Holy Sepulchre. Its original furnishings are still intact. Entry to the church can be gained via the office of the seminary, which is situated in the monastery.

A group of Jesuits were brought to the town of Nysa by Bishop Karol Habsburg. They proceeded to build the Baroque Jesuit **Church of the Assumption** (Kościół Wniebowzięcia NMP), which was constructed in 1688–92. The church has a magnificent twin-towered façade and its spectacular interior features paintings by Karl Dankwart. The church is just one of a group of buildings that are known collectively as the Carolinum College.

Basilica of Saints James and Agnieszka
🏛 Pl Katedralny 7
📞 774 33 25 05 🕐 Daily

Town Museum
⊛ 🏛 Pl Bpa Jarosława 11
🕐 9am–3pm Tue–Fri, 10am–3pm Sat & Sun (free Wed)
🌐 muzeum.nysa.pl

Church of Saints Peter and Paul
🏛 Ul Bracka 18 📞 77 448 46 70 🕐 Daily

Church of the Assumption
🏛 Pl Solny 🕐 Daily

→
The pretty city of Opole, beautifully illuminated at dusk

> The centrepiece of Pszczyna Palace is the extraordinary Hall of Mirrors, containing two vast mirrors, each with a surface area of some 14 sq m (150 sq ft).

Opole

Ⓐ C5 🚃🚌 🅸 Rynek 23; www.opole.pl

The origins of Opole, on the River Odra, go back to the 8th century. Once the seat of the Piast duchy, from 1327 it was ruled by Bohemia, from 1526 by Austria, and from 1742 by Prussia. Although it has been part of Poland only since 1945, it has always had a sizeable Polish population.

The town hall was built in 1936 in imitation of Florence's Palazzo Vecchio. Other buildings of note include the Cathedral of the Holy Cross, a Gothic church with a Baroque interior, and the late Gothic Franciscan church, containing the tombs of the dukes of Opole. The **Regional Museum**, covering the history of the area, is also worth a visit. On Pasieka Island, near the park's amphitheatre, stands the Piast Tower, all that remains of the Gothic ducal castle.

Regional Museum

⊗ 🏠 Ul św. Wojciecha 13
📞 77 453 66 77 🕐 9am–4pm Tue–Fri, 11am–5pm Sat & Sun (to 6pm Fri Jul–Sep)

Cieszyn

Ⓐ C7/D7 🚃🚌 🅸 Rynek 1 & Zamkowa 3B; www.cieszyn.pl

This delightful town on the Czech–Polish border was founded in the 9th century. From the 13th to 17th centuries it was the capital of a Silesian duchy and in 1653 fell under Habsburg rule.

Atop a hill, where there was once a castle, is the site of the 11th-century Romanesque Rotunda of St Nicholas (Rotunda św. Mikołaja), the Gothic-style Piast Tower and a hunting palace built by Karol Habsburg in 1838.

The Market Square has some fine town houses and a Neo-Classical town hall. Cieszyn is also home to the Protestant Church of Grace (Kościół Łaski), of 1709.

The town is well kept, with a number of pedestrianized streets. Czech as well as Polish is heard in its homely pubs, bars and restaurants.

Pszczyna

Ⓐ D6 🚃🚌 🅸 Brama Wybrańców; www.pszczyna.info.pl

On the edge of the ancient Pszczyna Forest, this town is named after a residence that was built within the walls of a Gothic castle in the area. The building, next to the forest and its wildlife, was used as a hunting lodge for centuries. From 1846 Pszczyna was ruled by the Hochbergs of Książ. The palace was rebuilt for them in 1870–76 in the French Neo-Renaissance style.

Today the palace houses the **Castle Museum** with an interesting and well-stocked armoury, a collection of hunting trophies and a fine array of period furniture. (Admission is free on Mondays from April to October, and on Tuesdays from November for March.) The centrepiece of Pszczyna Palace is the extraordinary Hall of Mirrors, containing two vast mirrors, each with a surface area of some 14 sq m (150 sq ft).

Castle Museum

⊗ 🏠 Ul Brama Wybrańców 1
🕐 Hours vary, check website
🌐 zamek-pszczyna.pl

Katowice

△D6 ☐☐ 𝒊 Rynek 13; www.katowice.eu

Long associated with factory chimneys, mine pitheads and Brutalist 1970s architecture, Katowice has re-emerged as a vibrant, fast-changing post-industrial city.

In the largely concrete and modern centre, the Spodek ("Flying Saucer"), a bulbous oval sports- and concert-hall opened in 1971, is outstanding.

North of the Spodek, the former Ferdynand coal mine is now the **Museum of Silesia**, with underground galleries revealing the history of the province in lively multimedia style. The Polish National Radio Symphony Orchestra's NOSPR Concert Hall, found nearby, is also worth a visit for its notable architecture.

Some 6 km (4 miles) south-east of the centre, the suburb of Nikiszowiec is a famous example of a pre-World War I model settlement, with a grid of red-brick miners' houses around a central square. A former mine on the outskirts now houses the **Wilson Shaft Gallery** (Galeria Szyb Wilson), a contemporary art gallery that hosts concerts.

Museum of Silesia

◎◎◎ ☐ Ul Dobrowolskigo 1 ☐ 10am-8pm Tue-Sun ⊠ muzeumslaskie.pl

Wilson Shaft Gallery

☐ Ul Oswobodzenia 1
☐ 9am-7pm daily
⊠ szybwilson.org

Gliwice

△C6 ☐ 𝒊 Ul Tarnogórska 129 ⊠ gliwice.eu/en

The third largest city of Upper Silesia after Katowice and Chorzów, Gliwice owes its wealth to iron and steel.

Villa Caro, the lavish home built by industrialist Oscar Caro in the 1920s, is found here, with period interiors and Caro's art collection.

Established in 1880 and later enlarged, the famous Palm House (Palmiarnia) is one of the city's most popular attractions. Another is the 1934 **Gliwice Radio Mast** (Radiostacja Gliwicka), in a park north of the centre, which dates from 1934. At 118 m (387 ft) it is thought to be the world's tallest wooden structure. On 31 August 1939 Nazi Germany staged an attack on the tower, which Hitler then blamed on Poland and used it as an excuse to initiate World War II. The on-site museum tells the story.

Villa Caro

◎ ☐ Ul Dolnych Walów 8a
☐ 9am-3pm Tue, 9am-4pm Wed, 10am-4pm Thu & Fri, 11am-5pm Sat, 11am-4pm Sun ☐ Mon ⊠ muzeum. gliwice.pl

> ## Did You Know?
>
> Katowice's Wilson Shaft Gallery is named after US President Woodrow Wilson.

→ The glow of sunset on the futuristic Spodek concert hall and sports venue

↑ A wooden church, one of the buildings at the Upper Silesian Ethnographic Park in Chorzów

Gliwice Radio Mast

 Ul Tarnogórska 129
May-Sep: 6am-10pm daily; Oct-Apr: 8am-8pm daily
muzeum.gliwice.pl

29

Chorzów

D6

Found just northwest of central Katowice, Chorzów's most famous attribute is the **Silesian Park** (Park Śląski), a vast green space laid out in the 1970s to provide the workers of Upper Silesia with a recreation area. Featuring open meadows, rose gardens and a high-wire activity park, it can be explored on foot or via the Elka Cableway (Kolejka Elka), a horizontal chair-lift that runs just above the ground. West of the park is the interesting **Upper Silesian Ethnographic Park**, an open-air museum home to traditional Silesian buildings dating from the late-18th to the early-20th centuries.

Silesian Park

Aleja Różana 2
en.parkslaski.pl

Upper Silesian Ethnographic Park

Ul Parkowa 25
Hours vary, check website
muzeumgpe-chorzow.pl

30

Brzeg

C5 brzeg.pl

This attractive town on the River Odra was the capital of the duchy of Legnica-Brzeg from 1311 to 1675. The town's most impressive building is the Gothic Castle of the Dukes of Legnica-Brzeg. The 14th-century chapel here contains a mausoleum to the Silesian Piasts, built in 1567. The castle was transformed into a Renaissance palace in the 16th century; today it houses the **Museum of the Silesian Piasts**, containing medieval art, weaponry and local crafts.

Other buildings of interest are the town hall, erected in 1570–77, the 14th-century Church of St Nicholas (Kościół św. Mikołaja) and the late-Baroque Jesuit church.

Museum of the Silesian Piasts

l Zamkowy 1
77 416 32 57
10am-5pm Tue-Sun

DRINK

Kafo
The best espresso in town.

Ul Wieczorka 14, Gliwice kafo.info

Kornel i przijacieli
A genteel bookshop café in an Old Town alley.

Ul Sejmowa 1, Cieszyn korneliprzyjaciele.pl

Biala Malpa
Multitap bar with a huge range of beers.

Ul 3 Maja 38, Katowice bialamalpa.pl

Lorneta z Meduza
Retro style, lots of character, and cheap drinks and snacks.

Ul Mariacka 5, Katowice

Jazz Club Hipnoza
A cult venue blending old-fashioned pub style and edgy bohemianism.

Pl Sejmu Slaskiego 2, Katowice jazzclub.pl

Picturesque Ulica Mariacka in Gdańsk, lined with amber shops

GDAŃSK

For more than 300 years Gdańsk was the capital of a Slav duchy in Pomerania, until it was taken over and enlarged by the Teutonic Knights in 1308. In 1361 Gdańsk became a member of the powerful Hanseatic League (a trade association of Baltic towns), further bolstering its economic development. From 1466 until the Second Partition in 1793, the city belonged to Poland and was the country's largest Baltic port and an important centre of trade with the rest of Europe. A very wealthy city, Gdańsk played a pivotal role in the Commonwealth of Two Nations. It also became a major centre of the arts – goldsmiths fashioned fine jewellery for the royal courts of Europe, and both the city's gemstone and amber workshops won great renown. From 1793 it was incorporated into Prussia, only becoming a free city under the Treaty of Versailles after World War I. It was in Gdańsk that the first shots of World War II were fired, a conflict that almost totally destroyed the city. A postwar rebuilding programme restored many of the city's finest buildings and much of its historic atmosphere. Gdańsk was also where Communism began to crumble, following the shipyard strikes of 1980. Today, together with the coastal resort of Sopot and the port of Gdynia, forms the conurbation known as Trójmiasto ("the Tri-City"), a huge metropolis stretching around the edge of the Bay of Gdańsk.

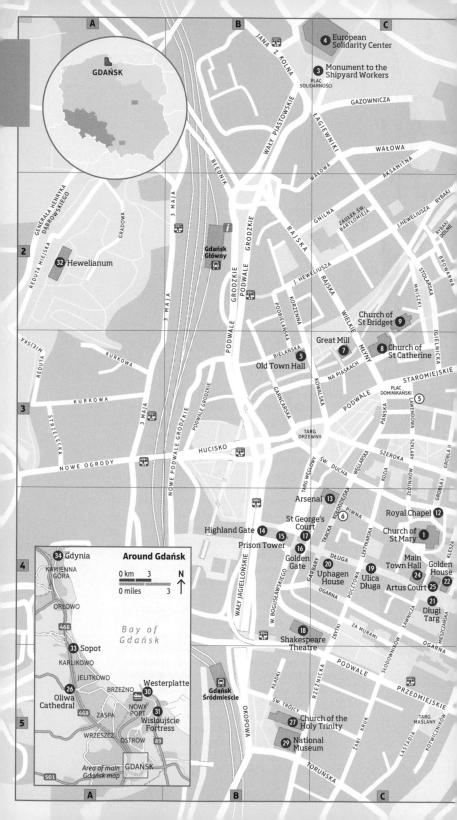

GDAŃSK

A

B

C

JANA Z KOLNA

4 European Solidarity Center

3 Monument to the Shipyard Workers

PLAC SOLIDARNOŚCI

GAZOWNICZA

WAŁY PIASTOWSKIE

ŁAGIEWNIKI

WAŁOWA

WAŁOWA

AKSAMITNA

GENERAŁA HENRYKA DĄBROWSKIEGO

GRADOWA

BŁĘDNIK

3 MAJA

GNILNA

RAJSKA

ZAUŁEK ŚW. BARTŁOMIEJA

J. HEWELIUSZA

RYBAKI

RYBAKI DOLNE

2

REDUTA MIEJSKA

32 Hewelianum

Gdańsk Główny

i

PODWALE GRODZKIE

GRODZKIE

PODBIELAŃSKA

KORZENNA

J. HEWELIUSZA

RAJSKA

WIELKIE MŁYNY

STOLARSKA

MNISZKI

BROWARNA

Church of St Bridget 9

KURKOWA

KURKOWA

3 MAJA

NOWE PODWALE GRODZKIE

PODWALE GRODZKIE

BIELAŃSKA

Great Mill 7

Old Town Hall 5

KOWALSKA

GARNCARSKA

NA PIASKACH

MEWY

8 Church of St Catherine

STAROMIEJSKIE

REDUTA MIEJSKA

STRZELECKA

NOWE OGRODY

HUCISKO

TARG DRZEWNY

PODWALE

PANSKA

PLAC DOMINIKAŃSKI

LAWENDOWA

5

SZKLARY

GROBLA II

3

TARG WĘGLOWY

ŚW. DUCHA

WĘGLARSKA

SZEROKA

KOZIA

MOKITRZOW

GROBLA I

Arsenal 13

KOŁODZIEJSKA

PIWNA

6

Royal Chapel 12

KLESZA

St George's Court

Highland Gate 14

17

TKACKA

LEKTYKARSKA

Church of St Mary 1

Main Town Hall 24

Golden House 22

25

Prison Tower 15

16

Golden Gate

DŁUGA

Uphagen House 20

POCZTOWA

19 Ulica Długa

Artus Court

WAŁY JAGIELLOŃSKIE

W. BOGUSŁAWSKIEGO

GARBARY

OGARNA

21

Długi Targ

ŁAWNICZA

MIESZCZAŃSKA

OGARNA

4

GDAŃSK

34 Gdynia

Around Gdańsk

0 km   3

0 miles   3

N

KAMIENNA GÓRA

ORŁOWO

Bay of Gdańsk

33 Sopot

KARLIKOWO

JELITKOWO

468

26 Oliwa Cathedral

BRZEŹNO

NOWY PORT

Westerplatte 30

31 Wisłoujście Fortress

ZA MURAMI

18 Shakespeare Theatre

Gdańsk Śródmieście

ŚRODOWIKÓW

PODWALE

RZEŹNICKA

PRZEDMIEJSKIE

KŁADKI

ZBYTKI

ZASPA

WRZESZCZ

OSTRÓW

89

Area of main Gdańsk map

GDAŃSK

501

OKOPOWA

ŚW. TRÓJCY

27 Church of the Holy Trinity

29 National Museum

ŻABI KRUK

TORUŃSKA

TARG MAŚLANY

LASTADIA

KOTWICZNIKÓW

5

A

B

C

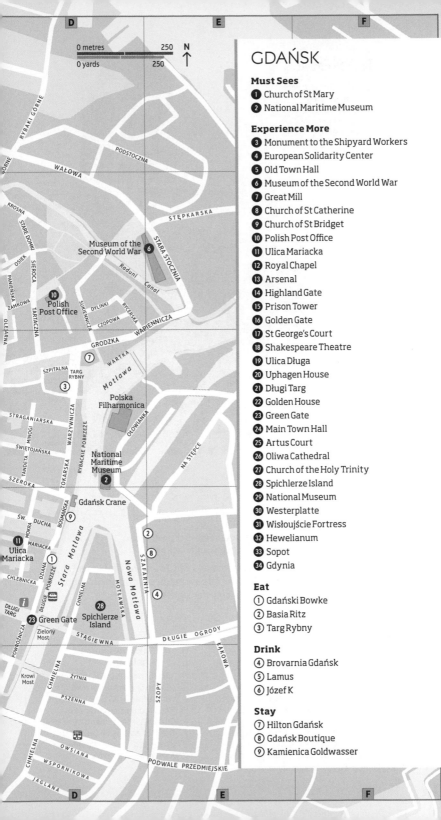

GDAŃSK

Must Sees
1. Church of St Mary
2. National Maritime Museum

Experience More
3. Monument to the Shipyard Workers
4. European Solidarity Center
5. Old Town Hall
6. Museum of the Second World War
7. Great Mill
8. Church of St Catherine
9. Church of St Bridget
10. Polish Post Office
11. Ulica Mariacka
12. Royal Chapel
13. Arsenal
14. Highland Gate
15. Prison Tower
16. Golden Gate
17. St George's Court
18. Shakespeare Theatre
19. Ulica Długa
20. Uphagen House
21. Długi Targ
22. Golden House
23. Green Gate
24. Main Town Hall
25. Artus Court
26. Oliwa Cathedral
27. Church of the Holy Trinity
28. Spichlerze Island
29. National Museum
30. Westerplatte
31. Wisłoujście Fortress
32. Hewelianum
33. Sopot
34. Gdynia

Eat
1. Gdański Bowke
2. Basia Ritz
3. Targ Rybny

Drink
4. Brovarnia Gdańsk
5. Lamus
6. Józef K

Stay
7. Hilton Gdańsk
8. Gdańsk Boutique
9. Kamienica Goldwasser

Did You Know?

In the 1980s, members of the banned Solidarity movement sought sanctuary in St Mary's.

CHURCH OF ST MARY

 C4 Ul Podkramarska 5 8:30am-5:30pm Mon-Sat (to 6:30pm Jul-Aug), 11am-noon & 1-5.30pm Sun bazylikamariacka.pl

Rising above the red-rooved houses of Gdańsk's Old Town, the monumental Church of St Mary (Kościół Mariacki) is the largest medieval brick-built church in Europe and one of the city's most spectacular sights.

Construction of the Church of St Mary began in 1343 on the site of an earlier wooden church, and took 150 years to complete. The final stage, completing the nave, was carried out by Henryk Hetzel. From 1529 until 1945, when it was destroyed during the carnage of World War II, St Mary's was a Protestant church. Like so many other parts of Gdańsk, it was rebuilt following the war. Compared with the weighty solidity of the exterior, the interior has a soaring, almost ethereal quality, painted all in white with clear glass side windows to fill it with light. It contains furnishings in the Gothic, Mannerist and Baroque styles.

GREAT VIEW
Take the Climbing Challenge

Tackle the 405 steps to reach the top of the church tower, which stands 78 m (255 ft) high, for sweeping panoramas of Gdańsk's historic centre and over the sea - sailors once used this tower as a valuable landmark. A small fee is payable.

↑ The buildings of the Old Town clustering around St Mary's Church

1 The Chapel of St Anne contains this 15th-century figure of the Virgin and Child by an unknown artist.

2 Plain whitewashing enhances the slenderness and grace of the church's columns and vaulting.

3 The astronomical clock, made by Hans Dürunger in 1464–70, shows the signs of the zodiac, the dates of movable feasts and the phases of the moon.

NATIONAL MARITIME MUSEUM

📍D3 🏠 Ul Ołowianka 9-13 🚌106, 111, 138
🕐 Summer: 10am-6pm daily; winter: 10am-4pm
Tue-Sun (to 3pm Dec) 🚫 Pub hols 🌐 nmm.pl

In the 17th century, Poland strove to be "master of the Baltic Sea" and her seafarers were dedicated to maintaining Poland's maritime presence. The fascinating history of these seafaring traditions is explored at the National Maritime Museum, housed in several buildings lining the River Motława.

There are four separate sections to the museum, two on either side of the river. The newly built Maritime Cultural Centre contains several permanent exhibitions, including a collection of small boats from around the world and an interactive exhibit of life in a working shipyard. Next door, the Gdańsk Crane is home to a number of exhibitions, including one that shows what harbour life was like during the 17th century, at the peak of Poland's attempts to dominate the Baltic Sea. Across the river, the Granaries contain waxwork exhibitions depicting the lives of Poles at sea, alongside an array of naval weapons that includes 17th-century Polish and Ruthenic cannon, as well as cannon from the Swedish warship *Solen*. You can also visit the *Sołdek*, the first Polish ocean-going ship to be built after World War II; constructed in the Gdańsk Shipyard in 1948, its holds are now used for exhibitions.

1 The Granaries on Ołowianka Island once stored goods including grain, salt, iron, anchors and millstones.

2 The museum's collection includes a variety of old cannons.

3 The interior of the *Sołdek* offers an insight into the living and working conditions aboard a coal-ore carrier.

HISTORY OF THE GDAŃSK CRANE

The Gdańsk Crane (Żuraw) is one of the city's finest buildings. A medieval structure almost unique in Europe, it was built in the 14th century and renovated in 1442–4, when it acquired its present appearance. Combining the functions of a city gate and a port crane, the wooden structure is set between two circular brick towers. It was operated by men working the huge treadmills within, and could lift weights of up to 2 tonnes to a height of 27 m (90 ft). The crane was used not only to load and unload goods but also to fit ships' masts. It burned down in 1945, but was reconstructed as part of the extensive citywide rebuilding programme after World War II.

←

The iconic Gdańsk Crane, dominating the cityscape at the edge of the river

EXPERIENCE MORE

❸

Monument to the Shipyard Workers

📍C1 🏛Pl Solidarności Robotniczej 🚌🚊

This monument was built a few months after the famous Gdańsk Shipyard workers' strike of 1980 and the creation of the independent Solidarity trade union. It was erected in honour of those shipyard workers who had previously been killed during the strike and demonstrations of December 1970; it stands 30 m (100 ft) from the spot where the first three victims fell. Its three stainless steel crosses, 42 m (130 ft) high, were both a warning that such a tragedy might happen again and a powerful symbol of remembrance and hope.

This distinctive monument was designed by a group of artists – among them the celebrated Polish sculptor, Robert Pepliński – alongside workers from the shipyard; the latter also assembled the monument. In the 1980s, the cross was the rallying point for Solidarity demonstrations.

❹

European Solidarity Centre

📍C1 🏛Pl Solidarności 1 🚌106, 111, 112, 123 🚊7, 8, 10 🕙10am–5pm Mon–Fri, 10am–6pm Sat & Sun 🚫Oct–Apr: Tue 🌐ecs.gda.pl

Dedicated to the history of Solidarity, the Polish Trade Union and Civil Resistance Movement, the European Solidarity Centre is located next to Gdańsk's shipyards.

The centre was built with the ambition of becoming a world hub for the ideas of freedom, democracy and solidarity.

Also a museum, it showcases the history of other opposition movements, many of which helped to instigate the democratic transformation of other countries in Central and Eastern Europe.

Visitors can enjoy views over the remains of the shipyards from the centre's viewing terrace or from its rooftop bar. The centre also regularly hosts workshops, events, concerts and a series of changing exhibitions.

SOLIDARITY

Solidarity was the first non-Communist trade union in Soviet-ruled Eastern Europe. Poland's Communist regime allowed the trade union to be founded, with Lech Wałęsa as its president, following the 1980 shipyard workers' strike. Its popularity spread, rendering the ruling regime more and more ineffective, until eventually they were forced to surrender control in 1989.

---

❺

Old Town Hall

📍B3 🏛Nadbałtyckie Centrum Kultury, Ul Korzenna 33/35 🚌106, 111, 112, 123 🚊2, 7, 10, 63 🌐nck.org.pl

Built by Antonis van Opbergen in 1587–95, the Old Town Hall is an outstanding example of Dutch Mannerist architecture. It is a compact, plain building with a defence tower. Beneath each bracket are two distorted masks personifying vice, and two smiling, chubby masks,

← Memorial to the shipyard workers at the European Solidarity Centre

→ Visitors looking at exhibits at the Museum of the Second World War in Gdańsk

> The building is a contemporary icon itself, a dramatically slanting structure that seems to be falling into the nearby canal.

personifying virtue. Inside, the painting, sculpture and furniture are very interesting, although little remains of the original decorative scheme of 1595. Of particular interest is the painted ceiling in one of the rooms by Hermann Hahn, a 17th-century Pomeranian artist. It was removed from a house at Ulica Długa 39 and transferred here some time after 1900. The ceiling paintings are allegorical: the one in the centre depicts *The Lord's Blessing*, in which a figure of Zygmunt III Vasa appears.

Museum of the Second World War

📍 D2 🏛 Pl Władysława Bartoszewskiego 1 🚌 100, 130 🕐 10am–7pm Tue–Fri, 10am–8pm Sat & Sun 🌐 muzeum1939.pl

Opened in 2017, this museum (Muzeum II Wojny Światowej) offers a fascinating, highly detailed account of the conflict. The building is a contemporary icon itself, a dramatically slanting structure that seems to be

falling into the nearby canal. The permanent exhibition covers all aspects of the war from the political tension of the 1930s to the ideological division of Europe after 1945. Tanks, aircraft and a re-created Warsaw street of 1939 are displayed. Particular attention is paid to the victims of war, with sections on the bombing of cities, the use of camps and slave labour, and the deliberate extermination of whole populations. The effect is profoundly moving.

Great Mill

📍 C3 🏛 Ul Wielkie Młyny 16 📞 58 305 24 05 🚌 132, 138, 154, 166 🚋 2, 8, 12, 63 🕐 Closed for renovation until late 2019

The Great Mill (Wielki Młyn), one of the largest industrial buildings in medieval Europe, was completed in around 1350. A two-storey bakery stood at the front, and beside the mill were large poles with millstones for grinding grain. The mill burned down in 1945, but was restored after the war.

EAT

Gdański Bowke
A roomy canalside pub-restaurant with traditional local cuisine focusing on seafood and house-brewed beer.

📍 D4 🏛 Ul Długie Pobrzeże 🌐 gdanskibowke.com

zł zł zł

Basia Ritz
For a stylish, modern take on Polish cuisine there are few better places. Fresh local ingredients are prepared with creativity and finesse.

📍 D4 🏛 Ul Szafarnia 6 🌐 restauracja-ritz.pl

zł zł zł

Targ Rybny
A pleasant seafood restaurant blending high standards of food with welcoming informailty.

📍 D3 🏛 Targ Rybny 6c 🌐 targrybny.pl

zł zł zł

The fine Church of
St Catherine, rising ↑
from the cityscape

DRINK

Brovarnia Gdańsk

Fronting the marina,
Brovarnia serves its
own beer and
Mediterranean food in
bright surroundings.
It also has live music
at weekends.

📍E4 🏠Ul Szafarnia 9
🌐brovarnia.pl

Lamus

This bohemian bar, with
an ironic retro interior,
has brought new life
(and a range of boutique
beers) to a hitherto
neglected corner of
the Old Town.

📍C3 🏠Lawendowa 8
📞58 691 97 40

Józef K

Characterful, kooky bar
on a busy street, with a
jumble of bird cages,
household implements
and unorthodox
lighting. The small
stone balcony is a good
place for people-
watching.

📍C4 🏠Ul Piwna 1/2
🌐jozefk.pl

 8

Church of St Catherine

📍C3 🏠Ul Profesorka 3
📞58 301 15 95 🚌132, 138,
154, 166 🚊2, 8, 12, 63
🌐muzeumgdansk.pl

The Church of St Catherine
(Kościół św. Katarzyny) is the
oldest and most important
parish church in the old town.
It was built in 1227–39 by the
dukes of Gdańsk-Pomerania.
Most of its Gothic, Mannerist
and Baroque furnishings were
pillaged or destroyed in 1945;
however, notable surviving
pieces include paintings by
Anton Möller and Izaak van
den Blocke, and the 1659
tombstone of the astron-
omer Johannes Hevelius.

The church's landmark
tower, standing 76 m (250 ft)
high, offers wonderful views
of the city. Housed within it is
the Gdańsk Science Museum,
part of the Museum of Gdańsk
(Muzeum Gdańska), containing an exhibt of tower clocks.

9

Church of St Bridget

📍C2 🏠Ul Profesorska 17
📞58 301 31 52 🚌132, 138,
154, 166 🚊2, 8, 12, 63

The Church of St Bridget
(Kościół św. Brygidy) was well
known in Poland in the 1980s
as a place of worship and
sanctuary for members of
Solidarity (p256). It was built
on the site of a 14th-century
chapel dedicated to St Mary
Magdalene, where in 1374 the
remains of St Bridget were
displayed. Soon afterwards
a monastery for the Sisters of
St Bridget was founded here.
The church built beside it was
completed in around 1514.

The brick shell of the Gothic
church contrasts with the
belfry, built in 1653 by Peter
Willer. The church's stark
interior is an effective foil for
the modern altars, sculptures
and tombstones that it now
contains. The most impressive
of these are the high altar and
the monument to Father
Jerzy Popiełuszko, who was
murdered in 1984 by Polish
security service officials.

10

Polish Post Office

📍D2 🏠Pl Obrońców Poczty
Polskiej 1/2 🚌100, 130
🕐May-Sep: 10am-1pm
Mon, 9am-4pm Tue-Fri,
10am-6pm Sat, 11am-
6pm Sun; Oct-Apr: 10am-
1pm Tue, 10am-4pm
Wed-Sat, 11am-4pm Sun
🌐muzeumgdansk.pl

This post office was the scene
of some of the most dramatic
events of the first days of
World War II. At daybreak on
1 September 1939, German
troops attacked the Polish
Postal Administration (in fact
the base of Polish intelligence
operations) in what was then
the free city of Gdańsk. For
15 hours the postal workers
resisted the onslaught, but
they were eventually over-
whelmed. On 5 October over
30 of them were executed by
Nazi soldiers at the Zaspa
Cemetery. Their heroism is

→

Ulica Mariacka, with
shoppers inspecting
amber items for sale

commemorated in the Post Office Museum, a branch of the Museum of Gdańsk, and by a monument depicting an injured postal worker atop scattered mail, handing over his rifle to Nike, the Greek goddess of victory.

Ulica Mariacka

📍 D4 🚌 106, 132, 166, 256 🚊 6, 7, 8, 63

Regarded as Gdańsk's finest street, Ulica Mariacka runs eastwards from the Church of St Mary to Długie Pobrzeże, terminating at the Mariacka Gate on the riverfront. Rebuilt from the ruins that resulted from World War II, the street contains outstanding examples of traditional Gdańsk architecture. Here, the town houses that were once owned by wealthy merchants and goldsmiths have tall, richly decorated façades; others are fronted by external raised terraces with ornamented parapets. It is small wonder that this picturesque street has for centuries inspired writers and artists.

During the long summer evenings, a number of musicians provide free open-air concerts, and welcoming street cafés stay open until late at night.

Royal Chapel

📍 C4 🏠 Ul św Ducha 58 📞 58 301 39 82 🚌 138, 154, 166, 178 🚊 2, 3, 6, 7

The Royal Chapel (Kaplica Królewska) was built by Jan III Sobieski as a place of worship for Catholics of the parish of St Mary's, which had become a Protestant church in 1529. The Baroque chapel was built in 1678–81 to designs by the great royal architect Tylman van Gameren. The interior is less ostentatious than the façade. The carving in the Kaplica Królewska is by Andreas Schlüter the Younger. The chapel itself is enclosed within a chamber and is situated on a raised floor.

Arsenal

📍 C4 🏠 Ul Targ Węglowy 6 🚌 138, 154, 166, 178 🚊 2, 3, 6, 7 🌐 asp.gda.pl

The Arsenal is perhaps the finest example of the Dutch Mannerist style in the whole of Gdańsk. Its red-brick and sandstone façade boasts

↑ The Arsenal building, adorned with figures and sculptures

original carvings by Wilhelm Barth. The building was initially constructed in 1600–9, probably to plans by Antonis van Opbergen in collaboration with Jan Strakowski. It has since been restored to its former glory following the damaged it sustained during World War II.

Today the ground floor of the former weapons and ammunition store is filled with shops, while the Academy of Fine Arts occupies the building's upper storeys.

14 Highland Gate

B4 **Ul Wały Jagiellońskie** 166, 200, 212, 256 2, 6, 8, 63

The Highland Gate marks the beginning of the Royal Way that, following Ulica Długa and Długi Targ, descends eastwards to the Green Gate. It was built by Hans Kramer of Saxony as part of the fortifications that were erected along the western limits of the city in 1571–6. Originally built in brick, the gate acquired its present appearance in 1588, when the Flemish architect Willem van den Blocke faced it with stone on its western side.

The gate's upper level is decorated with cartouches containing coats of arms: that of Poland, held by two angels flanked by the Prussian coat of arms, borne by unicorns; and those of Gdańsk, borne by lions.

→

Ulica Długa, looking towards the Golden Gate and PrisonTower

15 Prison Tower

B4 **Targ Węglowy 29** 166, 200, 212, 256 2, 6, 8, 63 muzeumgdansk.pl

The mix of architectural styles in the Prison Tower is the result of several rebuildings. The tower was originally built as part of the now-destroyed Ulica Długa Gate that was erected in the 14th century as part of the medieval fortifications of the Main Town. In the 15th and 16th centuries, the tower was heightened several times and the surrounding buildings altered accordingly. When the new fortifications were built in 1571–6, the complex lost its purpose and became a prison, court and torture chamber.

It was remodelled in 1604 by Antonis van Opbergen, who gave it a northern Mannerist form, and by Willem van der Meer, who added decorative detail. The tower was the scene of many blood-curdling interrogations. A whipping post on the western

> **The tower was the scene of many blood-curdling interrogations. A whipping post on the western wall was also the site of executions.**

wall was also the site of many executions.The Prison Tower now houses the Amber Museum, part of the Museum of Gdańsk, which tells the fascinating story of Batlic Amber and showcases a selection of jewellery.

16 Golden Gate

B4 **Ul Długa** 166, 200, 212, 256 2, 6, 8, 63

The Golden Gate was built in 1612–14 on the site of the medieval Ulica Długa Gate. The architect, Abraham van den Blocke, devised the new construction in the style of a classical Roman triumphal arch through which the Royal

←

The historic Prison Tower, now housing the Amber Museum *(inset)*

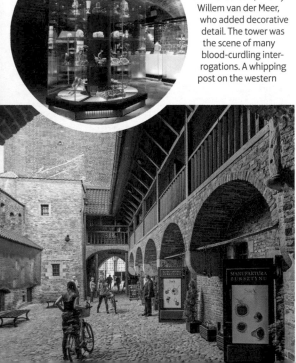

Way would enter the city. The arches of the gate are framed by Ionic columns in the lower tier surmounted by composite columns in the upper tier. Crowning the gate are statues carved by Piotr Ringering in 1648, reconstructed after the originals were damaged in World War II. Those on the outer side of the gate, facing away from the city, depict peace, freedom, prosperity and glory, while those facing the city, portray prudence, piety, justice and harmony. The decoration is complemented by inscriptions on the theme of civic virtue.

St George's Court

📍 B4 🚪 Ul Targ Węglowy 27 🚌 166, 200, 212, 256 🚋 2, 6, 8, 63 🔒 Closed to visitors

The fraternity of St George, an association of archers and the oldest of its kind in medieval Gdańsk, originally met in Artus Court. However, it later acquired its own premises, St George's Court, which was built in the Flemish style and completed in 1494.

The first floor contained an archery range and storerooms for equipment. Members met in the Great Hall on the first floor. The hall was also used for ceremonies, meetings and banquets, and as a theatre.

Shakespeare Theatre

📍 B4 🚪 Ul Bogusławskiego 1 🚌 112, 138, 166 🚋 8, 9 ⏰ Box office: 1pm–8pm daily 🌐 teatrszekspirowski.pl

Gdańsk has staged an international Shakespeare festival since 1993. In 2014, this annual event got a purpose-built home at this theatre. As well as hosting the festival, the theatre is a year-round venue for quality music and drama. The main performance space has a retractable roof and several tiers of balustraded boxes, mirroring the theatres of Elizabethan London.

Ulica Długa

📍 C4 🚌 111, 166, 200, 256 🚋 7, 8, 9, 63

Ulica Długa ("long street") is the Main Town's principal street. The houses that line it were once inhabited by the foremost burghers of Gdańsk, and virtually every one has a colourful history. Although the

oldest surviving houses on the street date from the Middle Ages, most were built during the heyday of the Hanseatic League. With their narrow façades crowned by a variety of decorative elements, they are typical of Gdańsk architecture. Sadly, their stepped terraces were removed in the 19th century.

After the carnage of World War II, almost every building was left in ruins. Although many of the houses were later reconstructed, only the finest buildings were rebuilt in architectural detail.

 The splendidly ornate doorway of Uphagen House on Ulica Długa

 20 ✦

Uphagen House

📍 C4 🏛 Ul Długa 12 🚌 111, 166, 200, 256 🚋 7, 8, 9, 63 🕐 10am–1pm Mon, 10am–6pm Tue–Sat, 11am–6pm Sun 🌐 muzeumgdansk.pl

The house that originally stood here was acquired by Johann Uphagen, a town councillor, in 1775. He had it demolished, and a new residence was built in its place. The architect, Johann Benjamin Dreyer, completed the project in 1787, creating an attractive building combining Baroque, Rococo and early-Neo-Classical features.

The sole ornamentation of the restrained façade is the Rococo decoration to the door, which is inscribed with the initial "A" for Abigail, the owner's wife. The splendid interiors are now part of the Museum of Gdańsk.

21

Długi Targ

📍 C4 🚌 111, 166, 200, 256 🚋 7, 8, 9, 63

This broad, short street that runs on from Ulica Długa and terminates at the Green Gate on the River Motława, is the final part of the Royal Way

leading from the Golden Gate through to the city centre. It also functioned as a marketplace, as well as a site for the public execution of aristocratic prisoners. The town houses on Długi Targ, like those elsewhere in the old town, were destroyed in 1945 but have now been restored.

The square's focal point is the Fountain of Neptune, which was installed outside Artus Court in 1633. According to legend, Neptune hit the water with his trident and shattered the gold coins in the fountain into fine flakes, creating the famous Gdańsk Goldwasser liquor. This wonderful herbal liquor is decorated with flakes of gold.

 22

Golden House

📍 C4 🏛 Długi Targ 41 🚌 111, 166, 200, 256 🚋 7, 8, 9, 63 🕐 Closed to the public

Also known as Speimann House or Steffens House after its owners, this building was constructed in 1609–18 for

3

The number of city gates that line the Royal Way in Gdańsk's Main Town.

the mayor of Gdańsk, Jan Speimann, a wealthy merchant and patron of the arts, and his wife Maria Judyta. The most impressive feature of the house is its fine façade, which is covered in intricate gilt carvings, and which luckily escaped the fires that ravaged the building in 1945.

Local people claim that the house is haunted; in one of the corridors the figure of the former lady of the house, Maria Judyta Speimann, is said to appear and whisper the words "A just deed fears no man". Today the building houses the Maritime Institute.

23 ✦

Green Gate

📍 D4 🚌 111, 166, 200, 256 🚋 7, 8, 9, 63 🏛 Długi Targ 24 🕐 10am–5pm Tue–Sun 🌐 muzeumgdansk.pl

With its pinnacled roof and decorative stonework, the Green Gate hardly resembles the usual city gate – in fact, it is far more like a mansion. There is good reason for this: the gate was actually intended to serve as an opulent residence for visiting royalty. In the event it was used for this purpose only once – when Maria Louisa Gonzaga arrived in Gdańsk from France in order to marry Władysław IV in 1646.

The gate was designed in the Mannerist style by the architect Johann Kramer from Dresden, and built in 1564–8 by Regnier from Amsterdam. From its windows there is a magnificent view of Ulica Długi Targ and the town hall in one direction, and the River Motława and Spichlerze Island in the other. The Green Gate now houses a branch of the National Museum (p254).

 →

The Main Town Hall, soaring above shoppers on Ulica Długi

Main Town Hall

📍 C4 🏛 Ul Długa 47 ☎ 58 573 31 28 🚌 111, 166, 200, 256 🚊 7, 8, 9, 63

Begun in 1327, the town hall had an elegant tower added in 1486–8, during one of several phases of rebuilding. After a fire in 1556, it was remodelled in the Mannerist style. The interior was lavishly decorated in 1593–1608 by the most prominent painters and craftsmen of the day, producing one of the finest town halls in all of northern Europe, proof of the city's wealth and power.

The highlight is without a doubt the Red Room, which was once the Great Council Chamber. The Renaissance fireplace is by Willem van der Meer and the centrepiece of the ceiling paintings is the *Apotheosis of Gdańsk* by Izaak van den Blocke. The town hall was rebuilt following World War II and many of its furnishings reconstructed. It now houses the **Museum of the History of Gdańsk**, a branch of the Museum of Gdańsk, which showcases the building's opulent interiors and has exhibits on everyday life in the city pre-World War II.

Museum of the History of Gdańsk

 🕙 10am–1pm Mon, 10am–6pm Tue–Sat, 11am–6pm Sun 🌐 muzeumgdansk.pl

㉕ Artus Court

📍 C4 🏛 Długi Targ 44 ☎ 78 944 96 54 🚌 111, 166, 200 🚊 7, 8, 9, 63 🕙 10am–1pm Mon, 10am–6pm Tue–Sat, 10am–6pm Sun

This court was a meeting place for Gdańsk's wealthy burghers, who were inspired by the chivalrous traditions of King Arthur and the Knights of the Round Table. Similar fraternities were set up across Europe, and were particularly fashionable in the Hanseatic League cities. Visitors came to discuss the issues of the day and to enjoy the fine beer served there in unlimited quantities. The first Artus Court in Gdańsk was formed in the 14th century, but the original building burned down in 1477. The present building opened in 1481. Its rear elevation

↑ The interior of historic Artus Court, set up as if for the old city burghers

preserves the original Gothic style, although the façade has been rebuilt several times since then. Despite wartime destruction, reconstruction has succeeded in recreating something of the historic atmosphere of the court, now a branch of the Museum of Gdańsk. A highlight of the interior is the intricately decorated 16th-century Renaissance tiled stove, 12 m (40 ft) high.

↑ The grand entrance to the 14th-century Oliwa Cathedral, which contains a famous organ

26
Oliwa Cathedral

 A5 🏠 Biskupa Edmunda Nowickiego 5 📞 58 552 47 65 🅿 🚌 117, 169, 171 🚋 2, 6, 11

Northwest of Gdańsk, the Oliwa district was once the base of wealthy Cistercians, who built a cathedral and monastery here. The present Gothic cathedral, built in the 14th century, replaced the original church destroyed by fire in 1350. While the exterior has survived without major alteration, the interior has been redecorated in a Baroque style. Its famous organ can be heard in recitals. The monastery now houses branches of the Diocesan, Contemporary Art and Ethnographical museums. Nearby Oliwa Park is a pleasant place for a walk.

27
Church of the Holy Trinity

🅱 B5 🏠 Ul św. Trójcy 4 📞 58 320 79 80 🚌 106, 111, 178, 186 🚋 8, 9

The imposing Church of the Holy Trinity (Kościół św. Trójcy) was built by Franciscan monks in 1420–1514. In 1480, the Chapel of St Anne was constructed alongside the church. Protestantism quickly spread to Gdańsk, and one of its most ardent proponents in the region was the Franciscan friar Alexander Svenichen. When congregations declined because of his activities, the Franciscans decided in 1556 to give the monastery to the city as a theological college. The head of the Franciscan order did not agree with the Gdańsk friars' decision to cede the monastery. However, the order's petitions to the Polish kings to have the property returned bore no result and the church was transferred to the Protestants. The grammar school that was established here later became the widely celebrated Academic Grammar School. It also came to house the first library in Gdańsk. However, centuries later, in 1945, it was returned to the Catholics, after the violence of World War II had reduced it to a ruin.

The aisled church has a distinctive exterior with ornamental Gothic spires. They crown the elongated presbytery, the façade and the walls of the adjacent Chapel of St Anne. The presbytery was separated from the aisles by a wall. Interesting features of the interior are the many tombstones that are set into the floor and the numerous works by Gdańsk artists. The very fine Gothic stalls were made by local craftsmen in 1510–11. Their carved decorations depict a variety of subjects, including a monkey, a lion fighting a dragon, and birds.

The church contains the oldest surviving pulpit in Gdańsk – it dates from 1541 and is another remarkable example of local woodcarving. In the north aisle is the marble tomb made by Abraham van den Blocke in 1597 for Giovanni Bernardo Bonifacio, Marquis d'Orii, a restless spirit and an avid champion of the Reformation who founded the Gdańsk library. "Bones long since thrown ashore here finally rest from their earthly wanderings" reads the poetic Latin inscription of the tomb. Beside the church is a half-timbered galleried house dating from the 17th century.

28
Spichlerze Island

 D4 🚌 106, 111, 112, 138 🚋 8, 9

Once joined to the mainland, Spichlerze Island was created when the New Motława Canal was dug in 1576. A centre of trade first developed here at the end of the 13th century,

↑ *The Last Judgement*, by Hans Memling, in the National Museum

beginning with a relatively small number of granaries. By the 16th century this had expanded to more than 300 granaries, each of which had a unique name and a façade that was decorated with an individual emblem. The purpose of digging the canal, and thus of surrounding the district with water, was not only to protect the granaries against fire, but also to help safeguard their contents against thieves.

Almost all of the granaries were destroyed in 1945. For a long time the island remained derelict, until a recent surge of regeneration projects totally changed its appearance. The remaining handful of red-brick granaries were restored, and the vacant lots between them filled with modern structures built in the same tall, steep-roofed style. Hotels and shopping centres are the principal tenants of this new urban landscape.

Running through Spichlerze Island is Ulica Stągiewna, leading to the **Amber Sky** ferris wheel, offering rides with a superb view of the Gdańsk skyline. At Stągiewna's other end are two impressive cylindrical 16th-century castle keeps, known as the "Milk Churns" (Stągwie Mleczne).

Amber Sky

 🏛 Ul Stągiewna
🕐 10am–10pm Mon–Thu & Sun, 10am–midnight Fri & Sat 🌐 ambersky.pl

29
National Museum

📍 B5 🏛 Ul Toruńska 1
🚌 106, 112, 138, 178
🚋 8, 9 🕐 May–Sep: 10am–5pm Tue–Sun; Oct–Apr: 9am–4pm Tue–Sun
🌐 mng.gda.pl

The collection held by the National Museum is laid out mainly in a former Gothic Franciscan monastery of 1422–1522. It contains a range of artifacts and art works in various media, from wrought-iron grilles to sculpture and painting. The museum's most prized piece is *The Last Judgement* by the Flemish painter Hans Memling (c 1430–94). In 1473, it was plundered by privateers from Gdańsk from a ship bound for Italy.

30
Westerplatte

📍 A5 🚌 106, 138, 606
🏛 During summer at Green Gate Guardhouse No 1

It was on this peninsula that the first shots of World War II were fired, on 1 September 1939. The German battleship *Schleswig Holstein* opened fire on Polish ammunition dumps in the Free City of Gdańsk. The Germans expected the capture of the Westerplatte to take a matter of hours, but the 182-man garrison under Major Henryk Sucharski held out for seven days; their heroism became a symbol of Polish resistance in the struggle against the Nazi invasion. Today, ruined barracks and concrete bunkers, together with a huge Monument to the Defenders of Westerplatte (1966), bear witness to that struggle. A permanent exhibit is also hosted here by the Museum of the Second World War *(p257)*.

↑ Westerplatte's moving Monument to Polish military heroism

EXPERIENCE Gdańsk

31
Wisłoujście Fortress

A5 **Ul Stara Twierdza 1** **106, 606** **Hours vary, check website** **muzeum gdansk.pl**

Fortifications were first built on this strategic point at the mouth of the River Vistula in the time of the Teutonic Knights. Construction of a brick tower began in 1482, and from here a duty was levied on passing ships using a simple and unavoidable enforcement method – a chain stretched across the river, preventing the ship's passage, which was released only when the captain had made payment. The tower was also used as a lighthouse.

In 1562–3 the tower was surrounded by a system of defences, and afterwards was repeatedly fortified as military technology advanced. During 1586–7 the entire complex was reinforced by adding four bastions and an outer moat. This was followed by the construction of a ditch in 1624–6. Also during the 17th century, the now-ageing tower was joined by an extra 15 tall barrack buildings.

Over the following years, constant building steadily enlarged the fortress. It withstood several sieges and was often used to accommodate visiting royalty.

A branch of the Museum of Gdańsk, this impressive fortress is today open to visitors and contains an impressive collection of weaponry.

32
Hewelianum

A2 **Ul Gradowa 6** **106, 132, 154, 189** **2, 3, 6, 7** **10am–4pm Tue-Sun** **hewelianum.pl**

An enthralling multimedia attraction devoted to science, the Hewelianum occupies the red-brick bastions of the 18th-century Góra Gradowa fort that overlooks the city centre from the east. The museum's name comes from Johannes Hevelius (1611-1687), the Gdańsk-born astronomer who was one of the first people to map the surface of the moon. Spread across several of the fortress buildings are displays on the formation of the earth, evolution, technology and physics. Exhibits have been carefully chosen so that all ages – young children, teens and adults – will find something of interest.

Located downhill to the southwest is a children's play area and fitness park.

33
Sopot

A5 **Plac Zdrojowy 2; www.sopot.pl**

Sopot, together with the neighbouring cities of Gdańsk and Gdynia, makes up the Tri-City, an extensive metropolitan area on the western shore of the Bay of Gdańsk. Sopot is the most popular resort on the Baltic coast and is easily explored on a day trip from Gdańsk. It was established as a sea-bathing centre in 1824 by Jean Georges Haffner, a physician in the Napoleonic army. Its heyday came in the interwar years, when it attracted some of Europe's richest people.

The city's pier is a continuation of the main street, Ulica Bohaterów Monte Cassino, colloquially known as Monciak. The pier is 512 m (1,680 ft) long and the bench encircling it is Europe's longest. The pier is lined with bars, restaurants and cake shops, as well as antique shops and boutiques selling amber. It is a pleasant place to enjoy a beer and some sea air. Or, visit the splendid Neo-Baroque 1920s Grand Hotel, which overlooks the beach, for a coffee. The Crooked

INSIDER TIP
Go Boating

Take to the water to admire the beauty of Gdańsk. Water trams (www.ztm.gda.pl) run from Green Gate to Westerplatte and Nowy Port. Some routes also cover Sopot and Gdynia.

↑ Visitors and locals strolling along a pedestrianized street in the resort of Sopot

House (Ul Haffnera 6) is one of the city's most famous buildings, and undeniably its quirkiest sight.

 34

Gdynia

📍A4 🏛️🚃 🚊Ul 10 Lutego 24; gdynia.pl

Alongide Gdańsk and Sopot, Gdynia forms part of the huge metropolitan area known as the Tri-City. As with Sopot, it can be easily explored on a day trip from Gdańsk.

When Poland regained independence in 1918 it was denied access to the sea at Gdańsk (which became an independent city-state) and chose the obscure village of Gdynia for its port and naval facilities. Gdynia grew into a

model city, characterized by straight boulevards and Art-Deco apartment blocks.

Today, it is a bustling mix of commerce and leisure. The main focus for visitors is the South Pier (Molo Południowe), where two museum ships are moored. The *Błyskawica* is a destroyer that saw action in World War II alongside Allied forces in Narvik and Dunkirk. Next to it is the 1909 *Dar Pomorza*, a three-masted training vessel.

At the end of the pier is a statue of Polish-British writer Joseph Conrad (1857–1924), a lifelong seaman. Also on the pier is the **Gdynia Aquarium** (Akwarium Gdyńskie), with an array of international sea and wetland creatures.

Leading south from the pier is a popular promenade lined with several cafés and restaurants. After 1 km (half a mile) it reaches Redłowo Beach, a golden strip of sand beneath Kępa Redłowska hill.

Gdynia was the departure point for ocean-going liners in the interwar years, and the Art-Deco passenger terminal has been transformed into the compelling **Museum of Emigration** (Muzeum Emigracji). It tells the story

←

The heavily fortified Wisłoujście Fortress on the Vistula estuary in Gdańsk

of Polish emigration – whether for economic or political reasons – through an engrossing mixture of mementoes, models and multimedia exhibits. It also deals with the impact of the Polish diaspora on the country itself.

On the southern outskirts of Gdynia, the **Experyment Science Centre** (Centrum Nauki Experyment) is an engaging hands-on attraction that educates children and introduces them to the joys of science.

Gdynia Aquarium

♿♿ 🚊Al Jana Pawła II 1 🕐10am–5pm daily 🌐akwarium.gdynia.pl

Museum of Emigration

♿♿♿ 🚊Ul Polska 1 🚌119, 133, 137 🕐noon–8pm Tue, 10am–6pm Wed–Sun 🌐polskal.pl

Experyment Science Centre

♿ 🚊Al Zwycięstwa 96/98 🚌119, 133, 137 🚊21, 24, 26 🕐10am–6pm, Tue–Fri, 10am–7pm Sat & Sun 🌐experyment.gdynia.pl

---

POLISH MUSIC SCENE

The port city of Sopot was the birthplace of Polish pop music. Here, merchant seamen frequently returned home bearing jeans and vinyl records, the latter inspiring new types of music. The city's beach resorts were the first places in Poland to have regular discos where beat music was played. The Sopot Festival, inaugurated in 1961, quickly emerged as a platform for new sounds, launching local stars such as Czesław Niemen, as well as hosting concerts by international guests.

A SHORT WALK
DŁUGI TARG
AND ULICA DŁUGA

Distance 700 m (765 yd) **Nearest station** Gdańsk Główny **Time** 15 minutes

Długi Targ and Ulica Długa, its continuation, are the most attractive streets in Gdańsk. Długi Targ leads westwards from the Green Gate on the River Motława to join Ulica Długa, which runs as far as the Golden Gate. These two pedestrianized streets are lined with old town houses that were once the residences of the city's wealthiest citizens. Most of the Main

Town's principal buildings, including the Main Town Hall and Artus Court, are on Długi Targ. Together the streets formed an avenue that was used for parades, ceremonies and sometimes public executions and, from 1457, for the processions that accompanied royal visits – which is why the two streets were known collectively as the Royal Way.

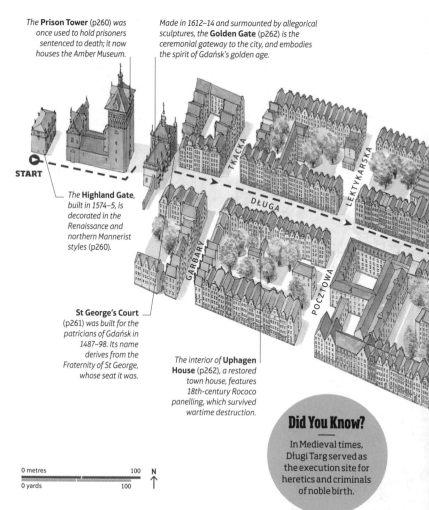

*The **Prison Tower** (p260) was once used to hold prisoners sentenced to death; it now houses the Amber Museum.*

*Made in 1612–14 and surmounted by allegorical sculptures, the **Golden Gate** (p262) is the ceremonial gateway to the city, and embodies the spirit of Gdańsk's golden age.*

START

*The **Highland Gate**, built in 1574–5, is decorated in the Renaissance and northern Mannerist styles (p260).*

St George's Court *(p261) was built for the patricians of Gdańsk in 1487–98. Its name derives from the Fraternity of St George, whose seat it was.*

*The interior of **Uphagen House** (p262), a restored town house, features 18th-century Rococo panelling, which survived wartime destruction.*

TKACKA · DŁUGA · LEKTYKARSKA · GARBARY · POCZTOWA

Did You Know?

In Medieval times, Długi Targ served as the execution site for heretics and criminals of noble birth.

0 metres   100
0 yards   100

N ↑

Locator Map
For more detail see p250

← The Golden Gate on Ulica Długa, with the Prison Tower rising behind it

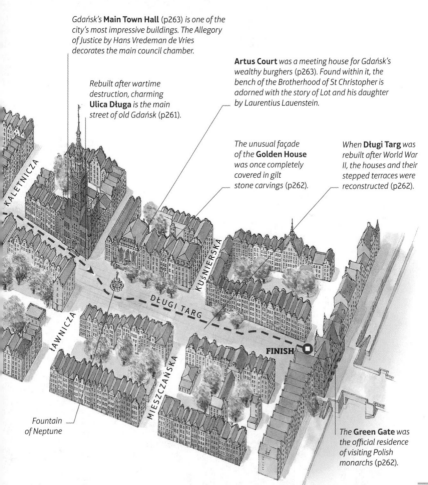

Gdańsk's **Main Town Hall** (p263) *is one of the city's most impressive buildings. The Allegory of Justice by Hans Vredeman de Vries decorates the main council chamber.*

Artus Court *was a meeting house for Gdańsk's wealthy burghers (p263). Found within it, the bench of the Brotherhood of St Christopher is adorned with the story of Lot and his daughter by Laurentius Lauenstein.*

Rebuilt after wartime destruction, charming **Ulica Długa** *is the main street of old Gdańsk (p261).*

The unusual façade of the **Golden House** *was once completely covered in gilt stone carvings (p262).*

When **Długi Targ** *was rebuilt after World War II, the houses and their stepped terraces were reconstructed (p262).*

KALETNICZA

ŁAWNICZA

KUŚNIERSKA

DŁUGI TARG

MIESZCZAŃSKA

FINISH ▢

Fountain of Neptune

The **Green Gate** *was the official residence of visiting Polish monarchs (p262).*

POMERANIA

Pomerania, a land of beautiful beaches, peaceful lakes and alpine scenery, is divided into the two regions of Western and Eastern Pomerania, each with an ethnically diverse population. During the 12th century, Christianity was introduced to Western Pomerania and the Duchy of Pomerania was established. Maintaining its independence for several centuries, the duchy secured economic development through its port cities, which were part of the Hanseatic League. The Thirty Years' War brought this independence to an end, with most of Western Pomerania coming under the rule of Brandenburg, while Szczecin and the surrounding area was engulfed by Sweden until 1713. In the 18th and 19th centuries, this area became first Prussian, then German, territory. It was returned to Poland in 1945 following the end of World War II. Eastern Pomerania was Christianized in the 10th century. Although it was originally part of Poland, it became an independent duchy from the 12th century, before being overrun by the Teutonic Knights in 1306. In 1466, after the Second Peace of Toruń, areas of Eastern Pomerania were ceded to Poland. However, during the Partitions of Poland, this region became part of Prussia, before again being returned to Poland in 1919.

POMERANIA

Must Sees

1. Szczecin
2. Malbork Castle
3. Toruń
4. Kashubian Switzerland

Experience More

5. Chełmno
6. Świnoujście
7. Stargard Szczeciński
8. Drawsko Lakes
9. Darłowo
10. Kołobrzeg
11. Słupsk
12. Słowiński National Park
13. Chojnice
14. Bytów
15. Hel Peninsula
16. Pelplin Abbey
17. Gniew
18. Kwidzyn
19. Bydgoszcz
20. Grudziądz
21. Golub-Dobrzyń
22. Ciechocinek
23. Stutthof Museum

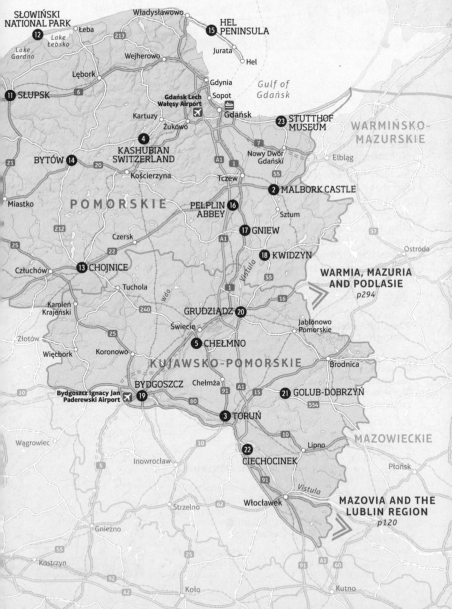

Karlskrona, Nynäshamm ↑

Baltic Sea

POMERANIA

SŁOWIŃSKI NATIONAL PARK
12 Łeba
Lake Łebsko
Lake Gardno
213 Władysławowo
HEL PENINSULA 15
Jurata
Hel
Wejherowo
Lębork
Gdynia
Sopot
11 SŁUPSK
6
Gdańsk Lech Wałęsy Airport
Gdańsk
Kartuzy
Żukowo
STUTTHOF MUSEUM 23
WARMIŃSKO-MAZURSKIE
4 KASHUBIAN SWITZERLAND
Kościerzyna
Nowy Dwór Gdański
7
A1
1
Elbląg
21
BYTÓW 14
20
Tczew
55
MALBORK CASTLE 2
POMORSKIE
212
Czersk
PELPLIN ABBEY 16
Sztum
25
22
GNIEW 17
A1
Człuchów
13 CHOJNICE
KWIDZYN 18
Tuchola
wda
55
Ostróda
57
Kamień Krajeński
240
1
16
WARMIA, MAZURIA AND PODLASIE p294
Złotów
25
GRUDZIĄDZ 20
Jabłonowo Pomorskie
Więcbork
Koronowo
Świecie
5 CHEŁMNO
KUJAWSKO-POMORSKIE
Brodnica
Wągrowiec
10
BYDGOSZCZ
Chełmża
91
A1
15
21 GOLUB-DOBRZYŃ
554
Bydgoszcz Ignacy Jan Paderewski Airport
19
80
MAZOWIECKIE
5
Inowrocław
10
3 TORUŃ
10
Lipno
Płońsk
22 CIECHOCINEK
91
Strzelno
62
Włocławek
Vistula
MAZOVIA AND THE LUBLIN REGION p120
Gniezno
25
Kostrzyn
55
92
A2
Koło
91
A1
60
Kutno
Miastko
Vistula
Gulf of Gdańsk

The colourful houses on the riverfront in Szczecin sparkling in summer

with finds from Western Pomerania. Among the many interesting exhibits are Gothic artworks and the costumes of Pomeranian princes.

Szczecin Philharmonic

🏠 Ul Małopolska 48
🕐 Ticket office: Tue–Fri 1–6pm; guided tours: 2pm on Fri 🌐 filharmonia. szczecin.pl

One of the most spectacular of Poland's 21st-century public buildings, Szczecin Philharmonic (Filharmonia w Szczecinie) looms like a cluster of opaque icebergs above Plac Solidarności. Designed by Barcelona's Studio Barozzi Veiga, the concert hall's angular white-clad exterior features a row of steep gables.

SZCZECIN

📍 A2 ✈️ 33 km N in Goleniów 🚉 Ul Kolumba
🚌 Pl Grodnicki ℹ️ szczecin.pl

Szczecin, on the river Odra, is a major port despite the fact that it is more than 65 km (40 miles) from the sea. It serves both ocean-going vessels and river traffic, and the river links it with Berlin. A castle and a fishing village existed here in the 9th century. It became the capital of a Pomeranian duchy, and later a major port. Szczecin suffered during World War II but restoration has been confined to its more important buildings.

①

The Upheavals Dialogue Centre

🏠 Pl Solidarności 1
🕐 10am–6pm Tue–Thu & Sat, 10am–4pm Fri & Sun
🌐 przelomy.muzeum. szczecin.pl

Part of the National Museum, the compelling Upheavals Dialogue Centre (Centrum Dialogu Przełomy) is devoted to Szczecin's modern history from 1939 to 1989, when it was affected by some of the 20th century's most significant events, wars and political movements. The building, which is designed by Robert Konieczny, is as dramatic as its content, a sloping grey slab that lies partly underground.

Inside, photographs, films and personal mementoes reveal the impact of totalitarianism and war on ordinary people. The Polish revolts against Communism are covered in detail, including the Szczecin shipyard strikes of 1970 when 16 protestors were killed by security forces.

---

②

National Museum

🏠 Ul Staromłyńska 27
🕐 10am–6pm Tue–Thu & Sat; 10am–4pm Fri & Sun (free Sat) 🌐 muzeum. szczecin.pl

This fascinating museum has an extensive collection of non-European artifacts, along

The all-white theme continues into the lobby, with its spiral staircase, while the main hall has a ceiling made of splinter-like wooden panels.

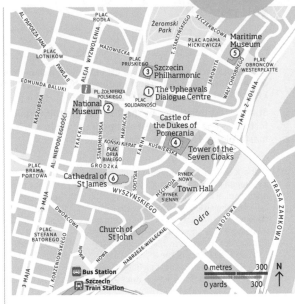

Castle of the Dukes of Pomerania

Ul Korsarzy 34 ◷11am-6pm Tue-Sun ⊠zamek.szczecin.pl

The large Castle of the Dukes of Pomerania was built in the mid-13th century and renovated in the Renaissance style in 1575–7. It has five wings with two interior courtyards and two towers. The east wing dates from the 17th century. After damage suffered during World War II, the castle had to be almost completely rebuilt.

In the former crypt of the dukes of Pomerania is a museum with an exhibition on the history and the restoration of the castle, as well as displays including the tin coffins of the last of the Gryfici dynasty. The castle balcony overlooks the Odra and offers a view of the Tower of the Seven Cloaks, the only remaining part of the city's medieval fortifications.

Across the road is the Royal Gate, one of a pair built under Swedish rule in 1726–8.

Maritime Museum

Ul Wały Chrobrego 3 ◷10am-6pm Tue-Thu & Sat, 10am-4pm Fri & Sun ⊠muzeum.szczecin.pl

Covering the long history of seafaring in the Baltic sea, this museum includes exhibits of amber and silver jewellery, and boats and fishing vessels displayed in a *skansen* behind the museum. There are also models of ships, nautical instruments and an ethnographical section. From the terraces, there is a fine view of the harbour below.

The Cathedral of St James

Św. Jakuba Apostoła 1 ◷Tower: 10am-7pm Mon-Thu, 10am-8pm Fri-Sun ⊠katedra.szczecin.pl

The spectacular Cathedral of St James (Katedra św. Jakuba) was erected in stages from the late 13th to the 15th centuries, but was almost completely destroyed by bombing in World War II; only the presbytery and west tower survived. It has since been rebuilt. The cathedral is home to several impressive Gothic altars, which were brought from other churches in Pomerania.

←
The dramatically modern, white exterior of the Szczecin Philharmonic Hall

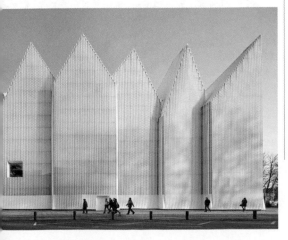

MALBORK CASTLE

🅐D2 🏠 Ul Kościuszki 54, Malbork 🚌🚉 🕐 May-Sep: 9am-7pm daily;
Oct-Apr: 10am-3pm daily (courtyard open 1 hr longer) 🔒 1 Jan, 8 Apr,
1 Nov, 25 Dec 🌐 zamek.malbork.pl

Strategically positioned by the River Nogat, this formidable fortress is one of the largest castles in the world and is a true masterpiece of medieval architecture.

Malbork, the castle of the Teutonic Knights, was begun in the 13th century. In 1309 it was made capital of an independent state established by the order. The first major phase of building was the Assembly Castle, a fortified monastery later known as the Upper Castle. The Middle Castle was built some time after 1310, and the Palace of the Grand Master in 1382–99 by Konrad Zöllner von Rotenstein. One of the greatest medieval battles took place here in 1410, when King Władysław II laid siege to the castle in an attempt to crush the power of the Teutonic Kights following the Battle of Grunwald (p61). In 1457 Malbork Castle was taken by Poland and used as a fortress. It was restored in the 19th century, and again after World War II; in December 1997, UNESCO declared the castle a World Heritage Site. Today this expansive complex is open for visitors to explore.

↑ View over the River Nogat to the impressive fortifications of Malbork Castle

The Golden Gate, built in the late 13th century, is enclosed by a porch; the keystone in the vaulting is carved with the figure of Christ.

Summer Refectory

Palace of the Grand Master

Upper Castle

Cloistered Courtyard

↑ Malbork Castle, a magnificent complex once home to the Teutonic Knights

💬 INSIDER TIP
Catch a Show

In summer, the castle's evening son-et-lumiere show sees lighting effects and music take over the central courtyard. Tickets should be purchased from the castle ticket office or online (www.zamek. malbork.pl).

① The four-storey Palace of the Grand Master was often thought to be one of the most splendid buildings in all of medieval Europe.

② Reenactments take place at Malbork Castle, with participants wearing the traditional battle dress of the Teutonic Knights: white cloaks marked with black crosses.

③ The castle's Summer Refectory has double rows of windows and late-Gothic palm vaulting supported on a central granite column. The Winter Refectory adjoins it on its eastern side.

Located in the Lower Castle, these partly reconstructed farm buildings, abutting the former Chapel of St Lawrence, have been converted into a hotel.

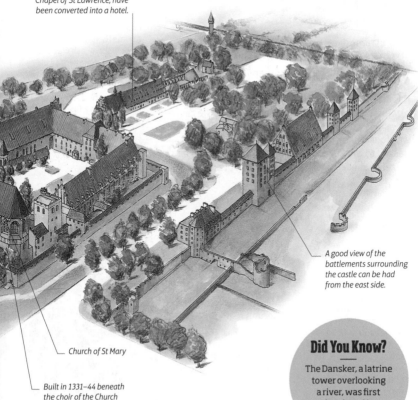

A good view of the battlements surrounding the castle can be had from the east side.

Church of St Mary

Built in 1331–44 beneath the choir of the Church of St Mary, the Chapel of St Anne contains the tombs of eleven Grand Masters.

Did You Know?

The Dansker, a latrine tower overlooking a river, was first developed in Malbork Castle.

The colourful
main street of →
Toruń at sunset

③

TORUŃ

☆D3 🚆 Toruń Główny, Ul Kujawska 1; Toruń Miasto, Pl 18 Stycznia 4 🚌 ℹ️ Rynek Staromiejski 25; www.torun.pl

While picturesque Toruń is perhaps best known as the birthplace of the astronomer Nicolaus Copernicus, it is also renowned for its architecture. The Old Town retains its medieval street plan and has a rare calm, since most of the streets are closed to traffic. Toruń was founded by the Teutonic Knights in 1233 but passed to the kings of Poland in 1454, after the city's citizens rebelled against the knights' rule.

It was expanded in the early 17th century by the Dutch-born architect Anthonis van Obbergen, who added a third floor designed in the style of the late Renaissance Mannerist movement, which was characterized by exaggerated elements. The lower parts of the 42-m- (138-ft)- high tower date from the 13th century. It commands a fine view over the city of Toruń.

The town hall now houses a museum featuring Gothic art, 19th-century paintings and

①

Wilam Horzyca Theatre

🏛️ Pl Teatralny 1 🌐 teatr.torun.pl/en/

This delightful theatre was built in 1904 by the Viennese architects Ferdinand Fellner and Hermann Helmer in the Art Nouveau style with Neo-Baroque elements. One of the town's leading cultural centres, the theatre hosts the Kontakt Theatre Festival each year in early summer, bringing together theatre performers from all over Europe, which draws large audiences to the varied performances.

②

Town Hall

🏛️ Rynek Staromiejski 1
🕐 Regional Museum: 10am–6pm Tue–Sun (to 4pm Oct–Apr); tower: 10am–8pm daily (to 6pm Oct–Apr) 🌐 muzeum.torun.pl

The town hall, an imposing building with an internal courtyard, was first built in 1391–9 with two storeys.

→

A statue of Toruń's famous son Nicolaus Copernicus outside the town hall

local crafts. The building's original interiors are also noteworthy, especially the vaulting of the former bakery and wool stalls on the ground floors of the east and west wings. The town hall also features a restaurant and a popular pub in the basement.

③ Church of the Virgin Mary

📍 Ul Marii Panny 📞 56 622 26 03

The Gothic Church of the Virgin Mary (Kościół NMP) was built for Franciscan monks in 1270–1300. It has an unusually richly ornamented east gable, with late 14th-century wall paintings in the south aisle, and a glorious 16th-century Mannerist organ loft in the north aisle, which is the oldest in Poland. By the presbytery is the mausoleum of Anna Vasa, sister of Zygmunt III. She was of royal blood but could not be buried at Wawel Castle because she was of the Protestant faith.

④ Old Market Square

The Old Market Square is the city's finest open space and still the vibrant heart of its historic district. While the centrepiece is the town hall, there are fine buildings on all four sides of the square. At No 7, on the south side, is the Meissner Palace. Built in 1739 for Jakob Meissner, mayor of Toruń, this structure was given a Neo-Classical façade in 1798. Many of the town houses now host a mix of restaurants, cafés and accommodation. The most attractive house in the square is Star House, at No 35 on the east side, built in 1697. It has a fancifully orna- mented façade, with motifs of fruit and flowers created in stuccowork. The Protestant Baroque Church of the Holy Spirit (Kościoł św. Ducha) in the square was built in the mid-18th century. A fountain has the figure of a raftsman who, according to legend, rid the citizens of Toruń of a plague of frogs. There is also a monument to Nicolaus Copernicus from 1853.

DRINK

Piwnica pod Antałkiem
This cosy bar is decorated with retro furnishings and pictures of historic Toruń. It has a semi- circular bar and a choice of boutique beers, plus a gingerbread-flavoured vodka – ideal for winter.

📍 Ul Ducha Świętego 1 📞 666 359 210

TUTU Jazz and Whiskey Club
A welcoming basement bar with photos of jazz greats lining the walls, TUTU is a great place to relax with a whisky as a jazzy-bluesy soundtrack or live band plays.

📍 Ul Rabiańska 17 🌐 kadr.torun.pl

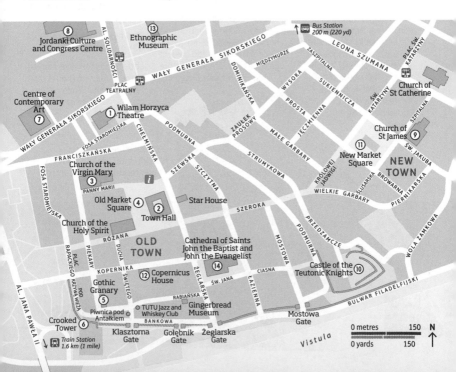

INSIDER TIP
Gingerbread

Toruń's gingerbread *(piernik)* is a much-loved local product that is sold throughout the town centre. Make your own and learn about its history at the Gingerbread Museum *(www.muzeum piernika.pl)*.

Gothic Granary

⌂ Ul Piekary 4

The most remarkable of the many Gothic granaries still standing in Toruń is that on the corner of Ulica Piekary and Ulica Rabiańska. Although the granary was rebuilt in the 19th century, it retains its towering ornamental gable with fine pointed arches.

Crooked Tower

⌂ Ul Pod Krzywą Wieżą

The Crooked Tower is one of Toruń's greatest attractions, and it leans significantly from the perpendicular. It is part of the town's old fortifications system, most likely built in the first half of the 14th century. Luckily, the floors that were added later are level; beer glasses in the pub

that it now houses can be set down on the tables without danger of sliding off.

Centre of Contemporary Art

⌂ Waly Gen. Sikorskiego 13
🕐 Jul–Aug: noon–6pm Tue–Sun; Sep–Jun: 10am–6pm Tue–Thu, 10am–8pm Fri, noon–6pm Sat & Sun
✖ Mon 🌐 csw.torun.pl

Occupying a modern building completed in 2008, Toruń's Centre of Contemporary Art (Centrum Sztuki Współczesnej) hosts high-profile exhibitions by international artists in its white-walled gallery spaces. The airy complex also boasts a chic daytime café, cinema and bookshop.

Jordanki Culture and Congress Centre

⌂ Aleja Solidarności 1–3
🕐 Box office: 1–7pm Tue–Sat
🌐 jordanki.torun.pl

The Jordanki Culture and Congress Centre (Centrum Kulturalno-Kongresowe Jordanki) is one of the boldest pieces of modern architecture in Poland. Completed in

2015, The playful exterior is an attractive jumble of geometric shapes, while the striking interior, home to the Toruń Symphony Orchestra, mixes bare concrete with red-brick mosaic.

Church of St James

⌂ Ul Rynek Nowomiejski 6
📞 56 622 29 24

The Gothic Church of St James (Kościoł św. Jakuba) was built in the first half of the 14th century as the new town's parish church. In the south aisle is a late 14th-century Gothic crucifix in the form of the Tree of Life, in which the figure of Christ is nailed to branches of a tree containing the figures of the prophets. Above the rood beam is a rare depiction of the Passion from about 1480–90, consisting of 22 scenes of the Stations of the Cross.

Castle of the Teutonic Knights

⌂ Ul Przedzamcze 📞 56 621 08 89

Little more than ruins remain of the castle that the Teutonic Knights built in Toruń when the city was their capital,

← The striking geometric buildings of the Jordanki Culture and Congress Centre

before the castle at Malbork (*p276*) was built. Constructed in the 13th century, the fortification it was destroyed in 1454 when the people of Toruń rose up in rebellion against the knights. Only the latrine tower – a tower overhanging a stream that acted as a sewer – was left standing, although part of the cellars and cloisters survive. The late Gothic house that was built on the site in 1489, probably with materials scavenged from the castle, was the meeting place of the Brotherhood of St George.

 ⑪

New Market Square

The new town emerged as a separate civic entity in 1264. Although it does not have as many historic buildings as the old town, there is a good deal of interest here. In the centre, where the town hall once stood, is a former Protestant church, built in 1824, probably by the German architect Karl Friedrich Schinkel. It is now a gallery of contemporary art. Fine houses, some with ornate façades, surround the square.

⑫ 🖾

Copernicus House

🏛 Ul Kopernika 15/17
📞 56 660 56 13 🕒 Oct-Apr: 10am-4pm Tue-Sun; May-Sep: 10am-6pm Tue-Sun
🌐 muzeum.torun.pl

Near the Old Town's main square, these two 15th-century Gothic town houses

↑ An atmospheric ruined gate, all that remains from the Castle of the Teutonic Knights

are excellent examples of Hanseatic merchants' houses. The painted façades and fine carving of the arched gables bear witness to the city's former wealth. Now these houses are more notable as a museum dedicated to Nicolaus Copernicus, who was supposedly born at No 17. This house belonged to his father, the merchant Mikołaj Kopernik. The museum has displays on Copernicus, as well as historic merchant life.

⑬

Ethnographic Museum

🏛 Ul Wały Gen Sikorskiego 19 🕒 Hours vary, check website 🌐 etnomuzeum.pl

The museum contains a range of exhibits, including fishing tools and folk art. There is also a *skansen*, in which wooden

houses from the region of Kujawy, Pomerania and Ziemia Dobrzyńska are displayed. Entry is free on Wednesdays.

⑭

Cathedral of Saints John the Baptist and John the Evangelist

🏛 Ul Żeglarska 16 📞 56 657 14 80

The origins of the Cathedral of Saints John the Baptist and John the Evangelist (Kościoł św. Jan.w) go back to 1250; the oldest surviving part is the presbytery. The interior is a treasury of art, with altars, chandeliers, stained-glass windows, sculpture and many paintings. In one of the side chapels in the south aisle is the Gothic font where Nicolaus Copernicus was baptized and a memorial to him from about 1580.

> ### NICOLAUS COPERNICUS
>
> Nicolaus Copernicus (Mikołaj Kopernik; 1473-1543), astronomer, mathematician, economist, doctor and clergyman, was born in Toruń, although he lived in Warmia for most of his life. He gained greatest renown for his astronomical observations, particularly for his heliocentric theory of the universe, which he expounded in *De Revolutionibus Orbium Celestium* (1543), which declared that the planets rotate around the sun.

 4

KASHUBIAN SWITZERLAND

🄰C1 🄰 Kashubian Landscape Park: Ul PCK 1, Kartuzy
🄾 Hours vary, check website 🅆 Landscape Park: pk.org.pl;
Ethnographic Park: muzeum-wdzydze.gda.pl; Museum:
muzeumaszubskie.gda.pl; CEPR: cepr.pl

Part of Kashubia, a region that has been inhabited
for centuries by the Kashub ethnic group, Kashubian
Switzerland (Szwajcaria Kaszubska) is an unspoiled
area of alpine valleys, pristine lakes and meadows.

 INSIDER TIP
Kościerzyna

If you end up stopping in
the town of Kościerzyna,
keep your eyes peeled
for the monument to
Józef Wybick - the
author of the Polish
national anthem - on
Ulica Wojska Polskiego.
The poet and political
activist was born in
Bedomin, a village in
Kościerzyna county.

To experience the best of the area's landscape,
visit the Kashubian Landscape Park, a protected area home to tranquil lakes and rolling
moraine hills. The region has its own distinctive language, and Kashubian culture is found
everywhere you go – especially in the area's,
festivals, cuisine and folk art (including paper
cutting, pottery and embroidery). For an introduction to the region's way of life, visit the
Kashubian Ethnographic Park or Wdzydze
Kiszewskie, an excellent *skansen* with a variety
of traditional buildings. The Kashubian Museum
in Kartuzy contains examples of the region's
distinctive embroidery, worked in only five
colours. There is also the unusual Centre for
Education and Regional Promotion (CEPR) in
Szymbar: part-*skansen*, part-theme park, it
contains reproductions of traditional buildings
alongside the area's quirkiest attraction, the
Upside-Down House.

← An autumn morning in the Kashubian Landscape Park and (inset) one of the peaceful lakes found within Kashubian Switzerland

① The Wdzydze Kiszewskie *skansen* is an open-air museum with an assembly of traditional buildings, including a windmill.

② Communist-era camping lodges are also part of the collection at the Wdzydze Kiszewskie *skansen*.

③ The Upside-Down House is one of the more unusual attractions that can be found at the Centre for Education and Regional Promotion.

Did You Know?

Most of the signposts in this area are bilingual, in both Polish and Kashubian.

EXPERIENCE MORE

5

Chełmno

 D2 🚌 🛈 Rynek 28;
www.chelmno.pl

The lands of Chełmno that Konrad, Duke of Mazovia, presented to the Teutonic Knights in 1226 were the beginning of the vast state that was eventually established by the order. The knights' first city, Chełmno, was founded in 1233 and was initially intended to be the capital of their state but this honour went to Malbork Castle (*p276*). Chełmno's medieval street plan and 13th- to 15th-century fortifications survive virtually intact. The town walls are set with 23 towers and a fortified gate, the Grudziądz Gate, which was converted into a Mannerist chapel in 1620. The town's finest building is the Town Hall, a late Renaissance structure of 1567–72 with traces of earlier Gothic elements. It houses the **Chełmno Museum**, which charts the history of the town. The 18th-century Baroque building on Ulica Franciszkańska once housed the Chełmno Academy.

Six Gothic churches have been preserved in Chełmno. The largest is the Church of the Assumption (Kościół Wniebowzięcia NMP) of 1280–1320, which contains early Gothic frescoes and stone carvings. Two monastery churches, the Church of St James (Kościół św. Jakuba) and the Church of Saints Peter and Paul (Kościół św. Piotra i Pawła), date from the same period. The Abbey of the Cistercian Nuns, established in the late 13th century, is a fine group of buildings. It was later passed to the Catholic sisters who now run a hospital here. The entrance, found on Ulica Dominikańska, leads to an internal courtyard, which in turn gives access to the Church of St John the Baptist (Kościół św. Jana Chrzciciela). It has two storeys, with the upper home to a nave once reserved for the choir of the Order of Teutonic Knights.

Chełmno Museum
♿ 🏛 Rynek 28 🕐 10am–4pm Tue-Sat (to 3pm on Sat Oct-Mar), 11am-3pm Sun 🚫 Apr-Sep: Sun 🌐 muzeumchelmno.pl

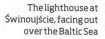

→
The lighthouse at Świnoujście, facing out over the Baltic Sea

EAT

Karczma Chełmińska
This charming restaurant, with exposed brick walls and flowers on the tables, serves traditional Polish food with modern style.

📍 D2 🏠 22 Stycznia 1, Chełmno 🌐 karczmach elminska.pl

6 Świnoujście

A1 🚆🚌 ℹ️ Ul Słowiański 6/1; www.swinoujscie.pl

The busy port and beach resort of Świnoujście stretches across two islands, Uznam and Wolin. The centre of town is on Uznam, while the train and bus stations, as well as the eastern suburbs, are on Wolin. A free passenger ferry shuttles across the Świna channel dividing the two. The German border is located on Świnoujście's western outskirts, and German visitors are frequent guests in the town, popping over for a

> **INSIDER TIP**
> **Sandy Shores**
>
> Spend a day hopping between beaches on the UBB, short for Usedomer Bäderbahn *(www.ubb-online.com),* the local railway that runs from Świnoujście to the genteel German seaside resorts across the border.

stroll along its long sandy beach. Świnoujście has been celebrated as a health resort for well over a century, and the town is home to a number of established spas and therapy centres.

Świnoujście was also an important Prussian fort in the 19th century, and remnants of the fortifications are scattered throughout the town. On the western side of the Świna, **Western Fort** (Fort Zachodni) and **Angel Fort** (Fort Anioła) preserve impressive red brick bastions. On the eastern side of the water, **Fort Gerhard** (Fort Gerharda) features tours and interactive shows with staff in 19th-century uniforms.

Western Fort

🏛️ 🚗 Ul Jachtowa 🕐 Hours vary, check website 🌐 fortzachodni.pl

Angel Fort

🏛️ 🚗 Ul Yachtowa 🕐 May-Sep: 9am-dusk daily; Oct-Apr: 10am-3pm daily 🌐 fortaniola.pl

Fort Gerhard

🏛️🏛️ 🚗 Ul Bunkrowa 🕐 May & Jun: 9:30am-5pm daily; Jul-Sep: 9:30am-7pm daily; Oct-Apr: 10am- 4pm daily 🌐 fort-gerharda.pl

7 Stargard Szczeciński

🏛️A2 🚆🚌 ℹ️ Rynek Staromiejski 4; www.stargard.pl

With its own port in the Szczecin Lagoon at the mouth of the River Ina, Stargard Szczeciński once rivalled Szczecin *(p274)* as a merchant town of the Hanseatic League.

Almost three-quarters of the old town was destroyed during World War II, but the impressive Gothic defensive walls survived. Most notable is the Gothic Church of St Mary (Kościół Mariacki); founded in the late 13th century, it was given its present appearance in the mid-15th. The rich decoration of glazed and moulded brick is quite striking. The magnificent town hall has a gable with intricate tracery. A good place for a morning coffee is the café in the former salt granary, a Gothic building overlooking a spur of the Ina.

The **Regional Museum** has militaria and an archaeological and ethnographical display.

Regional Museum

🏛️ 🚗 Rynek Staromiejski 3 🕐 10am-5pm Tue-Fri & Sun (to 4pm Sep-May), 10am-2pm Sat 🌐 muzeum-stargard.pl

Sunset at Chełmno's old town square, noted for its Renaissance town hall

8

Drawsko Lakes

 B2

The Drawsko Lakes are an oasis of quiet, unspoiled scenery. The largest of the lakes is Drawsko, on whose shores stands Stare Drawsko, with ruins of a once-impressive 14th-century Teutonic Knights' castle. In the delightful spa town of Połczyn Zdrój the mineral springs are surrounded by a park and there are some elegant early-20th-century sanatoria. The town of Złocieniec has outstanding Baroque architecture in the form of an 18th-century palace.

9

Darłowo

 B1 🅿️🚌 *i* Ul Pocztowa 6; www.darlowo.pl

Darłowo, set 2.5 km (1.5 miles) inland on the banks of the River Wieprza, is one of the most attractive towns of coastal Pomerania. In summer the waterfront swarms with tourists but the town's real charm lies in its old riverside district, where there are many historic buildings. The most prominent of these is the Gothic Castle of the Dukes of Pomerania. Founded in the 14th century, it was rebuilt several times and partially demolished in the 19th century; its surviving parts now house a museum.

10

Kołobrzeg

🅰️B1 🅿️🚌 *i* Ul Dworcowa 1 & Ul Armii Krajowej; www. kolobrzeg.pl

The fine sandy beaches of Kołobrzeg make it one of the most popular health resorts on the Baltic coast. It has a full complement of hotels, sanatoria, holiday homes and fried-fish stalls, but it is also a working fishing port. In the past it was a fortified coastal town of strategic significance. In summer the promenade, leading to the lighthouse, is crowded with holiday-makers.

The town's brick-built Cathedral of the Virgin Mary (Katedra NMP) was begun in 1255 and later altered and extended. Among its remark-able objects is a chandelier made by Johann Apengheter of Lübeck in 1327 depicting the Virgin and St John the Baptist. The Neo-Gothic town hall was built by the Berlin architect Karl Friedrich Schinkel in 1829–32. It is surrounded by alleys lined with old houses.

11

Słupsk

🅰️C1 🅿️🚌 *i* Ul Starzyńskiego 8; www.slupsk.pl

From 1368 to 1648, this town on the River Słupia was the capital of the Duchy of Western Pomerania. The Renaissance ducal castle was built by Antonio Guglielmo di Zaccharia in 1580–87. Today it is the **Museum of Central Pomerania**, which, besides items of local interest, has the country's largest collection of portraits by the painter and writer Stanisław Ignacy Witkiewicz (1885–1939), better known as Witkacy.

The watermill opposite the castle, dating from about 1310, is one of the oldest in Poland. Now a branch of the museum, it houses an ethnographical collection. In the Dominican Church of St Hyacinthus (Kościół św. Jacka) nearby are the black marble and alabaster tombs of Bogusław de Croy, the last of the dukes of Pomerania, and his mother, the Duchess Anna de Croy.

Museum of Central Pomerania

🕐🅿️ 🚪 Ul Dominikańska 5/9 🕐 Jul & Aug: 11am–3pm Mon, 10am–6pm Tue–Sun; Sep–Jun: 10am–4pm Wed–Sun 🌐 muzeum.slupsk.pl

12

Słowiński National Park

🅰️C1 🚌 *i* Rąbka, Łeba 84-360; www.slowinskipn.pl

Słowiński National Park is renowned for its large, shifting sand dunes, which move at a rate of about 9 m (30 ft) a year, leaving the stumps of dead trees behind them. The area

← Visitors relaxing on the shifting sand dunes of Słowiński National Park

Chrziciela), a superb example of a red-brick Gothic church. The one surviving part of Chojnice's fortifications is the towering Chłuchow Gate (Brama Chłuchowska), which is today home to the small **Chojnice Museum** displaying archeological finds.

Chojnice Museum

Ul Podmurna 15 ☐ Jul & Aug: 10am–5pm Tue–Fri, 11am–4pm Sat & Sun; Sep–Jun: 10am–5pm Tue & Thu, 10am–3pm Wed & Fri–Sun 🅦 chojnicemuzeum.pl

Bytów

📍 C1 🚌 i Ul Zamkowa 2; www.bytow.

Bytów, with nearby Lębork, was the westernmost outpost of the territory held by the Teutonic Knights. Established as a Polish fiefdom following its conquest in 1466, it was first ruled by the Pomeranian dukes, then by Brandenburg and Prussia. It has been part of Poland since 1945.

Few of Bytów's historic buildings survive. The most interesting is the castle of the Teutonic Knights, which was built in 1390–1405. It was one of the first castles in Europe to be adapted for the use of firearms. It has four circular corner towers and a residential wing was added in about 1570. It houses the **Museum of Western Kashubia**, which contains a collection of artifacts relating to the ancient Kashubian culture.

Museum of Western Kashubia

Ul Zamkowa 2 ☐ Sep–Apr: 10am–4pm daily; May–Aug: 10am–6pm daily (to 4pm Mon) 🅦 muzeumbytow.pl

was once a gulf – the glacial lakes of Łebsko and Gardno are vestiges of this. The park, a World Biosphere Reserve, is a haven for wild birds; more than 250 species, including the rare sea eagle, can be found here.

The main base for visiting the park is Łeba, a fishing village and beach resort with B&Bs and campsites. A path leads west from Łeba to Rąbka, 1.5 km (1 mile) away, where there is a park ticket office, bike hire and golf carts that take passengers further into the park for a fee. From here, the path goes westwards through beautiful forest.

After 3 km (2 miles) it passes Wyrzutnia ("Launchpad"), the place where German engineers tested rockets in World War II. Another 2 km (1 mile) further on is Biała Góra, the biggest of the shifting dunes. Visitors can climb up onto the dune and continue onwards to the nearby beach; much of the dune area is closed to the public to protect its unique ecosystem. In the hamlet of Kluki, on Lake Łebsko, is a *skansen* dedicated to the ancient local Slovincian culture. Fishing equipment and agricultural implements are exhibited in the farmsteads.

Chojnice

📍 C2 🚌 i Ul Podmurna 13a; www.turystyka-chojnice.pl

Fortified under the Teutonic Knights, and a prosperous market centre in the 19th century, Chojnice is one of the region's most attractive small towns. Most of the historic buildings are grouped around the Rynek. Oldest of the sacral buildings is the Church of John the Baptist (Kościół św. Jana

← Children playing at the fountain in front of the town hall, Darlowo

One of the beautiful beaches found on the Hel Peninsula, and Hel's Fisheries Museum *(inset)*

Hel Peninsula

D1 🚍🚉 **i** Ul Kuracyjna 26, Hel; 666 871 622

The Hel Peninsula is about 34 km (22 miles) long and in width ranges from just 200 m (650 ft) to 3 km (2 miles). It is made up of sandbanks formed by sea currents; in the 1700s it was no more than a chain of islets. The peninsula is now an area of outstanding natural beauty, Nadmorski Park Krajobrazowy. When the railway line to Hel was built in 1922, resorts began to appear on the peninsula. Their main attraction was the double beach – one part facing the sea, the other the Gulf of Gdańsk. At the base of the peninsula is the town of Władysławowo, named after Władysław IV, who founded a now-vanished fortress here.

Today the town boundaries embrace many resorts, such as Jastrzębia Góra, Cetniewo and Chałupy. Jastarnia is the most popular, as it still retains many of its original fishermen's cottages. The elegant resort of Jurata was established in 1928; Modernist hotels dating from the 1930s can be seen here. At the very end of the peninsula is the fishing port and tourist resort of Hel, with its towering lighthouse and timber-framed fishermen's cottages. The former Protestant church, built in the 1400s, is now the **Fisheries Museum**, which covers the history of Hel, Polish sea fishery and local boat building. From Hel, passenger and tourist boats cross to Gdynia and Gdańsk.

Fisheries Museum

🚹 🏛 Ul Bulwar Nadmorski 2, Hel ⏰ Jan & Dec: 10am-3pm Tue-Sun; Feb-Jun & Sep-Nov: 10am-4pm Tue-Sun; Jul & Aug: 10am-6pm Tue-Sun 🌐 nmm.pl

Pelplin Abbey

D2 🏛🚍 🌐 pelplin.pl

The Cistercian abbey at Pelplin is a fine example of Gothic architecture. Work on the monastery began in 1276, when the Cistercians came to Pelplin.

The brick-built church, now a cathedral, dates largely from the 14th century, although its late Gothic vaulting was not completed until the late 15th and early 16th centuries. The imposing triple-naved basilica has no tower; the interior contains an outstanding collection of finely crafted furnishings, including Gothic stalls with a rare carving of the Holy Trinity in which the Holy Ghost is depicted not as the customary dove but as a man. There are several paintings by Hermann Hahn, including a *Coronation of the Virgin* on the high altar. The monastery was dissolved in 1823, and in 1824 the church became the Cathedral of the Virgin Mary (Katedra NMP). The monastery buildings now house the **Diocesan Museum** whose carved gallery contains a handsome collection of ecclesiastical art as well as illuminated manuscripts. The most highly prized exhibits are a Madonna cabinet from Kolonowskie, a rare original Gutenberg Bible of 1435–55 and a 17th-century musical manuscript, the *Pelplin Tabulature for Organ*. A range of goldwork and liturgical objects are also displayed in the cathedral treasury.

Diocesan Museum

🚹🕐🏛 Ul Biskupa Dominika 11 ⏰ 9:30am-4:30pm Tue-Sun 🚫 Mon & religious feast days 🌐 muzeum.diecezja.org

17 Gniew

D2 www.gniew.pl

This little town on the River Vistula retains a medieval atmosphere. Founded by the Teutonic Knights in 1276, it was later the seat of a commander of the order and in 1466 became part of Poland.

The town's narrow alleys lead into the Market Square, which is lined with arcaded buildings. While most date from the 18th century, some, like the town hall, have Gothic elements. Traces of the 14th- to 15th-century fortifications that once protected Gniew from invaders still remain. The Gothic Church of St Nicholas (Kościół św. Mikołaja) towers over the town.

Probably built in the first half of the 14th century, it retains its magnificent interior, which includes Gothic vaulting and Mannerist, Baroque and Neo-Gothic altars.

The town's most distinctive feature is the castle of the Teutonic Knights. This imposing fortress was begun in 1283 and completed in the mid-14th century. The castle has a regular plan, with four corner turrets and the remains of a mighty keep in the north-eastern corner. It now houses the Zamek Gniew Hotel.

---

18 Kwidzyn

D2 www.kwidzyn.pl

From 1243 until 1525, the small town of Kwidzyn was the capital of the Pomerania bishopric, one of four to be established in the territory ruled by the Teutonic Knights. After the order was dissolved, the town passed in turn to Prussia, Germany and Poland.

The cathedral, standing on a high escarpment, and the castle attached to it are fine examples of Gothic architecture. The cathedral was built in the 14th century on the site of an earlier church;

only the narthex (a porch separated from the nave by a screen) remains. The porch dates from 1264–84.

In 1862–4 the cathedral was remodelled in the Neo-Gothic style by Friedrich August Stüler. The interior of this vast pseudo-basilica has Gothic murals, which unfortunately were excessively repainted in the 19th century. Many of the earlier furnishings are still in place, including a late Gothic bishop's throne from about 1510. The presbytery leads to the tiny cell of the Blessed Dorothy of Mątowy, who ordered that she be immured there in 1393. By the north nave is the Baroque chapel of Otto Frederick von Groeben, housing a tomb depicting the deceased and his three wives.

The castle, now the **Castle Museum**, was built in 1322–47 and partially demolished in the 18th century. Among the interesting features of the castle are the well tower and the exceptionally tall latrine tower, which is connected to the castle by a gallery supported on large arches.

Castle Museum
Ul Katedralna 1
55 646 37 80 or 646 37 97
May-Sep: 9am-4:30pm; Oct-Apr: 9am-2:30pm Tue-Sun

→
Resembling a knights' fortress, the Gothic castle at Kwidzyn

19

Bydgoszcz

 C3 🚌🚍 ℹ️ Ul Stefana
Batorego 2; www.
bydgoszcz.pl

This pretty city lies at the confluence of the River Brda and the Bydgoszcz Canal, which then both flow onward into the Vistula. Bydgoszcz was only briefly part of the state of the Teutonic Knights, after which its fate was linked with that of the rest of Poland. On 3 September 1939, the city was the scene of dramatic events when the town's German minority attempted to stage a coup. The Nazis took over the city shortly afterwards and massacred thousands of the Polish population.

The old town of Bydgoszcz is set on a bend of the Brda. It has several monumental town houses, the late Gothic church of Saints Nicholas and Martin (Kościół św. Mikołaja i Marcina), and two monasteries: a Bernadine monastery with a church of 1545–52, and the Church and Convent of the Poor Clares (Kościół Klarysek). Today, the latter houses a **Regional Museum**, home to folk art items and archaeological findings.

> On 3 September 1939, the city was the scene of dramatic events when the town's German minority attempted to stage a coup.

The half-timbered granaries on the banks of the Brda, built in the 18th and 19th centuries, were used to store the salt and wheat that the town traded, and also the beer for which it is renowned.

Regional Museum

🎟️ ☐ Ul Gdańska 4 ⏰ 10am–6pm Tue, Wed & Fri (to 4pm Nov–Mar), 10am–7pm Thu, 11am–6pm Sat & Sun (to 4pm Oct–Mar) 🌐 muzeum. bydgoszcz.pl

20

Grudziądz

 D2 🚌🚍 ℹ️ Rynek 3-5; www.grudziadz.pl

Grudziądz, situated on an escarpment overlooking the River Vistula, was once a major port. It was founded by the Teutonic Knights and became part of Poland in 1466. Due to the Partitions of Poland (p63), it became part of Prussia from 1772 and in 1918 was returned to Poland. Despite the damage it suffered during World War II, the town has some fine buildings. The Gothic Church of St Nicholas (Kościół św. Mikołaja) was begun in the late 13th century and completed in the second half of the 15th. It contains a late Romanesque font from the 14th century. The former Benedictine abbey, including the Palace of the Abbesses of 1749–51, is also of interest. Part of the

The spectacular interior of the Church of Saints Nicholas and Martin

abbey is now the site of the **Grudziądz Museum**, which has exhibits on the region's history, as well as archaeological discoveries. There is also an art gallery.

The huge complex of harbour granaries, 26 brick buildings built side by side along the waterfront, fulfilled a defensive function as well as being used for storage – seen from the river, the granaries appear to surround the entire hillside. They were built mostly in the 17th and 18th centuries, but some are much older.

Grudziądz Museum

🎟️ ☐ Ul Wodna 3/5 ⏰ Hours vary, check website 🌐 muzeum.grudziadz.pl

21

Golub-Dobrzyń

☐ D3 🚌🚍 ℹ️ Rynek 19; www.golub-dobrzyn.pl

This wonderfully picturesque town was originally two separate settlements, one on either side of the River Drwęca. During the Partitions, Golub was part of Prussia and Dobrzyń part of Russia (p63). Golub's main feature is the

↑ Colourful flowers blooming in Park Zdrojowy in the spa-resort of Ciechocinek

large **Castle Museum** built by the Teutonic Knights in 1293–1310. From 1466 Golub was part of Poland, and in the 17th century the castle became the residence of Queen Anna Vasa of Sweden, sister of Zygmunt III Vasa. The castle was rebuilt for the queen in 1616–23 in the Renaissance style. Highly educated, with an interest in botany and medicine, Anna Vasa was an unusual woman for her time. She remained a spinster, reputedly because of her perceived unattractive appearance. Today the castle hosts such events as jousting tournaments and oratory competitions, as well as New Year's balls, at which revellers say that the ghost of Queen Anna appears.

Castle Museum
♦ ♦ ♦ Ul PTTK 13 ☎ 56 683 24 55 ⏰ May–Sep: 9am–6pm daily; Oct–Apr: 9am–4pm daily

---

Ciechocinek

♦ D3 ♦ ♦ *i* Ul Zdrojowa 2; www.ciechocinek.pl

Ciechocinek is one of Poland's best-known spa towns, which grew and prospered thanks to its iodine-rich salt springs. It is not strictly part of Pomerania but of Kujawy, and has always been a Polish town. The town came into being in 1824, when Stanisław Staszic started to build saltworks and the first of three salt graduation towers. The "towers" are huge wooden frames filled with thorny brushwood which, washed with brine, accumulate salt crystals. Each "tower" is more than 1.7 km (1 mile) wide.

Other features of the town are the group of baths built in a variety of styles between 1845 and 1913, a fine park with a flower clock, a pump room designed by Edward Cichocki, a bandstand and open-air theatre, and numerous elegant boarding houses, sanatoria and hotels dating from the early 20th century.

Stutthof Museum

♦ D1 ♦ Ul Muzealna 6 ♦ ⏰ May–Sep: 8am–6pm daily; Oct–Apr: 8am–3pm ♦ stutthof.org

Found in the woods just outside Sztutowo, 40 km (25 miles) northwest of Elbląg, Stutthof began life as a labour camp for political prisoners from Poland and the rest of Nazi-occupied Europe. Treatment was brutal right and death rates were high. In 1943 the camp was included in Nazi plans for the Final Solution, and gas chambers were added. The total number of Stutthof's victims lies somewhere between 65,000 and 85,000. The display in the camp museum details life and death in the camp in harrowing detail.

A DRIVING TOUR
AROUND WOLIN

Length 100 km (62 miles) **Stopping-off points** Świnoujście; Wolin; Wolin National Park **Terrain** Mainly flat

The island of Wolin, off the northwestern coast, attracts walkers and photographers with its forests, deserted sandy beaches and picturesque coastal cliffs. An ancient Slav and Viking port, Wolin is awash with history, and the cathedral in Kamień Pomorski is one of the finest in Poland.

The renowned health resort of **Międzyzdroje** *was founded in 1830. It has a seafront promenade and a pier from which the cliffs can be admired.*

Wolin National Park

102

Kołczewo

Międzyzdroje

102

Wolin National Park

Kodrąb

Świnoujście

Kodrąbek

Osiedle Zachodnie

3

Unin

Łunowo

Lake Wicko Wielkie

3

93

Dargobądz

START

Lubin

Wolin

Szczecin Lagoon

111

Świnoujście *is an attractive coastal resort split across the islands of Wolin and Uznam. The only way between the two parts of the town is by ferry.*

Apart from its lakes and beaches, **Wolin National Park** *is known for its bison, which can be seen in a special reserve.*

In the early Middle Ages the small town of **Wolin** *was a major Baltic port. Today it has an open-air Viking museum with a re-created village, which also hosts workshops.*

0 kilometres   6
0 miles   6

N ↑

← Wolin National Park, known for its attractive sandy beaches

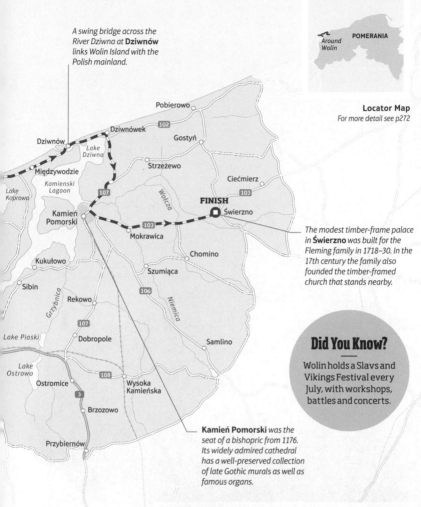

A swing bridge across the River Dziwna at **Dziwnów** links Wolin Island with the Polish mainland.

Pobierowo

Dziwnówek `102`

Dziwnów Gostyń

Lake Dziwna

Międzywodzie Strzeżewo

Kamieński Lagoon Ciećmierz `103`

Lake Koprowa `107` *Wołcza* **FINISH**
Świerzno

Kamień Pomorski

Mokrawica `103`

The modest timber-frame palace in **Świerzno** was built for the Fleming family in 1718–30. In the 17th century the family also founded the timber-framed church that stands nearby.

Chomino

Kukułowo Szumiąca

Sibin *Grzybnica* *Niemica*

Rekowo

`106`

`107`

Lake Piaski Dobropole

Samlino

Lake Ostrowo

Ostromice `108`

`3` Wysoka Kamieńska

Brzozowo

Przybiernów

Kamień Pomorski *was the seat of a bishopric from 1176. Its widely admired cathedral has a well-preserved collection of late Gothic murals as well as famous organs.*

Locator Map
For more detail see p272

POMERANIA

Around Wolin

Did You Know?

Wolin holds a Slavs and Vikings Festival every July, with workshops, battles and concerts.

→ The beautiful brick cathedral at Kamién Pomorski

WARMIA, MAZURIA AND PODLASIE

Known as the land of a thousand lakes, Poland's northeast is blessed with vast forests, undulating moraine hills, and a large number of lakes and rivers. Its three regions, Warmia, Mazuria and Podlasie, have had divergent histories. To the west is Warmia. Once inhabited by the early Prussians, in the 13th century it was taken over by the Teutonic Order. The area became part of Poland in 1466, but was transferred to Prussia under the Partitions; it was not returned to Poland until 1945. Mazuria was also once controlled by the Teutonic Order. In 1525, the region became known as ducal Prussia and was ruled by the Hohenzollern family, although until 1657 it was a Polish fiefdom. The area's subsequent history is linked to that of Germany, and it did not become part of Poland again until 1945. Podlasie, the region's eastern section, once belonged to the grand duchy of Lithuania. The area was covered in primeval forests, and three – the Augustów, Knyszyńska and Białowieża forests – remain today. The Biebrza valley also contains Poland's largest stretches of marshland and peat swamps.

0 kilometres 30
0 miles 30

Gulf of Gdańsk

Polessk

Pereslavskoye

Primorsk

Kaliningrad

Gvardeysk

Pravdinsk

Vistula Lagoon

BRANIEWO ⑥

③ **FROMBORK CATHEDRAL**

POMORSKIE

Nowy Dwór Gdański

S22

Gorowo Iławeckie

Bartoszyce

51

④ **ELBLĄG**

Orneta

LIDZBARK WARMIŃSKI ⑨

Bisztynek

592

KĘTRZYN ⑭

Pasłęk

527

S7

DOBRE MIASTO ⑧

RESZEL ⑪

⑬

Malbork

22

POMERANIA
p270

⑦ **MORĄG**

51

ŚWIĘTA LIPKA

Kwidzyn

Iławski Morąg

Barczewo

Mrągowo

Ukiel

Biskupiec

Lyna

16

⑩ **OLSZTYN**

Ostróda

WARMIŃSKO-MAZURSKIE

Iława

16

551

Olsztynek

Szczytno

53

Łasin

16

15

Lubawa

Jabłonowo Pomorskie

Nowe Miasto Lubawskie

⑫ **GRUNWALD**

Olsztyn Mazury Airport ✈

57

KUJAWSKO-POMORSKIE

Uzdowo

S7

⑤ **NIDZICA**

Brodnica

Kowalewo Pomorskie

15

Działdowo

Mława

MAZOVIA AND THE LUBLIN REGION
p120

Różan

61

60

WARMIA, MAZURIA AND PODLASIE

Must Sees
① The Great Mazurian Lakes
② Czarna Hańcza and Augustów Canal
③ Frombork Cathedral

Experience More
④ Elbląg
⑤ Nidzica
⑥ Braniewo
⑦ Morąg
⑧ Dobre Miasto
⑨ Lidzbark Warmiński
⑩ Olsztyn

⑪ Reszel
⑫ Grunwald
⑬ Święta Lipka
⑭ Kętrzyn
⑮ Tykocin
⑯ Biebrza National Park
⑰ Białystok
⑱ Białowieża National Park
⑲ Supraśl
⑳ Drohiczyn
㉑ Kruszyniany
㉒ Hajnówka
㉓ Grabarka

61

S8

Warsaw

17

①

THE GREAT MAZURIAN LAKES

🗺 F2 🚌🚉 🚗 Around 180 km (112 miles) SE of Gdańsk
ℹ Plac Wolności 7, Mikołajki; www.mazury.info

This area is known as the "land of a thousand lakes", a wilderness region with great forests, extensive woods and marshlands peppered with small towns and Gothic churches. It's a popular holiday spot in summer, but despite this, the countryside remains largely unspoiled.

Covering 52,000 sq km (20,000 sq miles), the Great Mazurian Lakes area encompasses over 2,000 lakes. The largest is Lake Śniardwy, and most of the activity is centred between here Lake Mamry. Interlinked by rivers and canals, the lakes are a delight to explore, either by car along the winding lakeside roads or onboard a cruise. Sailing dinghies, canoes and motorboats can be hired at Mikołajki, and there's a good regional museum at Pisz. Many rare plants and birds thrive here, including beautiful storks – in spring and summer you'll see more nesting here than anywhere else in Europe. It's also a paradise for ramblers and for anyone who enjoys messing around on the water.

WILD SWANS

Lake Łuknajno, listed by UNESCO as a World Biosphere Reserve, is one of Poland's finest nature reserves for wild swans. The lake is shallow, averaging only 1.5 m (4 ft) deep, making it easy for the birds to feed on the weed that grows on the lakebed. Lake Łuknajno attracts wildlife photographers from all over the world, eager for an unforgettable shot. To safeguard the habitat, boats are not allowed on the lake.

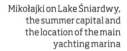
↑ The Pranie Forester's House Museum, the former home of poet Konstanty Ildefons Gałczyński on the shores of Lake Nidzkie

→ Mikołajki on Lake Śniardwy, the summer capital and the location of the main yachting marina

Must See

EAT

Smażalnia
On the popular fishing lake at Mikołajki, Smażalnia ("fry-up") is a simple café serving succulent freshwater fish in crispy batter.

🅰F2 📍Ul Mrągowska 14, Mikołajki
🌐 ryby-mikolajki.pl

Pod Kogutem
Traditional Polish cuisine is served with finesse; try roast goose or local lake or sea fish.

🅰D1 📍Wigilijna 8/9, Elbląg 📞55 641 2882

↑ Autumn colours at the Great Mazurian Lakes and *(inset)* families enjoying a day out at Lake Niegocin

CZARNA HAŃCZA AND AUGUSTÓW CANAL

Ⓐ F2/G2 **Ⓐ** 56 km (35 miles) N of Augustów **ⓘ** Wigry National Park: Krzywe 82, Suwałki; wigry.org.pl

EXPERIENCE Warmia, Mazuria and Podlasie

The picturesque Czarna Hańcza river and the historic Augustów Canal are two of the main attractions in Wigry National Park (Wigierski Park Narodowy), and together form one of the most beautiful canoeing routes in Poland. Although best explored by taking to the water in a canoe or kayak, the area can also be explored by car.

The Czarna Hańcza, the largest river in the Suwałki Region, rises at the beautiful Lake Wigry, which is peppered with tiny islands and home to a lovely old Camaldolite monastery. The river then twists its way through a variety of landscapes, from the dappled Augustów Forest to sprawling swamps and peaceful lakes. The river forks at the pretty village of Rygol, where the westward (or right-hand) branch joins the Augustów Canal. This marvel of 19th-century engineering has hand-operated locks that have remained almost unchanged since the time that they were built. The canal winds through lakes and locks until it reaches the handsome resort town of Augustów itself. This picturesque town is home to an elegant yachting marina, as well as many charming hotels and guest houses. It also features excellent restaurants and cafes.

> The river then twists its way through a variety of landscapes, from the dappled Augustów Forest to sprawling swamps and peaceful lakes.

↑ The Augustów Canal, its towpaths converted to hiking and cycling paths

↑ The Camaldolite Monastery overlooking the tranquil Lake Wigry

THE AUGUSTÓW CANAL

The Augustów Canal was built to connect the River Niemen with the River Biebrza, by linking a string of lakes in the Augustów region with manmade waterways; locks and weirs were constructed to overcome changes in level. Built in 1823–39 under the direction of General Ignacy Prądzyński, it was used to transport commercial goods such as timber, grain and salt, but with the arrival of the railways, it gradually fell into disuse. In the 1920s its potential as a tourist attraction was realised, and the canal was restored to accommodate pleasure boats and smaller leisure craft.

Did You Know?

Augustów Canal's locks were built from white and red bricks to represent Poland's national colours.

Visitors kayaking down the tranquil Czarna Háncza river in Wigry National Park ↑

FROMBORK CATHEDRAL

🅐D1 🅠Ul Katdralna 8, Frombork 🅒Cathedral: May-Sep: 9am–4:15pm Mon-Sat, Oct-Apr: 8:30am–3pm Mon-Sat; museum: May-Aug: 9:30am–4:30pm daily, Sep-Apr: 9am–4pm daily; planetarium: 9am–4pm Tue-Sun 🆆frombork.art.pl

Dominating Frombork town, this expansive complex has a history dating back to the 13th century, when it became a Warmian chapter (diocesan capital). The scholar Nicolaus Copernicus lived and worked here from 1510 to 1543.

Erected in 1342–88, the Gothic cathedral has an unusual form, with no towers on its west end, giving it the appearance of a Cistercian monastery. The Copernicus Tower was once the home of the celebrated astronomer; a museum dedicated to him is housed in the Bishops' Palace, and contains two copies of *De Revolutionibus Orbium Coelestium*, and medicine, instruments and replicas of the devices he once used.

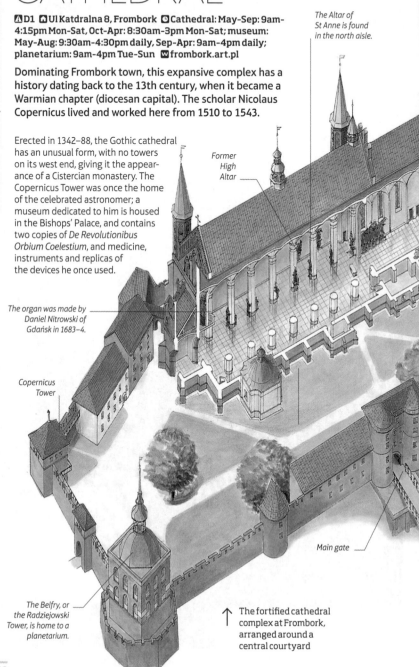

The Altar of St Anne is found in the north aisle.

Former High Altar

The organ was made by Daniel Nitrowski of Gdańsk in 1683–4.

Copernicus Tower

Main gate

The Belfry, or the Radziejowski Tower, is home to a planetarium.

↑ The fortified cathedral complex at Frombork, arranged around a central courtyard

↑ The cathedral's elegant interior, with the High Altar at the end

The High Altar was designed by Franciszek Placidi in 1742–52.

The Bishop's Palace now houses the Copernicus Museum.

Did You Know?

Lost for centuries, Copernicus's grave was rediscovered in this cathedral in 2005.

EXPERIENCE MORE

④ Elbląg

🅰D1 🔲🚍 *ⓘ* www.elblag.pl

Once a large port on a par with Gdańsk, Elbląg is today known for its large ABB engineering plant, its restored Old Town and for producing the beer Specjal. Founded in 1237 by the Teutonic Knights, the town was part of the Polish Republic from 1466 to 1772, when under the Partitions it passed to Prussian rule. After the devastation of World War II, only the most important old buildings of Elbląg were rebuilt. The Brama Targowa tower is all that remains of the former Gothic fortifications that surrounded the town. In the Old Town, just a few town houses survive but now buildings are being constructed in the style of the old Hanseatic merchants' houses, with stairways and gables, which is revitalizing this area.

The Gothic **Church of the Virgin Mary** with a double aisle was built for Dominican monks in the 14th century. After World War II it became the contemporary EL art

↑ The Brama Targowa tower in Elbląg's pretty Old Town

gallery. On Ulica Mostowa, the Church of St Nicholas (Kościół św. Mikołaja) was begun in the 13th century and completed in 1510. The interior includes a font from 1387 by Bernhuser, a *Crucifixion* ascribed to Jan van der Matten and a late Gothic altar with the Adoration of the Magi.

Church of the Virgin Mary
🈺 🅰Ul Kuśnierska 6
🕐10am–6pm Tue–Sat, 10am–5pm Sun 🔳galeria-el.pl

THE ELBLĄG CANAL

The Elbląg Canal is one of the most extraordinary feats of hydraulic engineering in Poland. A network of canals and locks connecting a number of lakes, it was built in 1848–72 by the Dutchman Georg Jacob Steenke. Including its branches, its length is 212 km (133 miles). Ingenious slipways enable barges to be hauled overland from one lake to another where the difference in the water levels is too high for conventional locks to be built. Canal boat trips take you through the Vistula Valley and Ilawa Lake District.

The Gothic Castle of the Teutonic Knights in Nidzica, rebuilt in the 1800s

 5

Nidzica

🅰E2 🏠🚌 *ℹ* Zamkowa 2; www.nidzica.pl

The main feature of Nidzica is the Teutonic Castle, which overlooks the town from a hill. It was built in the late 1300s and altered in the 16th century. Reduced to ruins, it was rebuilt in the 1800s and again after World War II. Part of it is now a hotel. Some of the town's medieval fortifications also survive.

The Tatars' Stone lies 2 km (just over a mile) south of Nidzica. This large rock, with a circumference of around 19 m (63 ft), marks the spot where, according to legend, the leader of the Tatars was

JOHANN GOTTFRIED VON HERDER (1744-1803)

Born in Morąg, German writer and philosopher Johann Gottfried von Herder was one of the great figures of the Enlightenment. He studied theology in the city of Königsberg (Kaliningrad) before entering the priest-hood. He understood the importance of nations in the making of history, and the role of culture and language in preserving national identity. While living in Riga, he recorded Latvian folk songs.

killed in 1656, thus sparing Nidzica from invasion in the same year.

 6

Braniewo

🅰E1 🏠🚌 *ℹ* Ul Katedralna 7; www.braniewo.pl

The fortified town of Braniewo was founded by the Teutonic Knights in 1240. The seat of the bishops of Warmia, it later became the diocesan capital of Warmia. The town was a member of the Hanseatic League with a busy port and grew prosperous through the linen trade. During the Counter-Reformation it played an important role as the first Jesuit centre in Poland: the Hosianum Jesuit College was founded here in 1565 and a papal college set up in 1578.

Braniewo is an important transit point for travellers crossing between Russia and Poland – it's located just 8 km (5 miles) from the Russian border. Although it suffered severe damage during World War II, several fine buildings still stand.

 7

Morąg

🅰E2 🏠🚌 *ℹ* Town Hall, Pl Jana Pawła II 1; www. morag.pl

Located in the lakelands of Iławski Morąg, the town of Morąg was founded by the

Teutonic Knights – like all other towns in the region. It received its municipal charter in 1327. Despite joining the Prussian Union, Morąg remained part of the state of the Teutonic Knights, and up until 1945 its history was linked to that of ducal Prussia. In the town are the remains of a 14th-century Teutonic castle, a Gothic town hall that was rebuilt after World War II, and the Church of St Joseph (Kościół św. Józefa), built in the 14th century and extended in the late 15th, with Gothic polychromes from that time.

Morąg is the birthplace of the German philosopher Gottfried von Herder. Housed in a Baroque palace, the **Johann Gottfried von Herder Museum** is dedicated to him.

Johann Gottfried von Herder Museum

♿ 🏠 Ul Dąbrowskiego 54 📞 89 757 28 48 🕐 9am-5pm Tue-Sun (to 4pm Oct-May)

→
Riverboat tour passing Warmiński's Bishop's castle; the castle's Rococo chapel (inset)

8

Dobre Miasto

 E2 ☐☐ ℹ www.dobre
miasto.com.pl

Founded in 1326, Dobre Miasto owes its historical importance to the fact that, in 1347, it became the seat of a college of canons of the diocese of Warmia. The vast Gothic collegiate church they established boasts an impressive interior, including two Gothic side altars as well as a Baroque high altar almost identical in design to that made by Franciszek Placidi for Frombork Cathedral (p302). The church possesses richly decorated Baroque stalls down each side, which have remarkable Gothic steps carved into them in the shape of lions.

9

Lidzbark Warmiński

E1 ☐☐ ℹ www.lidzbark-
warminski.pl

From 1350 to 1795 Lidzbark Warmiński was the main residence of the bishops of Warmia, and one of the area's major towns. Picturesquely set on a bend of the River Łyna, the town is dominated by the medieval Bishops' Castle, a massive edifice with corner towers built in the second half of the 14th century. Of special interest are the Palace of Bishop Grabowski and the Great Refectory in the east wing, the castle's Rococo chapel and armoury in the south wing, the Small Refectory in the west wing and the bishops' private apartments located in the north wing. The cloistered courtyard is decorated with murals. The astronomer Nicolaus Copernicus (p281) lived here as secretary and physician to his uncle, Bishop Łukasz von Wantzenrode, in 1503–10. The castle's rooms now house the **Warmia Museum**, and there is a bar and art gallery in the cellars. On display is a selection of Warmian art and a collection of icons from the Convent of the Old Believers in the village of Wojnowo.

On the opposite bank of the Łyna, in the historic town centre, stands the fine Gothic **Church of Saints Peter and Paul** (Kościół św. Piotra i Pawła). There are also remnants of the city walls, and the main gate, the Brama Wysoka, still stands. The former Protestant church (now Orthodox) nearby was built in 1821–3.

Warmia Museum

✥ ☐ Pl Zamkowy 1
🕒 Mid-May–Aug: 10am–6pm Tue & Wed, 9am–5pm Thu–Sun; Sep–mid-May: 9am–4pm Tue–Sun
ⓦ muzeum.olsztyn.pl

Church of Saints Peter and Paul

☐ Ul Kościelny 1 ☏ 89 767 23 15 🕒 9am–5pm Tue–Sun (to 4pm Sep–19 May)

Did You Know?

A poetry festival is held each year in the courtyard of Olsztyn's historic castle.

---

⑩

Olsztyn

Ⓐ E2 🚗🚌 *i* Ul Jana Pawła II; www.olsztyn.eu

Olsztyn is the largest city in Warmia and Mazuria and the main town of the two regions. It is a major city and a centre of academic and cultural life. It hosts the Olsztyn Summer Arts festival from mid-June to mid-September.

The Gothic Castle of the Warmian Chapter, which was built in the 14th century, formed the beginning of the city. The castle was built on a hill on the banks of the Łyna. It was a four-sided fortress of modest proportions with residential quarters in the north wing. The palace in the east wing was added in 1756–8. The finest part of the building is the refectory, which has intricate crystalline vaulting. On the cloister wall is a remarkable diagram of an equinox, probably drawn by Nicolaus Copernicus. The castle now houses the **Museum of Warmia and Mazuria**, which has a special section dedicated to Nicolaus Copernicus. The first floor contains an ethnographical

and natural history collection. The castle's fortifications were linked to the city walls, which were built after 1353 on the far side of the moat. The moat today has an open-air theatre that is often used for performances in summer.

In the picturesque Old Town of Olsztyn, set on a slope, are remnants of the walls and the High Gate. The quaint little Market Square surrounded by arcaded houses was built during the postwar recon-struction of the city, but the houses retain their original cellars, which today house bars, restaurants and cafés. Standing in the middle of the square is a Baroque town hall.

Another important building in the Market Square is the Gothic Cathedral of St James (Katedra św. Jakuba), most probably built between 1380 and 1445. The very fine crystalline vaulting was added in the early 16th century.

Halfway between Olsztyn and Nidzica lies the country's oldest *skansen*, **Budownictwa Ludowego Open Air Museum**, home to traditional wooden windmills, arts and crafts.

Museum of Warmia and Mazuria

⊗ 🏛 Ul Zamkowa 2 🕐 Oct-Apr: 10am–4pm Tue–Sat, 10am–6pm Sun; May & Sep: 10am–5pm Tue–Sat, 10am–6pm Sun; Jun–Aug: 10am–6pm Tue–Sun 🌐 muzeum.olsztyn.pl

Budownictwa Ludowego Open Air Museum

⊗ 🏛 Ul Leśna 23 🕐 Mid-Apr–Jun & Sep: 9am–5pm daily; Jul & Aug: 10am–6pm daily; Oct: 9am–4pm Tue–Sun; Nov–mid-Apr: 10am–2pm (outside only) 🌐 muzeumolsztynek.com.pl

---

⑪

Reszel

Ⓐ E2 🚌 *i* Rynek 24; www.reszel.pl, www.ugreszel.pl

This little town was once a major Warmian city. In 1337, Reszel was granted a municipal charter, and in the second half of the 14th century a Gothic castle was built here for the Bishops of Warmia. The castle's tower commands a splendid view over the town. The castle is now a hotel, but also houses the **Castle Gallery**.

There are two churches in the town: the Gothic Church of Saints Peter and Paul, built in

---

💬 INSIDER TIP
Lake Ukiel

This tree-shrouded, tranquil lake is a short walk from Olsztyn city centre. There is a sandy beach, boat hire and lots of scope for waterside walking and cycling. Fish is a speciality of the shoreline restaurants.

→

Exquisitely adorned interior of the Church of Saints Peter and Paul in Reszel

the 1300s with the addition of late-15th-century vaulting, and the Baroque Church of St John the Baptist, now an Orthodox church, built in 1799–1800.

Castle Gallery

⊛ ⊛ ⊚ 🄰 Ul Podzamcze 3 🄲 May-Sep: 9am-7pm Tue-Sun; Oct-Apr: 9am-4pm Tue-Sun 🅆 zamek-reszel.com

---

Grunwald

🄰 E2 🚌

The fields between Grunwald and Stębark (Tannenberg in German) were the scene of one of the major battles of the Middle Ages. On 15 July 1410, the forces of the Teutonic Knights – some 14,000 cavalry plus infantry commanded by Ulrich von Jungingen – faced 24,000 Polish-Lithuanian and Ruthenian cavalry and several thousand infantry led by Władysław II Jagiełło. The Knights suffered a resounding defeat, and the Grand Master himself was killed. Historians believe that during World War I, in August 1914, the German Field Marshal Hindenburg deliberately chose this site for his

victorious battle against the Russians in order to negate the memory of that defeat. The monument to the medieval Battle of Grunwald that stands on the site was designed by Jerzy Bandura and Witold Cęckiewicz and unveiled in 1960. Nearby is the small **Museum of the Battle of Grunwald in Stębark** which contains a collection of documents about the battle and archaeological finds from the site. For several years the battle's anniversary has been marked by enthusiasts re-enacting the engagement as it is described in chronicles.

Museum of the Battle of Grunwald in Stębark

⊛ 🄰 Stębark 1 🄲 10 Apr-Sep: 9:30am-6:30pm daily (to 8:30pm on 15 Jul) 🅆 muzeumgrunwald. fbrothers.com

---

Święta Lipka

🄰 E2 🚌

Święta Lipka has one of the most important shrines of the cult of the Virgin in Poland. The town's name means "holy lime" (or linden tree), and the legend that grew up concerns a miraculous sculpture of the Virgin carved by a prisoner in the 15th century and hung from a roadside lime tree.

> **Święta Lipka has one of the most important shrines of the cult of the Virgin in Poland.**

A chapel containing the statue of the Virgin was built on the site, although the structure was destroyed during the Reformation. In 1619 a temporary chapel was built here, followed in 1687–93 by a proper church, **St Mary's Sanctuary**. In 1694–1708 cloisters and outside chapels were added and the façade and belfry were completed in 1729.

Święta Lipka was a Catholic stronghold within Protestant ducal Prussia during the time of the Counter-Reformation. Large donations were made for decorating the church, resulting in one of the finest and most intriguing examples of Baroque art in Poland. The interior contains frescoes, including trompe l'oeil paintings in the dome by Mathias Mayer, and the high altar has an image of the Virgin dating from about 1640. The organ, with moving figurines of angels, is a great attraction.

St Mary's Sanctuary

🄰 Św Lipka 29 🄲 Apr & Oct-Nov: 6:30am-6pm daily; May-Sep: 6:30am-8pm daily; Dec-Mar: 9:30am-3:30pm daily 🅆 swlipka.pl

←

The atmospheric ruins of Olsztyn castle, perched on an isolated hill

14
Kętrzyn

E2 **i** Pl Piłsudskiego 10/1; www.it.ketrzyn.pl

From the 14th century, Kętrzyn was the seat of the Prosecutor of the Teutonic Knights, who built the castle that can still be seen today. Kętrzyn then passed to Prussia and later Germany, but continued to have a sizable Polish population. The original name for the town was Rastembork; in 1946 it was renamed in honour of Polish national activist Wojciech Kętrzyński. The Old Town was almost flattened during World War II: only the town walls and the Church of St George (Kościół św. Jerzego) survived. Its exterior is modest, but the interior is impressive – its finest decoration is the crystalline vaulting from around 1515.

A few kilometres east of Kętrzyn is Gierłoż, location of the "Wolf's Lair", the secret Eastern Front headquarters of the Germans in World War II. It consisted of dozens of reinforced concrete bunkers, an airfield, railway lines and a power station. Here, on 20 July 1944, the German officer Claus von Stauffenberg made an unsuccessful attempt on Hitler's life. The lair was never discovered by the Allies, and the bunkers were blown up by the withdrawing Germans in January 1945.

> **INSIDER TIP**
> **The Scenic Route**
>
> Running from Ełk, a lakeside town, to the village of Turów, the Ełk Narrow Gauge Railway (Ełcka kolej wąskotorowa) winds through a landscape of meadow and forest. Services run from June to August and there is a railway museum at Ełk station (www.muzeum.elk.pl).

↑ The parish church on Market Square, in the heart of Tykocin

15
Tykocin

F3 **i** Ul Złota 2; 85 718 72 32

This town owes its present appearance to renovation that was carried out after a fire in 1741. In the centre of the Market Square there stands a Baroque monument to Stefan Czarnecki that was carved between 1761 and 1763 by the court sculptor Pierre Coudray. The parish church on the east side of the square was built a little earlier, in 1750. The Baroque synagogue, which dates from 1642, is a relic of the town's former Jewish population. Inside, the walls are inscribed with religious quotations in Hebrew and Aramaic. The synagogue is home to the **Tykocin Museum**, with exhibits on the town's Jewish community.

Tykocin Museum
Ul Kozia 2 85 718 16 26 10am-6pm Tue-Sun (to 5pm Oct-Apr)

→ Wooden rowboat on the banks of the swampy Biebrza River

16
Biebrza National Park

F2 **i** National Park Management: Osowiec-Twierdza 8; www.biebrza.org.pl

Biebrza National Park is one of the wildest places in all of Europe, untouched by human activity. It stretches for 70 km (50 miles) along the banks of the River Biebrza and contains Poland's largest swamps, which are home to a wide variety of wildlife. A close encounter with an elk is a distinct possibility. But the greatest attraction of the swamps is their rich bird life; over 260 species live here, and bird-watchers from afar come

to the swamps to observe them. The most interesting swamp for bird life is Red Swamp (Czerwone Bagno), part of a strictly protected nature reserve accessible only by means of a wooden walkway. Walkways have also been installed in other parts of the park – a stroll along the red tourist trail. Visitors may hire a guide and tour the swamps in a punt, or descend the River Biebrza in a canoe, for which a ticket and the permission of the park management are required. In Osowiec, in the middle of the swamps, there is a beaver reserve. Nearby stand the partly blown-up walls of a Russian redoubt. Although it was impregnable, the Russians, fearful of the German offensive, abandoned it in 1915.

Did You Know?

Around half of Poland's elk population lives within Biebrza National Park.

Białystok

 G3 🚌🚂 ℹ Ul Kilińskiego 1; www.bialystok.pl

Białystok's population is both Polish and Belarussian, something that can easily be read in the cityscape: the domes of the Orthodox church rise up next to the towers of the Catholic church, and there are many Belarussian cultural institutions found here.

Białystok was once owned by the Branicki family and the the town is dominated by their former residence, Branicki Palace. The Baroque palace was built in the 17th century and extended by Jan Zygmunt Deybel – who gave it the appearance of a royal mansion – between 1728 and 1758. A formal park, with terraces, canals, fountains, summerhouses and sculptures, was laid out around it.

The **Historical Museum** (Muzeum Historyczne) has a charming display of domestic interiors through the ages. There's also a model of the city in the 18th century.

One of Białystok's most celebrated sons is Ludvik

Zamenhof (1859-1917), founder of the Esperanto movement. The **Ludwik Zamenhof Centre** (Centrum im. Ludwika Zamenhofa) recreates the multicultural city of Zamenhof's childhood with a compelling display of photographs, mementos, film and music.

Historical Museum
♿ 🏛 Ul Warszawska 37
🕐 9:30am–5pm Tue–Sun
🌐 muzeum.bialystok.pl

Ludwik Zamenhof Centre
♿ 🏛 Ul Warszawska 19
🕐 10am–5pm Tue–Sun
🌐 centrumzamenhofa.pl

EAT

Tatarska Jurta
This homely restaurant serves Tatar specialities such as *kibiny,* pastry pouches stuffed with vegetables or diced meat.

📍 G3 🏠 Kruszyniany 58
🌐 kruszyniany.pl

Babka
With an interior that mixes folk motifs with pop-art, Babka has made traditional cuisine fashionable again.

📍 G3 🏠 Ul Lipowa 2, Białystok
📞 690 273 707

Browar Stary Rynek
A large terrace and a broad menu make this a popular spot for locals. Good-value weekday lunchtime specials.

📍 G3 🏠 Rynek Kościuszki 11, Białystok
🌐 royal-hotel.pl/browar

Trees reflected in a pond in Białowieża National Park ↑

painstakingly re-created, as were its interior frescoes. Next to this is the **Icon Museum** (Muzeum Ikon), which contains holy images rescued from local village churches across the country and fascinating material on the important role of the icon in Orthodox spirituality.

Icon Museum

 🏛 Klasztorna 1 🕐 May-Aug: 10am-5pm Mon-Thu, 10am-6pm Fri; Sep-Apr: 10am-5pm Tue-Sun 🌐 muzeum.bialystok.pl

---

⑳

Drohiczyn

🅰 F4 🚌 🛈 Ul Kraszewskiego 13; www.drohiczyn.pl

Drohiczyn, set on a high bank of the River Bug, is today a small, quiet town. As early as the 13th century, however, it was a major centre of trade, and in 1520 it became the provincial capital of Podlasie. In 1795, with the Third Partition of Poland, it was demoted to the status of a village.
The Baroque Franciscan

---

⑱

Białowieża National Park

🅰 G3 🚌 🛈 Park Pałacowy 11; www.bpn.com.pl

The Białowieża Forest, covering 1,500 sq km (580 sq miles) or so, is Europe's largest natural forest. It lies partly in Poland and partly in Belarus. The larger – Belarussian – part is virtually inaccessible to tourists; the Polish part became a national park in 1932. Many parts of the park have preserved their natural character of a primeval forest.

The forest has an abundance of impressive flora and fauna. There are several thousand species of plants and 11,000 species of animals, including many very rare birds, such as the capercaillie, black stork and golden eagle. Larger mammals include elk, wolves, deer, roe deer, wild boar, lynxes and, most famously, the European bison.

Białowieża village contains a National Park Visitors' Centre and the multimedia **Nature and Forest Museum** (Muzeum Przyroniczo-Lesne). The parts of the forest immediately north are a strictly protected area that can only be entered with a guide, booked through the Visitors' Centre; choose

between a walking guided tour or a tour in a horse-drawn carriage. West of the village are areas that are not included in the protected area and can be entered without restriction. A bison-breeding centre can also be found west of the settlement.

Nature and Forest Museum

 🏛 Palace Park Botanical Gardens 📞 85 682 97 04 🕐 Mid-Apr-mid-Oct: 9am-4:30pm Mon-Fri, 9am-5pm Sat & Sun; mid-Oct-mid-Apr: 9am-4pm Tue-Sun

---

⑲

Supraśl

🅰 G2/G3 🚌 🛈 suprasl.pl

Situated on the edge of the Knyszyń Forest (Puszcza Knyszyńska), 16 km (10 miles) east of Białystok, the village of Supraśl is home to the Supraśl Lavra, an Orthodox Christian monastery founded in the 16th century. Approached through a splendid Eastern Baroque gate, the monastery's Church of the Annunciation (Cerkiew Zwiastowania) features fortress-like corner towers and intricate brick-work. Destroyed by the Nazis in World War II, it was then

---

> ### EUROPEAN BISON
>
> The European bison *(Bison bonasus)* is the largest mammal native to Europe. Hunting these animals has always been restricted, but by World War I (1914-18) the species faced extinction. In 1929, several bison were brought to Poland from zoos in Sweden and Germany to be bred in their natural habitat. The first were set free in Białowieża National Park in 1952. Today bison can also be seen in the other great forests of Poland, including Borecka, Knyszyńska and Niepołomice.

church dates from 1640–60 and is the oldest surviving church in the town. Originally a Jesuit building, the cathedral dates from 1696–1709.

The striking Benedictine church, begun in 1744, has a typically Baroque undulating façade and elliptical interior. To the east of the town, along the River Bug, lies a park, the Podlasie River Bug Gorge.

21 Kruszyniany

 G3 🚆

Kruszyniany and nearby Bohoniki count among their inhabitants the descendants of the Tatars who settled here in the 17th century. Although they became fully integrated into the community a long time ago, their Muslim faith and customs live on.

Kruszyniany boasts a charming wooden mosque, which originated in the 18th century and was rebuilt in 1843. The tombstones in the Muslim graveyard face Mecca.

22 Hajnówka

 G3 🚆 ℹ Ul 3 Maja 45; 85 682 4381

Hajnówka is a major centre of the local Belarusian population and home to striking Orthodox churches, including the ethereal Holy Trinity

Church (Sobór Świętej Trójcy), on Ulica Dziewiatowskiego. Its mushroom-like domes and tapering belfry give it an otherworldly appearance.

Just east of Hajnówka, the narrow-gauge **Forest Railway** (Kolejka leśna) was built by the German military in World War I. It now takes excursions into a magical landscape of wetlands and deep forest.

Forest Railway

 Ul Kolejki leśne
⏰ Departures 10am & 2pm on Sat mid-May–Jun; on Tue, Thu, Sat & Sun in Jul & Aug; Thu & Sat in Sep

23 Grabarka

 G3 🚗 🚆 ℹ www. grabarka.pl

For the country's Orthodox Christians, there is no more important place of pilgrimage than the Holy Mountain out-

↑ Votive crosses on the Holy Mountain, close to Grabarka town

side Grabarka. The story goes that in 1770, when the town was ravaged by an epidemic of cholera, the inhabitants of Grabarka were directed by a heavenly sign to erect a cross on the hill. The plague passed and the hill became a hallowed site. To this day its slopes are covered with hundreds of votive crosses. Each year, during the Orthodox Church's Feast of Transfiguration, 10,000 people visit the hill. The original wooden church, destroyed by an arsonist in 1990, was replaced by a brick-built church in 1998. The Orthodox convent next to it is the only one in Poland.

← Holy Trinity Church, one of many Orthodox churches in Hajnówka

NEED TO KNOW

Driving through autumnal foliage

BEFORE
YOU GO

Forward planning is essential for any successful trip. Be prepared for all eventualities by considering the following points before you travel.

AT A GLANCE

CURRENCY
Złoty (PLN)

AVERAGE DAILY SPEND

SAVE
250zł

SPEND
520zł

SPLURGE
800zł

BOTTLED WATER
3zł

COFFEE
8zł

BEER
10zł

DINNER FOR TWO
140zł

ESSENTIAL PHRASES

Hello	Cześć
Goodbye	Do widzenia
Please	Proszę
Thank you	Dziękuję
Do you speak English?	Czy mówi pan angielsku?
I don't understand	Nie rozumiem

ELECTRICITY SUPPLY

Power sockets are types C and E, fitting two-pronged plugs. Standard voltage is 230 volts.

Passports and Visas

For a stay of up to three months for the purpose of tourism, EU nationals and citizens of the US, Canada, Australia and New Zealand do not need a visa. Consult your nearest Polish embassy or the Polish **Ministry of Foreign Affairs** website if you are travelling from outside these areas.
Ministry of Foreign Affairs
w msz.gov.pl/en

Travel Safety Advice

Visitors can get up-to-date travel safety information from the **US Department of State**, the **UK Foreign and Commonwealth Office** and the **Australian Department of Foreign Affairs and Trade**.
Australia
w smartraveller.gov.au
UK
w gov.uk/foreign-travel-advice
US
w travel.state.gov

Customs Information

An individual is permitted to carry the following within the EU for personal use:
Tobacco products 800 cigarettes, 400 cigarillos, 200 cigars or 1kg of smoking tobacco.
Alcohol 10 litres of alcoholic beverages above 22 per cent strength, 20 litres of alcoholic beverages below 22 per cent strength, 90 litres of wine (60 litres of which can be sparkling wine) and 110 litres of beer.
Cash If you plan to enter or leave the EU with €10,000 or more in cash (or equivalent in other currencies), you must declare it to the customs authorities.
Limits vary if travelling outside the EU, so check restrictions before travelling. A licence is needed to export any item more than 100 years old or any artwork over 50 years old and exceeding 16,000zł in value. Visit the Polish **Ministry of Finance** website for more information.
Ministry of Finance
w finanse.mf.gov.pl

Insurance

It is wise to take out an insurance policy covering theft, loss of belongings, medical problems, cancellation, delays and adventure activities. Residents of the EU, the European Economic Area and Switzerland are entitled to free first aid and emergency treatment on production of an **EHIC** (European Health Insurance Card). Non-essential treatment and additional medicines will have to be paid for. Visitors from outside these areas must have private health insurance and may need to pay upfront for all treatment.
EHIC
🆆 gov.uk/european-health-insurance-card

Vaccinations

No inoculations are required for Poland.

Money

Major credit and debit cards are accepted in most shops, businesses and railway stations. They can't always be used in bus stations, cafés and restaurants outside the big cities, however, or at small B&Bs and hostels, so it is a good idea to carry some cash, too.

Cash machines can be found at most banks, shopping malls and railway stations. Cash can also be exchanged at a *kantor* (bureau de change) although rates often vary wildly.

Booking Accommodation

Poland offers a huge variety of accommodation, including boutique hotels in historic buildings, B&Bs, spa resorts and backpacker hostels. The country is also home to a large number of campsites, many of which are located in beautiful countryside. It is usually worth booking well in advance for the busy summer months (from June to September), at Easter, and around the 1 May and 3 May public holidays, when lodgings tend to fill up fast and prices rise.

Travellers with Specific Needs

Many main attractions and public buildings have wheelchair access, though it is recommended to call ahead to check accessibility.

In Warsaw and Kraków many trams and buses are wheelchair accessible; information is displayed on the electronic departure board at each stop to inform passengers when the next wheelchair-friendly service is due to arrive.

Hotels with four or more stars usually have wheelchair-friendly rooms, but these are often in short supply and ought to be booked well in advance.

Accessible Poland Tours organize trips for travellers with specific requirements including those in wheelchairs and the visually and hearing impaired.
Accessible Poland Tours
🆆 accessibletour.pl/en

Language

The official language of Poland is Polish, a Slav language related to Czech, Slovak and Russian. English is spoken widely in the main cities and throughout the tourist industry but the same cannot be said for rural areas. Many people in western Poland also know some German.

Closures

Mondays Most tourist attractions and museums are closed for the day.
Sundays Most businesses, malls and shops are closed, except for small convenience stores. Visiting times in churches may be restricted due to Sunday masses.
Public holidays Post offices, banks, shops and most tourist attractions are closed all day.

PUBLIC HOLIDAYS	
1 Jan	New Year's Day
6 Jan	Epiphany
Mar/Apr	Easter
1 May	Labour Day
3 May	Constitution Day
May/Jun	Pentecost Sunday / Whit Sunday
May/Jun	Corpus Christi
15 Aug	Feast of the Assumption
1 Nov	All Saints' Day
11 Nov	Independence Day
25 Dec	Christmas Day
26 Dec	St Stephen's Day

GETTING
AROUND

Whether you are visiting for a short city break or an expansive two-week tour, discover how best to reach your destination and travel like a pro.

Arriving by Air

Most Polish cities have international airports, ensuring that all regions of the country can be reached by air. Airports at Warsaw, Kraków and Gdańsk are connected to the city centre by train and bus. Most other airports are served by local bus lines.

Chopin Airport, Warsaw's main airport, is served by regular trains to both Warszawa Centralna and Warszawa Sródmieście, with a journey time of 30 minutes. The less frequently used Warsaw Modlin airport is connected by bus to Warszawa Centralna; travel time is 1 hour.

Kraków airport is connected by train to the central Kraków Główny train station. Trains depart every 30 minutes and take 20 minutes.

Gdańsk's Lech Wałęsa airport is connected to Gdańsk and Gdynia by train roughly every hour.

Poland's other airports rely on bus lines to and from their respective city centres; check individual airport websites for further details.

Train Travel

Long-Distance Train Travel

The railway network in Poland has improved considerably in recent years and is now a fast and comfortable way of getting from city to city. Trains are slower in rural regions, so visitors may find bus travel a better option.

Trains are run by a variety of companies. **PKP InterCity** runs express services connecting the main centres and is the best way of getting from Warsaw to Gdań sk, Kraków or other big cities. InterCity trains will have buffet facilities and Wi-Fi. **TLK**, part of the same company, also runs an express service; it is cheaper than InterCity but trains are slightly slower and with older, cramped carriages. A second-class single ticket from Warsaw to Kraków will be about 150zł on InterCity, 70zł on TLK , although discounts for online booking are available.

PolRegio runs a variety of cross-country and local trains, and is a useful way of getting to regional towns. Trains operated by regional companies such as **Koleje Mazowieckie** (central Poland) or **Koleje Dolnośląskie** (southwestern

GETTING TO AND FROM THE AIRPORT

Airport	Fare	Public Transport	Journey time
Warsaw Chopin	4.40zł	Train	30 mins
	50–60zł	Taxi	30 mins
Warsaw Modlin	33zł	Bus	1 hr
	200zł	Taxi	50 mins
Kraków John Paul II	9zł	Train	25 mins
	80–100zł	Taxi	50 mins
Gdańsk Lech Wałęsa	3.80zł	Train	45 mins
	70zł	Taxi	40 mins
Wrocław	10zł	Bus	40 mins
	60–80zł	Taxi	30 mins
Katowice Pyrzowice	27zł	Bus	50 mins
	100zł	Taxi	45 mins
Poznań Ławica	4.60zł	Bus	30 mins
	40–50zł	Taxi	25 mins
Lublin	5.30zł	Train	15 mins
	50–60zł	Taxi	25 mins
Łódź Władysław Reymont	4.40zł	Bus	35 mins
	40–50zł	Taxi	25 mins
Rzeszów	3.50zł	Bus	30 mins
	40–50zł	Taxi	30 mins

Poland) connect smaller places within the relevant region. Trains are usually comfortable and often offer additional services like Wi-Fi.

Koleje Dolnośląskie
ⓦ kolejedolnoslaskie.pl
Koleje Mazowieckie
ⓦ mazowieckie.com.pl
PKP InterCity and TLK
ⓦ intercity.pl
PolRegio
ⓦ polrego.pl

Local Train Travel

In Warsaw, the **SKM (Warsaw)** local train network is a good way of crossing the city from east to west. It is integrated into the city transport system and the same tickets and day-passes are valid.

The Tri-City area of Gdańsk, Gdynia and Sopot has a local train service called **SKM (Tri-City)**. Services connecting the main centres run every ten minutes during the day. Tickets are purchased from machines on the platforms. Tickets used for regular train services are not valid for SKM routes and vice-versa.

SKM (Tri-City)
ⓦ skm.pkp.pl
SKM (Warsaw)
ⓦ skm-warszawa.pl

Public Transport

Long-Distance Bus Travel

There is a country-wide network of bus services run by different companies. Cheaper than trains, buses also cover more destinations. Each town and city has a station where departures are listed and tickets sold. Some operators such as **Polski Bus** sell tickets exclusively online. Kraków's **MDA Bus Station** has an online timetable.

MDA Bus Station
ⓦ mda.malopolska.pl
Polski Bus
ⓦ polskibus.com

City Transport

Most major public transport networks, such as the **Kraków Municipal Transport Company** (Miejskie Przedsiębiorstwo Komunikacyjne), run integrated buses and trams. Some networks also operate electric trolleybuses and local trains. The **Gdańsk Public Transport Authority** (Zarząd Transportu Miejskiego) includes ferries, while the **Warsaw Public Transport Authority** (Zarząd Transportu Miejskiego) also boasts an underground metro system.

Individual tickets can be purchased from kiosks or from ticket machines (in Warsaw and Kraków, ticket machines are placed on platforms and also inside the trams), and then punched in machines when entering the vehicle. Day passes and three-day passes are usually available and offer huge savings if you use the system a lot.

Gdańsk Public Transport Authority
W ztm.gda.pl
Kraków Municipal Transport Company
W mpk.krakow.pl
Warsaw Public Transport Authority
W ztm.waw.pl

Boats and Ferries

Passenger steamers operated by **Żegluga Mazurska** on the Great Mazurian Lakes from Easter to late October are a good way to travel around the region and soak up fantastic views at the same time. There are also **Żegluga Gdańska** passenger ferries linking Gdańsk, Sopot, Gdynia and Hel.

River transport is available in a number of Polish cities from May to September. **Warsaw Water Trams** run up and down the Vistula, and additional free (and often very crowded) shuttle services link the east and west banks of the river. **Kraków Water Trams** have a scenic route along the Vistula to the suburb of Salwator. **Gdańsk Water Trams** run, in the summer, from the city centre to beach resorts east and west of the city.

Gdańsk Water Trams
W ztm.gda.pl
Kraków Water Trams
W tramwaywodny.net.pl
Warsaw Water Trams
W ztm.waw.pl
Żegluga Gdańska
W zegluga.pl
Żegluga Mazurska
W zeglugamazurska.pl

Taxis

Taxi ranks can be found at train and bus stations and at the main entrances to pedestrianized zones in city centres. Flagging down taxis on the street is rarely possible – it is best to go to a taxi rank or order one by phone. Well-known

Kraków taxi firms include **Barbakan** and **Wawel Taxi**, while Warsaw has **Super Taxi** and **MPT**. Taxi apps such as Uber also operate in most major Polish cities.

Most taxi journeys are metered, although you may be able to negotiate a fee if you are going a particularly short or long distance. Private taxis, which do not display a company name or phone number, should be avoided, and taxi touts at airports or train stations should be ignored, as their charges may be many times the official rate.

Barbakan
☎ 19661
MPT
☎ 19191
Super Taxi
☎ 19622
Wawel Taxi
☎ 19666

Driving

Driving to Poland

Poland is increasingly integrated into the European motorway network. However, routes from the west (through Germany) are faster than those from the south or east, where motorway construction is still lagging behind. The principal motorways that link Western Europe to Poland are the E30 (which links Berlin, Poznań, Łódź and Warsaw) and the E65 (which links Dresden, Wrocław and Kraków).

Car Rental

All major international car rental companies operate in Poland. To rent a car in Poland you must be over 21 or 25 years of age, depending on the hire company, and possess a valid driving licence. Driving licences issued by any European Union member state are valid throughout the EU. International driving licences are not needed for short-term visitors (up to 90 days) from North America, Australia and New Zealand. Visitors from other countries should check the regulations with their local automobile association before they travel. It is advisable to check the level of insurance cover provided by your rental company.

Driving in Poland

Poland is one of Europe's largest countries, and driving here can often involve covering long distances. Although the number of fast intercity highways is increasing – and travel times between the major centres are getting shorter – away from the main highways progress can be slow, with columns of traffic building up on popular routes.

The country's roads still vary widely in terms of quality. Although road surfaces in general are improving, rural routes may be bumpy.

In the event of a break down, **Emergency Road Services** will arrange a tow truck and advise on nearby garages.

Emergency Road Services
☎ 9637

Parking

Finding an on-street parking space can be very difficult in Polish cities and very often requires a parking permit purchased from local news kiosks. It is far better to find a parking garage or a guarded parking lot *(parking strzeżony)*, usually well-signed in Polish towns and cities. These rarely cost more than 40zł per day. Hotels sometimes have parking spaces for guests.

Rules of the Road

The wearing of seat belts is compulsory. Children under the age of 12 are not allowed to travel in the front of the car, and small children must be strapped into special child seats. It is obligatory for motorcyclists and their passengers always to wear helmets.

Headlights must be on, day and night, regardless of the weather conditions. Radar speed controls are frequent, and offenders will be given an on-the-spot fine.

The use of mobile phones while driving is banned unless the phone is a hands-free model. The permitted alcohol content in blood is so low in Poland (two parts per thousand) that drinking and driving should be avoided altogether.

Cycling

Long-distance cycling routes include the **Green Velo** cycle trail which winds through forested eastern Poland. Cities, too, are increasingly bike friendly, with a growing number of cycling lanes and signed routes. In urban areas, cycling on the pavement is allowed in areas without bike lanes, although you must give way to pedestrians.

Most major cities have bicycle hire schemes allowing you to pick up and drop off bikes at docking stations once you have registered with a credit card. These include Warsaw's **Veturilo**, Kraków's **Wavelo**, Poznan's **Poznanski Rower Miejski** and Lublin's **Lubelski Rower Miejski**. **SeeWrocław** rent out bicycles and run tours, while Gdańsk's **House of Bikes**, run by cycling enthusiasts, is an excellent all-round resource.

Green Velo
🆆 greenvelo.pl/en
House of Bikes
🆆 houseofbikes.pl
Lubelski Rower Miejski
🆆 lubelskirower.pl
Poznanski Rower Miejski
🆆 nextbike.pl
SeeWrocław
🆆 seewroclaw.pl
Veturilo
🆆 veturilo.waw.pl
Wavelo
🆆 wavelo.pl

RAIL JOURNEY PLANNER

Plotting Poland's major train routes according to journey time, this map is a handy reference for intercity rail travel. Journey times are for the fastest available service.

Białystok to Gdańsk	5 hrs
Gdańsk to Toruń	1 hr 45 mins
Kraków to Zakopane	2 hrs
Kraków to Zamość	3 hrs 40 mins
Lublin to Białystok	3 hrs 30 mins
Poznań to Wrocław	2 hrs 30 mins
Toruń to Poznań	2 hrs 30 mins
Warsaw to Gdańsk	3 hrs 45 mins
Warsaw to Kraków	3 hrs 45 mins
Warsaw to Lublin	2 hrs 45 mins
Warsaw to Poznań	3 hrs
Wrocław to Kraków	3 hrs
Zamość to Lublin	1 hr 20 mins

••• Direct train routes

PRACTICAL
INFORMATION

A little local know-how goes a long way in Poland. Here you will find all the essential advice and information you will need during your stay.

EMERGENCY NUMBERS

FIRE, POLICE AND AMBULANCE	MOUNTAIN RESCUE
112	**985**

TIME ZONE
CET/CEST. Central European Summer Time runs from the last Sunday in March to the last Sunday in October.

TAP WATER
Ordinary tap water in Poland is safe to drink. Outdoor taps not connected to the main supply will have a sign reading *woda niezdatna do picia* (not drinking water).

TIPPING

Waiter	10 per cent or round up
Hotel Porter	10zł per trip
Housekeeping	10zł
Concierge	20zł
Taxi Driver	10 per cent or round up

Personal Security

Poland is a generally safe country in which to travel and visitors are unlikely to encounter difficulties providing they take the usual precautions against petty crime. Crowded bars, public transport, major train stations and busy markets are the places where petty thieves and pickpockets are most active. Pickpockets frequently operate in gangs, and a sudden push or other distraction caused by them is hardly ever accidental. Car break-ins are common and valuables should never be left unattended in the car. Use guarded car parks rather than on-street parking wherever possible.

If you have anything stolen, report it to the police as soon as you can. Make sure you get a copy of the crime report in order to claim on your insurance. If your passport is stolen, contact your embassy or consulate immediately.

Health

Emergency treatment for citizens of the EU and Switzerland is free of charge *(p315)*. Popular remedies are available over-the-counter at Polish pharmacies but for more specific drugs and medicines you will need a prescription authorized by a local doctor. Minor health problems can often be dealt with in a pharmacy, where trained staff can provide advice. For more serious injury or illness, head for the emergency department of the nearest hospital.

Smoking, Alcohol and Drugs

Smoking is prohibited in all public places, cafés, restaurants and bars, with the exception of some bars which have a specific area for smokers.

The blood alcohol limit for drivers is 0.02 per cent, a very small amount which will be exceeded even if you only drink half a glass of wine – so it is best not to drink at all. Be aware that riding a bicycle while under the influence of alcohol is also a punishable offence.

Custodial sentences are frequently applied to those in possession of illegal drugs, especially if they are dealing or selling.

ID

Although checks on ID are rare in Poland, visitors are obliged to carry either their passport or national identity card at all times.

LGBT+ Safety

Although Poland has legalized homosexuality, it remains a conservative country in which LGBT+ communities have not always been met with acceptance. There are annual Equality Parades in Warsaw and Kraków, with both cities featuring a growing handful of hotels, bars and clubs that welcome members of the LGBT+ community. Elsewhere, same-sex couples may elicit a negative response from locals and business-owners.

Visiting Places of Worship

Poland is a devout Roman Catholic country and certain standards are expected when visiting churches. Visitors should refrain from making noise and use cameras discreetly. Strict dress codes apply: cover your torso and upper arms, and ensure shorts and skirts cover your knees. Shoes must be worn. There are working synagogues in a handful of big cities, some of which require male visitors to wear a black skullcap, available at the entrance.

Mobile Phones and Wi-Fi

Most hotels, cafés and bars offer free Wi-Fi to customers. There are also free Wi-Fi hotspots in main railway stations and in city centres, often around the main square. Visitors travelling to Poland on EU tariffs are able to use their devices without having to pay extra roaming charges on calls, text messages or data.

Post

Stamps can be bought from both post offices and newspaper kiosks. Allow up to ten days when sending post to Great Britain, and up to 15 days for the United States or Australia.

Taxes and Refunds

Poland's VAT rate is 23 per cent. Non-EU residents are entitled to VAT tax refunds, providing you request a tax receipt and regular retail receipt when purchasing your goods. These receipts must be presented to a tax refund office, together with your passport, when leaving the country.

Discount Cards

If you are a student, an **ISIC** (International Student Identity Card) will get you discounts at some tourist attractions and on public transport. Many Polish cities have passes offering free access to public transport alongside free access to or discounts at tourist attractions. These discount cards are usually valid for a set period of one, two or three days, and cover individuals as well as families. If you plan to visit a lot of attractions and use public transport to get there, these cards are well worth buying; they are available either online or from local tourist offices. The **Gdańsk Tourist Card**, the **Kraków Card** and the **Warsaw Pass** are among the best city discount cards.

Gdańsk Tourist Card
ⓦ visitgdansk.com
ISIC
ⓦ isic.org
Kraków Card
ⓦ krakowcard.com
Warsaw Pass
ⓦ warsawpass.com

WEBSITES AND APPS

Poland.travel
The country's official tourism site, www.poland.travel is a useful resource.

Warsaw Tourism
www.warsawtour.pl is Warsaw's official visitor information site.

Magic Kraków
Kraków's official tourism site can be found at www.krakow.pl.

Visit Wrocław
www.visitwroclaw.eu is one of the best of the city information sites.

Culture.pl
Run by the Adam Mickiewicz Institute, www.culture.pl focuses on Polish history and culture.

INDEX

Page numbers in bold refer to main entries

PHRASE BOOK

SUMMARY OF PRONUNCIATION IN POLISH

ą a nasal *"awn"* as in *"sawn"* but barely sounded
c *"ts"* as in *"bats"*
ć, cz *"ch"* as in *"challenge"*
ch *"ch"* as in Scottish *"loch"*
dz *"j"* as in *"jeans"* when followed by **i** or **e** but otherwise *"dz"* as in *"adze"*
dź *"j"* as in *"jeans"*
dż *"d"* as in *"dog"* followed by *"s"* as in *"leisure"*
ę similar to *"en"* in *"end"* only nasal and barely sounded, but if at the end of the word pronounced *"e"* as in *"bed"*
h *"ch"* as in Scottish *"loch"*
i *"ee"* as in *"teeth"*
j *"y"* as in yes
ł *"w"* as in *"window"*
ń similar to the *"ni"* in *"companion"*
ó *"oo"* as in *"soot"*
rz similar to the *"s"* in *"leisure"* or, when it follows **p**, **t** or **k**, *"sh"* as in *"shut"*
ś, sz *"sh"* as in *"shut"*
w *"v"* as in *"vine"*
y similar to the *"i"* in *"bit"*
ź, ż similar to the *"s"* in *"leisure"*

EMERGENCIES

Help!	**Pomocy!**	*pomotsi*
Call a doctor!	**Zawołać doktora!**	*zawowach doctora*
Call an ambulance!	**Zadzwonić po pogotowie!**	*zadzvoneech po pogotovee*
Police!	**Policja!**	*poleetsya*
Call the fire brigade!	**Zadzwonić po straż pożarną!**	*zadzvoneech po stras posarnAWN*
Where is the *nearest phone?*	**Gdzie jest budka telefoniczna?**	*gjeh yest nlbleezhsha najbliższą boodka telefoneechna*
Where is the hospital?	**Gdzie jest szpital?**	*gjeh yest shpeetal*
Where is the *police station?*	**Gdzie jest policji?**	*gjeh yest posterunek posterunek politsyee*

COMMUNICATION ESSENTIALS

Yes	**Tak**	*tak*
No	**Nie**	*n-yeh*
Thank you	**Dziękuję**	*jENkoo-yeh*
No, thank you	**Nie, dziękuję**	*n-yej jENkoo-yeh*
Please	**Proszę**	*prosheh*
I don't understand	**Nie rozumiem**	*n-yeh rozoom-yem*
Do you speak English? (to a man)	**Czy mówi pan po angielsku?**	*chi moovee pan po ang-yelskoo*
Do you speak English? (to a woman)	**Czy mówi pani po angielsku?**	*chi moovee panee po ang-yelskoo*
Please speak more slowly	**Proszę mówić wolniej**	*proseh mooveech voln-yay*
Please write it down for me	**Proszę mi to napisać**	*prosheh mee to napeesach*
My name is...	**Nazywam się...**	*nazivam sheh*

USEFUL WORDS AND PHRASES

Pleased to meet you (to a man)	**Bardzo mi miło pana poznać**	*bardzo mee meewo pana poznach*
Pleased to meet you (to a woman)	**Bardzo mi miło panią poznać**	*bardzo mee meewo pan-yAWN poznach*
Good morning	**Dzień dobry**	*jen-yuh dobri*
Good afternoon	**Dzień dobry**	*jen-yuh dobri*
Good evening	**Dobry wieczór**	*dobri v-yechoor*
Good night	**Dobranoc**	*dobranots*
Goodbye	**Do widzenia**	*do veedzen-ya*
What time is it?	**Która jest godzina?**	*ktoora yest gojeena*
Cheers!	**Na zdrowie!**	*na zdrov-yeh*
Excellent!	**Wspaniale!**	*wspan-yaleh*

SHOPPING

Do you have...? (to a man)	**Czy ma pan...?**	*che ma pan*
Do you have...? (to a woman)	**Czy ma pani...?**	*che ma panee*
How much is this?	**Ile to kosztuje?**	*eeleh to koshtoo-yeh*
Where is the... department?	**Gdzie jest dział z...?**	*gjeh yest jawuh z*
Do you take credit cards? (to a man)	**Czy przyjmuje pan karty kredytowe?**	*chi pshi-yuhmoo-yeh pan karti kreditoveh*
Do you take credit cards? (to a woman)	**Czy przyjmuje pani karty kredytowe?**	*chi pshi-yuhmoo-yeh panee karti kreditoveh*
bakery	**piekarnia**	*p-yekarn-ya*
bookshop	**księgarnia**	*kshENgarn-ya*
chemist	**apteka**	*apteka*
department store	**dom towarowy**	*dom tovarovi*
exchange office	**kantor walutowy**	*kantor valootovi*
travel agent	**biuro podróży**	*b-yooro podroozhi*
post office	**poczta, urząd pocztowy**	*pochta, ooZHAWNd pochtovi*
postcard	**pocztówka**	*pochtoovka*
stamp	**znaczek**	*znachek*
How much is a postcard to...?	**Ile kosztuje pocztówka do...?**	*eeleh koshtoo-yeh pochtoovka do*
airmail	**poczta lotnicza**	*pochta lotneecha*

STAYING IN A HOTEL

Have you any vacancies? (to a man)	**Czy ma pan wolne pokoje?**	*chi ma pan volneh poko-yeh*
Have you any vacancies? (to a woman)	**Czy ma pani wolne pokoje?**	*chi ma panee volneh poko-yeh*
What is the charge per night?	**Ile kosztuje za dobę?**	*eeleh koshtoo-yeh za dobeh*
I'd like a single room.	**Poproszę pokój jednoosobowy.**	*poprosheh pokoo-yuh yedno-osobovi*
I'd like a double room.	**Poproszę pokój dwuosobowy.**	*poprosheh pokoo-yuh dvoo-osobovi*
I'd like a twin room.	**Poproszę pokój z dwoma łóżkami.**	*poprosheh pokoo-yuh z dvoma woozhkamee*
I'd like a room with a bathroom.	**Poproszę pokój z łazienką.**	*poprosheh pokoo-yuh z wazhenkAWN*
bathroom	**łazienka**	*wazhenka*
bed	**łóżko**	*woozhko*
bill	**rachunek**	*raHoonek*
breakfast	**śniadanie**	*shn-yadan-yeh*
dinner	**kolacja**	*kolats-ya*
double room	**pokój dwuosobowy**	*pokoo-yuh dvoo-osobovi*
full board	**pełne utrzymanie**	*pewuhneh ootzhiman-yeh*
guesthouse	**zajazd**	*za-yazd*
half board	**dwa posiłki dziennie**	*dva posheewuhkee jen-yeh*
key	**klucz**	*klooch*
restaurant	**restauracja**	*restawrats-ya*
shower	**prysznic**	*prishneets*
single room	**pokój jednoosobowy**	*pokoo-yuh yedno-osobovi*
toilet	**toaleta**	*to-aleta*

EATING OUT

A table for one, please.	**Stolik dla jednej osoby, proszę.**	*stoleek dla yednay osobi prosheh*
A table for two, please.	**Stolik dla dwóch osób, proszę.**	*stoleek dla dvooh osoob prosheh*
Can I see the menu?	**Mogę prosić jadłospis?**	*mogeh prosheech yadwospees*
Can I see the wine list?	**Mogę prosić kartę win?**	*mogeh prosheech karteh veen*
I'd like...	**Proszę**	*prosheh*
Can we have the bill, please?	**Proszę rachunek?**	*prosheh raHoonek*
Where is the toilet?	**Gdzie jest toaleta?**	*gjeh yest to-aleta*

MENU DECODER

baranina	mutton, lamb
barszcz czerwony	beetroot soup
bażant	pheasant
befsztyk	beef steak
bigos	hunter's stew (sweet and sour cabbage with a variety of meats and seasonings)
bukiet z jarzyn	a variety of raw and pickled vegetables
ciasto	cake, pastry
cielęcina	veal
cukier	sugar
cukierek	sweet, confectionery
dania mięsne	meat dishes
dania rybne	fish dishes
dania z drobiu	poultry dishes
deser	dessert
flaki	tripe
grzybki marynowane	marinated mushrooms
herbata	tea
jarzyny	vegetables
kabanos	dry, smoked pork sausage
kaczka	duck
kapusta	cabbage
kartofle	potatoes
kasza gryczana	buckwheat
kaszanka	black pudding
kawa	coffee
kiełbasa	sausage
klopsiki	minced meat balls
lody	ice cream
łosoś	salmon
łosoś wędzony	smoked salmon
makowiec	poppy seed cake
naleśniki	pancakes
piernik	spiced honeycake
pierogi	ravioli-like dumplings
piwo	beer
prawdziwki	ceps (type of mushroom)
przystawki	entrées
pstrąg	trout
rolmopsy	rollmop herrings
sałatka	salad
sałatka owocowa	fruit salad
sok	juice
sok jabłkowy	apple juice
sok owocowy	fruit juice
sól	salt
śledź	herring
tort	cake, gâteau
wieprzowina	pork
wino	wine
woda	water
ziemniaki	potatoes
zupa	soup

HEALTH

I do not feel well.	Źle się czuję.	zhleh sheh choo-yeh
I need a prescription for...	Potrzebuję receptę na...	potzheboo-yeh retsepteh na
cold	przeziębienie	pshef-yENb-yen-yeh
cough (noun)	kaszel	kashel
cut	skaleczenie	skalechen-yeh
flu	grypa	gripa
hayfever	katar sienny	katar shyienny
headache pills	proszki od bólu głowy	proshkee od booloo gwovi
hospital	szpital	shpeetal
nausea	mdłości	mudwosh-che
sore throat	ból gardła	bool gardwa

TRAVEL AND TRANSPORT

When is the next train to...?	Kiedy jest następny pociąg do...?	k-yedi yest nastENpni pochAWNg do...
What is the fare to...?	Ile kosztuje bilet do...?	eeleh koshtoo-yeh beelet do
A single ticket to ... please	Proszę bilet w jedną stronę bilet do...	prosheh beelet v yednAWN stroneh beelet do
A return ticket to ... please	Proszę bilet w obie strony do...	prosheh beelet v obye strony do
Where is the bus station?	Gdzie jest dworzec autobusowy?	gjeh yest dvozhets awtoboosovi
Where is the bus stop?	Gdzie jest przystanek autobusowy?	gjeh yest pshistanek awtoboosovi
Where is the tram stop?	Gdzie jest przystanek tramwajowy?	gjeh yest pshistanek tramvi-yovi
booking office	kasa biletowa	kasa beeletova
station	stacja	stats-ya
timetable	rozkład jazdy	rozkwad yazdi
left luggage	przechowalnia bagażu	psheHovaln-ya bagazhoo
platform	peron	peron
first class	pierwsza klasa	p-yervsha klasa
second class	druga klasa	drooga klasa
single ticket	bilet w jedną stronę	beelet v jednAWN stroneh
return ticket	bilet powrotny	beelet povrotni
airline	linia lotnicza	leen-ya lotna-yeecha
airport	lotnisko	lotn-yeesko
arrival	przylot	pshilot
flight number	numer lotu	noomer lotoo
gate	przejście	pshaysh-cheh
coach	autokar	awtokar

NUMBERS

0	zero	zero
1	jeden	yeden
2	dwa	dva
3	trzy	tshi
4	cztery	chteri
5	pięć	p-yENch
6	sześć	shesh-ch
7	siedem	sh-yedem
8	osiem	oshem
9	dziewięć	jev-yENch
10	dziesięć	jeshENch
11	jedenaście	yedenash-cheh
12	dwanaście	dvanash-cheh
13	trzynaście	tshinash-cheh
14	czternaście	chternash-cheh
15	piętnaście	p-yEntnash-cheh
16	szesnaście	shesnash-cheh
17	siedemnaście	shedemnash-cheh
18	osiemnaście	oshemnash-cheh
19	dziewiętnaście	jev-yENtnash-cheh
20	dwadzieścia	dvajesh-cha
21	dwadzieścia jeden	dvajesh-ch a yeden
22	dwadzieścia dwa	dvajesh-cha dva
30	trzydzieści	tshijesh-chee
40	czterdzieści	chterjesh-chee
50	pięćdziesiąt	p-yENchjeshAWNt
100	sto	sto
200	dwieście	dv-yesh-cheh
500	pięćset	p-yENchset
1,000	tysiąc	tishAWNts
1,000,000	milion	meel-yon

TIME

today	dzisiaj	jeeshl
yesterday	wczoraj	vchorl
tomorrow	jutro	yootro
tonight	dzisiejszej nocy	jeeshAYshay notsi
one minute	jedna minuta	yedna meenoota
half an hour	pół godziny	poowuh gojeeni
hour	godzina	gojeena

DAYS OF THE WEEK

Sunday	niedziela	n-yejela
Monday	poniedziałek	pon-yejawek
Tuesday	wtorek	vtorek
Wednesday	środa	shroda
Thursday	czwartek	chvartek
Friday	piątek	p-yAWNtek
Saturday	sobota	sobota

ACKNOWLEDGEMENTS

The publisher would like to thank the following for their kind permission to reproduce their photographs:

(Key: a-above; b-below/bottom; c-centre; f-far; l-left; r-right; t-top).

123RF.com: Roman Babakin 260-1t; Wojciech Balsewicz 212-3b; Diesirae1 104-5b; pavel dudek 225t; Pawel Kazmierczak 190b; Patryk Kośmider 278br; Tomasz Mazoń 30t; Ewa Mazur 126-7b; Malgorzata Pakula 173br; Rochu2008 182b; seregalsv 146cra; udmurd 116b; whitelook 13br.

4Corners: Maurizio Rellini 96-7.

Alamy Stock Photo: A&P 301; Abbus Archive Images 75cla; AF archive 49cb; age fotostock 208t, 235clb, 241cl, 253bl, 283cb; Agencja Fotograficzna Caro 34-5t, 200-1, 201br, 224b, 231b, 244tl; Alltravel 228bl, 286-7b; Kobryn Andrii 8clb; Antiqua Print Gallery 62tl; Roman Babakin 269tl, 310tl; Religion / Stephen Barnes 265tl; Norman Barrett 147cla; Clive Barry 147tc; Jakub Barzycki 39tr, 56-7b; BE&W agencja fotograficzna Sp. z o.o. 35crb, 210cl, 216tl, 217b, 235tr, 283br; Arpad Benedek 95tl; Best View Stock 171ca; Bernard Bialorucki 44-5b; Philip Bird 113crb; Maciej Bledowski 232cb; Artur Bogacki 12t; Piotr Borkowski 106cl, 134-5t, 238tl, 299tl; Michael Brooks 22crb, 43c, 54-5b, 111cla, 205tl, 259tr; Magdalena Bujak 237tr; Timo Christ 8cl; Cultura Creative (RF) 256b; Luis Dafos 144bl; Ian Dagnall 84bl; Dario Photography 100-1b, 104tr; dbimages 24t; Mark Delete 33cla, 36tl, 124t, 173t, 191tl, 193tl, 202t, 210bl, 215t, 234-5t, 235br, 298cr, 311b; Design Pics Inc 171cra; V. Dorosz 308tr; DPA Picture Alliance 262tl; Robert Dziewulski 187tr, 290bl; East News sp. z o.o. 59tl; Jackie Ellis 76bl, 81br; Endless Travel 74bl; Celal Erdogdu 41b; Michal Fludra 52-3b; Peter Forsberg 103tr, 280b; Fotolandia / Stockimo 306-7b; James Freeman 267tl; Tony French 114b; Grzegorz Gajewski 127tl; Galind 277tc; Gary Eason / Flight Artworks 64bc; David Gee 1 177cla; Eddie Gerald 43br; Manfred Gottschalk 263b; Hemis 10ca; History and Art Collection 213br; Horizon Images / Motion 81t, 110cl; Hufton+Crow-VIEW 274-5b; Idealink Photography 113cra; Marek Idowski 213cla; imageBROKER 214bl, 277cra; incamerastock 42tl; Rafał Jabłoński 51br; marcin jucha 38-9b; Jacek Kadaj 113bl; Karol Kozlowski Premium RM Collection 128t; Pawel Kazmierczak 45crb; Padraig Knudsen 149cr; Christian Kober 28tl, 159t, 161tr, 174crb; Grzegorz Kordus 206cl; Henryk Kotowski 130tr; Slawomir Kowalewski 58cr;

Kamila Kozioł 232-3; kpzfoto 26crb, 307tr; Jakub Kwiatkowski 290-1t; Tuomas Lehtinen 253crb; David Lyon 163tr; mauritius images GmbH 155b, 300bl; Steven May 93br, 259b; John Michaels 175; Szymon Mucha 204b; Krzysztof Nahlik 162b, 226-7b; National Geographic Image Collection 106b, 126tc, 138tr; Old Images 60t; Sergiy Palamarchuk 155tl; Panther Media GmbH 293br; Jaroslaw Pawlak 186-7b; Pegaz 112-3t, 145cra; Photo 12 75ca; PjrTravel 206bl; pocholo 11crb; PRISMA ARCHIVO 63cra; Prisma by Dukas Presseagentur GmbH 83tl; Bart Pro 59cr; Peter Probst 255tl; Oleksandr Prykhodko 92b; Candice Pun 149tr; Realimage 239b; Simon Reddy 40bl; Przemyslaw Reinfus 162cl; Juergen Ritterbach 12-3b, 42-3b, 152cl, 226t, 241t; robertharding 53cl; Marcin Rogozinski 101cra, 134tl; RossHelen editorial 252-3t; Jan Rusek 277tr; Henryk Sadura 29tr; Alfredo Garcia Saz 77tl; Iain Sharp 145cb; Witold Skrypczak 28-9t, 29tc, 33tr, 139b, 160tr; Sławomir Staciwa 59clb; Piotr Stasiuk 32cra; Slawek Staszczuk 154bl, 183tr, 184tl; Ryszard Stelmachowicz 178t, 258tl, 263tr; Stepmark 135br, 303cra; Boris Stroujko 254-5b; Wojciech Stróżyk 26cr, 240bl, 281tr; Petr Svarc 56tl; Mariusz Świtulski 304-5b; Jerzy Szyper 213cra; Tetra Images 189bl; The Picture Art Collection 55cl, 63tr; travelimages 174br; Tomasz Trybus 236b; Georgios Tsichlis 77br; TTstudio 146-7b; Lucas Vallecillos 24cr, 79tr, 80b, 107tl, 150-1b, 156-7b, 161bl, 207tr; Ivan Vdovin 137tr; Dieter Wanke 260cl; Bogdan Wańkowicz 287tl; Mieczyslaw Wieliczko 133bl, 304tl, 305cr; Jan Wlodarczyk 22bl, 32-3t, 39cl, 110-1b, 180-1b, 292bl, 308-9b; David Wootton 174cra; WorldPhotos 61br; Gregory Wrona 12clb, 44-5t, 50-1t, 51cb, 101tl, 195, 300cra; Xinhua 117bc; yorgil 74clb; Zoonar GmbH 232bl; Marek Zuk 188tl; ZUMA Press; Inc. 113cl, 311tr.

Archives of National Forum of Music: Łukasz Rajchert 58clb.

Bridgeman Images: 61tl; Forum 61tr; Tarker 60cb; The Stapleton Collection 60br.

Bruno Fidrych / beethoven.org.pl: 59tr.

Conrad Festival: Edyta Dufaj 54-5t.

Depositphotos Inc: ajafoto 13cr; aleksander 37cr; MaciejBledowski 274tl; plrang 38tl; zi3000 11br.

Dreamstime.com: Bernard Bialorucki 37bl; Artur Bogacki 86-7; Castenoid 299ca; Ccat82 242-3bl; Bartłomiej Chudzik 21t, 270-1; Dennis

Main Contributors Jonathan Bousfield,
Małgorzata Omilanowska,
Jerzy S. Majewski
Senior Editor Ankita Awasthi Tröger
Senior Designer Owen Bennett
Designer William Robinson
Project Editor Rachel Laidler
Project Art Editors Dan Bailey, Ankita Sharma,
Priyanka Thakur, Stuti Tiwari Bhatia, Tania Gomes
Factchecker Carlos Canal Huarte
Editors Jackie Staddon, Penny Phenix,
Louise Abbott, Lucy Sara-Kelly, Elspeth Beidas,
Lauren Whybrow, Lucy Sienkowska
Proofreader Ben Davies
Indexer Hilary Bird
Senior Picture Researcher Ellen Root
Picture Research Ashwin Adimari,
Sumita Khatwani, Harriet Whitaker
Illustrators Andrzej Wielgosz,
Bohdan Wróblewski, Piotr Zubrzycki,
Paweł Mistewicz
Senior Cartographic Editor Casper Morris
Cartography Subhashree Bharati,
Rajesh Chhibber, Simonetta Giori, Dariusz Osuch,
Ewa i Jan Pachniewiczowie, Maria Wojciechowska
Jacket Designers Maxine Pedliham, Bess Daly
Jacket Picture Research Susie Peachey
Senior DTP Designer Jason Little
DTP George Nimmo, Azeem Siddiqui
Senior Producer Stephanie McConnell
Managing Editor Hollie Teague
Art Director Maxine Pedliham
Publishing Director Georgina Dee

MIX
Paper from
responsible sources
FSC
www.fsc.org FSC™ C018179

**The information in this
DK Eyewitness Travel Guide is checked regularly.**
Every effort has been made to ensure that this book
is as up-to-date as possible at the time of going to
press. Some details, however, such as telephone
numbers, opening hours, prices, gallery hanging
arrangements and travel information, are liable to
change. The publishers cannot accept responsibility
for any consequences arising from the use of this
book, nor for any material on third party websites,
and cannot guarantee that any website address
in this book will be a suitable source of travel
information. We value the views and suggestions
of our readers very highly. Please write to: Publisher,
DK Eyewitness Travel Guides, Dorling Kindersley,
80 Strand, London, WC2R 0RL, UK, or email:
travelguides@dk.com

First edition 2001

Published in Great Britain by Dorling Kindersley Limited,
80 Strand, London, WC2R 0RL

Published in the United States by DK Publishing,
1450 Broadway, 8th Floor, New York, NY 10018

Copyright © 2001, 2019 Dorling Kindersley Limited
A Penguin Random House Company
19 20 21 22 10 9 8 7 6 5 4 3 2 1

A CIP catalog record for this book
is available from the British Library.

A catalog record for this book is available
from the Library of Congress.

ISSN: 1542–1554
ISBN: 978-0-2413-6008-8

Printed and bound in China.

www.dk.com